CARSON McCULLERS

Books by Josyane Savigneau

Marguerite Yourcenar: Inventing a Life

Carson McCullers: A Life

CARSON McCULLERS

· A LIFE ·

Josyane Savigneau

Translated by Joan E. Howard

HOUGHTON MIFFLIN COMPANY

BOSTON · NEW YORK

2001

Originally published as *Carson McCullers: Un Coeur de jeune fille,*
copyright © 1995 by Éditions Stock
Translation © 2001 by Houghton Mifflin Company
ALL RIGHTS RESERVED

For information about permission to reproduce selections from
this book, write to Permissions, Houghton Mifflin Company,
215 Park Avenue South, New York, New York 10003.

Visit our Web site: www.houghtonmifflinbooks.com.

Library of Congress Cataloging-in-Publication Data
Savigneau, Josyane
[Carson McCullers. English]
Carson McCullers: a life / Josyane Savigneau ;
translated by Joan E. Howard.
p.   cm.
Includes bibliographical references and index.
ISBN 0-395-87820-9
1. McCullers, Carson, 1917–1967. 2. Women authors,
American — 20th century — Biography. 3. Southern
States — Biography. I. Title.
PS3525.A1772 Z8513 2001
813'.52 — dc21   [B]   00-046547

Printed in the United States of America

Book design by Victoria Hartman

QUM 10 9 8 7 6 5 4 3 2 1

Houghton Mifflin wishes to express its appreciation for assistance given by the government of France through the Ministry of Culture in the preparation of the translation.

Excerpts from the following published works of Carson McCullers are reprinted by permission of Houghton Mifflin Company: *The Heart Is a Lonely Hunter* (copyright 1940 by Carson Smith McCullers; copyright renewed © 1967 by Carson McCullers); *Clock Without Hands* (copyright © 1953, 1961 by Carson McCullers; copyright © renewed 1989 by Lamar Smith, Jr.); *Reflections in a Golden Eye* (copyright 1941 by Carson Smith McCullers); and *The Mortgaged Heart* (copyright © 1971 by Floria Lasky, Executrix of the Estate of Carson McCullers). The letter from Richard Burton to Carson McCullers is reprinted courtesy of Mrs. Sally Burton and the Estate of Richard Burton. Quotations from Tennessee Williams copyright © 1954, 1961, 1974, and 1975 the University of the South, reprinted by permission of the University of the South, Sewanee, Tennessee. Excerpts from Carson McCullers's writings are reprinted courtesy of Floria Lasky, Executrix of the Estate of Carson McCullers. The interview with Mary Mercer is reprinted by permission of Mary E. Mercer, M.D. Excerpts from the interview with John Brown are reprinted by permission of Dr. John L. Brown. Excerpts of the interview with Henri Cartier-Bresson are reprinted by permission of Henri Cartier-Bresson. Excerpts from the interview with André Bay are reprinted by permission of André Bay.

*For Bertrand Audusse, whose precious friendship
and professional vigilance have allowed me
to keep my mind free enough
to write this book*

I was thinking of the immense debt I owe to Proust.
It's not a matter of his "influencing my style" . . .
it's the rare good fortune of having always something
to turn to, a great book that never tarnishes, never
[becomes] dull from familiarity.

— *Carson McCullers, 1945*

ACKNOWLEDGMENTS

I WOULD LIKE to thank everyone who by providing information, advice, or support made it possible for me to write this book: Micheline Amar, Pascal Bancou, André Bay, Célia Bertin, John Brown, Henri Cartier-Bresson, Andrée Chédid, Florence Goude, Odile Jatteau, David Lustbader, Raphaëlle Rérolle, Dominique Rolin, Claude Roy, Maren Sell, Catherine Serre, Barbara Solonche-Lustbader, Béatrice Toureilles, Jacques Tournier, Marion Van Renterghem.

This work also owes a great deal to the knowledgeable and courteous librarians of the Harry Ransom Humanities Research Center of the University of Texas at Austin, who facilitated my research in the Carson McCullers archives.

I would like to extend special thanks to:

Marielle Bancou, for her memories, her documents, and her kind regard for this project.

Christiane Besse, a woman of infallible precision.

Professor Carlos Lee Barney Dews, whose intellectual generosity made it possible for me to acquaint myself with his work on Carson McCullers's autobiographical writings.

Jean-Marie Colombani, Edwy Plenel, Bertrand Audusse, Jacques Buob, Patrick Kéchichian, and *Le Monde*'s entire cultural team for their constant support, encouragement, and vigilance.

Claude Durand, who had confidence in me and approved this project.

Floria Lasky, Carson McCullers's literary executrix, who authorized me to quote from the unpublished texts and correspondence.

Dr. Mary Mercer, who agreed to meet, and talk, with me despite her distrust of biographers.

I must also pay tribute here to the memory of the novelist Marie Susini. Marie Susini was the first person to encourage me to write on Carson McCullers, persuaded before I was myself that her life, so totally unlike that of the writer whose biography I had just finished, Marguerite Yourcenar, would fascinate me for that very reason. Marie Susini died on August 22, 1993, when not a word had yet been written. This book, which she will never read, was nourished by her passion for Carson McCullers, by her enthusiasm for "this extremely fine writer, who had such grace" and whom she spoke of so marvelously, this "little sister" from another South, whose flights of enthusiasm, madness, and stubborn rejection of compromise she shared.

Finally, my gratitude goes most especially to two people without whom the completion of this project would not have been possible:

Valérie Cadet, an exceptional researcher and documentalist, who is responsible, in addition to her research, for compiling the notes, the index, and the bibliography.

Monique Nemer, for her tireless attention, her multiple rereadings, her translations of documents in English, her suggestions, and her patience.

TRANSLATOR'S NOTE

AT THE AGE of twenty-three, Carson McCullers burst onto the American literary scene with her prize-winning novel *The Heart Is a Lonely Hunter.* Almost no one could believe that a person so young had written such a book. The year was 1940, and Carson McCullers's novels and plays have held a special place among lovers of reading worldwide ever since.

France has long been a country of serious readers, so perhaps we should not be surprised that this new biography of a writer so strongly identified with the American South originated there. Carson also lived in France with her husband, Reeves McCullers, more than once in her short life, which may have whetted the French public's interest in her life.

Carson McCullers: A Life is the first major biography of this author for which the McCullers estate has granted access to many previously unpublished manuscripts and letters. Using these documents, a candid interview with Carson's psychotherapist and friend Mary Mercer, and a wide range of critical and biographical writings on Carson or Reeves formerly available only in French, Josyane Savigneau paints a vivid new portrait of a writer who never surrendered her "young girl's heart" — the biography's French subtitle is *Un Coeur de jeune fille* — and whose fiction is poignantly connected with the pain of growing up.

Obtaining the numerous primary texts on which this biography relies presented some surprising difficulties. Among those who helped out along the way, I would like to thank, first, Kate Giordano of the Portsmouth (New Hampshire) Public Library, interlibrary-loan specialist extraordinaire, who tracked down and furnished me with many an obscure published document. Thank you, too, to Tara Wenger of the Harry Ransom Humanities Research Center of the University of Texas at Austin, who kindly sent me reams of photocopied archival material, and to Suzy Kosh and her research team, who got many needles out of haystacks in that same location. I am grateful as well to Chris Carduff, formerly of Houghton Mifflin, for his many kindnesses during the early stages of this project and to Houghton Mifflin's Wendy Holt and Susanna Brougham for their thoughtful editorial attention to the translation manuscript. Thanks, finally, to Liz Duvall, also of Houghton Mifflin, for going over the page proofs with a fine-tooth comb.

CONTENTS

INTRODUCTION

C ARSON McCULLERS WOULD HAVE been eighty-four years old on February 19, 2001, an age that would have made her our absolute contemporary. But she died prematurely, in 1967, at age fifty. She published only eight books, plus a posthumous collection of short stories, essays, and poems. That doesn't sound like much to build an international reputation on. She attained one, however, and although she may not be very famous among the public at large, only rarely are serious readers unfamiliar with the work of this novelist from the American South. Could that be what annoys some of the people who knew and outlived her, causing them to minimize or obscure her writing, her status, her very existence?

John Brown, one of her first editors in the early 1940s, who became her friend and was a constant source of support during her stays in France (he was working at the time for the cultural service of the American embassy in Paris), seems to wonder what could possibly prompt a full-length biography of Carson McCullers: "Granted, there are some fine texts, but, even so, she was not really much of a writer."[1] "Moving, yes, but a minor author. And broken by illness at such a young age," adds the American playwright Arthur Miller.[2]

André Bay, who was Carson McCullers's French editor at Éditions Stock — he had read her work in 1945, on John Brown's recommendation — does not share this skepticism:

Obviously, if you use the entire history of American literature as a yardstick, and you line up the major works, you could conclude that Carson McCullers's four novels and her corpus of short stories make her "not really much of a writer." But there are "grand accidents." And they are essential. They are also what gives meaning to literature. Carson McCullers is one of the finest of those "accidents." No one has captured as she did the vast American sense of loneliness, and the suffering it causes, especially in the unreal, dreamlike South of her imaginings, which seems almost "bathed in rum." For me, it is also Carson McCullers, daughter of the South fascinated by snow that she was, who holds the answer to the question "When the snow melts, where does the whiteness go?" It is in her work.[3]

The view that Carson McCullers was merely a promising talent broken and unfulfilled has been strongly contested by another Southern writer, Tennessee Williams, one of her closest friends from the late 1940s on. In the foreword he wrote in 1974 for the major American biography of Carson McCullers by Virginia Spencer Carr, Tennessee Williams refuses to let commentators shut his friend away in her illness. No one can deny the suffering and infirmities that Carson McCullers had to live with for twenty years, but Tennessee Williams firmly states that the existence of a writer cannot be evaluated in terms of difficulties, any more than by the number of volumes produced. "When physical catastrophes reduce, too early, an artist's power, his/her admirers must not and need not enter a plea nor offer apology," he writes. "It is not quantity, after all, that the artist is to be judged by. It is quality of spirit and those occasions on which he/she was visited by assenting angels, and the number of those occasions is not the scale on which their importance is reckoned."[4]

Several years after her death, in another testimony to her reputation, Carson McCullers was the object of a monumental biography (during her lifetime, and with her assistance, one brief biographical essay, *The Ballad of Carson McCullers,* had been written by Oliver Evans). Carson had the most meticulous biographer one can imagine. Virginia Spencer Carr, a professor from the South who published *The Lonely Hunter: A Biography of Carson McCullers* in 1975, carried out an extremely methodical investigation, seeking to leave no moment of Carson McCullers's existence hidden, from her birth to her final day.[5]

Granted, Carr faced obstacles in documenting the life of her subject. McCullers's heirs refused to assist Carr in any way and barred her from citing the documents — unpublished texts and letters — preserved in the archives of the Harry Ransom Humanities Research Center at the University of Texas in Austin. At the time, Carson McCullers's sister, Margarita Smith; her lawyer, Floria Lasky (now her literary executor); and her agent, Robert Lantz, were hoping to find a biographer of their own choosing. Mary Mercer, Carson McCullers's doctor and friend during the last ten years of her life — a key figure for that period — also refused to speak with the biographer.

Virginia Spencer Carr nonetheless seems to have interviewed every other witness to Carson McCullers's existence — however minor or ephemeral. When she herself was not free to travel, she sent someone else to question people for her. Recollections were obtained from people who had met the American novelist only in passing — such as Simone de Beauvoir, who vaguely remembered an evening spent with her in Paris. By now, most of the women and men who provided information to Carr have died. No work on Carson McCullers could possibly be done without Carr's incomparably precise text, containing scores of comments now impossible to collect. Nothing can be written without referring to those unique testimonials, which is to say that we cannot but pay homage to the research of Virginia Spencer Carr.

And yet, despite an appearance of neutrality often found in American biographies — never a conjecture on points that are obscure or unexplained but a piling up of details, particulars, and testimonials as if all were of equal importance — Virginia Spencer Carr's work creates a rather negative image of Carson McCullers. *The Lonely Hunter* aims to be exhaustive, and it certainly comes close, but its portrait is cold, painted by a woman apparently unwilling to consider that a writer lives differently from people who don't write, organizes her existence according to other criteria, feels different feelings, thinks other kinds of thoughts. A writer is not someone who on the one hand loves, hates, rejoices, becomes outraged, or suffers and then writes in her free time. Not only is a writer's life partially refracted in fiction (that is, after all, what keeps the biographical enterprise from being inane), but the need to write fastens itself onto, indeed molds, every living moment. It is if not by that standard at least from that perspective that a writer's life must be judged. Virginia Spencer Carr shows little warmth — much less tenderness or compassion — for her subject, who, visibly, shocks her puritanism and moralism. Carson McCullers is too free with her passions and her words, too independent, and too adept at surviving come what may so that she can continue to write.

A few years after Carr's American summa, in 1979, Jacques Tournier, a French writer and translator as well as a great admirer of Carson McCullers, published a new biographical essay, *Retour à Nayack* [*sic*] (Return to Nayack), at Éditions du Seuil.[6] It is an intimate, enthusiastic, and passionate work inspired by a journey Tournier made, following in Carson McCullers's footsteps, from Columbus to Nyack via Paris. A slightly revised version of this book appeared in 1990 at Éditions Complexe. Called *À la recherche de Carson McCullers* (In search of Carson McCullers), it is an emotion-filled and sentimental quest for Reeves McCullers, Carson's husband, who dreamed of being the writer that his wife alone became.

For Jacques Tournier, though he denies it and though his passion for Carson McCullers is undoubtedly sincere, everything must be read in relation to Reeves. The film he made on Carson for French television in 1995, like his book, proves it. According to Tournier, Carson's life after the death of her husband — that is, for fourteen years — was nothing more than intense despair over his absence, a long lament, nights spent imagining that Reeves's ghost had returned to roam in the garden of the author's Nyack home.

◆　◆　◆

Happily, alongside the skeptics Carson McCullers had some real friends who outlived her: Floria Lasky; Dr. Mary Mercer; Marielle Bancou, her other intimate during the 1950s and 1960s, a young designer at the time; and the photographer Henri Cartier-Bresson, a witness of the 1940s. The photos that Cartier-Bresson took of Carson in 1946 show both the admiration and the real tenderness he had for his subject. When these people speak of Carson McCullers, they evoke a person who is first and foremost a writer, a novelist entirely attached to her work. "Writing is my occupation," Carson often said as she was fighting to continue her work at the height of her physical suffering. "I must do it. I have done it for so long." Her devotion to her work served as proof of the exceptional talent, lucidity, and maturity already in evidence when, at twenty years of age, she started writing her first novel, *The Heart Is a Lonely Hunter*.

Much more than a woman destroyed by the death of the man she loved — and she loved James Reeves McCullers, that much is certain — Carson McCullers, in her life and in the comments of her friends, resembles the touching adolescents — irritating, too, at once generous and egotistical, weak and yet uncommonly strong — who are featured in two of her novels, *The Heart Is a Lonely Hunter* (Mick) and *The Member of the Wedding* (Frankie). Adolescence seems to have remained intact in Carson, indestructible despite all the experiences of life — the loves, the losses, and the afflictions of a body broken by illness — preserving in her a young girl's heart, with its angry outbursts and its torments. Society does not easily tolerate that kind of person, which may account for the obvious or latent hostility that Carson McCullers can arouse among those who have commented on her life. Further fanning the flames of jealousy and disapproval, she was a remarkable writer: she amassed in a small number of years the experiences of a long life, even marrying the same man twice; she achieved great successes and met with failures no less dizzying, became a triumphant Broadway playwright, and saw one of her novels being made into a film by John Huston, with Marlon Brando and Elizabeth Taylor as its stars. Through it all, with inconceivable determination, she held on against the torments of the body and the heart.

It might well irritate these naysayers to find that the adolescent spirit at the heart of Carson's work — the very mark of Carson McCullers — is precisely what keeps her writing fresh. From one generation to the next, young readers are moved by Mick and Frankie, those girls who shot up too fast and refused to enter a world that didn't suit them, rejecting the lies and the compromises of adult life.

Paul Bowles, an American writer who lived in the same house as Carson did in Brooklyn during the 1940s, very aptly described "the essentially childlike woman she [was] all her life," insisting on the word *childlike*, which is nothing like *infantile*, to evoke the "born writer" spoken of by the British writer Edith Sitwell after she had read the novels of Carson McCullers. With "this exaggerated simplicity," said Paul Bowles in 1970 to Virginia Spencer Carr, who had come to visit him in Tangiers, where he was living, "went a total devotion to writing and subjugation to it of all other facets of her existence. This undeviating seriousness did not give her the air of an adult, but rather that of a prodigious and slightly abnormal child who refused to go out and play because she was busy writing in her notebook."[7]

Within the space of this peculiar paradox we must seek, more than thirty years after her death, the closest possible likeness of this strange woman-child, this writer so accomplished in her youth who never really grew up, who was seductive till the end, even when she was paralyzed and almost incapable of speaking, besieged by illness, and withdrawn into a thick fog of alcohol: Carson McCullers. We will have to find her in her books, in her stubborn will to keep on writing until the final day, which she did — she was working on her autobiographical papers when she died. We must avoid the trap that others fell into when they set out in search of her and managed to conceal her instead, or almost made her disappear, as if Carson McCullers — the accomplished writer and the "woman still a child" — constituted a frightening chimera, foreign to the world as it should be, a ceaselessly improper, permanently unacceptable personality.

MARY

L ATE ONE MORNING in 1958, Dr. Mary Mercer was awaiting a
new patient, Mrs. Carson McCullers, who had been referred
by her colleague Dr. Hammerschlag. A friend of Carson's, Dr.
Ernst Hammerschlag had decided that the author needed regularly
scheduled psychotherapy sessions and thus a doctor, if possible, who
lived in her own town of Nyack, since a serious physical impairment
made it hard for her to get around. He had thought of Mary Mercer,
even though she specialized in treating children. No matter — the
American practice of child psychiatry in the 1950s often led to an extension of therapeutic treatment to adults.

Mary Mercer had agreed to a first meeting on that basis. It was certainly not a passion for literature that swayed her, nor a taste for the
supposed psychic complexity of writers, nor even curiosity about a celebrity. Mary Mercer had not read one book by Carson McCullers.
She remembered only having seen a play written by her some eight
years back in New York that had been a great success on Broadway. It
was *The Member of the Wedding,* the story of a Southern adolescent
who wants to be included in her brother's wedding, to form a threesome with him and his brand-new bride and join the newlyweds on
their trip north. It had been a lovely play, superbly performed, on a
subject that was not without interest. But it had not prompted Dr.
Mercer to buy Carson McCullers's novels. She did not read works of
that type; they were beyond the scope of her immediate concerns.

Had she been told that the writer lived in Nyack when she moved to that small New York city in 1953? Perhaps, but if so, she had paid no attention. Ernst Hammerschlag had been rather laconic on the subject of Carson McCullers. Mary Mercer had carefully pointed out, however, that she did not know McCullers's work. Hammerschlag paid that detail little mind, announcing that Carson McCullers would arrange her own appointment, or so he hoped. The phone call had been long in coming. Then one day, a short while ago, a woman with a strong Southern accent had called, very timidly, mentioning Dr. Hammerschlag and asking to see Dr. Mercer. It was Mrs. McCullers. And Mary Mercer was waiting.

The person coming up the walkway, tall and very thin with short-cropped hair, was using a cane. From a distance Dr. Mercer had taken her for a young man. Could this be Mrs. McCullers? No one had thought to inform Mary Mercer about McCullers's infirmity. She had been told that Mrs. McCullers was barely forty years old. If the person just arriving was indeed the famous writer, why was she using a cane to get around? Had she just been in an accident? Someone could have warned her, after all.

As she made her way with difficulty toward Dr. Mercer's home, Carson McCullers for her part was prepared for the worst. Hostile to the idea of undergoing psychotherapy, she had nonetheless allowed her friends to talk her into it — especially Hammerschlag, because he was a doctor, and Tennessee Williams, because he himself was in analysis and she had faith in his judgment. For several weeks now she had really been feeling awfully bad. Things simply could not go on the way they had. It was clear to her that she was in danger, even though her housekeeper, Ida, tried to make her see things differently. Ida was wary of "head doctors" and kept pleading with her every day, "Don't go, Sister. You're not crazy and they're going to hurt you."

Yet Carson sensed that she could not make it through the winter, could not cope with her loneliness, could not abide her incapacity to write. Her novel in progress, *Clock Without Hands,* had stopped dead, as if it had vanished from her psyche. She thought about it ceaselessly, to no avail. Not one sentence came to her, not one inkling of where the plot might go, not a single one of the "illuminations" that had seized her in the past, when, for instance, the main character of *The Heart Is a Lonely Hunter* had appeared to her, or when she had realized that Frankie Addams desperately wanted to be a "member" of her brother's wedding. This time, absolutely nothing came. It seemed the writer inside her had died. You might as well say that she herself was dying. What was left of her other than a woman aged beyond her years and very ill? Paralyzed on the left side by a stroke, unable to live on her own, in need of constant assistance for the simplest tasks of daily living. Unable to travel by herself. Unable even to leave the house alone to take a walk. Reeves, the deplorable and marvelous Reeves, was no longer there to gather her up in his arms to catch a train or a boat. Nor Marguerite, her mother, to meet her plane at the airport. It was entirely too much to bear.

Seeing a psychotherapist would not likely change anything. But she had to make an effort of some kind. So she had finally called Dr. Mary Mercer, as Hammerschlag had recommended. She was no longer sure, though, that she had done the right thing. She would never be able to forget the psychiatrist at the Payne Whitney Psychiatric Clinic who had informed her, ten years ago now, that writing itself was a form of neurosis and that she would have to rid herself of it. That doctor had come very close to killing her. This Mary Mercer would probably have similar views. For several days Carson had been wondering what Dr. Mercer might look like. She had asked several of her friends, but no one knew her. She would almost certainly be ugly, curt, argumentative, uncultivated, boring, and obsessed with "normalcy." Finally, Carson had set up an appointment. She might as well see her once, if only to show Hammerschlag and Tennessee that her rejection of the doctor and her treatment was not the mark of an incurable ill will.

When the door opened and Carson McCullers entered Dr. Mercer's office, she was dumbfounded. The woman standing before her was magnificent: slightly older than she was perhaps, though it was difficult to judge her age exactly — she might be forty or forty-five years old (she was in fact forty-seven). She was tall and slender, with blue eyes and brown hair that framed her face, even features, and a demeanor at once gentle and firm. "Her hair is dark, her eyes gray-blue and her skin very fair," Carson McCullers would write some years later. "Most of all, her face reflects the inner beauty of her noble and dedicated mind."

◆　◆　◆

"Yes, Carson seemed quite surprised when she first saw me," Mary Mercer recalls. "Almost immediately she said to me, 'Dr. Mercer, I have lost my soul.' I said simply, 'I do not believe that you have lost your soul, Mrs. McCullers, but perhaps you have mislaid it.' That is how it all began."[1]

♦   ♦   ♦

Everyone who had seen Carson McCullers during the months before that meeting, including her doctors, was convinced that she did not have much time left. A year. Maybe two.

She lived nearly ten more years, she was well enough to travel — and, most important of all, she was well enough to write.

I

COLUMBUS, GEORGIA, 1917

WILLIAM FAULKNER WAS not yet twenty years old. The South's greatest writer and one of the great writers of the twentieth century — born on September 25, 1897, in New Albany, Mississippi — was still just Billy Faulkner, a young man from a good Southern family marked by defeat in the Civil War. He had written a few poems, and the year 1917 would see his first publications, not of texts but of drawings, in the magazine of the University of Mississippi. In another Southern state, Georgia, on the banks of the Chattahoochee River in Columbus, a singular compatriot would soon enter the world who would one day be compared with Faulkner, more often than not by those who found the two authors equally worthy of reproach: her name was Carson McCullers.

Europe was in the grip of the Great War, a slaughter from which several young, rebellious contemporaries of Faulkner would emerge as major writers in France, such as Louis Aragon, André Breton, and several others. Their world was a very long way from Faulkner's South. Those Europeans and Americans were not destined to cross paths, except by way of their literary legacies and in the minds of their readers.

Columbus at that time was a small Georgia city with fewer than thirty thousand people; as was typical of the Deep South, its economy was based on cotton mills. On February 14, 1916, Marguerite Waters, born in Dublin, Georgia — her ancestors had emigrated from Ireland — married a watch repairman and jeweler named Lamar Smith, a native Alabamian who had recently moved to Columbus and was descended from French Protestants named Gachet. Theirs was a very simple marriage between a woman with a romantic spirit who loved music and a man entirely devoted to his work. The young couple, who did not have much money, lived with Marguerite's mother, Lula Caroline Waters, right in the center of Columbus at Thirteenth Street and Fifth Avenue, a neighborhood that by the late 1910s had already begun to decline, though it was still considered respectable. It soon would not be, a fact that led white middle-class residents to migrate to the outskirts of the city.

Later on, Carson McCullers would describe a town much like Columbus

> in the middle of the deep South. The summers were long and the months of winter cold were very few. Nearly always the sky was a glassy, brilliant azure and the sun burned down riotously bright. Then the light, chill rains of November would come, and perhaps later there would be frost and some short months of cold. The winters were changeable, but the summers always were burning hot. The town was a fairly large one. On the main street there were several blocks of two- and three-story shops and business offices. But the largest buildings in the town were the factories, which employed a large percentage of the population. These cotton mills were big and flourishing and most of the workers in the town were very poor. Often in the faces along the streets there was the desperate look of hunger and of loneliness.[1]

Lamar and Marguerite Smith's first child came into the world on February 19, 1917. It was a girl, and they named her Lula, after her Grandmother Waters, and Carson, after the same grandmother, whose family name had been Carson before she married Charles Waters. This practice of using the last name of one branch of the family as a middle name — Carson's sister was called Margarita Gachet Smith — spawned the first legend about Carson McCullers, a pointless attempt to romanticize her birth. A few months before Carson was born, near the end of 1916, Carson's mother traveled to Atlanta to attend a concert given by Enrico Caruso. Dazzled by the tenor, she decided that if she had a son, she would call him Caruso. From that time on, it seems, articles and films on Carson McCullers have explained at considerable length how Marguerite Smith, disappointed — of

course — because her baby was a girl and could not be named
Caruso, turned the *u* upside down and moved it to the end of the
word, thereby straying as little as possible from the name she had originally chosen, and called her infant daughter Carson. A glance at the
Waters family tree reveals that there's no truth to this tale, as an autobiographical account written by Carson McCullers in the last decade
of her life confirms: "Lula Carson," said Grandmother Waters to her
daughter Marguerite, "is a hard name for a baby to bear."

> "I hate double names even if they are old fashioned. [It] could have
> been worse, though."
> "Lula Carson is named after you, and it's a beautiful name."
> "Could have been worse, though. Remember the time Lamar
> took you to Atlanta to see Caruso. You were wild about him.
> Wanted to name the baby Enrico Caruso. An innocent child with a
> dago name, even if she des have a golden God sent voice. Lamar
> was very concerned and hurt."
> "Lamar hurt!"
> "[W]hat did you expect him to be? If it was a boy he naturally
> expected to have him named after himself. Yes he was hurt and you
> never even noticed."[2]

Carson's grandmother's comments confirm Marguerite Smith's desire to call her son Caruso — with complete disregard for tradition —
but, more notably, they indicate her relative indifference toward her
husband from the moment the baby appeared. Such an attitude is not
at all exceptional; still, it is interesting that Carson McCullers made
note of it many years later in remembering her grandmother, who
supposedly went on to say, "You're so distracted with Lula Carson and
the coming baby that you have no mind for Lamar or even little
Lamar Jr."[3] These memories corroborate what various witnesses have
said about the Smiths' life in Columbus during the 1920s: Marguerite
Smith was primarily concerned with her children, especially her two
girls, and most of all her elder daughter.

The "Caruso affair" has led some to conclude that Carson
McCullers was subject to artistic predestination. Considerable attention has also been paid to the personality of Marguerite Smith — not
so much to her tastes or her artistic sense, which may in fact have influenced her daughter, as to her conversations with neighbors and

friends. From Carson's earliest infancy, Marguerite supposedly announced to all who would listen that the child would be a musician, a famous one, and that the whole world would know her name. Needless to say, such remarks take on meaning only in light of who that child grew up to be.

For the time being the little girl was Lula Carson Smith. At home they called her "Sister," as Southern families often do. A brother, Lamar Jr. — "Brother Man" — was born on May 13, 1919, and a sister, Margarita Gachet — "Baby Sister," later nicknamed Rita — arrived on August 2, 1922. The early years of Lula Carson's life were spent in the downtown house belonging to Grandmother Waters, who lived there with her children and grandchildren. Commentators have placed so much emphasis on the role of Carson McCullers's mother that her grandmother's part has been underestimated. In Carson's unfinished autobiographical works, "Illuminations Until Now" and "Illumination and Night Glare," however, Carson speaks of her love for Lula Waters, who also had a very particular affection for her "grayeyed grandchild," like the "grey sea," with the same "grey eyes as Helen," her own daughter who had died when she was young.[4] Carson also tells — twice — the juicy tale of a visit made by a battalion of women from the Woman's Christian Temperance Union (WCTU), come to convince Mrs. Waters that she drank too much and should modify her habits:

> I loved an old lady who smelled always of lemon verbena sachet and whom I adored. I slept with her and cozied in the dark. Often she would say, "bring up the chair, darling, and climb to the top drawer of the bureau," and there I would find some goody. A little cup cake, or once, to my delight, some cumquats. This first love was my grandmother, whom I called Mommy.
>
> Her life had not been a happy one, although she never complained. Her husband had died of alcoholism after years of being tended by a strong manservant who could control his sudden fits. However, Mommy never had bad feelings against alcohol. Once, towards the last of her illness, some ladies from the WCTU came to call. There were so many it looked like a delegation.
>
> "I know what you're here for," Mommy said. "You're here to arrange about that badge, purple and gold, to put over my body, but I tell you now I won't have it. I come from a long line of drinking

men. My father drank, my son-in-law [Lamar] who is a saint drinks also. How sad it makes me when I hear that 'POP,' and I know that all his home brew has exploded. And I drink also.

The ladies said in shocked voices, "You could not Mrs. Waters!"

"I do every night — [Lamar] fixes me a toddy, and moreover, I enjoy it."

"Well! Mrs. Waters," the delegation said aghast.

When daddy came into the room, Mommy said mischievously, "is it time for my toddy yet [Lamar]? I think it would be delicious now."

"Would any of you ladies like to join us?" Daddy asked.

But already the WCTU were fleeing in horror.

"To tell you the truth [Lamar], those WCTU ladies are awfully narrowminded, although I guess it's wicked of me to say so."[5]

That happy childhood, sheltered by a gentle complicity with the grandmother whose first name the little girl bore, came to an end in November 1923, when Lula Waters died of pernicious anemia. Carson McCullers's two autobiographical works recount the event in slightly different ways. In "Illuminations Until Now" the news of Grandmother Waters's death arrives by way of a telephone call from Marguerite Smith to her sister Martha (Martha Elba, who is called "Mattie," "Mat," or "Leih"), at whose home Carson stayed while her grandmother was dying. In that account it is not clear who informs the child. In "Illumination and Night Glare" it is the gardener who speaks to Lula Carson. But in both manuscripts the central point is the little girl's refusal to kiss the corpse when her mother asks her to.

Carson was clearly upset and confused by her grandmother's death. "Aunt Leih had a wonderful Scupernong arbor and many fruit trees," she wrote in "Illumination and Night Glare."

There was always Tuppelo honey at the breakfast table and often ripe, peeled figs over which we would pour fresh, thick cream. On Sundays we always had ice cream, and I was allowed to churn it and of course, lick the dasher. I hardly realized it when the gardner told me that my grandmother was dead. So we were driven home in the old Dodge car by Aunt Leih.

At home, when I saw the wreath on the door, I knew that something strange and uncanny had happened. I flung myself to the floor in the hall and some moments later I had a convulsion. Mother wanted me to kiss my grandmother, but I said firmly, "she's dead isn't she, and you don't kiss dead people." Though my grand- mother was dead, her spirit still lives with me, and I've always had a picture of her on my wall. A young, beautiful widow with five children.

Mother and Daddy I also loved, but Mommy was someone al- ways special to me.[6]

Carson never spoke much of her father beyond saying that he was very nice, indicating the importance in her life of certain gifts that were apparently his idea (a piano and a typewriter) and recounting her childhood fascination with his jewelry shop, its clocks and watches, their inner workings, and the curious sense of time she sometimes felt in that place. Her mother, by contrast, would be at Carson's side throughout most of her adult life, especially after the death of her fa- ther in 1944; and, although no written record of their relationship ex- ists (none of their letters have been saved), we know that Marguerite Smith was one of the key figures in Carson's life.

In those early years Carson always felt that she had been lucky, that she had been "on the good side" in the small city marked by poverty where she grew up. The misery in which a large part of the population of Columbus lived was so present for the little Lula Smith that it would form the backdrop of young Carson's first novel. It is difficult to understand *The Heart Is a Lonely Hunter* without grasping that the town, whose name is never specified, is also a character and unques- tionably one of the story's essential elements.

The town is located in the very western part of Georgia, bordering the Chattahoochee River and just across the boundary line from Al- abama. The population of the town is around 40,000 — and about one third of the people in the town are Negroes. This is a typical factory community and nearly all of the business set-up centers around the textile mills and small retail stores.

Industrial organization has made no headway at all among the workers in the town. Conditions of great poverty prevail. The aver- age cotton mill worker is very unlike the miner or a worker in the automobile industry — south of Gastonia, S.C., the average cotton mill worker has been conditioned to a very apathetic, listless state.

For the most part he makes no effort to determine the causes of poverty and unemployment. His immediate resentment is directed toward the only social group beneath him — the Negro. When the mills are slack this town is veritably a place of lost and hungry people.[7]

"We were rich, but we were not like the richest people in town," Carson wrote in "Illuminations Until Now."

More than anything I wanted a pony, . . . but I knew without asking we were not rich enough to have a pony.

Aunt Mat and Uncle Gray were richer than we were. Their house in the suburbs was a brick house with blue hydrangeas bordering the front porch. They had a gramophone you could crank up and hear Pallachi and Home to My Mountains. And — marvel of marvels — they had a piano. The piano was an upright one, and from time to time my cousins would bang on it. But I would only look at it, and it seemed that between myself and the piano there was a secret. I would touch one note and let it echo. Then when everybody else was away from the house, I would bunch notes together and pick out little tunes. Yes, there was a secret between the piano and myself. And when I touched it, I was always alone. I touched it in this [way] as often as possible that summer. It was as [though] it was magic. And one magic leads to another. One afternoon that summer I thought I was Aladdin.[8]

Although she states in her autobiography that "soon after Mommie's death, Daddy bought a piano," the purchase does not appear to have been made before 1925 or 1926.[9] It was during the summer of 1925 that, faced with the rapid decline of the downtown area, Lamar Smith, having bought a small coupe, rented a house on Wynnton Road and moved his family to the suburbs.

Lula Carson entered third grade at Wynnton Elementary School. She also started going to the Baptist church — of her own accord, believing that her grandmother would have wanted her to (her parents made no such demands on her). She would ask to be baptized the following year, in 1926, at the age of nine, along with her friend Helen Jackson, who described the event to biographer Virginia Spencer Carr. When Helen said she felt no different after the baptism than she had before, Lula Carson reportedly replied: "But we *are* different, Helen, no matter how we feel. . . . When we die, we'll go to heaven now."[10]

Lula Carson attended church and Sunday school regularly until she was fourteen. Then she quit going and stayed at home on Sunday mornings, reading or playing the piano with her mother, while her brother and sister continued their religious education. In the Wynnton Road house, the piano really entered Lula Carson's life, becoming her refuge from an irritating little sister who intruded on her space — even though Lula Carson was clearly her mother's favorite — and from a loneliness due at once to family rules (she was not allowed to play with neighborhood children except for Helen Jackson, whom the Smiths viewed as an acceptable companion for their daughter) and to her own not very sociable nature. When the piano that Lamar Smith had bought for his children arrived, Lula Carson remembered another piano, the one she had played at her aunt's house:

> My Aunt [Leih] had a piano and I had touched it gingerly and even arranged a few chords, so when *my* piano arrived I sat down immediately and began to play. To my parents this seemed a miracle.
>
> "What was I playing?" they asked me.
>
> "A tune I had made up," I told them.
>
> They decided that I ought to have a music teacher, and so they asked Mrs. Kierce to give me lessons twice a week.
>
> I did not much like the lessons, and still preferred to make up my own tunes. Mrs. Kierce was impressed, and very conscientiously wrote down the music.[11]

An almost identical account, but with added details and more of the little girl's own impressions, appears in "Illuminations Until Now":

> It was not a secret piano, but my own. I settled myself on the stool and played for the first time: *Yes Sir That's My Baby.* I played it with both hands and the time was right. The family was as amazed as I was. Then I tore into *Yes, We Have No Bananas.* Again, I was as amazed as my family. Then I began to make up little tunes and these I liked best. This was my own music. "Just made it up like that," Daddy marveled. Then there crossed my daddy's face an expression I had seen many times: pride, and the fear of new expenses. Finally he said to Mama, "I guess we ought to go see Miss Helen

[her name was actually Alice; Carson McCullers must have had a memory lapse] Kierce tomorrow."

"I can play the piano!" I said. I was still amazed. However poorly or well I played, it was the illumination in my life. It came as suddenly as a comet that shoots across the August sky. The comet lasts only in memory, but my music even when I could not longer play the piano myself lasts forever. But at that time I only said to myself, "I can play the piano! Jazz tunes and made up tunes also."[12]

Mrs. Kierce gave Lula Carson piano lessons until 1930. But she was quickly surpassed by her pupil, who was already composing small pieces of her own and was very good at improvising. To the amazement of family members, she could also reproduce instantly and instinctively songs she had heard only once — to perfection when they were simple and most acceptably when they were more complex.

In the meantime the Smiths had moved into a home of their own. In January 1927 they left Wynnton Road for a house at 1519 Starke Avenue that Lamar Smith had just purchased and where he would spend the rest of his life. A modest but comfortable home with the traditional front steps, veranda, and small yard, it would serve as a model for the setting of one of his daughter's novels, *The Member of the Wedding*: "Frankie's room was an elevated sleeping porch which had been built onto the house, with a stairway leading up from the kitchen."[13] According to Virginia Spencer Carr, who gathered firsthand accounts during the early 1970s in Columbus (where no one ever really appreciated the personage that Carson McCullers became), little Lula Carson deplored her parents' social status.[14] Their servants worked only by the day, whereas most neighbors had several full-time maids — black ones, of course, as they were at the Smiths' and everywhere else.

At 1519 Starke Avenue in the late 1920s the piano became the focus of everyone's attention. That instrument was the sign of Carson's indubitable talent, and it crystallized all the ambition, all the dreams of success held by the young girl's mother, Marguerite Smith. Her daughter would likely be a brilliant music student and become a professional musician, a soloist perhaps. Why not a concert artist, or a great international pianist, darting from continent to continent, concert to concert, ovation to ovation? The celebrity she so desired for Lula Carson, having failed to achieve it for herself, was on its way.

And Lula Carson did play for several hours every day, though her new passion, reading, was also beginning to take up a lot of time.

> My librarian cousin once remarked that I didn't only read books, but libraries. It is true that my nose was in a book from the time I was ten until this day.
>
> When I was about eleven my mother sent me to the grocery store and I carried a book, of course. It was by Katherine Mansfield. On the way I began reading and was so fascinated that I read under the street light and kept on reading as I asked for the supper groceries. . . .
>
> Thomas Wolfe is another author I love, partly because of his wonderful gusto in describing food.
>
> The next and possibly one of the strongest influences in my reading life is Dostoeveski — Tolstoy, of course, is at the top.
>
> As I grew older my love for Katherine Mansfield somehow was lost, and I seldom read her now, but I must add here that as a critic she is often dead right.[15]

"The stories I liked best when first I learned to read were those that had something to eat in them," Carson wrote in an article for *Harper's Bazaar*. "One in particular I recall. It was about a little boy whose eyes were larger than his stomach, and who died after stuffing down candy, cake, and a mountainous platter of ice cream. There was a picture of him kneeling on the floor, with all those goodies spread out around him, dressed in a sailor suit and pop-eyed with gluttony. I loved him. And to this day I still, when I am hungry, like to feast vicariously — with the 'Satyricon' of Petronius; or Rabelais, or Mr. Pickwick, or the novels of Thomas Wolfe."[16]

Fortunately, Lula Carson had her books and her piano to combat loneliness. "My childhood was not lonely because when I was six years old my Daddy bought a piano," she wrote in "Illumination and Night Glare."[17] But boredom weighed on her like a yoke, like the summer heat in her hometown of Columbus. She described the atmosphere magnificently in *The Ballad of the Sad Café*:

> The town itself is dreary; not much is there except the cotton mill, the two-room houses where the workers live, a few peach trees, a church with two colored windows, and a miserable main street only a hundred yards long. On Saturdays the tenants from the nearby

farms come in for a day of talk and trade. Otherwise the town is lonesome, sad, and like a place that is far off and estranged from all other places in the world. The nearest train stop is Society City, and the Greyhound and White Bus Lines use the Forks Falls Road which is three miles away. The winters here are short and raw, the summers white with glare and fiery hot.

If you walk along the main street on an August afternoon there is nothing whatsoever to do. The largest building, in the very center of the town, is boarded up completely and leans so far to the right that it seems bound to collapse at any minute. The house is very old. There is about it a curious, cracked look that is very puzzling until you suddenly realize that at one time, and long ago, the right side of the front porch had been painted, and part of the wall — but the painting was left unfinished and one portion of the house is darker and dingier than the other. The building looks completely deserted. Nevertheless, on the second floor there is one window which is not boarded; sometimes in the late afternoon when the heat is at its worst a hand will slowly open the shutter and a face will look down on the town. It is a face like the terrible dim faces known in dreams — sexless and white, with two gray crossed eyes which are turned inward so sharply that they seem to be exchanging with each other one long and secret gaze of grief. The face lingers at the window for an hour or so, then the shutters are closed once more, and as likely as not there will not be another soul to be seen along the main street. These August afternoons — when your shift is finished there is absolutely nothing to do; you might as well walk down to the Forks Falls Road and listen to the chain gang.[18]

"Yes, the town is dreary," writes Carson McCullers at the end of her story. "On August afternoons the road is empty, white with dust, and the sky above is bright as glass. Nothing moves — there are no children's voices, only the hum of the mill. . . . There is absolutely nothing to do in the town. Walk around the millpond, stand kicking at a rotten stump, figure out what you can do with the old wagon wheel by the side of the road near the church. The soul rots with boredom."[19]

The little girl who languished in summer's too stifling heat beneath a too glaring sun, described later in almost all her books, was looking at what went on around her. She was playing the piano, reading, and observing — the severity of the climate, the Southerners' harshness, and the violence of social relations, which Carson would later address in a text comparing the world described by Russian writers with that of the South she knew as a child:

> In Faulkner's *As I Lay Dying,* . . . [t]he author reports this confusion of values but takes on himself no spiritual responsibility.
>
> To understand this attitude one has to know the South. The South and old Russia have much in common sociologically. The South has always been a section apart from the rest of the United States, having interests and a personality distinctly its own. Economically and in other ways it has been used as a sort of colony to the rest of the nation. The poverty is unlike anything known in other parts of this country. In social structure there is a division of classes similar to that in old Russia. The South is the only part of the nation having a definite peasant class. But in spite of social divisions the people of the South are homogeneous. The Southerner and the Russian are both "types" in that they have certain recognizable and national psychological traits. Hedonistic, imaginative, lazy, and emotional — there is surely a cousinly resemblance.
>
> In both the South and old Russia the cheapness of life is realized at every turn. The thing itself, the material detail, has an exaggerated value. Life is plentiful; children are born and they die, or if they do not die they live and struggle. And in the fight to maintain existence the whole life and suffering of a human being can be bound up in ten acres of washed out land, in a mule, in a bale of cotton.[20]

Racism was part of everyday life in the South, of course. Lula Carson was sensitive to it at a very early age. She grew up in a family that was not militantly racist, even if her parents were not as liberal or progressive as she herself would be throughout her life. In her autobiography she recounts an incident she never forgot:

> I remember one time during the depression when there were ten cent taxis. Our maid Lucille, who was one of the kindest and youngest of our nurses, she was only fourteen and a marvelous cook, had called a cab to go home. Brother and I were watching as she left, and the taxi refused to drive her.
>
> "I'm not driving no damn nigger," he bawled.
>
> Seeing Lucille's embarrassment, and feeling the ugliness of the

whole injustice, [Lamar] ran under the house, (I must explain here that under the house is almost like a separate room that goes from the front door to the middle of the house. There's a special smell to under the house. The dirt is blacker, and the smell is acrid and bitter.) Brother was weeping under the house, but I was torn with fury and I screamed to the taxi man, "You bad, bad man." Then I went to join my brother, and we held hands in order to comfort ourselves, because there was nothing, nothing else we could do. Lucille had to walk a good mile home.

Black and white people in those days [were] rooting in garbage cans. People, kind, sweet people who had nursed us so tenderly, humiliated because of their color. I do not wonder now, as my father used to wonder, why I was a great believer of the Communist party when I was seventeen, although I never joined it, and eventually I became disenchanted with the workings of the Communists also.

We were exposed so much to the sight of humiliation and brutality, not physical brutality, but the brutal humiliation of human dignity which is even worse. Lucille comes back to me over and over; gay, charming Lucille. She would stand at the window and sing a current tune which went "Tip Toe to the Window." Blues tunes were not her taste as she was much too gay for them. . . .

Then in the middle of the depression, mother thought she could do her own work and cooking, and so let Lucille go with every fine recommendation. She should of looked into the family Lucille was going to work for because they were abnormal, and accused Lucille of poisoning them. Lucille, with her good cooking! On their word she was sent to the penitentiary. There she was a cook and she also learned to sew and practice reading and writing. I think she got a pretty liberal education there, and the experience did not harm her. Mother and daddy testified as to her character and cooking ability, but the other people were so insistent and as he was an alderman, she had to remain there for almost a year. But she sewed and cooked and got on with her reading and writing. She wrote us several letters, and daddy sent money for the prison canteen. When she was released she went to Chicago and met and married a fine, upstanding brick mason who made a good salary. Not too long ago Lucille visited me. She had found out my Nyack address. Although it was an August afternoon she had over her arm a beautiful fox fur, and was lavishly dressed. We embraced each other and talked bout the old days and her new prosperity. I, too, had become a little prosperous, in that I was making a living with my writing which was a great pride to Lucille.[21]

Lula Carson's childhood, which nourished the novelist's tales, might look rather banal, resembling that of many other children whose families started out in the lower middle class. Hers was the childhood of a much-loved daughter, punctuated by school, music, reading, and dreams, particularly dreams of winter and snow in a part of the country where it never got cold and in summer was decidedly too hot. Perhaps that is why Carson McCullers wrote so many pieces about Christmas over the course of her lifetime, as her sister, Margarita Smith, reflected:

> Christmas was Carson's favorite holiday and fall and winter her favorite times of the year. Often her work evokes a longing for the cold and snow as seen in Frankie Addams' dreams of Winter Hill, or she summons the autumn with her descriptions of a "hunting dawn," the making of cane syrup, or slaughtering day after the first frost. Mother's fruitcakes were baked before Thanksgiving and were so famous that the time our house burned down when we were children, the only thing that our brother thought was valuable enough to save were a few freshly baked fruitcakes soaking in good bourbon and wrapped in linen napkins and not to be cut until Christmas.[22]

"Christmas Eve was the longest day, but it was lined with the glory of tomorrow," recalled Carson in a piece published in 1949.

> The sitting-room smelled of floor wax and the clean, cold odor of the spruce tree. The Christmas tree stood in a corner of the front room, tall as the ceiling, majestic, undecorated. It was our family custom that the tree was not decorated until after we children were in bed on Christmas Eve night. We went to bed very early, as soon as it was winter dark. I lay in the bed beside my sister and tried to keep her awake. . . .
>   At twilight I sat on the front steps, jaded by too much pleasure, sick at the stomach and worn out. The boy next door skated down the street in his new Indian suit. A girl spun around on a crackling son-of-a-gun. My brother waved sparklers. Christmas was over. I

thought of the monotony of Time ahead, unsolaced by the distant glow of paler festivals, the year that stretched before another Christmas — eternity.[23]

Carson rounded out these recollections in "The Discovery of Christmas," published in 1953: "It was our family custom to have fireworks on Christmas night. Daddy would light a bonfire after dark and we would shoot Roman candles and skyrockets."[24]

School was easy for Lula Carson and everything went smoothly; as soon as classes were done, she concentrated on her music. But as time passed, she grew more and more isolated and began to resemble the strange adolescent in several of her novels: "School was all right as I learned easily & went straight to the piano in the afternoon," she observed in her autobiography. "I spent practically no time on homework. I passed every grade, but that was all. I liked to climb a tree in the backyard & sit in a tree house my brother & I had made. We had an elaborate signal system for the cook, who was awfully nice to fasten a string in a basket & bring up goodies. Years later when I was troubled I would still take refuge in that same tree house."[25]

2

I WAS EIGHTEEN YEARS OLD,
AND THIS WAS MY FIRST LOVE

In February 1930 Lula Carson Smith celebrated her thirteenth birthday and entered high school in Columbus, without enthusiasm. The rigid schedules, the constant restrictions, the need to take classes with people not of her own choosing taught by teachers who were forced on her — she liked none of this. Why should she not be free to structure her daily routine in her own way, according to her personal rhythms, so she could have the time alone that allowed her to concentrate? "I had heard horrifying things about high school," she remembers. "Mother dressed me in a pink wool suit & I set out for that scary high school."[1]

Without overanalyzing every detail of her childhood, we can see the significance of an incident from Carson's first year at the high school that the writer recorded in her autobiography long after the event occurred:

> The first week at school I was literally captured by a girl when I was in the basement. She threw me to the floor & said "Say fuck three times."
> "What is it" I asked.
> "Never mind what it is, you lily pure innocent, just say it."
> All the time she was grinding my face against the cement floor.
> "Well fuck" I said.
> "Say it 3 times"
> "Fuck, fuck, fuck" I said quickly, and she let me go.

I can still feel her foul breath on my face & her sweating hands. When I was released I ran straight home but did not tell my parents because I knew it was something ugly & wicked.

"What happened to your face?" my mother asked.

"Just one of the things in high school" I said. Although nothing else that dramatic ever happened to me, the dullness of school was a dreadful experience. When I graduated at 17, I didn't even attend all the ceremonies, but asked the principal to keep my diploma, as my brother would pick it up the next day.[2]

In fact it seems that Carson's dislike for high school met with her parents' sympathy — or at least with understanding from Marguerite and weary resignation from Lamar:

I still wanted to be a concert pianist so my parents did not make me go every day. I just went enough to keep up with the classes. Now, years later, the high school teachers who taught me are extremely puzzled that anyone as negligent as I was could be a successful author. The truth is I don't believe in school, whereas I believe very strongly in a thorough musical education. My parents agreed with me. I'm sure I missed certain social advantages by being such a loner but it never bothered me.[3]

Fitting in at the high school was not made any easier by the adolescent's physical appearance. In the space of a few months she grew to be a long-limbed, gangly teenager who wasted no time reaching, prematurely, her full adult height of five feet nine inches. The experience was likely not an easy one, but it increased Lula Carson's sense of her own singularity — indeed, so much so that a lanky adolescent ill at ease with herself and in the world became the central figure in several of Carson McCullers's novels, beginning with the first, *The Heart Is a Lonely Hunter*. The model for Mick Kelly, and later Frankie Addams in *The Member of the Wedding*, was the young high school girl from Columbus who "shot up too fast":

Biff sensed that someone was standing in the entrance and he raised his eyes quickly. A gangling, towheaded youngster, a girl of about twelve, stood looking in the doorway. She was dressed in khaki shorts, a blue shirt, and tennis shoes — so that at first glance she was like a very young boy. . . . He remembered Mick. He wondered if he should have sold her the pack of cigarettes and if it were really harmful for kids to smoke. He thought of the way Mick narrowed her eyes and pushed back the bangs of her hair with the palm of her hand. He thought of her hoarse, boyish voice and of her habit of hitching up her khaki shorts and swaggering like a cowboy in the picture show.[4]

"Although I was awkward, I was the best roller-skater for all the blocks around," asserts Carson. "I was always coming home with scabbed knees or hurt arms."[5] It was this tomboy who departed in July for a visit with her uncle Elam Waters in Cincinnati, Ohio, and who on her way home from this journey decided to shorten her name from "Lula Carson" to the single word "Carson." Was she trying to assert and distinguish herself? No doubt she was, just as Frances Jasmine Addams does when she decides she will no longer be called "Frankie," opting first for "F. Jasmine" and then simply "Frances." Did Carson wish to be deliberately ambiguous in taking a first name that kept people from knowing for certain her gender? Perhaps, but we surely can't compare the brand-new Carson Smith — who came to look more and more like a young man between the ages of fifteen and twenty — to her "amazon" contemporaries in 1930s Europe, who cultivated their sexual indeterminacy and dressed in men's clothes to conquer women. Carson remained a girl of the Deep South, awkward, shy, unsociable, and withdrawn. But she already knew that she wanted something more than the dreary life of a Columbus housewife, and she already dreamed of having a destiny. For the time being, however, the young Carson was not at all sure of herself and far from being much of a conqueror. She was merely "a queer young girl who looked like a boy."

What distinguished her even more than her physique, and justified her dreams of glory, was her talent as a pianist. With her first teacher, Mrs. Kierce, she was getting nowhere. Fortunately, Carson attended a concert featuring a highly skilled instrumentalist, Mary Tucker. She found out that Mrs. Tucker was married to an officer at Fort Benning, a military base on the outskirts of Columbus, and that by audition she accepted a few select students. With the help of Mrs. Kierce, who knew that she had nothing more to teach her student, Carson was able to schedule an audition with Mrs. Tucker, who then took her on as a pupil. "The work I played for my new teacher was the 2nd Hungarian

Rhapsody," Carson McCullers recalled many years later. "She once said it was the fastest, loudest Hungarian Rhapsody she had ever heard, and she accepted me as a pupil. Not only as a pupil — I spent every Saturday at her home, and she started me on Bach, whom I had never heard before."[6]

For nearly four years Marguerite Smith drove her daughter to Fort Benning every Saturday and returned to pick her up every evening.

Mary Tucker was obviously more than a piano teacher for Carson and had a strong influence on her. Carson stayed at the Tuckers' on Saturdays well beyond the end of her music lesson. She grew friendly with her teacher's daughter, Gin, who was a few months younger than she. Carson felt very much at home in the Tucker family. Mrs. Tucker's refinement was extremely appealing. But to conclude, as other commentators have, that Mary Tucker was Carson's first female love (supposing that there really were others) is quite a leap. Every adolescent who has a crush on her teacher does not grow up to be an adult with a taste for women. There has been, and will no doubt continue to be, a stream of contradictory speculations about Carson's love life and desires. In the case of Mary Tucker at least, it is more than probable that Carson wallowed in a romanticism not unusual for her age, a time when girls take pleasure in the pain of an impossible passion — and there is no way to be sure that she ever abandoned this mode of behavior. An almost filial relationship, but a chosen one, and a wish to be adopted, to belong, to be a "member of," also colored her friendship with Mary Tucker and existed throughout Carson's life and in the lives of her heroines.

Though Carson Smith still wanted to become a concert pianist, and though music had now become incarnate for her in Mary Tucker, reading, a favorite pastime for several years, had gained a new place, taken on an altered status in her life. She describes it very clearly in "Books I Remember":

> Often there comes a time in early adolescence when books suddenly take on a new meaning. The books that most of us enjoy in childhood are the ones through which we can enjoy some outward, physical adventure that is not likely to befall us in everyday life. Or we like the sound of words put together in a pleasant way. But then all at once neither outward experience nor jingles can satisfy us alto-

gether, and we are drawn to the richer and more dramatic adventures of the soul. With me this change came when, at thirteen, I first read the great Russians.

The books of Dostoevski — "The Brothers Karamazov," "Crime and Punishment," and "The Idiot" — opened the door to an immense and marvelous new world. For years I had seen these books on the shelves of the public library, but on examining them I had been put off by the indigestible names and the small print. So when at last I read Dostoevski it was a shock that I shall never forget — and the same amazement takes hold of me whenever I read these books today, a sense of wonder that cannot be jaded by familiarity. Along with Dostoevski the stories of Chekhov have for me the same powerful fascination. The hot lazy Russian summers, the lonely villages on the steppes, the old grandfathers who sleep with the children on the stove, the white winters of Saint Petersburg — these are as close to me as scenes from my own home town. And of course there are "War and Peace," "Anna Karenina" and some of the shorter works of Tolstoy. "Dead Souls" by Gogol and all the works of Turgenev are books that can keep me at home almost any evening.

Sometimes it seems to me that the grandeur of Russian literature lies in the fact that the Russian writers, more perhaps than any others, have been able to accept the conditions of human existence. Life by them was reckoned as a unit, and they knew the necessity of death. Yet the dominant attitude of the great Russians is not one of cynicism.[7]

In the same piece she discusses her sudden enchantment with the fate of the dancer Isadora Duncan, whose *My Life* she had read: "'My Life' by Isadora Duncan affected me like the rash. It made me want to take on the responsibility of the whole family and traipse with them to Chicago and Paris and Greece. It made me sicken for the hectic radiance of concert halls and starvation in dubious hotels. This book also was the cause of a School of the Dance in our neighborhood. And for a whole week I managed, by strategy and bribes, to keep a little gang of sweaty children draped in sheets and hopping hopelessly around the back yard."[8]

She returned to the subject in her autobiography:

When I was fourteen years old, the great love of my life which influenced the whole family, was Isadora Duncan. I read My Life, not only read it but preached it. My daddy, who believed with my mother, that a child should read without censorship, could not help but be amazed by my preaching of free love to the family at large, and anyone else who would listen. One nosy neighbor criticized my parents for letting me speak so precociously about Isador Duncan and her love life. I can only guess what the other neighbors thought. I begged my father to let me run away to Paris, and I told him I would dance there for the family's living. Running away to Paris — and worse still, me, awkward as I was, supporting the family by dancing, was beyond my father's wildest imagination.[9]

Though she did not know it at the time, 1932, the year she turned fifteen, would be pivotal for Carson, in ways both good and bad. On the good side, her father gave her a typewriter on which she amused herself by writing stories, an activity for which she developed an exceptional fondness. And on the bad, she contracted an illness, the secret precursor of the attacks that would punctuate her life, leaving her physically disabled. Early in the winter of 1932, Carson fell gravely ill. She saw several doctors, all of whom remained baffled by her condition. They eventually diagnosed it as pneumonia with complications and ordered complete bed rest until Christmas. What she had was not pneumonia, however, and it took nearly thirty years for doctors to realize that it had probably been rheumatic fever, an affliction that, undetected and untreated, did severe internal damage to the girl.

It is difficult to pinpoint when Carson decided to devote herself to writing, but her friend Helen Jackson, already in college, said that when she went to see Carson during her winter vacation, the still convalescing teenager announced her intention to abandon the idea of a career in music in favor of becoming a writer. But others have recalled that when Carson left for New York in 1934, she was planning to take music classes there. Carson herself says in her autobiography that she arrived in New York intending to become a writer. But she made that disclosure some thirty years after the fact, as an accomplished writer who was most likely not inclined to attribute the origin of her career to the vagaries of chance.

What we can confirm, by contrast, is that during 1933 and early 1934 Carson continued to visit Fort Benning every Saturday for her piano lesson at Mary Tucker's house and that her teacher encouraged her to enroll in a prestigious school of music, either the Juilliard

School in New York or the Curtis Institute of Music in Philadelphia. A choice had to be made, for 1933 was her final year of high school. Carson was quite pleased to have it over with. She did not get along very well with young people her own age. She was not one to go out with other girls or flirt with boys.

Carson's classmates from that time have described her as "eccentric," "bizarre." Her skirts were apparently longer than fashion permitted. Instead of girls' stockings and pumps she donned high socks and walking or tennis shoes — not always very clean ones, rumor has it. Some say she was intentionally provocative. It is more probable, though, that Carson Smith simply did not care what people thought of her and was thoroughly indifferent to their social gaze. She was a person apart and hard for anyone to label. Certain fellow students or teachers remember her as "stubborn and often highly argumentative"; others recall that she was timid, not extremely sociable, and very talented but that she spent too much time playing music to be able to exploit her other gifts. Her English teachers call her a passionate reader. In high school, right around her sixteenth year, she stepped up and diversified her reading. To the great Russian novelists, already read in abundance, she added writers she had never tried before, such as Flaubert, Joyce, and Faulkner.

At the same time, she began to write more regularly, not snatches of text here and there but full stories. They were essentially short plays, which her brother and sister would perform for an audience of family members. She describes these events in "How I Began to Write":

> In our old Georgia home we used to have two sitting-rooms — a back one and a front one — with folding doors between. These were the family living-rooms and the theatre of my shows. The front sitting-room was the auditorium, the back sitting-room the stage. The sliding doors the curtain. In wintertime the firelight flickered dark and glowing on the walnut doors, and in the last strained moments before the curtain you noticed the ticking of the clock on the mantlepiece, the old tall clock with the glass front of painted swans. In summertime the rooms were stifling until the time for curtain, and the clock was silenced by sounds of yard-boy whistling and distant radios. . . .
>
> As the eldest child in our family I was the custodian, the coun-

ter of the cakes, the boss of all our shows. The repertory was eclectic, running from hashed-over movies to Shakespeare and shows I made up and sometimes wrote down in my nickel Big Chief notebooks. The cast was everlastingly the same — my younger brother, Baby Sister and myself. . . .

The sitting-room shows ended when first I discovered Eugene O'Neill. It was the summer when I found his books down in the library and put his picture on the mantlepiece in the back sitting-room. By autumn I was writing a three-acter about revenge and incest — the curtain rose on a graveyard and, after scenes of assorted misery, fell on a catafalque. The cast consisted of a blind man, several idiots and a mean old woman of one hundred years. The play was impractical for performance under the old conditions in the sitting rooms. I gave what I called a "reading" to my patient parents and a visiting aunt.

Next, I believe, it was Nietzsche and a play called *The Fire of Life*. The play had two characters — Jesus Christ and Friedrich Nietzsche — and the point I prized about the play was that it was written in verses that rhymed. I gave a reading of this play, too, and afterward the children came in from the yard, and we drank cocoa and ate the fallen, lovely raisin cakes in the back sitting-room by the fire. "Jesus?" my aunt asked when she was told. "Well, religion is a nice subject anyway."[10]

When she was sixteen Carson wrote her first short story, "Sucker," which was repeatedly rejected by magazines and did not appear until thirty years later on September 28, 1963, in the *Saturday Evening Post*. Though it lacks the compositional mastery that her fiction would later acquire, "Sucker" is a compelling story about the loss of almost brotherly closeness between two boys who live together, sixteen-year-old Pete and his twelve-year-old cousin, nicknamed Sucker because he tends to swallow every yarn that people spin. Pete suffers his first heartbreak in love, and Sucker enters into an unhappy adolescence. Like Carson, Sucker goes through a rapid spurt of growth: "Sucker has grown faster than any boy I ever saw. He's almost as tall as I am and his bones have gotten heavier and bigger."[11] The childhood camaraderie and complicity that Pete and Sucker once shared become a thing of the past. Pete has to call Sucker by his real name now, Richard. Remaining are only regrets: "I miss the way Sucker and I were for a while in a funny, sad way that before this I never would have believed," says Pete.[12]

In 1934, the year after she wrote "Sucker," Carson experienced both her first adolescent heartbreak and her first adult friendship. She met Edwin Peacock, who would become one of Carson's closest friends, thanks to Mary Tucker. Peacock, a great music lover, had heard that Rachmaninoff was giving a concert in Atlanta, a hundred miles from Columbus. He asked Mrs. Tucker if she knew of anyone who was going and might be willing to take him along. She and Carson were already planning to travel to Atlanta for the concert in an automobile belonging to a neighbor of the Tucker family, who readily agreed to take on another passenger. "It was at a concert of Rachmaninoff that I met my first adult friend," Carson reported: "He was twenty-three and I seventeen and we could talk about all sorts of things together. Not only music, but he introduced me to Carl Marx and Engels, and that probably was the dawn of social consciousness in me. I had realized so often during the depression, when I saw Negros rooting through the garbage pails at home, and coming to the house to beg, that there was something fearful and wrong with the world, but I had not in any way thought of it intellectually." She continued, "My new friend, Edwin Peacock, came every Saturday afternoon, and his visits were a joy to me. I was not 'in love,' but it was real friendship, which has indeed lasted throughout all my life."[13]

Peacock, as it happened, was also a great reader with a passionate interest in literature and politics (he later opened a bookstore in Charleston, South Carolina, with his friend John Zeigler). Carson was boundlessly curious, and Peacock widened the scope of her readings. Carson liked Walt Whitman and Hart Crane in particular, but she also took great pleasure in the works of D. H. Lawrence. During this time Carson read Lawrence's lovely short story "The Prussian Officer," whose theme is not unrelated to that of one of her future books, *Reflections in a Golden Eye;* she would even be accused of having plagiarized the book, by the *New Yorker* magazine on January 15, 1941.

Although Peacock was living at Fort Benning when he met Carson, he was not a military man. He belonged to the Civilian Conservation Corps, created by President Roosevelt to provide work for unemployed young people. Some time later he left the base and took a room in downtown Columbus. He and Carson were then able to see each other almost every evening. She went to his room to listen to music and to "remake the world," as young people so often do, generation after generation. But in 1930s Columbus — and elsewhere — nice girls did not go to a man's room alone. The small-minded provincials of Columbus were scandalized by the conduct of "the elder Smith girl." Rumor had it that on certain evenings Carson dressed up like a boy and went abroad in the town with Peacock and that sometimes they left Columbus for Phenix City, Alabama, otherwise known as "Sin City," where Fort Benning soldiers went looking for girls. Fortunately for Carson, her parents were unfazed by small-town gossip. Marguerite, who always thought highly of her daughter, wanted Carson to be free to do exactly as she chose.

In her biography Virginia Spencer Carr dwells on every account that presents Carson Smith as a girl with a masculine first name who wore men's clothes in a more or less conscious attempt at self-disguise. But might this not be going too far? Would it be outrageous to suggest that Carson may have favored outfits that resembled men's simply because they looked good on her and were well suited to her androgynous physique? Looking back, we can say that Carson was simply ahead of her time, more like the young people of the 1970s and 1980s than she was like respectable young girls from the South of the 1930s.

Whatever people may have been saying about her did not affect Carson, who was happy finally to have found a friend who listened to her, gave her support, and encouraged her to write. But Carson knew that she would have to leave Columbus if she was going to build a life for herself rather than simply submit to one. And she could not make up her mind. The indispensable break with the scene of her childhood was no doubt made easier by the departure of Mary Tucker, whose husband had just been transferred to Maryland in the spring of 1934. That separation from her "other family" was certainly traumatic for Carson — the wound left its mark in *The Member of the Wedding* — and it is true that she would not see Mrs. Tucker again for more than fifteen years.

Many have laid stress on the "great rupture" between the young Carson and the object of her impossible passion. Others have gone so far as to trace Carson's decision not to become a musician back to Mary Tucker's departure — while several accounts, among them

Helen Jackson's and Carson's own, place the decision long before that event, and still others recall its taking place long afterward.

More than anything else, Mary Tucker's leaving represented for Carson childhood's end. It compelled her to learn that reality sometimes, even often, stands in the way of desire. It is also possible that Mrs. Tucker took advantage of her relocation to assert her need for distance, to sever Carson's adolescent passion, to bring her "adoption" to a close. And everything that tended to make Carson understand that adolescence — with its rejection of compromise, its refusal to reconcile itself to the real — was a transitory state seemed to her an outrage, an abomination.

The shock of that unwelcome separation, which felt so much like an abandonment, probably did hasten Carson's decision to go north and study in New York. She took a steamer from Savannah, Georgia, in September, and laid eyes on the ocean for the first time. But what was she planning to study once she got to the big city? In 1942 she explained that she had come to New York "with the idea of going to classes at Columbia and at the Institute at Juilliard [the Juilliard Foundation]." But on her second day there, she went on to say, "I lost all my tuition money on a subway. I was hired and fired for various part-time jobs and went to school at night."[14]

Quite a different version of the story appears in her autobiography:

> I yearned for one particular thing; to get away from Columbus and to make my mark in the world. At first I wanted to be a concert pianist, and Mrs. Tucker encouraged me in this. Then I realized that Daddy would not be able to send me to Juillard or any other great school of music to study. I know my Daddy was embarrassed about this, and loving him as I did, I quietly put away all thoughts of a music career, and told him I had switched "Professions," and was going to be a writer. That was something I could do at home, and I wrote every morning.
>
> My first book was called "A Reed of Pan," and it was, of course, about a musician who really studied and accomplished things. However, I was not satisfied with the book and did not send it to New York, although I'd heard of agents and so forth. I was sixteen years old and kept on writing. This time the book was called "Brown River." I don't remember very much about it except it was strongly influenced by [D. H. Lawrence's] "Sons and Lovers."

My grandmother had willed "to her gray-eyed grandchild" the only article of value that she had; a beautiful emerald and diamond ring. I put it on my hand just once, because I knew that I had to sell it. My Daddy, who was a jeweler in the town, sold it so that I was able to go to New York and take a course in creative writing and philosophy.

So, at last, I was leaving home and going to study. A girl I'd never met before was taking courses at Columbia, and she invited me to share her room with her. Daddy took one look at her and was dubious about the arrangements, because the girl had dyed hair, at a time when only "fast" girls dyed their hair. However, he let me go.

I travelled by boat from Savannah to New York, so for the first time I saw the ocean, and later, marvel of marvels I saw snow.[15]

We know only one thing for sure: the cash from Lula Waters's emerald and diamond ring had disappeared. What really happened? Either Carson lost the money herself, or the friend to whom she entrusted it did so. That friend may even have seized the cash for her own purposes, declaring it lost.

Carson's sister, Margarita Smith, suggests that the exact details of what happened are not really important. In her preface to the posthumous collection *The Mortgaged Heart,* she quotes Tennessee Williams's unpublished essay "Praise to Assenting Angels," in which the playwright gives his version of the story with his usual humor:

> The great generation of writers that emerged in the twenties, poets such as Eliot, Crane, Cummings and Wallace Stevens, prose-writers such as Faulkner, Hemingway, Fitzgerald and Katherine Anne Porter, has not been succeeded or supplemented by any new figures of corresponding stature with the sole exception of this prodigious young talent that first appeared in 1940 with the publication of her first novel, *The Heart Is a Lonely Hunter.* She was at that time a girl of twenty-two who had come to New York from Columbus, Georgia, to study music. According to the legends that surround her early period in the city, she first established her residence, quite unwittingly, in a house of prostitution, and she found the other tenants of the house friendly and sympathetic and had not the ghost of an idea of what illicit enterprise was going on there. One of the girls in this establishment became her particular friend and undertook to guide her about the town, which Carson McCullers found con-

fusing quite imaginably, since even to this day she hesitates to cross an urban street unattended, preferably on both sides. However a misadventure befell her. Too much trust was confided in this mischievous guide, and while she was being shown the subway route to the Juilliard School of Music, the companion and all of her tuition money, which the companion had offered to keep for her, abruptly disappeared. Carson was abandoned penniless in the subway, and some people say it took her several weeks to find her way out. . . . [R]egardless of how much fantasy this legend may contain, the career of music was abandoned in favor of writing, and somewhere, sometime, in the dank and labyrinthine mysteries of the New York subway system, possibly between some chewing-gum vendor and some weight and character analysis given by a doll Gypsy, a bronze tablet should be erected in the memory of the mischievous comrade who made away with Carson's money for the study of piano. To paraphrase a familiar cliché of screen publicity-writers, perhaps a great musician was lost but a great writer was found.[16]

So Carson no longer had the money that should have covered her college expenses for the year. She would have to work if she wanted to remain in New York. She did not alert her parents, convinced that they would simply send her a bus ticket home. But finding work was not easy in those years following the Great Depression. And Carson was somewhat lost in the city. She would often spend the afternoon reading in a telephone booth at Macy's department store because she felt safe there. At night she barely slept, for she was frightened all alone in a room that she supposedly shared — with a girl who was always somewhere else. If she really planned to spend a year in New York City, where she had started attending night classes at Columbia University, she would have to move. "Then finally, I thought I would go to the Dean of Women at Columbia, and ask her advice," she wrote in her autobiography.

"How old are you?" she asked me.
    "Seventeen," I said proudly.
    "You're much too young to be living alone in the city," and she suggested a Women's Club for students.
    I got my belongings together and moved into the Parnassus

Club. There, for the first time in more than a week, I slept. I slept
for twenty hours.

A girl at the Club was practicing a Bach Fugue, and I felt completely at home. I made friends easily and thankfully. When my
first and special friend told me that she was going to move to the
Three Arts Club, I decided to join her.[17]

Approximately 150 girls, most of them planning to enter professions in the arts, resided at the Three Arts Club. Carson made one or
two friends at these residences for young women with whom she occasionally went out for the evening. Still, she tended to steer clear of the
different groups that formed. She read and wrote a great deal. Every
day she mailed a letter to her mother, receiving one with the same
regularity. Those letters have been lost, and they are sorely missed by
everyone who seeks to understand the strange relationship between
Carson and Marguerite Smith. We know, however, that the mothers
in Carson McCullers's novels — except for the first one, where Mick's
mother remains very much in the background — have all disappeared. Only after 1955, the year Marguerite Smith died, do mothers
reappear in Carson's texts.

To earn money for her living expenses, Carson found various odd
jobs, as she would later call them, but no employer ever kept her very
long. She did quite well as an accompanist for dance lessons. But her
post at the magazine *More Fun and New Comics* went nowhere —
"Me, a tragic writer, editing the funny papers," she exclaimed ironically in "Illumination and Night Glare":

The job was to be the front man for, as I soon discovered, the magazines were being sued. I was sincerely grateful when they fired me
after a couple of months.

Then I was faced with the job situation again, and I found one
with Mrs. Louise B. Fields, who insisted on calling me a Real Estate
salesman. I checked with customers about apartments in New York.
The main part of the job, I remember, was that Mrs. Fields would
send me out for sour cream. She would eat the sour cream with a
long ice tea spoon. But once, when I was reading Proust behind the
ledger and got involved in a long Proustian sentence, Mrs. Fields
caught me. She picked up the ledger and banged me over the head
with it. Her parting, venomous shot was you will never amount to

anything in this world, and [she] banged me again with the ledger. So, under such circumstances, I was fired again.[18]

Every one of Carson McCullers's biographers relates this particular episode. What a pleasure for a writer, after the fact, to have lost a mediocre temporary job for the love of Marcel Proust, for being totally absorbed in *Swann's Way*!

A short story called "Court in the West Eighties" attests to those lean times. Though very well written, it was never published during Carson McCullers's lifetime.[19] In the story an eighteen-year-old girl arrives in New York from out of town and, living in a rather shabby building, from her window observes her neighbors — a young couple, a cellist, and a man with red hair. She sees them coming and going, living their lives, moving out never again to be seen. She knows their quirks, their petty annoyances, the problems they have tolerating each other, their distress, and sometimes their rage.

◆   ◆   ◆

While Carson was enjoying her first taste of independence, Edwin Peacock, back in Columbus, met a young, very handsome serviceman from Fort Benning, and the two became friends. "Meanwhile, my friend Edwin in Columbus, had written me that while he was at the library he had met a young man and had invited him to his house for drinks," Carson recalled. "He said he was charming, and he thought that I would like him very much and we would get together when I came home."[20] Peacock introduced his new friend, James Reeves McCullers — who, like Carson, used only his middle name — to the Smith family. Marguerite was captivated, adopting Reeves as she had Edwin Peacock and including him in the circle of young people she was fond of receiving in her home.

Carson did not return to Columbus until June 1935. She had begun writing classes with Dorothy Scarborough and Helen Rose Hull in February at Columbia. At the end of the academic year she departed for the South and, immediately upon arriving home, decided to start working for the local newspaper, the *Columbus Ledger*.[21] She did not last long. Her intention had been to learn something about journalism and to maintain the regular writing habits that she had developed in her classes. The attempt was an utter failure. She was much too

dreamy to be a reporter and totally immune to the excitement of
working on a news story. And she hated it, profoundly. Later on she
told her first biographer, Oliver Evans, that she had been unable to
meet even the minimal requirements of the job and persisted, for example, in referring to "the murderer in the city jail," even though she
was told every time to write "the alleged murderer."[22] Such a profession, in her view, was fit only for people who were totally lacking in
imagination. In leaving the *Ledger,* Carson loudly broadcast how she
felt: "I'd starve to death before I'd do what you do," she announced to
Latimer Watson, the woman's editor of the paper.[23]

Despite the unpleasant surprise provided by Carson's brush with
journalism, the summer of 1935 also yielded "the" encounter of her
life. "So in June I went home and met Reeves McCullers at Edwin
Peacock's apartment," Carson wrote.

> There was a shock, the shock of pure beauty, when I first saw him;
> he was the best looking man I had ever seen. He also talked of Marx
> and Engels, and I knew he was a liberal, which is important, to my
> mind, in a backward Southern community. Edwin, Reeves and I
> spent whole days together, and one night when Reeves and I were
> walking alone, looking up at the stars, I did not realize how time
> had passed, and when Reeves brought me home, my parents were
> distressed, as it was two o'clock in the morning. However, my
> mother was also charmed by Reeves, and he would bring her rec-
> ords of music. At that time he was a clerk in the army at Ft.
> Benning, Georgia. We both loved sports and often Reeves would
> borrow Edwin's bicycle and we would go off to the Girl's Scout
> Camp, about thirty miles away. Mother would pack a lunch and
> we'd ride side by side, stopping off now and then for a cold coke.
> Chess was his great hobby, and after swimming in the brown, cool
> water, we would play a game, (he would always beat me.) Then
> swimming again and then the long ride home. I was eighteen years
> old, and this was my first love.[24]

Corporal McCullers was twenty-two years old, but he looked more
like eighteen. Born on August 11, 1913, in Wetumpka, Alabama, he
had spent his early childhood in Jesup, Georgia, and then returned to
his home state. Carson for her part was eighteen, but though practically as tall as Reeves, she could easily have passed for three years

younger. The two young people were constant companions that summer. With Edwin Peacock they formed a threesome of inseparable friends, to the delight of Marguerite Smith. Reeves was charming, and Marguerite did not wait to ask Carson what she thought before making him one of her intimates. Every time he came to call, Reeves brought flowers, which Mrs. Smith particularly appreciated, as well as candy and fruit for the children. After meeting Carson, he never failed to bring the beer and cigarettes she was so fond of whenever he paid her a visit.

In 1931, after graduating from high school, Reeves had enlisted in the army for three years and was stationed at Fort Benning. In November 1934 he signed on for another three-year hitch. In Wetumpka, before joining the army, Reeves had been everything that Carson was not: a leader, well liked by his fellow students, admired for his charm and his physique, envied by boys because girls found him attractive, good at football, and good in class. Yet little James Reeves McCullers Jr. had had a difficult childhood, tossed back and forth between an unstable father who had tried his hand at everything — and drank too much — and a mother who was totally absorbed by her efforts to cope. Jessie McCullers (1888–1964) was vigorous and solid, but she often had to dispatch her children (of which she bore five between 1913 and 1921) to other members of the family because life was so tough at home. In the McCullers clan women were strong and men weak. Perhaps Reeves would later see himself as a victim of that gender inversion. Nor were things much different in Carson's family, for that matter. Aware of these patterns, Carson would try early in their liaison not to dominate Reeves and to bolster his sense of virility.

The portrait of Reeves drawn by Oliver Evans — which surely owes a lot to Carson McCullers, since that first biographical essay was written and published during her lifetime — makes him sound like a highly attractive young man:

He was . . . of Irish ancestry, and handsome in a virile kind of way — blond, with grey-blue eyes, unusually regular features, and a hard, well-knit body which he kept in perfect condition. His height — fairly short for a man — was approximately Carson's own. He had not gone to college — this was to be a source of dissatisfaction to him later — but he was intelligent, well-read and well-spoken. There was even something a little disconcerting about his charm — not that it was "professional" in any sense (on the contrary, it was supremely natural) nor that he "traded" on it, at least not consciously, but nearly everyone who knew this man, whose career was destined to be such a tragic one, agrees that there was something almost uncanny about the way he attracted people to him — all kinds of people, and animals as well. This was one of the ways in which he and Carson were different: she did not make friends easily (though she was fiercely loyal to them when she did), while Reeves would not have found it easy, even if he had tried, to make an enemy.[25]

In their social relations Carson and Reeves were in fact very different. But in their way of looking at the world and viewing their existence they had many things in common, beginning with an unbridled fondness for literature — not as a form of entertainment but as a way of reading the world, and perhaps of trying to write it. Nonetheless, Reeves was much more a teller than a writer of tales. He told stories magnificently, and people listened to him with passion. But that was not enough for him. Was it during that summer of 1935 spent side by side, with Carson writing nearly every day, that Reeves began expressing his desire to be a writer so he might "become someone"? "I'd been writing for a couple of years and Reeves said he was going to be a writer also," Carson McCullers would write.[26] Had she already developed the habit of preparing full Thermoses of "hot sherry tea" for herself in the morning, containing more sherry than tea? And did Reeves already drink too much himself? The Smith family would not likely notice — no one there shied away from alcohol, an unexceptional state of affairs in the South of that era. Were Carson and he already drinking together? No doubt they were, but as people do at a never-ending party, talking ceaselessly late into the night. That kind of drinking had nothing to do with the pathology that developed later on.

But from the moment they first met, beyond their identical tastes and their mutual attraction, there existed between those two young people a more profound, more irrational bond, a strange twinning that no one will ever really understand. Commentators have desperately striven to prove who was to blame for their common disaster, eagerly seeking to reveal the couple's demons — malice, an urge to destroy, a will to harm — while failing to notice that from 1935 until Reeves's death (that is, for nearly twenty years) the two were never really able to separate.

As often happens, fiction, with its freedom to "authentically invent," provides the most accurate description of their resemblance, their secret attachment. The young French novelist Linda Lê devoted one of the four narratives that make up her fascinating *Les Évangiles du crime* (The four gospels of crime) to a certain "Reeves C.," husband of a famous American novelist. She tells their story with great sensitivity, often coming closer to the mark than those who claim to tell it objectively:

> The man who played destiny's mediator was named Edwin. One day he decided to introduce his two friends, Carson and Reeves, to each other. . . . They met on a summer's day. Reeves was wearing his military uniform, Carson a pair of men's trousers and a jacket that was too large for her. . . . In the beginning Edwin never left them alone; his presence kept them from getting to know each other completely, left them feeling as if they were still strangers. . . . Edwin eventually slipped away. . . . Carson put her hand in Reeves's, and they sat together in silence. If I had passed the window of their room and seen them as they were at that moment, hand in hand with a smile on their lips, I would have said to myself: those two kids, looking like a couple of orphans with no need for anybody else, are whetting the hangman's imagination. . . . Reeves declared his love for her. . . . He said he loved her like a brother with an ill-fated future loves his somewhat shady little sister. . . . Carson gazed at him with her sad, frantic eyes. She was usually the one who behaved this way, the one who summoned others to love her, but in a way that caused them to reject her. She believed that she alone was afflicted with such pride. She believed that she alone, ham actor and vandal all at once, could beg for affection the way Reeves was doing. She had met her double, and when that double declared to her his love, it was as if he were making a threat.[27]

Reeves had heard so much about Carson that he may already have been a little in love with her before the two met, according to Edwin Peacock. Peacock retained a dazzling memory of those summer months in 1935. Throughout his life, whenever he described them, he recalled a season "outside of time" with retrospective indulgence and emotion for fleeting youth: he was suddenly strong, master of his fate, capable of acting on the real. Together, Edwin Peacock remembers, the three companions had never-ending talks about literature and politics. Mr. Smith loaned them his four-cylinder cabriolet. They would put a phonograph on the backseat and drive around the outskirts of Columbus. On certain days, when Edwin wasn't free, Carson and Reeves would go swimming together in the nearest pond — as lovers. But "we had never made love sexually because I told him I did not want that experience until I was clear in my mind that I would love him forever," Carson McCullers was careful to state.[28] This is a far cry from the triumphant, provocative amazon, the cavalier enthusiast of self-disguise that others have depicted on more than one occasion.

When Carson left again for New York in September, she considered herself practically engaged to Reeves. At the Washington Square College of New York University, she signed up for two semesters of writing classes with Sylvia Chatfield Bates, a professor with an excellent reputation for artistic sensitivity, open-mindedness, and an ability to discover and encourage young talent. It is surely thanks to her that Carson definitively made the decision to become a writer. In so doing, she not only took a risk but also commenced an endeavor requiring strength, resistance, and a capacity to persevere. Sylvia Chatfield Bates made Carson understand that she was truly gifted, to the point of being able to "embark on the adventure." We see this in Mrs. Bates's comments on the short story "Poldi," the first in a long series of tales of nonreciprocal love — this time between the little pianist Hans and the cellist Poldi Klein.

This is an excellent example of the "picture" story — which means full dramatization of a short time scheme, the picturing of an almost static condition the actual narrative elements of which are in the past or in the future. The situation is rather trite, but not very. You can rescue it from triteness — as Willa Cather did in *Lucy Gayheart* — by the truth, accuracy and freshness of detail. Many a story sells on its detail; yours, so far as I have seen them, may be that sort. These details are good. Very vivid. Also a special knowledge story has a bid for success, and your special knowledge of music exhibited here sounds authentic. A musician can judge that better than I.

The average reader will want more than your static picture vividly presented — movement forward, at the very least suggested for the future. But I like this as it is. For what it is it need not be much better done.[29]

A similar acknowledgment of Carson's literary qualities by her professor can even be found in Mrs. Bates's reading of what might be called a premonitory text, depicting a scene between two alcoholics, a husband and wife. Sylvia Chatfield Bates did not like "Instant of the Hour After," whose plot struck her as too thin and insufficiently developed. She could not see why we "should . . . be given all these rather disagreeable details, only at the end to hear his [the husband's] love is so great it will destroy him."[30] To her, the story needed to be reworked, perhaps even completely rewritten. But the first paragraph of her commentary clearly shows how highly she regarded her student's talent:

> I like this the least of anything you have done, so you see I do not always praise you! The good points first: If I had never seen anything you had done I should have to comment on the great vividness, the acute visibility of your writing. The dramatization of every little detail is excellent, and fresh. And the characters come through the objective scenes beautifully. The "feature" of the story is the delightful little "element of artistic piquancy," the two persons in the bottle. That is memorable and good.[31]

◆   ◆   ◆

Reeves was bored in Columbus after Carson left. He, too, was growing more and more eager to head north — all the more so since his friend John Vincent Adams had just moved to New York to further his studies and perhaps, he said, to write. But getting out of the army, in which Reeves had re-upped the year before, would cost him approximately $1,500, and he did not have one red cent. So he tried to forget his dreams of leaving, of studying, of books, and settle down to being simply Corporal McCullers again. Once he had decided, under duress, to resign himself to his fate, one of his aunts died, in January 1936, leaving him a bit of money — enough, at any rate, to buy his way out of the army. Reeves was therefore able to free himself from his military obligations and a few months later, having returned to civilian life, move in with John Vincent Adams at 439 West Forty-third Street in New York. He then enrolled at Columbia, in anthropology and journalism, for the fall term.

Meanwhile, in June, Carson returned to Columbus, exhausted by her year at college. But the idyllic summer of 1935 was not to be repeated: Sylvia Chatfield Bates had recommended that her student take a summer course at Columbia given by Whit Burnett, an excellent professor who, in addition to teaching, directed *Story* magazine with his wife, Martha Foley. This periodical was renowned for the high-quality short stories it published and for its propensity to discover new authors.

"It is scarcely possible to overestimate the importance of this magazine in the Thirties and Forties," notes Oliver Evans,

> which published the first stories of William Saroyan, J. D. Salinger, Tennessee Williams, Jesse Stuart, Frederick Prokosch, Truman Capote, Nelson Algren, and Norman Mailer, and which numbered among its regular contributors William Faulkner, Sherwood Anderson, and Erskine Caldwell. At one time or another Gertrude Stein, William March, Kay Boyle, James T. Farrell, and Richard Wright had all appeared in it, as well as a good many writers from across the Atlantic: Frank O'Connor, Graham Greene, Seán O'Faoláin, and, in translation, Ignazio Silone and two distinguished Nobel Prizewinners, Luigi Pirandello and Ivan Bunin.[32]

Thanks to Whit Burnett, Carson Smith would be published for the first time in *Story* in December 1936. The magazine bought "Wunderkind," the story of a fifteen-year-old child-prodigy pianist believed to have a bright future ahead of her who suddenly understands that she will not be a great musician. This was Carson's way of abandoning once and for all her mother's dream — which for a time had been her own — that she would become a concert pianist. With the $25 she received — proof that she was really a writer, a professional — she bought chocolate cakes, a bottle of wine, and a book by Thomas More. Whit Burnett also bought "Like That," another story written by Carson Smith. But he never published the piece (discovered in the archives of *Story* magazine, it did not appear during Carson

McCullers's lifetime), judging this account of a painful, anxious puberty described by a child who watches with alarm as her older sister becomes an adult, complete with a discussion of girls' periods, to be unpublishable in the mid-1930s. It would have to wait, in his view, for more liberated times.

Before experiencing her first success and the beginning of a writing career, Carson again fell very seriously ill, in November. Reeves, who was taking courses at Columbia, left school to take her back to Columbus. She was believed to have tuberculosis, and once again Carson's rheumatic fever went undiagnosed and untreated. Carson urged Reeves to get out of Columbus and return to his life in New York. During her long convalescence she embarked on a large-scale project — namely, a novel. Though weakened by her illness, she worked long hours, eating almost nothing and smoking some three packs of cigarettes a day. Her every thought was focused on the book. Its hero was first called John Minovich, then Harry Minowitz — a character by the same name would appear in the published version of the novel four years later, but he was no longer the hero — and finally John Singer, a deaf-mute.

Once all the elements were firmly in place, Carson experienced what became her customary modus operandi as a writer: For a time she would get nowhere, groping in the dark, writing things down for days that made no sense to her or, in any case, bore no relation to what she was trying to achieve. Then suddenly she would have one of the "illuminations" she evoked whenever she was asked to explain her creative method. Carson McCullers described these events, "the grace of labor," in a passage from "The Flowering Dream: Notes on Writing":

> I understand only particles. I understand the characters, but the novel itself is not in focus. The focus comes at random moments which no one can understand, least of all the author. For me, they usually follow great effort. To me, these illuminations are the grace of labor. All of my work has happened this way. It is at once the hazard and the beauty that a writer has to depend on such illuminations. After months of confusion and labor, when the idea has flowered, the collusion is Divine. It always comes from the subconscious and cannot be controlled. For a whole year I worked on *The Heart Is a Lonely Hunter* without understanding it at all. Each char-

acter was talking to a central character, but why, I didn't know. I'd almost decided that the book was no novel, that I should chop it up into short stories. But I could feel the mutilation in my body when I had that idea, and I was in despair. I had been working for five hours and I went outside. Suddenly, as I walked across a road, it occurred to me that Harry Minowitz, the character all the other characters were talking to, was a different man, a deaf mute, and immediately the name was changed to John Singer. The whole focus of the novel was fixed and I was for the first time committed with my whole soul to *The Heart Is a Lonely Hunter.*[33]

3

THE BIRTH OF CARSON McCULLERS

W HEN REEVES RETURNED to New York for a new academic term at Columbia, Carson still had not recovered from what was thought to be tuberculosis. He had been reluctant to head north again without Carson, whom he now called his fiancée, but she insisted, promising to write almost daily. Reeves moved in as before with his friend John Vincent Adams and, finally, was living the student's life he had dreamed of. It lasted for a full term — the only one of his life. When classes let out in the spring, the two young men rented a country cottage on Lake Katona in Golden Bridge, some fifty miles north of New York City. A room was reserved there for Carson, who joined them as soon as she felt strong enough to make the trip. Reeves drove into New York to pick her up. But their desire to share a peaceful spring holiday as lovers, alone, far away from family members, was abruptly confounded: Carson had hardly spent two weeks in Golden Bridge when she again fell ill and sought her mother's care, as she always did when she was unwell. With Reeves by her side, Carson took the steamer back to Georgia.

John Vincent Adams and Reeves McCullers had hatched a plan to spend some time living in Mexico. That land of adventures and legends, with its long, serpentine history, would make an inspirational setting for his first novel, Reeves declared. But Adams for his part seems at least to have deferred his ambition to write the next great American novel, his professed aspiration five years earlier when he and Reeves had met at Fort Benning. He decided to marry and abandon the prospect of a Mexican journey. Then Reeves, too, began thinking about marriage — to Carson, of course. Except that he would need a little money. He would have to find a job, no mean feat in those tough economic times. After various fruitless attempts in several cities, Reeves went to Charlotte, North Carolina, where one of his uncles, John T. Winn Jr., lived very frugally with his wife and two young sons. Reeves was hoping to become a reporter at the local daily, the *Observer*. Yet again, he struck out.

Despite the roadblocks he encountered, mobilized by his desire to marry Carson, Reeves did not become discouraged. He kept on chasing leads no matter how improbable and in the spring of 1937 secured a position as credit investigator for the Retail Credit Corporation. He would be paid almost entirely on commission to place loans after investigating both the needs and the creditworthiness of potential borrowers, which required making forays into other people's lives, a task not at all to his liking. Though he complained about the job to John Vincent Adams, finding it as unstimulating as it was unprofitable, in his letters to Carson he emphasized the joy of earning the money they needed for their marriage and the pleasure of living in Charlotte, whose climate, much less scorching and less stifling than that of Columbus, agreed with him: an asthmatic, he had finally gotten rid of the constant attacks that had previously made his life miserable.

Carson, too, found herself dreaming about marriage that summer and was apparently charmed by the idea. She recuperated more quickly than usual from her illness. And not only did she try to earn a little money by giving lectures on music to several women of leisure from the cultured society of Columbus, but she let people know that she hoped to buy a wedding trousseau with her earnings. Never before had anyone heard her show interest in linens or clothes, though later on, she would develop a sensual taste for soft, expensive fabrics, white silk in particular. She wrote to Reeves with great regularity, sharing with him every detail of her daily life, every encounter. She was particularly taken by one of the women who attended her music lectures, Kathleen Woodruff, who had just returned from a European sojourn. Kathleen had lived in Paris for a time on that famous Left Bank where intellectuals and artists congregated. Paris was a city made for writers, and she and Reeves would go live there soon, Carson affirmed with quiet conviction. The weather was delightful, the setting magnificent, and near Saint-Germain-des-Prés one dined outdoors. In Paris "a writer could always find grist for his mill," she was told. "I'm going to be very famous," she concluded in her imperious and stubborn child-like way.[1]

Was it Carson who, before her future husband, forged the "European dream"? That conclusion seems a bit risky: from what was little more than an offhand conversation, she came away with a match between Paris and literature. In her mind the city was simply a stereotypical backdrop, a writers' fantasy — as such, she imagined her presence there as both necessary and inevitable. People laughed at her in those days, more or less openly, when Carson spoke of her literary future. Few believed that she was truly determined to become a writer or that such a destiny might be within the reach of this young woman from the South, this sickly daughter of the jeweler Lamar Smith and his fanciful wife, Marguerite.

◆　◆　◆

When his train arrived at the station in Columbus early in the day on September 20, 1937, Reeves McCullers knew that he had not saved enough money to marry Carson Smith, not by a long shot, especially since he had wrecked his car in an accident and had had to pay an extremely high repair bill. Still, he was resolved to go through with the wedding and wanted to get on with it immediately. It took place that very day, in the Smiths' home, with only Carson's family and Edwin Peacock in attendance. Carson and Reeves spent a matter of minutes making up their minds; the Baptist minister was asked to come at noon. Anywhere else such a scenario would have been totally outlandish, but extravagant events were more the rule than the exception at the Smiths'.

Marguerite, as usual, took everything completely in stride. Reeves wore a very simple suit; Carson bought a tailored ensemble but did not give up her heavy, flat shoes — heels would have made her taller than Reeves — or her white knee socks. It had been decided that the bride and groom's entrance into the living room would be accompanied by a passage from one of their favorite recordings, Bach's Concerto for Two Violins in D Minor. Legend has it that Peacock placed the album on the gramophone wrong side up and started playing a movement much too rapid for the occasion, further heightening the strangeness of the ceremony. Legend also has it that Marguerite Smith, extremely attached to Carson despite loving Reeves almost as if he were the son she had hoped for, calmed her fears regarding her daughter's marriage by repeating to herself these words from an old tune: "A son is a son 'til he gets a wife; a daughter's a daughter the rest of her life."[2] Typically, no account mentions Lamar Smith except to say that he was present. That same evening Reeves McCullers and Carson — who from that day forth, for the rest of her life and for posterity, would call herself McCullers — took the train to Charlotte. He was twenty-four years old and she just barely twenty.

Why marry Reeves? This is a question that Carson McCullers would have to answer many times. One of her most frequent responses was simply "because he was the first man who kissed me." She was not unaware that, for her readers, this remark could not fail to call to mind a scene she had written shortly after getting married, in her first book, *The Heart Is a Lonely Hunter.* While that scene is not a direct transposition, it is difficult to avoid mentioning it here, particularly since there is absolutely nothing in what Carson McCullers later wrote or in the life that she was known to lead, to refute the kind of bodily discomfort or to lessen the weight of a first kiss that Mick Kelly essentially disowned, instantly erasing it from consciousness. Such a kiss "leads straight to . . . sin," as Mollie said much later in *The Square Root of Wonderful.*[3]

"Maybe we better start back if we want to be home before dark."

"No," he said. "Let's lie down. Just for a minute."

He brought handfuls of pine needles and leaves and gray moss. She sucked her knee and watched him. Her fists were tight and it was like she was tense all over.

"Now we can sleep and be fresh for the trip home."

They lay on the soft bed and looked up at the dark-green pine clumps against the sky. . . .

They both turned at the same time. They were close against each other. She felt him trembling and her fists were tight enough to crack. "Oh, God," he kept saying over and over. It was like her head was broke off from her body and thrown away. And her eyes looked up straight into the blinding sun while she counted something in her mind. And then this was the way.

This was how it was. . . .

"We got to understand this," Harry said.

He cried. He sat very still and the tears rolled down his white face. She could not think about the thing that made him cry. An ant stung her on the ankle and she picked it up in her fingers and looked at it very close.

"It's this way," he said. "I never had even kissed a girl before."

"Me neither. I never kissed any boy. Out of the family."[4]

If Carson had to marry, it may have been for reasons that she never chose to clarify fully at any time throughout her life. She decided to live in the North, but never once did she spend any length of time in New York without falling ill. First of all, of course, because her health was not good. And because of the climate. But her almost pathological incapacity to live — and especially to sleep — alone cannot be totally dismissed as a factor in Carson's decision to marry. "We shared . . . the same room that looked out on the same holly tree and Japanese magnolia, and for the first twelve years of my life, the same mahogany bed," writes her sister in her introduction to the posthumous collection *The Mortgaged Heart*.[5] Throughout her life Carson liked nothing better than to slip unannounced into the beds of her friends. Some of them reacted with visible embarrassment or even discomfort, though it never took anyone long to realize that her actions were by no means sexual advances but indications of a childish need to snuggle up to someone. Generally, Carson liked to touch the people she talked to. It was a way of feeling closer, to be truly "with" them. "Now she had what she had wanted so many nights that summer; there was somebody sleeping in the bed with her. She lay in the dark and listened to him breathe, then after a while she raised herself on her elbow. . . . Then she breathed deeply, settled herself with her chin on his sharp damp shoulder, and closed her eyes: for now, with somebody sleeping in the dark with her, she was not so much afraid."[6]

During the first eight months of their marriage, Carson and Reeves were poor and happy — this seems to sum up, a bit ironically, the various accounts of the period provided by the couple's friends. Toward the end of her life — at a time when her view of her common existence with Reeves was far from idyllic — Carson herself described it in a way that, while emphasizing their poverty, also lets a kind of happiness show through:

On Saturday night, the house shining and my pencils sharpened and put away, we went to the wine store and bought a gallon of Sherry, and occasionally Reeves would take me to the S & W, which was an inexpensive restaurant in town. I could feel in Reeves none of the unhappiness or dissatisfaction that later lead to his ruin and death. . . .

At 4:00 AM one morning, after about two years of marriage, and with my full consent, Reeves . . . set out for the city, while I waited at home. Home was not a pleasant place without him. I was more aware of the miserable surroundings after he left.

It was a one family home, divided into little rabbit warrens with plywood partitions, and only one toilet to serve ten or more people. In the room next door to me there was a sick child, an idiot, who bawled all day. The husband would come in snd slap her, and the mother would cry.

"If I ever get out of this house," I would say to myself, but the words dwindled after the scream of the sick child, and the poor mother's useless efforts to calm her. I hated to go to the toilet because of the stench. I know my parents would have helped if they had seen me in such misery, but I was too proud.[7]

Despite legitimate suspicions that their marriage was less than blissful, it does seem that the months spent in Charlotte were the only period of their common life when Reeves and Carson were quite happy together, or at least untroubled. Carson came to know the unfamiliar rhythm of life as a couple. Reeves was handsome and charming, and he had a taste for literature. He believed in his wife's future as a writer. He himself planned to become one. The two experienced a kind of mutual fraternity, a feeling in fact that never left them despite everything that would divide them in the future and that they probably foresaw. As Linda Lê wrote in *Les Évangiles du crime*, "They lived this moment with exaltation; at the same time they were afraid. They were afraid of one another, they were afraid for one another. If they were called upon to meet, it was as two little lambs who were summoned to be led side by side to the sacrifice."[8]

In her letters to her friends, the young Mrs. McCullers recounted that she had just married a marvelous man. She embroidered somewhat on her husband's biography; embellished his childhood; explained that, like her, he wrote; and made up studies that he had supposedly completed. She was more precise in her physical description of Reeves. He was slim with curly blond hair — in a word, an extremely handsome man. She even stressed the fact that he was slightly taller than she, a highly desirable state of affairs for a couple (though his height exceeded hers by less than an inch). Reeves for his part annoyed those around him by posing as an intellectual. A few months of course work in journalism and anthropology in New York hardly gave him the right to look down on North Carolina's working men and women. That said, decades later this singular couple was described by people who had known them during that year of 1937 as "very much ahead of their time."

They might have said "modern" if the twentieth century's end were not marked by moralistic, puritanical, and familialist decline. Indeed, Carson and Reeves were more like a pair from the 1960s or 1970s, a time when more people believed that a couple could create life anew rather than passively conform to old models and narrow conventionality. In that spirit, the two struck a deal, a writer's pact: one after the other, they would each devote a year to writing; the nonwriting spouse would be responsible for earning a living for the couple that year. It was a dangerous promise, a vow made by twin adolescents who could not see beyond their enthusiasm or their desire for fusion and impossible equality: "In love one must never encounter one's double," the novelist Lê continues. "Two friends who resemble one another always reach an understanding: One of them chooses to remain behind, to play the role of the easy-going double who knows he's lost the race before it even starts; he will serve his alter ego as confidant, factotum, sole legatee. A pair of inseparable friends makes a reassuring spectacle. But a couple of lovers in which each one keeps a lookout on the other for an apparition of him- or herself is a spectacle that promises to be bloody."[9]

Writing: Carson would go first. She had already been published and had a manuscript in progress, and Reeves had a salaried position that he could not risk losing. But in their cramped two-room apartment Carson could not find a good place to work. The kitchen was too small to accommodate even the refrigerator, which encroached on the bedroom. Bookcases took up an inordinate amount of space, and Reeves hated sealing books away in boxes or banishing them to the attic. Carson wrote every day, and in the evening she supposedly read her day's work to her husband. The listening Reeves quickly became, for those who would reduce or even deny Carson's creative powers, a correcting Reeves who directed the work of the young writer. In any case, the two seem to have shared a real literary complicity.

They also spent evenings playing chess and, since there was no way to make music — Carson complained a great deal about the lack of a piano — listening to some on the Victor Electric phonograph. There were also cooking and cleaning to contend with. Carson, who had always had servants, did not know how to do anything, and Reeves's income was too small for them to hire an occasional housekeeper. Trying all the while to instill in Carson some housekeeping basics — wastebaskets should be emptied, for example — the young husband transformed himself at the end of his workday into a cook and handyman, and with no apparent displeasure — or at any rate without expressing any, as his aunt and uncle remarked with considerable chagrin. They were highly shocked by Carson's meager "feminine qualities," as they were by her appearance. They had found her likable at their first meeting despite her surprising getup — a loose-fitting embroidered shirt with long sleeves worn underneath a man's jacket; but as time passed, they were surprised that Reeves did not disapprove of his wife's unusual outfits.

Early that winter of 1937 the newlyweds moved into a more spacious apartment, where Carson could finally have a real work table. She wrote every day but was sometimes so cold that she took refuge in the local library. In letters to her friends Carson confided that the couple liked to drink and listen to music in the evening. They had a large demijohn of sherry, which they tried to make last. Reeves also liked wine, she noted, but had stringent standards, drinking it only when the quality was high. Reeves seemed to enjoy those times as well, though he was less passionate than Carson about music. Carson was particularly fond of Bach, but on the piano only, since she hated the harpsichord. As for opera, she enjoyed the melodies but detested the voices.

Reeves seemed happy to be able to tell friends such as John Vincent Adams that Carson was writing with great regularity and making constant progress. Although he had no time to devote to writing now, he declared himself serene, certain that his day would come. Yet the evenings were already less calm than they appeared in the couple's letters.

Alcohol was already too large a presence in their lives. Certain nights were much like those Carson described in the short story that Sylvia Chatfield Bates had not liked because its plot was too fuzzy and not fully developed. "Instant of the Hour After" is nonetheless the very fine — and no doubt highly revealing — description of a dreary night of drunkenness in which, etched between the lines, appear the first signs of destruction.

It came to her that she must have drunk more than she realized, for the objects in the room seemed to take on a strange look of suffering. . . .

When she stood above him once more, waiting for him to rise, she felt a moment of pain for the drained pallor of his face. For the shades of darkness that had crept down halfway to his cheekbones, for the pulse that always fluttered in his neck when he was drunk or fatigued.

"Oh Marshall, it's bestial for us to get all shot like this. Even if you don't have to work tomorrow — there are years — fifty of them maybe — ahead." But the words had a false ring and she could only think of tomorrow. . . .

With a shiver she got up from the couch and moved toward the whiskey bottle on the table. The parts of her body felt like tiresome appendages; only the pain behind her eyes seemed her own. She hesitated, holding the neck of the bottle. That — or one of the Alka-Seltzers in the top bureau drawer. But the thought of the pale tablet writhing to the top of the glass, consumed by its own effervescence — seemed sharply depressing. . . .

[The whiskey] made a sharp little path of warmness down into her stomach but the rest of her body remained chill. . . .

[Marshall's] white face sank into his hands.

Slowly, with a rhythm not of drunkenness, his body swayed from side to side. His blue sweatered shoulders were shaking. . . .

Tiredly she reached out for his head and drew it to her. Her fingers soothed the little hollow at the top of his neck, crept up the stiff shaved part to the soft hair at the top, moved on to his temples where again she could feel the beating there.

"Listen — " he repeated, turning his head upward so that she could sense his breath on her throat.

"Yes Marshall."

His hands flexed into fists that beat tensely behind her shoulders. Then he lay so still that for a moment she felt a strange fear.

"It's this — " he said in a voice drained of all tone. "My love for you, darling. At times it seems that — in some instant like this — it will destroy me."[10]

After eight months spent in Charlotte, Carson and Reeves were forced in May 1938 to move to Fayetteville, still in North Carolina, where Reeves had been transferred after receiving a promotion. He was put in charge of the local branch of the Retail Credit Corporation there. That small town of fifteen thousand inhabitants — most of them poor — apparently set down by some unseen hand in the midst of a sadly flat landscape, annoyed them from the outset. The air was always humid; it was harder to breathe there than in Columbus. They missed the hills and the coolness of Charlotte. Despite his reservations, Reeves attempted to integrate himself into the Fayetteville community and made a few connections to help his business thrive.

Carson did little to help him, however, and avoided small-town social events like the plague. Even when she attended them, she could not keep from making disagreeable remarks about the town and how boring it was, remarks whose effect was scarcely less disastrous than her absence. On top of her outlandish style of dressing, which gave rise to sharp whispered comments, Carson behaved in a way that was openly judged scandalous: she had been seen in the street speaking to blacks, that is, engaging them in conversation. A black man had been spotted entering her house — and he appeared to be a guest, not a servant. Clearly, there could be no question of associating with a woman so indifferent to the social codes that ruled the little town. Carson for her part openly detested the mediocre society of Fayetteville and could not stand the neighborhood they lived in: it was dirty, squalid, and foul-smelling, and their building, whose walls were too thin, was unbearably noisy. Assuming that there really had been a honeymoon period for Carson and Reeves, it was decidedly over in Fayetteville. Their relations deteriorated, and Carson kept repeating how unhappy she was far from her mother, the latter's daily letter notwithstanding. Despite her growing exasperation, however, Carson kept working every day on her manuscript.

Just before their move to Fayetteville, Carson had sent a synopsis (known today as "Author's Outline of 'The Mute'") and six chapters of her novel to the Boston publishing house Houghton Mifflin.[11] She had previously submitted her work to her former professor, Sylvia Chatfield Bates. Bates had recommended that she show it to the novelist William March, to whom she had introduced Carson back in New York. An enthusiastic William March could hardly believe that this text, given its style and maturity, was the work of an unpublished beginner. Buoyed by these reassurances, Carson had sent her manuscript to Houghton Mifflin with a little less anxiety. The response, long in coming, arrived in early summer: a contract and the promise of a $500 advance — $250 right away and the balance on publication of the book.

Carson had taken the important first step toward accomplishing her plan — and had dealt a stinging refutation to her doubters. She was even able to celebrate the good news with her mother, whom she had not seen since the day of her wedding nearly a year before. Reeves had managed to get a week's vacation in July, which the young couple spent in Columbus at the home of Marguerite and Lamar Smith. Carson would not let her check, the first installment on her advance, out of her hands, showing it off as if it were a trophy.

Political discussions at the Smiths' house were lively in that summer of 1938. For several years now Carson had been interested in politics, particularly politics in Europe, where war was starting and threatening to spread. Carson and Reeves, determined antifascists and antiracists, were convinced that the conflict would spread to all of Europe, and they hoped for U.S. involvement in the joint battle against Nazism. Lamar Smith, by contrast, feared seeing his country enter the fray. Carson's brother, Lamar Jr., who was nineteen years old, and her sister Rita, seventeen, were interested in the discussion and stuck close to home during that week.

Carson would have liked to stay on in Columbus a short while without her husband. But before returning to Fayetteville, Reeves planned to attend a conference in the mountains at Blowing Rock. The trip sounded too pleasant to pass up, and it was. On the way back home Carson and Reeves stopped in Charlotte, where Reeves's mother and sister were spending a few days with the Winns — the aunt and uncle who had helped Reeves get his bearings in Charlotte. The time had come for Carson to meet them. Reeves's sister was reticent before her singular sister-in-law, but his mother, Jessie McCullers, developed an immediate fondness for the odd girl that her older — and favorite — son had married. The fondness was reciprocal. Carson was attracted to her mother-in-law's energy, her zest for life despite a not-so-happy marriage, and her way of discouraging pity or condescension.

Back in Fayetteville, Reeves and Carson looked for an apartment that would better suit them, and in early autumn they moved to a more affluent neighborhood. Their bad reputation followed them, however: they listened to loud music late into the night, they drank, they fought. Edwin Peacock came to see them in December. As always, they were charming hosts and warm-hearted friends — Carson even cooked. But Peacock saw that something had changed between the two young people. Like those who spent time with the couple much later in France, he spoke of tension between them, with the exception of New Year's Eve, when Reeves suggested that the three go out to celebrate. On that night Peacock found his old friends to be exactly as they had always been, laughing a good deal, glad to be alive, resolutely optimistic in a nonetheless difficult world.

The year 1939 should have been Reeves's turn to write, but since Carson had a contract, it was she who kept on. Reeves understood that they had given up on the romantic but unrealistic idea of taking turns, and that for Carson, writing would probably always come first. Reality suddenly imposed itself: his strange wife-child was a writer — though at that time she had published only one short story in a magazine — and what mattered to her most was what she wanted to write. Everyone else's idea of "real life" would have to take a backseat.

The Mute was finished in April, and the manuscript conformed in all respects to the description provided in McCullers's "General Remarks," with which her "Author's Outline of 'The Mute'" begins:

> The broad principal theme of this book is indicated in the first dozen pages. This is the theme of man's revolt against his own inner isolation and his urge to express himself as fully as is possible. Surrounding this general idea there are several counter themes and some of these may be stated briefly as follows: (1) There is a deep need in man to express himself by creating some unifying principle or God. A personal God created by a man is a reflection of himself

and in substance this God is most often inferior to his creator. (2) In a disorganized society these individual Gods or principles are likely to be chimerical and fantastic. (3) Each man must express himself in his own way — but this is often denied to him by a wasteful, short-sighted society. (4) Human beings are innately cooperative, but an unnatural social tradition makes them behave in ways that are not in accord with their deepest nature. (5) Some men are heroes by nature in that they will give all that is in them without regard to the effort or to the personal returns.

Of course these themes are never stated nakedly in the book. Their overtones are felt through the characters and situations. Much will depend upon the insight of the reader and the care with which the book is read. In some parts the underlying ideas will be concealed far down below the surface of a scene and at other times these ideas will be shown with a certain emphasis. In the last few pages the various motifs which have been recurring from time to time throughout the book are drawn sharply together and the work ends with a sense of cohesive finality.

The general outline of this work can be expressed very simply. It is the story of five isolated, lonely people in their search for expression and spiritual integration with something greater than themselves. One of these five persons is a deaf mute, John Singer — and it is around him that the whole book pivots.[12]

After sending off her final manuscript, Carson started complaining to her friends. It supposedly took her publisher a long time to acknowledge receipt of her text, and she waited in vain for the second half of her author's advance before understanding that it would not be paid until the book was published. She had evidently been asked to make many changes, which she claimed to have refused with the exception of a few minor points. What the publisher recalls is how enthusiastic readers were about this first novel and the excitement and exaltation of having discovered a young, promising author. The only important change suggested by the publisher — and accepted by Carson McCullers — appears to have been that of the title. *The Heart Is a Lonely Hunter* comes from a poem by William Sharp, "The Lonely Hunter," in which this verse appears: "But my heart is a lonely hunter that hunts / On a lonely hill."[13]

Exhausted, in a semidepressive state, Carson left alone for Columbus. She wanted to be coddled by her mother — and to flee the reproaches of Reeves, who began to be openly annoyed by the sloppy state of the couple's apartment, by the accumulating disorder that seemed to escape Carson's notice.

But Carson would soon return to Fayetteville, where she spent two months writing a short text, *Army Post,* which would eventually become *Reflections in a Golden Eye.*[14] For the first — and only — time in her life, she had the feeling that writing was a breeze, that the work got done all by itself. "Afterward I was so tired but I couldn't stop," she told Tennessee Williams, "so I wrote *Army Post,* which took about two months. Wrote just like eating candy. Suddenly all the characters came to me. . . . then when I finished that I put it in the drawer."[15] She never even gave a thought to possibly publishing one day what she referred to as "a fairy tale," apparently based on an incident described by Reeves: at Fort Bragg, near Fayetteville, a young soldier was arrested as a voyeur, caught peering through the windows of the married officers' quarters. "Whereas Reeves had labored with her over *The Heart Is a Lonely Hunter, Army Post* was entirely her own creation," affirms Virginia Spencer Carr.[16] Nonetheless, it was the book whose authenticity would be most severely contested: some people have the opinion that only a man's eye and a man's imagination could capture and express life at a military post.

When she was writing, Carson was far removed from such debates, and she was entering a period of great productivity. Her confidence was bolstered by the successful completion of her first substantial project: *The Heart Is a Lonely Hunter.* And she needed to escape a situation that was weighing on her mind: Reeves's growing dissatisfaction. Still, Reeves was trying to avoid a promised transfer to Savannah, Georgia, for fear that Carson would not follow him into the Deep South. With the arrival of fall Carson returned to Columbus, where she confided to her mother that her marriage had begun to deteriorate. When Carson did not feel well, physically or psychologically, her mother was always the refuge.

In Columbus Carson also got some unfavorable professional news. Her literary agent, Maxim Lieber, wrote to her on November 10 to explain that two of her stories, "Sucker" and "Court in the West Eighties," had been rejected by so many magazines that they should give up trying to publish them:

I am sorry to say that your manuscripts SUCKER and COURT IN THE WEST EIGHTIES have been rejected by the following magazines respectively; The Virginia Quarterly, The Ladies' Home Journal, Harper's, Atlantic Monthly, The New Yorker, Redbook, Harper's Bazaar, Esquire, American Mercury, North American Review, Yale Review, Southern Review, Story, and; The Virginia Quarterly, The Atlantic Monthly, Harper's, The New Yorker, Harper's Bazaar, Coronet, North American Review, The American Mercury, The Yale Review, Story, The Southern Review, Zone, Nutmeg.[17]

Lieber returned the stories to McCullers. Nothing, however, seemed capable of breaking Carson's momentum in that fertile year. She began a new project, which she referred to as *The Bride and Her Brother* — an early version of *The Member of the Wedding* — whose genesis probably lay in her childhood despair at the departure of her piano teacher, Mary Tucker. She went back to Fayetteville to work, chaining herself every day to her typewriter. But the hours went by — and nothing happened. She could not find the central core of her novel, the focal point around which to build the story. "When I started writing *The Member of the Wedding*," she confided again to Tennessee Williams, "it was the most difficult and exacting work I have done so far. I . . . just couldn't get into it. Every day I'd write for hours but got nowhere. . . . I thought of this work as a prose poem. I don't think there should be any distinction between prose and poetry — I hate the word 'prose' — hate the word 'poetry' too. . . . I was trying to recreate the poetry of my own childhood."[18]

In the spring of 1940 Marguerite Smith came to Fayetteville to visit "her children." Marguerite had maternal feelings for Reeves, and he viewed her as his mother, as he did Jessie McCullers, whom he saw much less often. Marguerite felt as though the marriage was failing, and she wanted to do whatever she could to remedy the situation. Her presence lowered the tension between Carson and Reeves, and certain evenings she found them to be as mischievous and joyful as they had been in Columbus.

But Carson's mother was hardly in any position to teach her daughter to take a share in household tasks. She herself had little fondness for housekeeping chores. And her husband never had reason to complain, since the presence of servants had always made it possible for him to come home from the jewelry store to an impeccably maintained house. Such was not the case for Reeves, who for his part had to transform himself into a housekeeper, a cook, and sometimes a nurse when he came home from work. At least the presence of Marguerite Smith spared him the daily task of getting meals. For a reprieve Marguerite suggested that the three of them spend a weekend in Charleston at Edwin Peacock's.

It was a beautiful city, but Carson was in no mood for tourism when they arrived. She preferred to stay on the island where Peacock made his home, playing or listening to music in the house. Those few days nonetheless improved relations between "the children," and when the family trio returned to Fayetteville, the atmosphere was not as heavy as before. Straightaway, Reeves tried to get a job further north, still in a retail credit firm, and if possible in New York. He knew that nothing would give Carson more pleasure than to leave the South for good.

On June 4, 1940, *The Heart Is a Lonely Hunter*, dedicated to Reeves McCullers and Marguerite and Lamar Smith, appeared in bookstores. Carson, who had turned twenty-three in February, was the literary discovery of the year — of the decade, some would say. Despite a few reservations among critics — though acclamations carried the day by a very wide margin — everyone recognized that this book revealed a new tone, a true writer's sensibility: in short, that the young Carson McCullers was a real find. "*The Heart Is a Lonely Hunter* is a first novel," Rose Feld wrote in the *New York Times Book Review* of June 16, 1940. "One anticipates the second with something like fear. So high is the standard she has set. It doesn't seem possible that she can reach it again." Reviewers were amazed by the accuracy of her tone, by her profound knowledge of human solitude, by the way she portrayed the entire little world of a Southern town. They praised the quality of her portraits, the strength of her characters: John Singer, the deaf-mute around whom the narrative revolves; Mick Kelly, a gangly adolescent who wants to become a musician (and behind whom lurks the profile of the little Carson Smith, who had shot up too fast); Biff Brannon, owner of the café where the characters cross one another's paths; Benedict Copeland, the black doctor, a Marxist intellectual; Jake Blount, the alcoholic rebel. "We have waited a long time for a new writer," observed May Sarton in the June 8, 1940, *Boston Evening Transcript,* "and now one has appeared it is an occasion for hosannahs. . . . It is hard to think that we shall have to wait a year or two before we can expect another book from this extraordinary young woman."

The Heart Is a Lonely Hunter is a magnificent novel that seems to have been written by a seasoned writer with a firm grasp of how to balance tragedy and humor, feeling and political analysis, rebellion and passion. Adolescents of all times and places can identify with the figure of Mick Kelly. A reader need know nothing at all about the Deep South to recognize old Doctor Copeland. Jake Blount is at once pathetic and comical, with his air of "a man who had served a term in prison or had been to Harvard College or had lived for a long time with foreigners in South America. He was like a person who had been somewhere that other people are not likely to go or had done something that others are not apt to do."[19] John Singer is a hyperbolic figure of isolation: a deaf-mute, he is separated early on in the story from his sole companion, another deaf-mute. He becomes the confidant of all the other characters. But he himself can confide nothing, and it kills him.

In a very fine article in the August 5, 1940, issue of the *New Republic,* the black writer Richard Wright, whom Carson McCullers would meet a few months later, compares her to Faulkner while stressing the qualities that are hers alone: "To me the most impressive aspect of 'The Heart Is a Lonely Hunter' is the astonishing humanity that enables a white writer, for the first time in Southern fiction, to handle Negro characters with as much ease and justice as those of her own race. This cannot be accounted for stylistically or politically; it seems to stem from an attitude toward life which enables Miss McCullers to rise above the pressures of her environment and embrace white and black humanity in one sweep of apprehension and tenderness."

Less than two weeks after the book's release, Reeves and Carson left Fayetteville with jubilation. They sent all their bags by train and boarded the *Atlantic Coast Line Champion,* bound for New York. There they moved into a fifth-floor Manhattan walkup at 321 West Eleventh Street, with the firm intention never again to make their home in a Southern state. Carson for her part was launched. Her dream of worshipful celebrity became in part a reality. Everyday life ceased to be a dismal series of boring obligations and finally matched her desires: she was being talked about; "important people" wanted to meet her; she was invited to parties; strangers recognized her on the street. She and Reeves went for walks in the city, hand in hand, stopping in front of all the bookstores to savor the display windows dedicated to Carson and the piles of books topped by photos of the young novelist wearing one of her husband's shirts. Readers' widespread amazement that such a young author had produced a book so mature, so well composed, sometimes so hard, turned to absolute stupor when Carson McCullers appeared on the scene. She was viewed by all as a child prodigy, for no one could believe that she had just turned twenty-three — Carson looked sixteen or seventeen at the very most.

Reeves seemed to share Carson's joy, yet he must have understood that the die had been cast. Between the two of them, she was the writer. And even if he finally got down to a project, if he followed it successfully through to the end, he would always wind up in second place. Besides, who could imagine two writers of the same generation using the same name? Carson had appropriated his. He would have to use a pseudonym. Had he already taken the full measure of his failure? At the literary level, no doubt he had. But he still believed in his own inner strength, in his ability to keep pace with Carson and become "someone," as he had decided he would during his adolescence. He did not resign himself, as he would some years later, to the idea that she would dominate him once and for all.

While Carson and Reeves enjoyed their beautiful spring in New York, war was spreading in Europe. After a "phony war," France gave way to Nazi occupation. But on June 18, General Charles de Gaulle, who had taken refuge in London, called on his fellow countrymen to resist the enemy and refuse defeat. While London became the center of the Resistance, New York became a home for exiles. The new celebrity Carson McCullers would meet some of the European intellectuals who sought refuge in the United States, among them two of the German author Thomas Mann's children: thirty-four-year-old Klaus and his older sister Erika, who, to obtain a British passport allowing her to travel more freely, had married, sight unseen, the English poet W. H. Auden, also in New York at the time.

In his personal journal Klaus Mann noted on June 26: "Another curious encounter, with the young Carson McCullers, author of that fine book *The Heart Is a Lonely Hunter.* Just now arrived here from the

South. A strange mixture of refinement and wildness, 'morbidezza' and naïveté. Perhaps very gifted. The book she's working on now will be the story of a Negro and a Jewish émigré: two pariahs. Could be interesting." Carson made friends with the Manns. In *Decision,* the literary magazine he created in the United States, whose first issue appeared on December 18, 1940, Klaus Mann published her work, along with that of other Southern writers such as Eudora Welty. Among the contents of the June 1941 issue, Mann mentioned in his journal on June 2, 1941, was "an extremely curious short story, melancholy and burlesque, by Eudora Welty, whose name is one to remember. (She comes from the Deep South, like Carson McCullers and like Faulkner, whose influence both of them — Welty and McCullers — have been subject to.)"[20]

Over the course of that 1940 springtime, according to biographer Virginia Spencer Carr, the timid Carson, growing bolder, tucked her book under her arm and without deliberation called on Greta Garbo, whom she had admired all her life. Wrapping Carson in simplistic stereotypes, Carr suggests that Carson cherished Garbo for her "male" side and her not very feminine style of dress. According to Carr, Carson declared her passion, asking for her idol's friendship, and Garbo courteously turned her away.[21] If the meeting did in fact take place, it's likely that Carson and Greta Garbo simply realized that they did not have much to say to each other.

However, through her European acquaintances, Carson did make friends with a thirty-two-year-old Swiss woman, Annemarie Clarac-Schwarzenbach, who would be one of the most troubling and important figures in her life. The two had made plans to meet in a bar because Annemarie, who had read *The Heart Is a Lonely Hunter* and found it "good but nothing more," wanted to meet the book's author. She sought to grasp why America, where she felt very much a foreigner while war was destroying the Europe she loved, had become so intensely infatuated with young talent. Carson was immediately conquered by Annemarie's androgynous beauty and believed she had found in the Swiss woman one of the doubles she was constantly searching for.

"She had a face that I knew would haunt me to the end of my life," wrote Carson. "Beautiful, blonde, with straight short hair. There was a look of suffering on her face that I could not define. As she was bodily resplendent I could only think of Myschkin's meeting with

Natasha Philopla ? in the 'Idiot,' in which he experienced 'terror, pity and love.' She was introduced by Erica as Madame Clarac. She was dressed in the height of simple summer fashion, that even I could recognize as a creation of one of the great Paris couturiers. . . . She asked me to call her Anna Marie right away, and we became friends immediately."[22]

Annemarie, too, had been published for the first time at the age of twenty-three, attracting notice. She herself had financed the publication of her book *Les Amis de Bernard* (Bernard's friends) — an account of what would later be referred to as "the lost generation" — in early 1931. The book received critical if not mass-market acclaim in Germany and sparked real enthusiasm in Switzerland. Annemarie, too, had played the piano since childhood and was a highly talented musician; she, too, had an exalted love of literature and found it difficult to face reality.

Annemarie had everything it took to instantly enchant the young Southerner, but far from being her double, she was almost her exact opposite. Married in 1935 to Claude-Achille Clarac, from whom she quickly separated, Annemarie was the daughter of a wealthy silk merchant, one of those refined and cosmopolitan upper-middle-class intellectuals who were protagonists and witnesses of a world and way of life that disappeared with World War II. Here is what Klaus Mann wrote about the young woman he called "our Swiss child" and described as the "eccentric scion of a patrician house":[23]

> She is proud and delicate and grave; she has an adolescent's pure forehead beneath soft ash blond hair. Is she beautiful? When she dined with us for the first time, in Munich, the Magician [Thomas Mann, in his children's sobriquet], who kept looking at her out of the corner of his eye with a mixture of uneasiness and pleasure, finally observed: "It's curious, if you were a *boy*, you would have to be considered *extraordinarily* handsome." But she *is* beautiful, even as a girl. The French poet Roger Martin du Gard well knew what he was thanking her for when he inscribed one of his books: "For Annemarie — whom I thank for meandering about this earth with the lovely face of an inconsolable angel."[24]

She was undoubtedly beautiful, in a curious way. "Her head was a Donatello David head," Carson wrote in an unpublished essay, "her blonde hair was smooth and cut like a boy's; her blue eyes dark and slow moving; her mouth childish and soft with shily parted lips."[25] Annemarie had traveled extensively and seen everything that Carson had dreamed of. Her father had found it convenient to dress Annemarie as a boy when she accompanied him on trips, letting her pass for one of his sons. How could Carson not have fallen crazily in love? Some biographers maintain that Carson threw herself at Annemarie; others claim that the young Swiss woman, ill at ease in America and using too many drugs, clung to Carson. Of course, in tales of seduction there are always *two* players, neither one fully in control. In her essay Carson attempts, legitimately, to paint herself as the well-balanced character at the side of a poor little rich girl who cried a great deal, drank even more, and took drugs for good measure. Annemarie was used to being wooed and no doubt took pleasure in Carson's admiration. She probably enjoyed at least somewhat the adulation of the touching child that Carson seemed to be. But her own sights were firmly set on seducing Erika Mann; Annemarie did not wish to be bothered by an adolescent who loved with the insistence of a girl with little amorous experience, though she spent long evenings with Carson that spring.

Reeves, meanwhile, was feeling abandoned. He had met Annemarie, and the two had gotten on extremely well together; but Carson, this time, had no wish to form a trio. Annemarie was certainly the first and most important of the women that Carson and Reeves called Carson's "imaginary friends," women who contributed much to the decline of their amorous relationship. Reeves put up with his wife's passions, according to Virginia Spencer Carr, "so long as they stopped short of the bed," but where Annemarie was concerned, he could no longer be certain of anything.[26]

And so here again, the matter of Carson's lesbianism, or rather bisexuality, arises. Some see a banal sentence spoken by Biff Brannon in *The Heart Is a Lonely Hunter,* "by nature all people are of both sexes,"[27] or the writer's claim to have been "born a man" as evidence of her bisexuality. It is just as easy, however, to make the opposite claim. Carson and Annemarie wrote in letters that they loved each other "like brothers" — not a terribly amorous phrase. Much later, when describing the last time the two women met, Carson said, "As I went out the door Anna Marie followed me, 'Thank you, my liebling,' she said and she kissed me. It was the first and last time we ever kissed each other."[28] How likely are two lovers who never shared a passionate kiss?

The labels *lesbian* and *bisexual* have been used by those who denigrate any form of marginality to distance themselves from Carson McCullers by categorizing her as an "abnormal artist." They have also been used by partisans of homosexuality — both male and female — who would appropriate the writer for their cause. This eagerness to label is more apt to obscure than to throw light on the romantic and sexual dynamics that motivated Carson. What no one seems to challenge is the notion that all beings are endowed with a penchant for the pleasures of the flesh. And yet, where in Carson's work or in her life or in her letters is there a description, or even a suggestion, of the physical pleasures of love, "deviant" or otherwise? Romantic crushes, by contrast, abound. She no doubt had an adolescent and quite bothersome way of pursuing women of whom she was enamored — to the point of causing them to flee her advances. Some, she failed to recognize, had absolutely no romantic interest in women, as was true of Katherine Anne Porter. But her romantic obsessions show little or no evidence of sexual desire. Rather, they reveal a wish to love in a kind of troubadourish manner that must have been present at the time of her meeting with Annemarie — and even earlier. Illness, too, may have affected the way in which Carson sought to love and be loved. Is it not within the realm of possibility, moreover, that Carson's desires were not strongly sexual and that, because they shared her gender, women may have struck Carson as less highly sexed and less sexually demanding than men? If one man nonetheless became the object of her infatuation — her French doctor, Robert Myers — it may well have been because Dr. Myers's profession formally ruled out any kind of sexual intimacy, placing Carson at a distance that may have seemed comfortable to her.

In Carson's novels sex is almost always linked to shame, repulsion, violence. As the American essayist Alfred Kazin points out, "In McCullers what fills the space usually occupied by man-and-woman love is a sensitiveness that charges other people with magical perceptions. She radiated in all her work a demand for love so total that another was to become the perfect giver, and so became magical. The world is so bleak that it is always just about to be transformed. . . . McCullers had the intuition that human beings could be in psychic states so absolute and self-contained that they repelled each other sexually."[29]

In addition to the disastrous bicycle ride with Harry Minowitz in

The Heart Is a Lonely Hunter, during which Mick makes love — so badly — for the first time, Miss Amelia of *The Ballad of the Sad Café* gets married and refuses, from her wedding night on, to be touched. A few days later, when her husband puts his hand on her shoulder, before he can even open his mouth, "she . . . swung once with her fist and hit his face so hard that he was thrown back against the wall and one of his front teeth was broken."[30] "There are the lover and the beloved, but these two come from different countries," Carson writes in *The Ballad of the Sad Café.*

> Often the beloved is only a stimulus for all the stored-up love which has lain quiet within the lover for a long time hitherto. And somehow every lover knows this. He feels in his soul that his love is a solitary thing. . . .
>
> It is for this reason that most of us would rather love than be loved. Almost everyone wants to be the lover. And the curt truth is that, in a deep secret way, the state of being beloved is intolerable to many. The beloved fears and hates the lover, and with the best of reasons. For the lover is forever trying to strip bare his beloved. The lover craves any possible relation with the beloved, even if this experience can cause him only pain.[31]

That the act of "stripping bare" — of taking something away rather than adding something on, such as pleasure or vitality — should be placed in such close contact with "relation" indicates at the very least the major risk of unlawful seizure that Carson seemed to dread in sexuality.

Largely, it has been individuals outside mainstream scholarly publishing who have addressed Carson's unrequited passions and her fear of the body, among them Jean-Pierre Joecker in the French periodical *Masques,* a "journal of homosexualities":

> For Carson love is not that of Eros, it is friendship-love, which is every bit as difficult to live. Carson is horrified of sex, yet it is constantly present in her books. . . . There is a kind of gap for Carson between sexuality and love, between fornication and beauty. Reeves was a beautiful man, and she loved him like a twin brother. . . . Bodies in Carson McCullers seem unaware of one another, though desire is right there on the surface. . . . Beauty and sex cannot coexist. Thus Miss Amelia in *The Ballad of the Sad Café* married Marvin

Macy, "the handsomest man in [the] region," but pushed him violently away when he tried to slip into her bed. She accepted physical contact only with her cousin Lymon, the little, ageless hunchback. . . . Sensuality prevails over sexuality. Friendship-love ends up being unlivable, and "abnormal" characters render symbolically the impossibility of finding love.[32]

Carson's taste for dressing like a man was noted by Anaïs Nin in her journal of 1943: "I saw a girl so tall and so lanky I first thought it was a boy. Her hair was short, she wore a cyclist's cap, tennis shoes, pants." This description highlights Carson's attire as a way of remaining adolescent, of refusing to join the ranks of women rather than a provocative display of sexual preference.[33] Writing about Annemarie Schwarzenbach, Carson describes herself as feeling at ease with "the kind of girls who do not give the impression that they want to be ladies, creatures who judge a man by the way he lets you pass first or picks up something you have dropped."[34] She wanted to be one of them.

Thus 1940 was the summer of Carson's passion for Annemarie. It was also the summer when the beginning writer discovered her peers. Thanks to Louis Untermeyer (Carson had read his autobiography, *From Another World,* that year), who was the first artist in the United States to consider her a great writer, Carson was invited to participate that August in the Bread Loaf Writers' Conference, an annual literary gathering at Middlebury College in Vermont. The towering figure of the poet Robert Frost dominated this intellectually exalting moment. Eudora Welty, another writer from the South and Carson's elder by nearly ten years, was also there — delicate, elegant, and silent, as was her way. Welty, an exceptional short story writer, a good daughter of the South who had stayed "home" — in Jackson, Mississippi — timidly described how she had gone boating with William Faulkner (he would choose her to present him with the gold medal for the novel of the American Academy of Arts and Letters in New York in 1962, the year of his death).

Carson was surely just as timid as Eudora Welty, if not more so. But in contrast to Welty's restraint, so prized by William Faulkner, Carson conducted herself in a way that could not fail to attract attention, with her young boy's body and her men's shirts — which she changed three times a day — with the way she drank, her passions, and her cruel texts. She drank gin in orangeade glasses. Louis Untermeyer dubbed her "the flower of evil" and predicted that she would die young. Untermeyer confided that their relationship that summer had been "a platonic affair intensified by not-so-platonic embraces." "We had been drinking a bit and going over passages of *Reflections* [*in a Golden Eye*]," he recounted. "The party inside was breaking up — it was well after midnight — and Carson gave me a goodnight kiss. Then she said, 'Would you like to sleep with me?' I said (ungallantly but honestly), 'I'm afraid I'm too tired.' 'Me, too,' said Carson. 'But I thought it would be nice to ask.'"[35] The response denotes an adolescent awkwardness, a kind of inadequacy where sexual matters are concerned, more than a casual ease.

Carson enjoyed her time at Bread Loaf. But she missed Annemarie and invited her to visit. Annemarie did nothing of the kind. She was on the New England island of Nantucket, where her friend Baroness Margot von Opel owned a house. She told Carson that she was deeply engrossed in her work and could not take her mind off it. In fact, she was not doing well: her relationship with the baroness was going sour, and Carson's insistence weighed on her mind. She had already confided her uneasiness to Klaus Mann in a letter written in July:

> It will probably be very difficult for you to understand that it is young Carson McCullers who has sparked such a violent crisis; she is seriously ill and lives in an imaginary world so bizarre, so remote from reality that it is absolutely impossible to get her to listen to reason. I thought I had acted with all due caution and had treated her gently, but she is waiting for me to arrive from one day to the next, convinced that I am her destiny. And now her husband has left her because of it. Naturally, Margot is right to say that one is not entirely blameless in such matters.[36]

In late August, upon leaving Middlebury, Carson had to stop in Boston for a visit with her editor, Robert Linscott, at the offices of Houghton Mifflin. Yet again, she tried to drag Annemarie along with her. The Swiss woman asked Robert Linscott to take care of Carson, suggesting that he accompany her to Cape Cod by way of consolation, and above all help her come to grips with reality. "It upsets me not to be in a position to do anything for Carson. I have a great affection for her and I would like the world to be different, for her to be able to face up to it more easily. I would like to be capable of never wounding her. But she is very candid and cannot accept the difficulties posed by the real."[37] When Carson returned to New York after her visit with Linscott, she was feeling extremely unwell. Progress on *The Member of the Wedding* had come to a halt. She discovered that Annemarie had had a long talk with Reeves, and Carson held it against her. She even accused her of "taking Reeves's side."

George Davis, editor in chief of *Harper's Bazaar* — before becoming that of *Mademoiselle,* where Carson often published — bought *Reflections in a Golden Eye* for $500 in August 1939. The novel, written when she was still in Fayetteville with Reeves earlier that year, would appear in two installments, in October and November. Davis invited Carson to come to a big house he had rented in the very nice neighborhood of Brooklyn Heights. In September, Carson left Reeves for what both hoped would be a healing separation and moved in at 7 Middagh Street, which for several years would be home to a community of intellectuals and artists. In addition to George Davis, who had taken the initiative to rent the house — after the composer Kurt Weill's death he would marry Weill's wife, the actress Lotte Lenya — occupants would include Richard Wright and his wife, Klaus and Erika Mann, Benjamin Britten, Jane and Paul Bowles, Wystan Auden, and the striptease artist Gypsy Rose Lee, who fascinated Carson by being so much the opposite of Annemarie, with her beauty in full bloom and her distaste for the tragic or for tedious relations.

Gypsy did have strange dealings, however, with a certain Mr. Wechsler, who came often at the most peculiar hours in a black, chauffeur-driven Packard with thick, smoked-glass windows and with "two very husky men on each side of him." One day he left a thousand dollars underneath the doormat, at a time, observes Carson, "when a thousand dollars was a thousand dollars."[38] The amorous gangster was killed two streets over from their house, Carson goes on to say, still visibly amused nearly twenty years later by that film-noir episode.[39]

The Swiss writer Denis de Rougemont, whom Golo Mann (another son of Thomas Mann) brought to Davis's house the following year, described it as "an unlikely household — Kafka and the 'Enfants Terribles' — with an atmosphere that was definitely old New York."

Some of the residents were writing, some were composing, some were doing sculpturing, and the piano students were always practicing with their doors ajar. They all had their meals together around a very long table served by two or three enormous black women. Wystan Auden, the greatest English poet since Eliot, presided over the table with malicious dignity. At the other end George Davis, the editor of *Harper's Bazaar,* played a proprietary role. Benjamin Britten and Paul Bowles represented the new music, Gypsy Rose Lee, the dance and striptease, and all the others with one title or another were "creative people" who talked of Kierkegaard, Jung, the ballet, or pre-Columbian sculpture. I am convinced that everything new in American literature, American music, American painting, and American choreography passed through that house in Brooklyn, the only center of thought and art that I found in any one of that country's big cities.[40]

Even Salvador Dali and Gala could sometimes be found in what Carson called that "campy" abode, which bulldozers destroyed at the end of the war. In 1945 buildings at that end of Middagh Street were razed to make room for an expressway that would facilitate access to the Brooklyn Bridge. Today number 7 no longer exists, and the neighborhood is submerged in noise from the expressway. But a bit farther down is a still tranquil quarter, which looks across the river at the southern tip of Manhattan. Carson's description in her article "Brooklyn Is My Neighbourhood" still evokes the place:

> Brooklyn, in a dignified way, is a fantastic place. The street where I now live has a quietness and sense of permanence that seem to belong to the nineteenth century. The street is very short. At one end, there are comfortable old houses, with gracious façades and pleasant backyards in the rear. Down on the next block, the street becomes more heterogeneous, for there is a fire station; a convent; and a small candy factory. The street is bordered with maple-trees, and in the autumn the children rake up the leaves and make bonfires in the gutter. It is strange in New York to find yourself living in a real neighbourhood.
>
> Comparing the Brooklyn that I know with Manhattan is like comparing a comfortable and complacent duenna to her more brilliant and neurotic sister. Things move more slowly out here (the street-cars still rattle leisurely down most of the main streets), and there is a feeling for tradition.
>
> The history of Brooklyn is not so exciting as it is respectable. In

the middle of the past century, many of the liberal intellectuals lived here, and Brooklyn was a hot-bed of abolitionist activity. Walt Whitman worked on the *Brooklyn Daily Eagle* until his anti-slavery editorials cost him his job. Henry Ward Beecher used to preach at the old Plymouth Church. Talleyrand lived here on Fulton Street during his exile in America, and he used to walk primly every day beneath the elm-trees. Whittier stayed frequently at the old Hooper home.

She concluded, "Here in Brooklyn there is always the feeling of the sea. On the streets near the water-front, the air has a fresh, coarse smell, and there are many seagulls."[41]

In the bars on Sand Street there were odd women, "old dowagers of the street," who went by names such as "The Duchess" or "Submarine Mary." "In one bar," wrote Carson, "there is a little hunchback who struts in proudly every evening." These quick sketches may be viewed as early silhouettes of Miss Amelia and Cousin Lymon. The months spent in Brooklyn were for Carson an "other life," a brief interlude of freedom and peace that would never recur, even when she came back to live in the same house. "From the windows of my rooms in Brooklyn there is a view of the Manhattan sky-line. The sky-scrapers, pastel mauve and yellow in color, rise up sharp as stalagmites against the sky," she wrote in "Look Homeward, Americans," which in December 1940 was her first publication in a magazine since "Wunderkind" in 1936. "My windows overlook the harbour, the grey East River, and the Brooklyn Bridge. In the night, there are the lonesome calls of the boats on the river and at sea. This water-front neighbourhood is the place where Thomas Wolfe used to live, and Hart Crane. Often when I am loafing by the window, looking out at the lights and the bright traffic crossing the Bridge, I think of them. And I am homesick in a way that they were often homesick."[42]

Reeves did not live at 7 Middagh Street, but he visited frequently, leaving there more often than not with a great deal of liquor under his belt. He and Carson also saw each other in Manhattan, at the Brevoort Hotel, since destroyed, on Fifth Avenue at Eighth Street, which would always be one of their favorite haunts, the one where all their reconciliations took place over a cocktail with lemon called a "stringer." Carson tried to work on the manuscript of what would become *The Member of the Wedding* but made little progress — which suited Reeves just fine. To his way of thinking, it meant that Carson could not work without him near. Then suddenly on Thanksgiving Day she had one of those illuminations, as she called them, that gave structure to her work. "Frankie is in love with her brother and the bride!" she exclaimed, "and she wants to be a 'member of the wedding,'" a phrase that would become the book's title. "It was Thanksgiving. We had just finished dinner — in Brooklyn," Carson related to Tennessee Williams. "Gypsy Rose Lee was there. Suddenly we heard fire engines — Gypsy loved fires. Suddenly I said: Frankie is in love with her brother and the bride. Then I cried and cried. Then I was able to get back — The illumination had focused the whole book. I couldn't use any approximations. I wanted the language to be pure . . . worked on it five years."[43] She spoke often of those "revelations" or "outpourings," which occurred after long spells of groping around in the dark and were "the grace of a writer's labor."

The satisfaction of finally making progress on her manuscript did not prevent Carson from falling ill with the onset of a harsh northern winter. Her mother rushed to her bedside, and as soon as she was well enough to travel, they left for Columbus, shortly before Christmas. Relations between Carson and Marguerite Smith were highly complex and are poorly understood. Virginia Spencer Carr describes Marguerite's short stay in New York at considerable length but comes up with only the most banal facts: Marguerite was a mother proud of her daughter's success; Carson was a fragile daughter torn between her need to be protected and her wish to be free. Marguerite passed up no opportunity to tell people she met about her "little prodigy," taking umbrage if they remained unaware of her recent celebrity. Marguerite was both a source of assistance for Carson and an intrusion into her new life — hardly an unusual state of mother-daughter relations. Most of the people who liked Carson also liked her mother, Carr observes. Only a few of them, such as Janet Flanner, the famous *New Yorker* columnist, viewed her as harmful to the young woman; Flanner described Marguerite as an abusive, catastrophic, and "abysmal" mother.[44]

Rita Smith, Carson's sister, also had the feeling that the tie between Marguerite and her favorite child was stranger than it seemed. When

Carson was living, she notes in her preface to the posthumous collection *The Mortgaged Heart,*

> her papers were no concern of mine . . . and I had no idea what she had saved. I have been just as surprised by what is there as by what is not there. I can't find any letters from our mother who wrote her every day they were separated, but all the valentines from a year were committed for keeping. So it would seem that these archives are partially due to accidental circumstance — dependent on Carson's health and the whim of any part-time secretarial help she had from time to time. Those of us concerned with her estate hope that these files will go to a library before much longer and be made available for further study. Even then, scholars will find it difficult to distinguish the truth.[45]

Indeed, the fact that there remains no trace of such a sustained correspondence would seem to have less to do with "accidental circumstance" — the same accidental circumstance would likely have allowed a few letters to survive — than with a firm intent whose nature is a mystery.

At about the time Carson fell ill, in late November, Annemarie Schwarzenbach was hospitalized in a Connecticut psychiatric clinic. She had been taking drugs and making suicide attempts for several years. Her friends ascribed her current depression not only to her difficult love affair with Baroness von Opel but also to her feelings of guilt for not returning in early November to Switzerland, where her father had just died. Carson wrote to Annemarie but had no way of knowing whether her letters were passed on to her. Hospital visits being absolutely prohibited, Carson let herself be persuaded to return to Columbus with her mother. She was there a few weeks later, early in 1941, when she learned that Annemarie had taken refuge at a friend's house in New York after escaping from the clinic. Carson took the first train north and went to join her. But in no time at all the police, accompanied by a doctor, located the fugitive and had her hospitalized at Bellevue in White Plains — an asylum with a sinister reputation. Carson returned to Columbus, and shortly thereafter Annemarie went back to Europe: the two friends would resume their letter writing, but they had seen each other for the last time.

Although she no longer socialized with New York's intelligentsia,

Carson McCullers was still the writer everyone was reading in early 1941. In its January 1, 1941, issue *Vogue* published her short piece "Night Watch over Freedom," which appealed for solidarity between the United States and Europe.[46] Then on February 14, Valentine's Day, *Reflections in a Golden Eye* — dedicated to Annemarie Clarac-Schwarzenbach — appeared at Houghton Mifflin. Five days later Carson turned twenty-four years old. Louis Untermeyer wrote an endorsement for the novel, which appeared on the jacket: "It is a story which flows in every paragraph, flows with strange and sinister twists and sudden humorous flashes, but flows always to its predictable and incalculable end . . . I find it utterly unlike anything produced in our time . . . It is one of the most compelling, one of the most uncanny stories ever written in America."

Reflections in a Golden Eye may be Carson McCullers's strongest book. It is the most provocative in any case, and the most controlled. Tight and dry, it is surely the most meticulous in its observation of the everyday and of the cruelty of human relations. It is also the most devoid of sentimentalism, the most tight-lipped, the most serenely merciless. Carson's account of the closed world of this barracks in peacetime — marked by the mortal attraction of Captain Penderton for Private Williams; by the personality of the captain's wife, an excellent horsewoman who holds the soldiers in thrall; and by the pathetic Alison Langdon, the major's wife — starts off like this: "An army post in peacetime is a dull place. Things happen, but then they happen over and over again."[47] Everything has already been suggested in these first few words: the confinement, the boredom, and the madness that can stem from such conditions underneath the strictest appearance of decorum.

Reflections in a Golden Eye was disturbing, even shocking. The reviews tended to be unfavorable but concealed their profound aversion for this book behind quasi-technical arguments and comparisons with *The Heart Is a Lonely Hunter*. Fred T. Marsh, in the *New York Times* of March 2, 1941, expressed measured disappointment. "Mature people of very diverse literary tastes and sympathies have found it [*The Heart Is a Lonely Hunter*] unforgettable. The present much shorter and slighter novel exhibits to some degree the same quality. But it is vastly inferior." Marsh even suggested that the book had been written before *Heart* and was "unwisely pressed into service" by Houghton Mifflin to keep Carson McCullers in the public eye. In addition to an insufficiently polished style — the book was written too quickly, some said — *Reflections in a Golden Eye* was accused in the main of exhibiting too great a taste for the morbid and bizarre, an exaggerated penchant for the abnormal and deformed, and an overabundance of perversity. Some critics went so far as to advise their readers to forget about this book straightaway. In her *New York Herald Tribune* piece of February 16, Rose Feld, one of the most enthusiastic voices when *Heart* was released, judged that Carson had progressed in her ability to master the construction of a narrative, but she remained perplexed by the meaning of certain details — the horse Firebird, for example, that Captain Penderton rode very poorly. In particular, she says:

> Mrs. McCullers has been compared to William Faulkner; here, indeed, she seems almost deliberately to be seeking something that could match him at his most morbid. Her success does not, however, add anything to her power as an artist. One is merely impressed with and offended by her arrogant and pitiless fearlessness which, besides giving an unpleasant effect, betrays her youth. . . .
>
> "Reflections in a Golden Eye" is a literary adventure into an emotional underworld and, as such, interesting. But one still hopes that Carson McCullers will use her very real powers to write a book that does not depend completely upon the grotesque and the abnormal for its effect.[48]

These sententious objections to her taste for "abnormality" led Carson McCullers to explain her perspective on *Reflections in a Golden Eye,* and the question of "the normal" in literature more generally, on multiple occasions. She attempted to sum up her thoughts in "The Flowering Dream: Notes on Writing":

> One cannot explain accusations of morbidity. A writer can only say he writes from the seed which flowers later in the subconscious. Nature is not abnormal, only lifelessness is abnormal. Anything that pulses and moves and walks around the room, no matter what thing it is doing, is natural and human to a writer. The fact that John Singer, in *The Heart Is a Lonely Hunter,* is a deaf-and-dumb man is a symbol, and the fact that Captain Penderton, in *Reflections in a Golden Eye,* is homosexual, is also a symbol, of handicap and impotence. The deaf mute, Singer, is a symbol of infirmity, and he

loves a person who is incapable of receiving his love. Symbols suggest the story and theme and incident, and they are so interwoven that one cannot understand consciously where the suggestion begins. I become the characters I write about. I am so immersed in them that their motives are my own.[49]

She returned to the subject in 1967, shortly before her death:

[*The Heart Is a Lonely Hunter*] was a rather long book, in which I had faced many moral problems; the problems of prejudice and of poverty in the South. I had indeed taken my stand as a Southerner on the white-Negro "Problem." It would never be necessary to ask what I thought about the progress of the Negro. I had taken my stand for liberalism in the South. That was a purely moral issue, but it was exhausting. Without realizing I yearned to play, to write language for the sheer joy and beauty of words.

At that time my husband casually mentioned that there was a voyeur at Ft. Bragg, an Army Base near our town in Fayetteville. I heard nothing more about it, but the idea stuck in my mind. . . . I busied myself with housework, cleaned our small apartment every day until it was immaculate. I was tired, I didn't want to start another book, but against my will the idea of the peeping-tom soldier had taken possession of me, so that I began, "An Army Post in peacetime is a dull place." The locale established, the characters one by one, asserted themselves. . . . the tale had taken over my life, and I had never written with such pleasure.

The style of the story was of prime importance, and every day I thrilled with the marvel of words. My usual writing average was one page a day, but with this story, to my surprise and delight, I found myself finishing three, four and sometimes even six pages a day.[50]

If today most American university critics agree, according to Margaret B. McDowell, that *The Member of the Wedding* and *The Ballad of the Sad Café* are Carson McCullers's two most accomplished works, there is still lively debate as to which of her first two novels, *The Heart Is a Lonely Hunter* and *Reflections in a Golden Eye*, is the better — and *Reflections* has very staunch supporters.[51] At the time only Otis Ferguson, in the *New Republic* of March 3, 1941, seems to have grasped what Carson McCullers was trying to accomplish and the extent to which she had succeeded:

If this quiet, subtle and thorough treatment of human passions seems a *tour de force* in spite of its atmosphere of strange-but-true, its etched background of the army post, the customs, the look and feel of the weather, the key to it is in [the book's] two principals. They are ranged against each other by such extreme peculiarities of temperament and moved by such dumb, obscure forces, that almost anything could be made logically to happen to either. Whereas in the sense of the dramatically inevitable, nothing *has* happened by the ending, in release or final expression, vengeance or atonement. The reader is never identified with anyone in the book; and it seems that the price of such perfection in having everything come out exact and even is that you have to play with a special deck of cards, deliberately leaving the hearts out of it.[52]

Ferguson's assessment stood alone until 1950, when Tennessee Williams took a first step toward the reevaluation of *Reflections* in his preface to the New Directions edition of the novel. For Williams this second text was markedly better than *Heart:* "Discerning critics should have found it the opposite of a disappointment since it exhibited the one attribute which had yet to be shown in Carson McCullers' stunning array of gifts: the gift of mastery over a youthful lyricism." He spoke of the austerity and "Grecian purity" of this novel, of the "lapidary precision" of its style. Referring to Joyce and Faulkner, he wrote, "*Reflections in a Golden Eye* is one of the purest and most powerful of those works which are conceived in that Sense of The Awful which is the desperate black root of nearly all significant modern art, from the *Guernica* of Picasso to the cartoons of Charles Addams."[53] Essayists would follow his lead, all of them contradicting the first impression given by the press.

In point of fact, the scandal when the book was released was not so much literary as it was moral. And although journalists, except for the most openly conservative ones, chose to limit themselves to a supposedly aesthetic evaluation whose moral roots (consciously or unconsciously) they kept hidden, the general public and certain pressure groups denounced the novel's assertion of independence and its refusal to conform to societal norms, particularly disturbing since it had been written by a young woman. "It got me into a lot of trouble," Carson confided to Tennessee Williams. "Mary Tucker is a friend and music teacher. I was about 12 years old at the time. Dad threw the book across the room when he read it. General Marshall wrote to Mary: What is your private life in Fort Benning like really? Did the whole post go to pot when I left or is there something in the girl herself?"[54] One night in Columbus, where Carson was staying when *Reflections* came out, a Ku Klux Klan member called her parents' home to issue the order that she leave town immediately or else he and his friends would come "get her" before morning: "'We know from your first book that you're a nigger-lover,' the voice said, 'and we know from this one that you're queer. We don't want queers and nigger-lovers in this town.'"[55] Carson's father spent the night sitting on his front porch with a loaded shotgun, but nothing came of the threat. Still, middle-class Southerners could never forgive one of "their" writers for taking such liberties and proceeded to disseminate the legend of an obnoxious, heedless Carson McCullers. In his *À la recherche de Carson McCullers,* Jacques Tournier describes his visit with Edwin Peacock in Charleston and his encounter with a woman who, learning of his interest in Carson, remarked sharply: "People claim she was obnoxious. . . . Is it true?" "She pursed her lips," Tournier comments, "and used the word 'bitch,'" which makes one wonder why he felt he had to translate that woman's remarks euphemistically instead of just saying, "People claim she was a bitch."[56]

More than any other work, *Reflections in a Golden Eye* was seized upon by everyone who hoped to show that Reeves McCullers may have written the books that his wife signed. In Columbus, where a bad opinion of Carson McCullers was indelibly etched — but in how many small towns do people think highly of good writers? — they refused to believe that Carson was the author of her books, explains Virginia Spencer Carr. When Carson first began to write, old people, remembering that Marguerite had been fond of telling stories ever since she was a child, believed that she was the real author of her daughter's novels. Only after Marguerite died, when they saw that Carson kept on publishing, did certain people in Columbus finally concede that "it must have been little Lula Carson after all."[57]

Beyond the aversion with which Carson herself was regarded and outside the common tendency, sometimes not explicitly expressed, to challenge any starkly original artistic feat, what gave rise to all the rumors about authorship that circulated then and later on? Reeves's desire to become a writer and the "year-on, year-off" writing pact that he had made with Carson are certainly part of the answer to this question, as is the constantly repeated anecdote about Carson reading her day's work to Reeves every evening, first in Charlotte, then in Fayetteville. And the fact that in 1945, with Reeves back on American soil after World War II, she finished *The Member of the Wedding* very quickly after having been obstructed in her work for several months added fuel to the fire. But no one thinks to mention, regarding this last sequence of events, that Reeves was fighting in Europe, that Carson was undoubtedly distracted by the constant fear that he would be killed over there, or that she went to finish her manuscript in a place where, precisely, Reeves was not.

Jacques Tournier begins his discussion of the matter by saying how absurd the rumor is "that Carson may have been nothing but a surrogate pen":

> You can find articles today in some American periodicals to this effect. One of them would even have us believe that *Reflections in a Golden Eye* was entirely Reeves's and that the military authorities, after becoming aware of the manuscript, threatened to bring him before a war council if he published it under his name. And so someone supposedly proposed that they use Carson's name to avoid — what, exactly? In October 1940, when *Harper's Bazaar* prereleased the book, Reeves had been out of the army for more than four years. What risk would he have been taking? And so what if he did? I don't believe in writers sacrificing themselves out of love, or allowing themselves to be deterred. From 1940 on there was nothing to stop Reeves from writing. He did not have a job, and Carson was earning enough money for them both. People say that Carson stifled those close to her. But one had to let oneself be stifled. What writer has ever stopped his or her brother, sister, husband, wife, or children from writing? Look how many wives or children there are, on the contrary, who trail along behind someone else's glory without going to the trouble of making a name for themselves. By giving his last name to Carson, Reeves signed her books along with her, affirming his role as a sounding board.[58]

And yet, speaking specifically of *Reflections in a Golden Eye*, Tournier adds:

> I have almost reached the point of believing the rumors that the book was really written by Reeves. He is in there, that much is cer-

tain. Far more present than in *Heart*. He is there in the images of Fort Benning, with everything he experienced at that post for four years, which he alone could have known. Granted, Carson went there every Saturday but only to the Tuckers to make music with Mary. . . . As for the rest — the camp, the barracks rooms, the soldiers' life, everything that makes this inward-focused world of men real — Reeves was the one that made it possible for her to describe it. And Reeves's recollections. And maybe his notebooks, if he kept any. When I say you get the impression that it's someone else, it comes across so clearly that she never returned to that milieu again. Everything she wrote from then on had its source within herself.[59]

What a curious way to prove a point: it is not at all clear why the fact that Carson never reused the barracks setting in her work should mean that she was not the book's author. The "outskirts of Carthage" do not appear frequently in Flaubert's oeuvre. Does this mean, then, that since he wrote *Madame Bovary*, he did not write *Salammbô* — or the other way around? This logic also assumes that a writer must have lived an experience to be able to transform it into art, a variation on the tired old theme of a direct causality between the man and the work. Though Reeves may well have supplied Carson with some details of his military life, to give those details precedence over the writing would make the literary act almost meaningless.

The dynamics of literary creation within couples have received a good deal of attention lately. Jacques Tournier, along with a few others, has inaugurated something of a trend in reporting on — or imagining — the symbiotic lives of literary couples. Today we hear not that Simone de Beauvoir wrote the works of Jean-Paul Sartre — not yet anyway — but that Beauvoir's firm belief that she was not a creative philosopher was not a proof of clear thinking (which she nonetheless displayed in abundance) but the result of her submission to that little man, who "ruled" her.[60] Bertolt Brecht, we are told, most certainly did not write his plays. At best, he put "final touches" on the work of his wives and mistresses — at worst, he merely appended his slave-driver's signature.[61] For all this we may thank a pseudofeminist demagogy that does nothing to further the cause of women, that denies women exercise of their own free will, and that limits the relations between the two sexes to pure, mechanical male domination.

In the case of Reeves and Carson, this simplistic pattern supposedly existed in reverse. Proponents of this theory would have us believe that a fragile and tyrannical woman-child forced a weak but talented man to work for her. Doesn't this seem a bit far-fetched? Granted, the relationship between Reeves and Carson's writings was clearly complex, and Reeves's place in Carson's creative process still remains open. But though Carson wrote two books at Reeves's side, with him, perhaps attended by him, she subsequently wrote in spite of him, against him, and for years after his death.

If certain critics insist on contesting Carson's originality, they might do better to explore the effects of her literary readings on her work. Comparing *Reflections* with D. H. Lawrence's short story "The Prussian Officer" (not to show, as some have tried, that Carson McCullers plagiarized Lawrence, which she did not) could help us understand the confluence of literary resources that in part shaped her development as a writer. Oliver Evans takes this tack in a chapter humorously called "Not Even the Horse Is Normal."[62] Moreover, a book that, like *Reflections in a Golden Eye,* meditates on voyeurism cannot fail to call to mind the fiction of Faulkner, a monumental Southern writer who might carry more weight for a fellow novelist than Carson's conversations with her husband.

Though she was a long way from New York — and a long way from the debates surrounding her novel — Carson fell ill once again in late February. All of a sudden she began having terrible migraines accompanied by a loss of vision. She was frightened and particularly fearful that she would no longer be able to write. Yet again the doctors in Columbus had only a vague idea of what was going on. Clearly, they could not imagine that at twenty-four years of age Carson had just had a stroke — the first in a series of attacks that would profoundly alter her existence. No one knew at the time that her health had been decisively affected. Little by little, she regained her strength, and her vision was restored. In a month or so everything returned to normal, and Carson believed that the danger had passed.

Reeves arrived in Columbus — on Marguerite Smith's orders he had been waiting for Carson to recover before coming to join her in the South — and the two left together for New York City in April. Carson returned to the apartment on West Eleventh Street, which Reeves had continued to occupy after their most recent separation. It was at that time, on April 1, 1941, that *Harper's Bazaar* published "Books I Remember," in which Carson discusses with great simplicity and insight the books, literarily important or more ephemeral, that played a role in forming her sensibility. "These, then, are a few of the books I remember just now," Carson concludes. "And yet 'remember' is hardly the word, for there is implied the possibility that one might forget. While books that one loves are a part of oneself, like a muscle or a nerve. And in thinking back at random one is likely to overlook the books that are dear above all others. A moment ago I realized I had not mentioned a book that I have come to understand in the past couple of years and that now I like to read in almost every evening — the Bible. That, also, is a book to be remembered."[63]

In New York, on the recommendation of a woman she had met in Columbus, Carson arranged to meet Elizabeth Ames, director of Yaddo artists' colony in Saratoga Springs, New York, a place (founded in 1900) to which artists can retreat to work in peace, generally for short periods of time. When Elizabeth Ames saw the "shy, sweet girl from Columbus" who had been recommended to her, she discovered that the writer had lost her voice: "I have been so frightened at meeting you," Carson murmured. Charmed, Elizabeth Ames offered Carson, who struck her as a very young girl, the rare privilege of spending the entire summer at Yaddo to work on her two manuscripts in progress, *The Ballad of the Sad Café* and *The Member of the Wedding*.[64]

The Middagh Street residents, for their part, found Carson to be in a rather bad way that year when she dropped by to join them for a drink. She was coughing a lot and seemed unable to get by without her syrup, containing codeine, which she was too dependent on. Happily, a new friend was about to appear, whose affection would restore her energy. In early May, Muriel Rukeyser introduced Carson to a young composer, David Diamond. He appealed to Carson right away and the feeling was mutual, so much so that the first time they met, he took a ring off his finger and gave it to her. He would later say that Carson had a curious power: no sooner did she admire some object than its owner was possessed of an irrepressible desire to hand it over to her right then and there. Diamond would also become friendly with Reeves. The three friends often went out together in the evening, drinking a great deal.

One night when Carson was talking about writers she admired, she mentioned loving Djuna Barnes and said she wanted to take her a bottle of champagne on the spot. Did she act on that desire? And if so, was it at that very moment, in the middle of the night? Legend would have it that Carson did go to Djuna Barnes's place, begging the author to open the door and let her in, but that Barnes, unswerving in her wish never to see anyone again (she lived for forty-odd years shut away in her New York apartment), remained unmoved. Djuna Barnes's biographer recounts that impromptu visit somewhat less spectacularly:

> [Unlike Anaïs Nin], Carson McCullers did not admire Barnes from a distance or in print. She attempted to storm her apartment, but Miss Barnes was practised in privacy and quite capable of simply ignoring insistent pressing of the entrance bell when there was no one she was expecting. Stories are told of McCullers crying and moaning on the stoop to be let in. (McCullers had done the same thing to Katherine Ann Porter whom Barnes, by the way, knew casually and thought very vulgar.) There was silence, except for one occasion when Miss Barnes called down to her: — *Whoever is ringing this bell, please go the hell away.* She did go away, though eventually the two had a perfectly uneventful meeting years later, when Barnes was inducted into the American Academy of Arts and Letters in 1959 and was seated at the lunch afterwards with McCullers and Thornton Wilder.[65]

When she arrived at Yaddo on June 14, Carson fell in love with the place right away, with the woods, where she loved to go walking before breakfast; with the two lakes; with Yaddo's whole landscape of calm and repose. Scattered about the estate were the main house — where the common areas were located, including the dining room — several smaller dwellings, and some farmhouses. Some of them had kitchens, which gave their occupants more autonomy, since they were not obliged to take communal meals. Elizabeth Ames, the benevolent director, hated it when people failed to show up promptly at mealtime.

Carson did not know most of the musicians, painters, and writers who arrived the same time she did, except for her Southern compatriot Eudora Welty, whom she had met a year earlier at Middlebury, and one other writer from the South, at that time the most well known artist present: Katherine Anne Porter. She was also the oldest and most beautiful, a woman resplendent in her fifties. Quite small, she was slender and elegant. Porter had been at Middlebury the previous year as well, but Carson had not even dared speak to her. She had simply "fallen in love" with the elder writer, in the highly particular way in which she tended to do so. This time she planned to simply tell her, "I love you, Katherine Anne," making it her duty to follow her everywhere.

Katherine Anne Porter, who died in 1980, remembered that episode for Virginia Spencer Carr in 1971. Rather humorlessly, she explained that her own husband had strong opinions about Carson: "That woman is a lesbian. . . . I can tell from the author's mind in that novel [*The Heart Is a Lonely Hunter*] and by what she makes her characters do and say." Though Katherine Anne Porter denied having been convinced by her husband's remarks, she admitted to feeling increasingly uncomfortable around Carson, a discomfort aggravated by Carson's ill-considered actions and her curious habit of wearing men's clothes — a detail that seemed to support her husband's claims. "But perhaps I simply misunderstood Carson," she confided thirty years later, stressing the fact that in *Heart* she had seen "the mark of genius." "I have many friends who are homosexual," she added, "and the fact does not bother me at all, but with Carson then, the thought seemed intolerable."[66]

Unfortunately, she pursues her reflection no further. Had the incident disturbed her? Had it annoyed her that the person she was faced with was not a woman admitting to a penchant she could either consent to or refuse but a demanding child whose neurosis and instability were immediately apparent? It is quite possible that Carson played on her androgynous physique and her ambiguous, indeterminate appearance; she was clearly sensitive to the beauty of women and experienced deep emotional attachment to some of them. But it seems reasonable not to exaggerate her awareness of those feelings or, especially, the amount of control she had over them. One afternoon, according to Katherine Anne Porter, Carson came knocking at her door, trying to engage her in conversation. Without getting up from her work table, Porter cried out that she did not wish to be disturbed and refused to open the door. But when she saw that it was nearly six-thirty, and well aware that Elizabeth Ames did not take kindly to latecomers at dinner, she had to leave her room. When Porter ventured forth, Carson was lying there in the hall: "I merely stepped over her and continued on my way to dinner. And that was the last time she ever bothered me."[67] After that the two women ceased to speak to each other.

Carson nonetheless made a new friend at Yaddo, Edward Newhouse, who wrote short stories for the *New Yorker* and always remembered her with kindness. Unlike Katherine Anne Porter, he spoke in a most amusing way of that summer. While acknowledging that "sometimes husbands feared for their wives," Newhouse described Carson as "*childlike,* although people who didn't like her thought her *childish,*" and emphasized her adolescent way of attaching herself to people or dropping them. He also recalled her constant desire to talk about herself and be listened to, although she herself, like a child, had only a limited capacity to pay attention to others.[68] She had a tremendous aptitude for making up stories that she wanted people to accept for the truth, in which she herself wound up believing. She claimed, for example, to have written a letter several hundred pages long to Greta Garbo, declaring her love. According to Edward Newhouse, there were several ways to interpret that story: "One, she actually wrote it. Two, she didn't. Three, the letter had been several thousand pages long. Four, it ran to nine pages. Five, today is Wednesday. As I told you, our girl was given to saying pretty much anything that came into her head. If I were given the choice of writing her biography or being shipwrecked on a desert island with Spiro Agnew . . . Well, I don't know."[69] Though Newhouse keeps on smiling, even when suggesting that it was sometimes difficult to tolerate Carson, her ego, her crushes, her grandiloquent assertions of self-worth, of her importance as an author, others, such as Gore Vidal, admitted that she infuriated them. Vidal found her "vain, querulous, and a genius — alas, her presence in a room meant my absence: five minutes of one of her self-loving arias and I was gone."[70] His conclusion: "An hour with a dentist without Novocain was like a minute with Carson McCullers."[71]

All of this would be rather pointless, saying more about Carson McCullers's personality and neurosis than about her value as an artist, had the young writer's stay at Yaddo not been marked by intense creative labor. After her morning walk in the woods and breakfast, she returned to her room at nine-thirty with a beer, a Thermos bottle of her famous hot sherry tea, and a snack for lunch. She did not leave her desk before five o'clock in the afternoon, at which time she joined friends for a drink before dinner at six-thirty. She worked this way all summer, with great discipline, on her two primary manuscripts, *The Ballad of the Sad Café* and *The Member of the Wedding,* while composing some short stories on the side. She was extremely proud when one of them, "The Jockey," was published on August 23 in the *New Yorker,* thanks to her new friend Edward Newhouse.[72] Did that prestigious publication fuel her desire to keep up the pace? Two other stories, "Madame Zilensky and the King of Finland" and "Correspondence," were bought by the *New Yorker* that same summer.[73]

"Madame Zilensky," the wild tale of a woman composer, in Carson McCullers's humorous vein, is as comical as "The Jockey" is dark. "The Jockey" is a bitter account of the trials and tribulations of a undersized man whose physical appearance is not unrelated to that of Cousin Lymon in *The Ballad of the Sad Café.* "Correspondence" has been read as a story born of Carson's lack of contact with Reeves during that summer. A skillful stylistic composition, full of humor, it consists of four letters that a female student has written to a Brazilian correspondent whose name she found on a list posted at her school.

Carson was also writing more than fiction. The July 15 issue of *Vogue* published her political piece "We Carried Our Banners — We Were Pacifists, Too"; an article, "The Russian Realists and Southern Literature," also appeared in July, in Klaus Mann's magazine, *Decision;* and in November Carson published a poem, "The Twisted Trinity" (which David Diamond would put to music in July 1946). These achievements make it abundantly clear that the young Carson McCullers was beginning, in a rather prestigious way, a fine career as a recognized writer.[74]

"We Carried Our Banners" shows, concisely and efficiently, a young American going off to war and reveals his understanding of why he must go. In "The Russian Realists and Southern Literature" Carson ponders problems close to her heart, challenging the convenient label "Gothic School" typically attached to writers from the South, beginning with her:

> In the South during the past fifteen years a genre of writing has come about that is sufficiently homogeneous to have led critics to label it "the Gothic School." This tag, however, is unfortunate. The

effect of a Gothic tale may be similar to that of a Faulkner story in its evocation of horror, beauty, and emotional ambivalence — but this effect evolves from opposite sources; in the former the means used are romantic or supernatural, in the latter a peculiar and intense realism. Modern Southern writing seems rather to be most indebted to Russian literature, to be the progeny of the Russian realists. And this influence is not accidental. The circumstances under which Southern literature has been produced are strikingly like those under which the Russians functioned. In both old Russia and the South up to the present time a dominant characteristic was the cheapness of human life. . . .

Southern writers have reacted to their environment in just the same manner as the Russians prior to the time of Dostoievsky and Tolstoi. They have transposed the painful substance of life around them as accurately as possible, without taking the part of emotional panderer between the truth as it is and the feelings of the reader. The "cruelty" of which the Southerners have been accused is at bottom only a sort of naïveté, an acceptance of spiritual inconsistencies without asking the reason why, without attempting to propose an answer. Undeniably there is an infantile quality about this clarity of vision and rejection of responsibility.

But literature in the South is a young growth, and it cannot be blamed because of its youth. One can only speculate about the possible course of its development or retrogression. Southern writing has reached the limits of a moral realism; something more must be added if it is to continue to flourish. As yet there has been no forerunner of an analytical moralist such as Tolstoi or a mystic like Dostoievsky. But the material with which Southern literature deals seems to demand of itself that certain basic questions be posed. If and when this group of writers is able to assume a philosophical responsibility, the whole tone and structure of their work will be enriched, and Southern writing will enter a more complete and vigorous stage in its evolution.[75]

The analytical rigor and literary sophistication shown in such writing underline again the astonishing partition within Carson: on the one hand an indisputable intellectual maturity and on the other a tangle of adolescent urges that propelled her in the realm of emotions.

Reeves McCullers was not doing well that summer. His wife's sudden embrace by a milieu whose recognition he, too, would have enjoyed was probably related to his despondency. Carson's departure for 7 Middagh Street, then for Yaddo — even though she did spend a few weeks with him in the meantime — signified to Reeves in a spectacular way the divergence of their two destinies. In addition, he had confided to David Diamond that Carson and he "simply [were] not husband and wife any more" and therefore had no reason to keep living together if it was only to hastily cross paths at some hour of the day or night in a shared apartment.[76] He lost himself in high-flown speeches like Jake Blount's in *Heart,* to the point of tiring even his faithful friend Diamond, who dedicated his 1941 ballet, *The Dream of Audubon,* to the couple and who had once written in his journal that life with Carson would certainly be difficult but that "it would doubtless be a more successful liaison than a permanent relationship with Reeves would be."[77] Reeves lived with David Diamond in Rochester until mid-November and may have had a brief affair with him, whether out of genuine attraction or vengeance. Carson had decided to divorce Reeves when she found out that, forging her signature, he had cashed several of her checks, in particular the one she got from the *New Yorker* for her story "The Jockey."

Before returning to New York to pursue divorce proceedings, Carson used her summer at Yaddo (where she stayed until September 30) as a pretext for treating herself to a late-August trip to Quebec with two new Yaddo friends, the essayists Newton Arvin (author of a Hawthorne biography and later Truman Capote's great love) and Granville Hicks. It seems to have been a rather banal excursion, which reveals a gap between the enthusiasm Carson expressed in the letters she sent at the time and the way she behaved with her traveling companions. She almost never went anywhere with them — not even on their trek to Île d'Orléans; instead she stayed in her room, drinking and dreaming.

Divorce seemed inevitable to Carson, but she found the process repugnant. Since mutual consent did not exist as grounds for divorce, she had to use the unpleasant grounds of adultery. She also well knew that a simple legal act would not resolve the deep problem of her relationship with the man she had married — each of them being like the other's bad twin, at once destructive and perhaps indispensable. Her refuge, of course, was Columbus. But on the very day of her departure, in mid-October, a curious incident occurred: Just as she was leaving the Brevoort Hotel, "their" favorite, Carson was unable to sign the check to pay her bill. She had to call her friend Muriel Rukeyser, who vouched for her identity and helped her write her name.[78] Events such as this one, it seems, are what gave rise to the idea that Carson McCullers suffered not from strokes but from recurring psychosomatic ailments — that she responded to all crisis situations with behaviors bearing the mark of hysteria. To get from there to the belief that she was simply a hysteric and that all her maladies, including her paralysis, were psychosomatic, is a rather large step, but many commentators have taken it, holding Carson personally responsible for the state of her health.

The disturbing Brevoort episode was quickly forgotten in Columbus. Carson once again let herself be soothed by the family atmosphere and by the mild Southern autumn. She played the piano and got up very early each day, two hours before sunrise, to take advantage of the quiet before dawn. But by December 1941 she was gravely ill again, for the second time that year, with pleurisy and double pneumonia. The doctors feared for her life. Then the incredible life force of that long, lean young woman, seemingly so fragile, was revealed. Contrary to all expectations, Carson quickly recovered, started eating again — she had been ordered to gain twenty pounds — and in early February 1942 finished the first part of what became *The Member of the Wedding,* a part called "The Listener," which she would rewrite five times. She then began the central part, "The Nigger with the Glass Blue Eye." (These chapter headings would be cut from the final version.)

It seemed that Reeves had completely disappeared from Carson's horizon. On March 19 he reenlisted in the army. At the end of November he was once again at Fort Benning, the post he had left with such relief six years earlier. Reeves had a harder time than Carson did in adjusting to the divorce; he missed her and began to admit that she was much stronger than he was. On several occasions, beginning at that time, he described her as "indestructible," with a mixture of admiration and exasperation. The novelist Linda Lê, some fifty years later, probably comes closest again to describing the two forces at work:

Carson resembled a small animal curled up on itself, with a nucleus of suffering buried in the pit of her coiled body. She may be wounded, pierced by knife blows, but no weapon could cut into the concentrated strength she had within her. Reeves, though, could not stop falling to pieces. He had no resistance. Every blow cracked his face. It was drama he yearned for; he was not prepared for continual humiliation, for daily proof of his own impotence and her tenacity. He was witnessing the realization of his dream — living in nearness to creation — but he who would himself have been an actor full of panache was reduced to the status of a voyeur, a watchman, one who stands guard before the entryway but has no access to the secret. He finally had hold of something, and at the same time they were telling him he had no right to it. Little Carson was moving away; she turned her eyes upon him of course, but she had already gone beyond him. She did not yet suspect that she was seeking a means of escape — why should she burden herself with a double who lags behind and does nothing but whine and beg for tenderness so that he might put his foiled ambitions out of his mind?[79]

Carson's sentimental preoccupation in early 1942 was once again Annemarie Schwarzenbach. They had been writing to each other a lot since autumn 1941, and Annemarie's letters, which often took more than two months to reach their destination, were more than warm: "We were both spoiled and silly last year. We should not cheat at our destiny. Don't forget my tenderness for you."[80] Those letters came from places that Carson could not even imagine: the Belgian Congo, a boat on the Congo River, another boat that had just left Angola and was headed for Lisbon, Lisbon itself, the French consulate in Tétouan, Morocco. Annemarie's letters were long and effusive, recounting her day's activities or her latest "philosophical" considerations on life and creation. She also encouraged Carson to write, to let nothing distract her from the work she must unflaggingly construct.

I am so happy to think that you are at work — writing, living only for this, and in the enclosure of lovelyness — your life must be almost the same than mine, and I started with the first part of my new manuscript on October 22nd, the birthday of my father. . . .

Carson, I talk so easily to you — about things which really are the subject of my book. I think it deals with our *nun* heritage, our relation to men, to what we call nund and enemy — our bitter loving fight with the world first then with the angel who leads us back to the reborn calm of death + eternity. . . .

Sometimes I would like to be with Erika, Klaus, Freddy, at N.Y.

and in sad + lonely hour. I think of how close + with infinite tenderness you and I would understand each other. You are the only writer who thinks about the hard tasks + process of our profession in the same way as if we were brothers. . . .

I also think that you will be the only one to translate my book which you will like — and I hope to translate yours [*Reflections in a Golden Eye*]. Your poem the twisted trinity could be the motto of my book, — which starts with a man looking at a tree, trying to find the instant symetry of the tree, his soul and god's silence.

all my affection to you[81]

Annemarie Schwarzenbach's book, never published, was to be called *The Miracle of the Tree,* and, curiously, after Annemarie had written to her at length about the project, Carson interrupted her work on *The Member of the Wedding* and set about writing a story with themes that echoed her friend's. "A Tree. A Rock. A Cloud" is not one of Carson McCullers's great stories, though it appeared in the *O. Henry Prize Stories* anthology for the year 1942. The story meant a lot to her because it dated from the time of her recovery and was linked to her passion for Annemarie Schwarzenbach.[82] With heavy symbolism, Carson reveals her concerns about love and love's connection to pleasure through a discussion in a café between a little twelve-year-old newsboy and a vagabond.

> "I meditated on love and reasoned it out. I realized what is wrong with us. Men fall in love for the first time. And what do they fall in love with?" . . .
>
> "A woman," the old man said. "Without science, with nothing to go by, they undertake the most dangerous and sacred experience in God's earth." . . .
>
> "They start at the wrong end of love. They begin at the climax. Can you wonder it is so miserable? Do you know how men should love?" . . .
>
> "Son, do you know how love should be begun?" . . .
>
> "A tree. A rock. A cloud."[83]

Crowning that positive period — of restored health, regular, fond letters from Annemarie, and continual work, allowing her to finish the first draft of *The Member of the Wedding* — Carson learned on March 24 that she was to receive a Guggenheim fellowship, a prestigious award since out of fifteen hundred candidates there were only eighty-two winners, among them John Dos Passos. She wanted to use it to finance a working stay in Mexico with her friends David Diamond and Newton Arvin, but the doctors and foundation trustees dissuaded her, judging her health too fragile for such an adventure. George Davis invited her back to Middagh Street, but she chose to go to Yaddo, no doubt on account of the comforting presence of the director, Elizabeth Ames. She stayed there from July 2, 1942, until January 17 of the following year. It was a time of concentrated reading — Yeats, Chekhov, Jane Austen, Djuna Barnes, Céline — one that attests to a remarkable literary acuity on the part of a young woman with no university training in this area. She played the piano and listened to music. Her favorite piece that year was Mahler's second symphony. She also got many letters — among them a noteworthy one from Henry Miller, whom she had not yet met, expressing his admiration for her sense of psychology; with it he sent her his own books.

Still, the year came to a very bad end. On December 1, at Yaddo, Carson heard from Klaus Mann that Annemarie Schwarzenbach had just died at her home in Sils, Switzerland: she had taken a serious fall from a bicycle on November 6; three days later she fell into a deep coma, and she died on November 15. Rumors of all possible kinds circulated about the circumstances of that death. Had there been a drug overdose? Was it suicide? It seemed no one could believe that this uncommon young woman could have died in such a commonplace way. "Annemarie, our dear 'Swiss child,'" wrote Klaus Mann.

> A bicycle accident, they're now telling me it was. Yes, an ordinary bicycle that bolted like a wild horse. In Engadine there are very steep roads with many sharp curves — that's how it happened. Our Swiss child had lost control of the contraption, and it threw her into a tree, in Switzerland, and her head — her dear, beautiful head, with her "lovely face of an inconsolable angel" — smashed into it in the most abominable way. She did not die right away.[84]

Annemarie Clarac-Schwarzenbach had turned thirty-four years old on May 23. Carson McCullers was only twenty-five. She did not know that her life was already half over, but she did understand that the death of Annemarie had brought her youth to a tragic, unalterable end.

4

A WAR WIFE

D URING THE EARLY months of 1943, Richard Wright found
that Carson McCullers's tendency to self-destruction had become impossible to overlook. She returned from Yaddo and
moved back into the house on Middagh Street, where Wright and his
family rented rooms. George Davis had not expected Carson before
sometime in February, and he was in the process of refurbishing the
entire house, which smelled strongly of fresh paint. When she arrived
on January 17, she found her room devoid of furniture and waiting to
be painted. Conveying as it did the impression that "her place" was no
longer hers, her empty room may have heightened her discomfort, her
sense of precariousness, her unease. Carson began to take up too
much space. She drank too much, she talked too much, she constantly
complained, and she spoke of no one but herself, said Richard Wright,
who had once been so touched by the timid little Southerner suddenly
propelled toward success. For him, she destroyed the harmonious atmosphere that had previously reigned in that house, and he immediately began to seek alternative lodgings.

Anaïs Nin, who visited Middagh Street for the first time in March
1943, seems to have shared Wright's highly critical view. In her journal
Nin notes both the pleasure of her discovery of George Davis's "little
museum of America" and the displeasure of her encounter with Carson McCullers, who had nonetheless wanted to meet her, or so Davis
says. As for the pleasure: "An amazing house, like some of the houses
in Belgium, the north of France, or Austria." George Davis had "filled

it with old American furniture, oil lamps, brass beds, little coffee tables, old drapes, copper lamps, old cupboards, heavy dining tables of oak, lace doilies, grandfather clocks. It is like a museum of Americana, which I had never seen anywhere before." As for the displeasure: "Carson came in . . . and pushed through the group like a bull with its head down, looking at no one, not saying a word. I was so put off by her muteness, and by her not even looking at me, that I did not even try to talk with her."[1]

This account and others launched a battle of interpretations. Carson's friends point to the writer's shyness and emphasize that she was often ill at ease. Her detractors claim that she always had to be the center of attention and that if someone else stole top billing — Anaïs Nin could well have done so that day among the group at Middagh Street — she clammed up. It is also possible, however, that she was subject to both attitudes, one after the other or at the same time, or that Carson and Anaïs Nin — who surely was not pleased when she was not the "star" of a gathering, either — may have experienced "hate at first sight," which seems quite likely. If there were nothing more to it than personality conflicts or the clashing of two egos, the whole affair would be simply anecdotal. But as Richard Wright correctly sensed, Carson McCullers was psychologically unstable, not to mention chronically depressive, a condition she attempted to offset with alcohol, thereby making it worse. She was also in failing physical health.

In leaving Yaddo for Middagh Street, Carson began to feel extremely unwell, as she did every winter. An infected tooth rapidly declared itself, followed by a bout with the flu. As always, Marguerite Smith made the journey north to care for her daughter. But when she tried to bring her daughter back to Columbus with her, Carson refused, claiming that she had to stay in Brooklyn to work. So Marguerite went home by herself — Carson did not follow until late April.

In the meantime Reeves had reestablished contact by way of a tender, touching, and rather adolescent letter, coming from a man who was thirty years old. Written on February 23 at the Camp Forrest training center in Tennessee, where Reeves — now a lieutenant — was preparing to join the war effort in Europe, it was mailed to Yaddo and forwarded to Middagh Street. Reeves's letters — sixty or so of them — are on file at the Harry Ransom Humanities Research Center at the University of Texas in Austin. They are often long, handwritten for the most part with a fountain pen, and in a handsome script. That first letter after two years of separation was a new declaration to Carson and a shy request for love, or at least attention:

I must write to you again, I have to. Even though the letter be returned unopened or I never know if you received it. . . .

Almost two years have gone by since that rainy, dismal, horrible afternoon when I last saw you. Many things have happened to both of us and each of us has probably changed some but there has not been one day during which your image has not appeared in my mind. You have always been first with me and I know now that no one else could ever mean what you did. That sort of talk may make you uncomfortable so I should say no more.

I have not talked with or heard from any one in several months who had news of you. I don't know where you are or what you are doing but I concentrate on you and wish you well and hope you have been able to make some adjustment to the times we live in. . . .

I am rather deeply involved in this war and after spring maneuvers expect combat orders. Although I don't want to die I should be glad to get overseas and away from the States. I know I am a good soldier and I believe I am a good officer to my men, so I have nothing to fear except the normal fear one undergoes in his baptism of fire. I think I know pretty well about that already.

Someone has said that this generation was conceived in pathology and raised in despair and that may be true. . . .

But battles are so sickening and repulsive and horrible, Carson, that they cause one to lose every human attribute. I have become everything that I would not desire in a person, although it is for a good cause.

If I come out of the war in one piece I should like to live in Europe for several years if I can get a job. If I can't live in France then probably one of the Scandanavian countries. Failing that I have a job waiting in China. I have a feeling the States will be depressing, but then to breathe clean, free air again will probably be good in any country. It would be good to sit with you then and have drinks and talk. If we ever meet again can't we talk together?

This is about the most pleasant night we have had since I have been stationed here and that is why I decided to write to you. . . .

. . . Somewhere way back in a little corner of your mind I want you to wish me well. I am not religious but that may help.

One other thing I will mention before closing. I wonder how you are fixed for money. I make more than I need and I agree with my Colonel who says it is amazing how few things there are to buy on a battlefield. If you can use any money I would be glad to re-pay some I owe you by having some sent from Washington each month. There are no strings attached to that offer and if you have all you need well and good.

I must be up at 3 A.M. to go on a field problem so I should turn in.

I wish the best for you always, Carson.[2]

Not only did Carson respond, but she and Reeves struck up a very regular correspondence. None of Carson's letters from that time have reached us, since the soldiers had to destroy all their mail before they departed for Europe. Reeves thanked her for her long letters and sent her richly detailed ones of his own. He talked about the war and the "fiendish" acts committed in the name of Nazism, about "times so tragic and so atrocious that it will be several years before men can raise their heads." He recalled their life together, calling it "so mixed, hectic and insecure."

We have come a long way since then, and I feel that I have finally grown up. We seem to be much closer and more understanding of each other than in any of the days before. . . .

I will never let anything mar or affect the love and friendship that have survived our unhappy times. . . . I am strong now and [can] be depended upon.

. . . You sound encouraging and confident about your book and I think New York is the place for you to be right now. . . .

Carson, work is a precious burden. Most of the time you have known me I had no work. It is only in the past three years that I have learned its value and meaning to the soul. . . .

. . . But Carson, you have your craftmanship and genius and work right at hand and in the very present, so do not go wander-ing off.

. . .

To have dinner with you in a sidewalk cafe on Fifth Avenue and to go to all the places I love in New York has become an obses-sion. . . .

I think of you every day and I will always be your friend and will always love you deeply and tenderly.[3]

To that private correspondence, of which only Reeves's loving letters survive, Carson added a spectacular public declaration. In April she gave *Mademoiselle* "Love's Not Time's Fool," named after Shakespeare's sonnet number 116, which she signed, anonymously and symbolically, "By a War Wife":

You will be fighting as a unit in an army which is fighting a machine determined to extinguish all of our concepts of life, of moral integrity, and of love. You are not only fighting for our own personal love, but for the rights of all human beings to love and live in a world of order and security. However hard it may be, your fight is a struggle which is planned and directed, and your duty is at all times clear. That is your contribution to the preservation of our love. We have to admit within ourselves that this contribution may be total. In any case, your part in our fight to preserve our love will take the utmost of the strength and power in you.

I know that always, during these times, you have put yourself in my place. Your part in this war, in this fight for our love, is more immediate than mine. But I, and all other women whose loved ones are fighting in this war, have a struggle also — and it is not an easy one. . . .

First, there is one white lie that I shall not utter, either to you or myself: that I do not feel fear. Fear is one of the prime realities of these times. When we were too lazy or too ignorant to know our enemy and fear him, we came near losing the world that is blessedly ours. It is right to fear, when it brings courage and fury to a job that must be done. . . .

. . . I want you to know that my love for you has given my life, my capacity for all experience, an intensity and vigor that I would not have otherwise. I want you to know that because of you my love for others, my faith in the ultimate triumph of the human spirit, has been nourished and sustained. And I want you to know that I will fight with all that is in me to preserve this love — just as you will be fighting your part in this battle, somewhere far away. We know what we are fighting for. We know that it will not be easy, that the obstacles ahead of us are real and tragic obstacles. But love such as ours has the tenacity and power to overcome even the conditions with which we are now faced. Tonight I keep thinking of the sonnet you love so well:

> Let me not to the marriage of true minds
> Admit impediments. Love is not love
> Which alters when it alteration finds —

Our love *is* an ever fixed mark, which we will work toward and fight for. And in spite of separation, a separation the length of which we cannot know, our love is not time's fool. And in the final victory I know we will have won our own triumph — the preservation of our love, our life together.[4]

April was a good month for Carson that year. On the ninth she learned that she was to receive a grant of $1,000 from the American Academy of Arts and Letters. On the twenty-second she arrived in Columbus and prepared to see Reeves, who was writing to her often. On Easter Day he went to mass, and it

> was good to hear the clear, strong voices ringing the old, rich religious songs. I have been looking and looking for a letter from you but none has come though. . . . Since I have found you again I consciously worry more about you. As long as I am in the States I want to know where you are, how you are and what you are doing. I say "in the States" because that is the land of possibility — after I leave the States there will be only darkness and silence until after the war. Believe me, it is not a possessive feeling I have for you; I don't think there is a person living who could completely possess you. It is only that I love you, Carson, deeply, strongly and in a way that I hope you understand.[5]

He suggested that the two get together, and they made plans to meet on May 5 in Atlanta. The reunion was a happy one, but Carson did not even wait to be sure that it would be before inviting Reeves to come spend his five-day leave in Columbus. "I will feel very strange going back to Columbus," he wrote, "but if you say it is all right then I will be at ease."[6]

Getting back together again in Columbus, in the house where they had married in 1937, was no doubt a good way to find out where things really stood between them. Or, rather, it would have been a good one at any time other than wartime. In Carson's eyes and those of her parents — who welcomed him again like a son — Reeves was more than just himself in that springtime of 1943. He was the face of America going to the aid of a wounded Europe that was under threat of death. Even before his war exploits, he was already almost a hero. He was one of those sons, one of those husbands that the press was praising to the sky, and his status as a symbol had certainly played a part in his invitation to Columbus. It almost seems, moreover, that Carson found a momentary form of equilibrium in the solidarity of wartime, one attested to by her "letter from a war wife" in *Mademoiselle:*

> If you could see me some mornings walking the three blocks along our street toward the subway, with a nod here, a hello there, a gay wave of the hand to the little candy-store man at the corner, you would blink and . . . well, laugh *at* and *with* me. Yet I would hate to see this new neighborliness go, when the war is over. . . . Neither you nor I are exactly folksy types, but I know, from your letters about the men with you, and from what I'm feeling about people these days, we are better off, more genuinely you and me, now that we are no longer on the sidelines. . . . It's odd, but these days I am with you not only when I am listening to our Mozart quintet, but when I am explaining her ration card to that deaf old lady three doors down.
>
> This leads me to the thing that constantly I keep in mind. I am not alone. All around me I see other women who are faced with exactly my situation. And as a soldier can find protection in the spirit of camaraderie that always accompanies the horrors of war, so those of us who are working together here at home can find strength in the knowledge that our emotions are shared by all of those around us. These are the times when people must reach out to each other. We must feel that we are a necessary and integral part of something larger than ourselves. We must assume our individual responsibilities to the limit of our capacity. We must give all that is in us.[7]

There can be no doubt that the "we" of Carson and Reeves received ample reinforcement from the collective "we" into which Carson integrated herself with apparently sincere enthusiasm.

Carson's friends recalled that in her letters she emphasized Reeves's strength and his training, adding that she had not seen him in such good physical shape for years and that he had managed to get sober. "Reeves was here, on his furlough, last month," she wrote to Edwin Peacock, who was in the navy. "He is now with the Rangers. He is in good shape, in every way. But oh, Edwin, it was sad — thinking back over the old days and realizing that a certain kind of relation which we once had is a thing of the past, and that we must each of us face life alone."[8]

As for Reeves, he needed to be comforted, to feel supported, cared about, and loved — even beyond the genuine love and admiration that he had felt for Carson ever since they first met. He needed to know that he was not an isolated soldier going off to war with no one to worry about him, that he would not soon be forgotten. It must have been the combination of all these feelings that caused him to dwell on past times so tenderly — to the point of occasional amnesia — and that above all made him anxious to renew his attachment to Carson. The very day of his return to Camp Forrest, on May 16, 1943, he sent her an emotional thank-you letter:

> There have been few days in my life that were so soothing, calming and satisfying. I can now face the really hard days to come with renewed hope and patience. . . . You give me an added dose of strength, moral courage and a drive that I could get from no other person.
>
> Although I have the manner of a stern grandmother toward them the men were glad to see me on my return. They had had a tough week. . . .
>
> My stoicism seems to be a comfort to them. When the going gets rough and serious, I never grumble and bitch and neither do they. They have an almost fanatical faith and trust in me and it nearly frightens me at times. . . . You said something when I was with you which I have thought about many times and with which I disagree. You said that Frankie was the expression of your failure as a person. I do not wish to influence what you want to write about but to me you are not and have never been a failure as a person. When I was with you you were the best wife a man could have — coming home from work, in the evenings, in the bed, of hurried early mornings, at the market, in times of trouble — you were the most considerate, lovely and compatible person I could ever hope for as a life companion. It is not your fault that we aren't still married and don't

own a pleasant home somewhere near New York. I don't know if we could ever have any life together near New York but I daresay if we were cast up on a Pacific island with fifteen fairies you and I could live together. But I don't suppose that will ever happen.

What I want to say is that I could love you at any time and in any way you would need love and comfort. You always have Beloved Bebe[9] but as long as I am alive you must *never* feel lost and lonely and cut off away from any *one* for you will always be the first and most dearest person in my life. . . . Stay where you are as long as you can work at ease. Don't be hasty or rush your writing. Yours is a creativeness that must come in a slow psychic flow of rhythm. When you are ready go to Yaddo and finish your book as you feel you must. . . .

And Carson followed Reeves's advice — which she had not done for a long time. On June 1 she left Columbus for New York, where she remained for only a few days before leaving for Yaddo, staying there until August 12. The war atmosphere that reigned throughout America then meant that Yaddo was more or less deserted for an entire summer. But Carson had taken the precaution of coming with her friend Alfred Kantorowicz. The weather was splendid, and they felt as if they were on vacation. They took hikes, went swimming in the lakes, talked, played, and read. Carson began reading Karl von Clausewitz in an attempt to better understand the war. And every morning she resumed her work on *The Member of the Wedding* manuscript. The month of July brought a few return residents to Yaddo, among them Alfred Kazin, who took a liking to Carson and years later, in 1971, would be one of the few people who described her to Virginia Spencer Carr without excess of either devotion or resentment.

From the moment I met her at Yaddo during the war, I was moved by her *Southern* feeling against injustice. . . . She had such an intense need of love, and we were so sympathetic to each other in a funny kind of way, that there is almost nothing to say but that we "loved" each other. My relationship with Carson was personal without being intimate, sentimentally intense. She was unhappy to the point of catastrophe — and when we met I was so grateful for her sympathy, as for her art, that it was great being together. But we weren't together very often, actually, or very long; a deep part of her life — her sexuality — always a mystery to me and perhaps to her — was outside of my ken, as were a lot of her friends.[10]

Kazin's friendship was precious to Carson during the weeks after they met, as she dealt with an unpleasant incident that Kazin himself called "a tempest in a teapot" but that greatly troubled Carson. In August *Harper's Bazaar* published *The Ballad of the Sad Café*, which the magazine had purchased a few months earlier. Carson received an anonymous letter accusing her of anti-Semitism on account of this passage about Morris Finestein:

> It was not a common thing to have an unknown hunchback walk to the store at midnight and then sit down and cry. Miss Amelia rubbed back her hair from her forehead and the men looked at each other uncomfortably. All around the town was very quiet.
>   At last one of the twins said: "I'll be damned if he ain't a regular Morris Finestein."
>   Everyone nodded and agreed, for that is an expression having a certain special meaning. But the hunchback cried louder because he could not know what they were talking about. Morris Finestein was a person who had lived in the town years before. He was only a quick, skipping little Jew who cried if you called him Christkiller, and ate light bread and canned salmon every day. A calamity had come over him and he had moved away to Society City. But since then if a man were prissy in any way, or if a man ever wept, he was known as a Morris Finestein.[11]

Shattered, she wrote to nearly all her Jewish friends who had read the manuscript before it was published in *Harper's Bazaar* to ask why they had not said something to her about that passage. Perhaps, they replied, it was because they were personal friends and therefore knew full well that she was in no way anti-Semitic. She nonetheless anxiously inquired as to whether the passage might offend readers who did not know her and declared her desire to defend herself, even though all her friends tried to talk her out of it. She wrote an open letter detailing her opposition to fascism, explicitly asserted in her first book, and tried to get *Harper's Bazaar* to publish it. The magazine chose not to print her long self-justification, which everyone found disproportionate to the incident. The anonymous accusation was undoubtedly unfounded; still, it is easy to see why that anecdote may have been judged unseemly during the worst days of World War II. The anti-Semitic trait depicted here, not of Carson McCullers herself but of a small American community, adds nothing to the singular story of Miss Amelia, Marvin Macy, and the hunchback Cousin Lymon — impeccably told by Carson McCullers — and historical circumstances no doubt should have dictated that it be left out.

In August Carson returned to Columbus from Yaddo, stopping off on the way in New York. Her father was not well. He had had a heart attack, and the doctors had ordered him to stop drinking. Carson looked after him, rationing his doses of alcohol with a rigor that she was never able to apply to herself. Reeves kept on writing letters to Carson, worrying about her and lamenting the idea that he would not see her again before the end of the war. He also sent money. She answered his letters regularly. In late September Reeves and his company were sent to Fort Dix, New Jersey. They would soon be leaving for Europe. In October Reeves and Carson wrote to each other frequently — great, long letters, as if they had to take stock of everything before the momentous departure. October 16 alone brought two letters from Reeves. In them he related the events of his day. He spoke of his men, with great respect and warmth, and as always of his desire to have Carson at his side: "In a way I, too, wish you were a man and were in my company. You would make a good soldier and get along well with the men." He reviewed his postwar ambitions and plans — beyond American shores — engaging in a bit of self-analysis that is not without lucidity, and then plunged into fantasy.

> Do you understand . . . why I have to leave the States after the war? It isn't escapism at all . . . it is only that I seem never to have fully identified myself in America.
>
> I love deeply so much of this country but I have never found a place in it, mostly because of an uprooted home in youth and a wild adolescence with no serenity. There was also a complete lack of personal love until I knew you. After I was with you I coasted on your identity until I became disgusted with myself and became alcoholic that year in New York. But the shock of our being apart straightened me out quickly and I have been of right mind since last spring. . . .

He encouraged Carson to work, to write. "You are the complete master of two of your styles of writing. I don't know which of the two will make you immortal. You must work and not be unduly upset by these times." He spoke again and again of his love. "It is quite clear what you mean to and are to me but I am not sure what I am to you. . . . My life is not nearly complete but knowing you has made it so full. Through you I know tenderness and the real meaning of love."

Reeves wanted Carson to come see him before he left — "It would mean so much to me" — and she did so during the last week of October. In the meantime she had told David Diamond and Newton Arvin that Reeves and she had spoken of remarrying, on her initiative. "In the important ways I am closer to you that any husband has ever been to a wife," Reeves answered.[12] He gave her directions to Fort Dix, where Carson stayed for a week and saw Reeves every day. He got a two-day leave, which they spent in New York visiting their mutual friends — David Diamond, George Davis, Alfred Kantorowicz — one last time before Reeves and his unit would have to set sail.

> You know, I think, how I feel about marriage. . . . When we were no longer friends and were entirely apart I was almost destroyed. . . .
>
> However, I do not love you as a fresh youth of twenty odd [he was thirty years old]: I love you with a maturity, depth and understanding and tenderness that is beyond ordinary personal love. But I don't have to tell you that again. . . .
>
> Our marriage would indeed give a certain "rightness" to our situation. . . .
>
> Even if there will not be enough time for us to be married seeing you and the personal vows would nearly mean the same thing — though not quite. . . .
>
> Oh, my precious Carson I want to hold you close and look at you and to tell you I love you. I want ten minutes, an hour, a day with you — whatever God will grant us.[13]

In the end Carson and Reeves decided not to get married right away but to wait until the war was over before making plans for the future. Carson returned to Columbus, and the two corresponded right up until Reeves left at the end of November.

"My Darling, my beloved Carson," Reeves wrote in an undated letter,

> I have just finished reading again the three letters you have written since being back home. . . . Somehow the letters we have written each other during the past three seasons and the times we have been

together have cancelled and blotted out the terrible and agonized feelings I used to have in the past. . . .

In each of your last letters you repeat that you think it wise that we did not remarry. In fact you seem a little concerned in emphasizing this. . . . What you say in your last letter about our hard-won individual wholeness . . . and the absolute necessity for each of us maintaining a definite separate freedom for our own different types of expression — in our personal lives as well as in our individual work — all that I know to be true. . . . A domestic or marital tie isn't for us. It simply isn't necessary and I always want you to realize that I know that it is not. In the important ways I am closer to you than any man has ever been to a wife. . . .

Tonight there was a sad little ceremony when I burned your letters of the last nine months (we must not take anything that will identify us as a separate unit). . . .

Oh, my Precious Girl, you have been so good and kind to me. I will always have letters from you and forever will I carry memories and associations of you and of us in my heart. Whenever I hear music I think of you first.[14]

The two final letters mailed in the United States were dated November 13 and 15, 1943. Reeves had not heard from Carson for ten days.

Mail has apparently been held up at the base censor's office. . . . Not getting your letters as often as before is just an adjustment I will have to make. . . .

I hope you have had some good working days since I last heard from you. When I get very tired and the men are exhausted and it seems we can't go much further I remember that your work is just as hard. I know, too, that your heart is with me and with us. . . . I realize fully that it takes courage and great strength of mind to write and create in these times. . . .

I am studying German and French now at every opportunity so there will be no language barrier. I would like to think of us being in Europe together in whatever country my job might carry me — but of course you could come and go as you pleased. . . .

I will always give everything I have to something I believe in and know to be right but I am able to give so much more when we are near each other.

If it were not for the renewal of our love and friendship last spring I would not be the soldier I am now or have faith in the peace and new world as I do.

Before saying goodbye, as a kind of incantation Carson and Reeves made a date to meet after the war on the terrace of the Brevoort Hotel, the site of all their reconciliations. When she wrote to Edwin Peacock on November 15, Carson was full of affectionate admiration for her future hero:

> He is in splendid trim, and a wonderful soldier. . . . Reeves is so handsome, it fills me with a sort of horror to look at him and to know the danger he must face. I am glad, though, that we had this visit together. We have been through such sorrow together, such ties of mutual destruction, and somehow those last days made all those dreadful doings seem far away. He was so glad to have me. So proud for me to see his company, and meet the men he has been training with. I have always loved him so tenderly. Now, knowing the Rangers will see so much action ahead of them, it will be very hard to wait between letters. God help him.[15]

Like many American soldiers on November 23, 1943, Reeves McCullers did not know exactly where he was headed, other than to Europe to fight. In fact, his battalion was sent to England — he arrived on December 2, 1943 — where he, along with others, went through intensive training for the D-day landings on the beaches of France, whose date, of course, was at that time still unknown. The Second Rangers found themselves in Bude, then in Tishfield and Folkestone.[16] As soon as he could spare a few minutes — and there were very few to spare — Reeves wrote — to Carson, essentially. Occasionally he wrote to his mother, Jessie McCullers, now living in Baltimore, Maryland, and, more rarely, to friends.

Although Carson and Reeves would write to each other often until Reeves was safely back on American soil in the spring of 1945, it is impossible to say they had a normal correspondence, in which one letter responded to another. Letters arrived irregularly and often were lost before they reached their destination. As for Carson's letters, only some of those written after the Normandy landings of June 6, 1944, have survived — those that came back to America with Reeves. The ones received in England between January and June 1944 were destroyed, as was customary, before the soldiers left English soil.

Both Carson and Reeves tended to return in their letters to the same subjects: fear, absence, the anguish of knowing nothing about the other. This is especially true of Carson, for reasons not hard to understand. For one, she was the person who was "waiting," and for another, it would not have been appropriate for her to say too much about a mode of daily life that, although the United States was at war, bore no resemblance to a soldier's existence, or even to life in a country under threat or occupation. Reeves, in addition to repeated expressions of his feelings, had much to say. Despite the harshness of the times, he was discovering a new continent and finding out what war was like for an average soldier on a day-to-day basis. He clearly enjoyed describing his experiences, supplying all the details. In England he was "billeted with another officer from the Battalion in the home of a widow who was blitzed out of London." He took pleasure in giving her "charming little daughter" his weekly ration of chocolate. The country seemed "magnificent," its rural landscapes enchanted him. "Some time ago a friend of mine came accross English editions of your books in a stall in Bristol and bought them," he rejoiced on December 5, 1943. "It was a pleasant feeling to know your name in Briton was not that of a stranger and that people still buy your books."

Carson continued to bring up the question of remarriage, as if to vindicate herself for having been the one to suggest and then postpone it, since Reeves answered her at length in February, holding fast to his position: "It seems you misunderstood me about our relationship and marriage. My proposed plans did not entail any possession for each of us is alike in the sense that neither would tolerate possession. . . . Although our marriage was a disaster, I don't think it was in any way wrong that we ever knew each other and were close to each other. I still feel close to you."[17]

In the autobiographical narrative she began four months before her death, Carson engaged in a "rereading" of her relationship with Reeves that was not devoid of certain distortions: "All the time during World War II, Reeves' letters were constantly harping on marriage. I was still reluctant about remarriage, although the subject was always uppermost in our letters. I think if I had just had a friendly, non-possessive relationship with Reeves, his life would not have ended in such disaster. But he was most determined to possess me."[18]

It is not accurate to say that Reeves's letters were marked by an obsession with remarriage. He talked about it, certainly, but it is excessive to view his remarks as a kind of harassment. Reeves was trying to become a responsible adult, urging Carson to be patient — about the mail, about her work:

> You are young and there will be time for what you want to do. I trust you in everything. . . . You are well disciplined, too. If it takes another year, two — even three more for this book — you will also come through. . . .
>
> I have loved you for many years, Carson. . . . I know of the wild bird that flutters in your heart at times. There is little I can say about that except that I understand, Dear. I am no diagnostitican and I have never attempted to give you a definite answer. . . .
>
> Since things went topsy-turvy that summer in New York I have never deceived myself in thinking the normal situation possible for us. That did not alter my feeling for you in the least. There is something in my nature that you possibly do not understand — or perhaps overlook. Although you wish all happiness for me the fact is simply that I do not need and do not really *want* a woman. That isn't included in my requirements for happiness.
>
> It can't be possible nearly eight years since you, Edwin and I took Sunday rides and walks and came back to his place for wine and talks and music. Oh Carson, we have had many pleasant, happy times together.[19]

In Columbus, where she spent the whole winter, Carson was once again seriously ill. Her doctors diagnosed pleurisy. As soon as Reeves learned of it, in a letter from Marguerite Smith, he pleaded with Carson to take care of herself. "Darling, darling please don't ever be sick again. For God's sake give your body a chance and don't have your mind worrying or nervousness torture it any more."[20]

In February Reeves fractured his wrist in a motorcycle accident, but he recovered in time to resume training. On the night of June 5, 1944, despite uncertain weather and after the endless equivocating of which we have since heard so much, Lieutenant James Reeves McCullers boarded ship with thousands of other men — their destination, Omaha Beach.

On the boat that transported him to the Normandy coast, he described that extraordinary deployment of forces for Carson:

> Most of last night and all during the day we have been sailing in a vast armada from England towards France to attack Germany. As

far as the eye can see there are ships and crafts in the thousands of every design and type. On the perimeter are the heavy escort vessels. Overhead aeroplanes lazily turn and spiral like protective but insistent sheepdogs leading us on our way.

It is the time we have all been waiting so long for. The pulse of every [man] aboard throbs with excitement and eagerness to be at the Hun. On my craft we have a secret thing designed to surprise him. Our main concern right now is the weather. We pray for the heavy sea to go down.

It is just past supper time and I have finished reading some letters to the men from their leaders — Canham, Bradley, Montgomery, Eisenhower, and the President. They are simply worded notes of advice and encouragement to help them face the horrible, terrifying, miserable days and nights to come. . . .

I must stay up all night with the ship's skipper but I have a last bottle of scotch saved for the occasion to sip on and think and plan. It is a bit chilly tonight but I have on the blue sweater you gave me under my army jacket and that keeps me warm. . . .

I don't believe there is a group of men in the entire expedition more willing and anxious to do their job. Many of us will be killed but we will leave something behind. By killing as many Nazis as possible we will leave a little more freedom on earth. Our Battalion Commander heard General Montgomery make a little talk just before we left. He spoke calmly and factually and said that Germany would be out of the war in six months and that six months after that Japan would be defeated. Half of the forty principal cities of Germany are now destroyed and within a few months the other halves of these cities will be rubble; and she cannot fight a war on three fronts with the possibilities of another opening up when Russia breaks through the Balkans. So much for the war. . . .

This afternoon I was looking at two pictures of you I have — one taken at your home as you were sitting by the piano in which there is a quiet loveliness and calm in your face. The other is from a magazine and was taken at Yaddo I suppose. There is a faint smile on your face about something. . . .

This may be the last letter I will be able to write in some time for only God and the Commanding General know when we will get a rest period. But you will be in my heart and thoughts always.[21]

That letter may not have differed much from hundreds of others written the same night by men who in many cases would never return, but there is something powerful about the conjunction of such a singular personal destiny and such an intense moment of collective history. Reeves was in danger, that much is certain. But he may also have been his best self in that time of combat, feeling internally reconciled and unified by a project and collective will not subject to the uncertainty of his own individual contradictions.

Reeves's battalion was part of the first wave of landings: the Rangers had been charged with storming Pointe du Hoc under the command of Lieutenant-Colonel James Earl Rudder, while one company was to land on Omaha's "Charlie" beach and strike enemy positions at Pointe de la Percée. Lieutenant Dutch Vermeer recounted the saga of Pointe du Hoc. He noted that Lieutenant J. R. McCullers was the only man who succeeded at getting a supply boat loaded with explosives and munitions — the Rangers' only munitions for the entire time they would remain on the point — near the shore. After indicating how much the company owed to Reeves, Dutch Vermeer ended his otherwise purely military account by noting that Reeves's wife was Carson McCullers, the author of several best-selling books.

Amid great loss of life, Reeves's company seems to have been spared the worst enemy fire. No one was killed, though twenty-nine soldiers were wounded — one of them Reeves, who suffered a slight injury to his hand: "The wound isn't serious and I will be well and back on the job in about a week."[22] Indeed, on June 20 Reeves was back at the front, where he served as a company commander. From June 12 through 16 the Rangers advanced toward Vierville-sur-Mer and Grandcamp-les-Bains and then headed for Valognes: "The past 14 days have been the hardest and most horrible I have ever known," he wrote to Carson. "It was just as bad as we had expected — they threw everything at us except the kitchen sink. There was no turning aside or stopping but only to go on and on and on. We accomplished our mission but at a certain price."[23]

◆ ◆ ◆

Since June 15 Carson had been at Yaddo, where she hoped to make better progress on the *Member of the Wedding* manuscript than she had during her stay in Columbus — a hope that was not realized. Needless to say, she was rather preoccupied under the prevailing circumstances. It was to Yaddo that Reeves mailed a July 9 letter typed "on a German typewriter in former German officers' quarters."

It is damn good to be alive, and to be in a building again with a roof over one's head, a bunk to sleep on, and a cheerful stove going in the corner of the room. I have just had my first hot, total submersion (with the exception of D-day when I was in the ocean for twenty minutes) bath in over two months.

I have your second letter written from Yaddo. It isn't dated but I assume it to have been written about a week after the other. Dear, you are still using my old APO number. This means a delay of a week or more. . . . I am concerned about your not having heard from me since we landed. There is absolutely no communication here except letters. I have tried. I have written many times . . . In case my letters haven't reached you I will repeat. I was slightly wounded but I am sound and entirely well now and back for duty on the line. I have command of a company again and some of the old men are still with me. That is just as it should be and I do not wish to be in New York, China or anyplace else except just exactly where I am. I am in this with whole heart and soul until the finish but I sure do want it to finish soon. . . . I wish we had been together more after the bad time was over and we had seen each other that last time in Columbus.

That, I believe, was the turning point in my life. . . . Life was so clean and sweet and my future was held so firmly and surely in my hands, I felt certain of realizing my life just as I wanted it. That could never have been until I had come to terms with myself and become friends with you again. If you had not realized the change and given your love again something vital in me would be dead now.

I will apologize for writing in the past tense but I have told you one just cannot comprehend the future in a situation like this: you live only in the very present. . . .

Modern war must be different from others. Confusion, of course, is supreme; it is fantasic, incredible, at times funny, and naturally gory and horrible. A few days ago I spent several hours in Cherbourg talking with the returning natives and those who had stuck it out.

You and I have known for many years what the Nazis are like and we were further enlightened by what refugee friends and acquaintances had to say but I did not grasp the immense perpretration and exacting fiendish detail of their revolution until I had talked to German prisoners of the different types. Those little stories are among the nastiest I have heard, including things done to the Jews. . . . It is the personal story of a real victim told just to you that makes the war real — [more so] than bullets and shells flying all around you.

It will take three generations to remove from the German soul what Hitler has put into it.

My own little one, I know that the tension right now is almost unbearable for you, but there is nothing I can do to alleviate it. These times are harder for you than for me right now. I know that. I can only repeat that I love you and want more than anything else to come back to you.

Keep always some of the freshness which you have had since I have known you. Let each morning be new and vital and different from any other day the world has known. Work.

Before this time next year I hope to knock on the door of the house wherever you are staying and ask if Carson McCullers is in.

In Normandy Reeves discovered coffee laced with Calvados, "a distillation from apples — something like applejack, only better," whose virtues he vaunted to Carson, suggesting she substitute it for her traditional mixture of sherry and tea. He also described the first "liberated" Bastille Day:

> The people were out in their Sunday best, walking arm in arm along the streets and walkways. One almost wept to watch their timid smiles and air of pride. It is the first time in four years they had celebrated this day. They are still shy and timid and it is hard to say whether they are still inwardly shaking from the noise and hell the Americans made to liberate them — or whether they still feel the effect of the Boche. In any event after you talk with them a few minutes they are cordial, very human and probably the most charming people on earth.[24]

And in his letter of August 21 he extolled his mission as a liberator: "France's hours of agony are almost over and she is beginning to live again. It is good to watch the rebirth of a nation."

It was at Yaddo, on August 1, that Carson heard the news of her father's sudden death from a heart attack. Lamar Smith had been closing up his jewelry shop for the night when he collapsed, dying instantly. He was fifty-five years old. Carson returned to Columbus, where she stayed on after the funeral.

Reeves had heard the news and spoke of it in his August 21 letter:

I am deeply shocked and grieved by your father's death. He was such a kind and gentle person. No man loved his family as he did. I wish I were able to be there with you, Bebe and Rita.

It is wise that Bebe stayed with you and Rita for a while — later on there will be a time when she will be very lonely and will need you. Please give her my deep and tender love.

Carson's mother did not wish to remain in the South, especially since Rita had moved that spring to New York, where she had started working as assistant editor of *Mademoiselle*. Marguerite Smith, who had been hospitalized the day after her husband was buried, did not even want to set foot in the Starke Avenue house again. After being released from the hospital and before heading north, she stayed with her sister. On September 4 Carson, Marguerite, and Rita moved to Nyack, New York, about an hour outside the city on the banks of the Hudson River. They rented a house at 127 South Broadway, directly across from the library, where Marguerite regularly supplied herself with mysteries and detective novels, which Carson often read to relax — "for a change of pace," she said. After selling the Starke Avenue house in Columbus, in May 1945 Marguerite Smith acquired the house at 131 South Broadway that Carson would buy from her in 1951 with money she received when Stanley Kramer bought the movie rights to *The Member of the Wedding*. Both Marguerite and Carson would end their lives in that beautiful, two-story Victorian home with its garden and terrace overlooking the Hudson. Years later Carson spoke in a radio interview of how much she loved that "peaceful community of ten thousand people":

Although not a typical commuters' suburb of New York, the town is wide open to the world. Nyack is internationally famous because of the work of the Tolstoy Foundation, which has directly resettled 13,000 persons from troubled foreign countries to a new way of life in America. . . .

But the strongest and most lasting communication between any people and the world is in its art. Our community, Nyack and its environs, is indeed proud of its artists, and for the best of reasons. Henry Varnum Poor, one of the greatest artists of our time, moved to South Mountain Road in the hills west of Nyack decades ago, when the country was still primitive. He built his own house almost single-handed from the native stone of a quarry near Nyack. In its individuality and beauty it is surely one of the loveliest houses of the world. A long two-story house with an outside studio and kiln, his pictures on the walls, and the long table set with his beautiful ceramics — every object in the house has the hallmarks of this great artist.

Near Henry Poor lives Maxwell Anderson, who wrote his play called *High Tor* about this region. . . . The actors, Katharine Cornell and Burgess Meredith, live around this region too.

In Upper Nyack, Ben Hecht the writer, and Helen Hayes the actress with her writer-husband Charles MacArthur, live in neighboring houses with rose gardens and terraces reaching down to the Hudson River. . . .

Nyack is my adopted home, where I have lived for more than ten years. When I wanted to establish my family near New York, I wanted to live near the city but not in it or in a typical suburban town. I did not want to live in a self-conscious "arty" community. Nyack, while proud of its artists, is not a self-conscious town.[25]

While Carson was getting settled in Nyack, Reeves was at the height of the war. Most difficult for him was seeing men in his battalion lose their lives. Every death revived his fear and distress in the face of that fatal lottery, and in one letter he eventually alluded to his own possible demise: "The greatest shock was losing Meltzer. He was the one close friend I had made in years and I feel like a brother is gone. He was so very real and vital. . . . [A]nd he was so anxious to know you."[26]

According to documents concerning the Second Rangers preserved at the World War II Memorial in Caen, Robert Meltzer was a Hollywood screenwriter who had joined the company commanded by Reeves ten days after the Normandy landings. On September 23, 1944 — that is, not long after Meltzer's death — the American magazine *Collier's* published a juicy account written by him, relating one of many "bar patrols" launched by American soldiers in search of Calvados. This particular episode features Mac the Steady Drinker, alias James Reeves McCullers, who regularly took part in such forays.

> Such patrols, not to be found in the military texts and not countenanced by any staff directives, are composed generally of at least one steady drinker and one soldier who is able to make certain basic desires known in French.
>
> I happen to know French, which explains how, just after the fall of Cherbourg, I found myself in one such patrol. Besides the Steady Drinker, Mac, there were the battalion Intelligence officer, Dutch, and the sad-eared jeep driver who was known as Pony Boy.[27]

The patrol visited a bistro that was ruled with an iron hand by a female proprietor "who had obviously been tyrannizing her family and employees since the Fall of the Bastille." There is no Calvados, she snorted violently — which sparked an indignant reaction on the part of a passing "Parisian," who, recalling Sedan and Verdun and invoking de Gaulle, pleaded that "it was one thing to hide her stock of Calvados from the Nazis but quite another to deny it to our friends, our liberators, the Americans." The Calvados was forthwith removed from its hiding place. "Calvados is also known as *Eau de Vie du Cidre* and might be compared roughly to vodka or tequila. It's clear and white and was mistaken by the Steady Drinker for nitroglycerin when he tossed off his first glass" — a first glass followed by many others. Copiously intoxicated, the "Parisian" proposed raiding an enemy position two kilometers away, a suggestion that his new companions, equally tanked, accepted. Happily, considering the state the crew was in, they did not find any Germans; but in a nearby farm they did find more bottles of Calvados, which extracted from Reeves/Mac the Steady Drinker a "long and profane apostrophe" about the virtues of that "damned wonderful, belly-burning, gut-tearing, mind-searing concoction."[28]

That "Normandy Interlude" — as the title of the article called it — ended agreeably. Not all of them did. The copy of the article preserved at the Caen memorial is accompanied by a typewritten note saying, "After a period of rest in Normandy, Meltzer and McCullers embarked on another escapade in Brittany similar to the one described here, during which Meltzer was killed."

The fighting intensified, and each day that he remained alive seemed like a miracle to Reeves. He wrote to Carson,

So many miracles have accurred during the past thirty-six hours that I don't know just where to start in telling you about what has happened. . . . First of all — I am alive. I am alive. I enjoy writing that. JRM is alive. Verily that is a miracle. . . . When we were relieved I slept for 22 hours without even turning over. . . .

I mailed a package to you today in care of Rita's address. God knows when or if it will reach you. I suppose one would call it booty, although the contents were freely given to me by a German naval officer, Otto Levovdowsky, we captured. He heard one of the men mention my name and he asked me if I had written *The Heart is a Lonely Hunter.* I told him who wrote it and we sat down and had a few drinks together. He had picked up the book in France last winter and liked it.[29]

On October 5 Reeves's heading was just "somewhere in Europe":

This is the first chance in nearly three weeks I have been able to write you. . . . I know this lapse of communications has worried you but it couldn't be remedied. . . .

Great battles rage on . . . wide fronts. At times I get involved in one. . . . Each day of being alive is a little miracle in itself. I have been in so much action the past four months and shot at so many times I can't see how the next bullet misses me. . . .

Death and danger are present in every square foot of surface.

I can't be cheerful or hopeful where I am now. I can only say I hope I survive and see you again some day.

Somehow lots of people you know will return from the war — I must be one of them. . . .

The same day Reeves wrote a second letter to ward off the first one's pessimism: "I wasn't very happy in the note I wrote you earlier today. The tension is the worst thing. Very difficult to bear." As if trying to distance himself somewhat from what he was going through, he wrote:

[We are still in a barn.] One week we live worse than dogs — then comes a rare day or two when we resemble human beings in mode of existence.

In the past month I have lived in a vacuum and able to think or consider only the few immediate hours ahead of me. But there is always you — Carson, Carson, somewhere back in my mind.

A peaceful feeling comes when I am able to think of you.

The last wartime letters that we have from Reeves, written between October 10 and November 8, were mailed from Luxembourg — the Rangers arrived in Belgium in early October, then joined the fighting in Luxembourg on the twenty-first of that month before returning to Germany, where the battles were extremely severe.

Of the letters Carson wrote to Reeves between November 8 and Reeves's return to the States in late February 1945, we have only those that Reeves brought back with him or that were returned by the post office. "There is time for a note before going out to make my rounds," Reeves explained on October 10. He wanted his letters to be "closely spaced," to say precisely what he was doing at what time of day, as if the act of writing and describing were proof of his survival.

It is so useless for them to continue to resist but the fanatics are still in power. We hope it ends before winter sets in. Winter fighting is so slow and difficult.

Right now I am in one of the most beautiful areas in Europe. The war has not smitten the people here so hard. They are quite friendly and make things as easy as possible for the troops. . . .

I long for a letter from you. It has been way over a month since I had one. I know you write regularly — they just haven't been able to catch up with me.

How I long to sit and talk quietly and be with you.

I am anxious to get started on a real future.

Later the same day he wrote a new letter describing the late afternoon and that place, which he could have loved so dearly if it were not then a battleground.

When times are different life is so pleasant and uncomplicated here. The people are about the same as they have been for years and years.

Even if I am dead in twenty four hours from now I have had a very happy afternoon. We rode for a while on business then stopped at a cozy inn in a border town. It was one like Kay [Boyle] described in *Avalanche* on the French border. Clean, fresh, with white table cloths. . . . It was so good to sit quietly drinking schnopps. . . . What a pleasure it is to be alone an hour or two and have your own free thought. It is one of the terrors of combat that impressions are forced on one and there is no freedom of mind and thought or time for the willing acceptance of impressions. Nights are the most horrible of all times — even if there is no firing. . . .

I suppose the war is changing me and will make other changes but I won't grow too old. As you do, so do I hope to keep a freshness and expectancy of life.

On October 17 he was in one of those little cafés that would make him nostalgic for Europe after his return to the States. It was a beautiful day.

The only thing missing to have it nearly perfect is you.

We *will* see each other again, won't we dearest. . . . There are so many things for us to see and do together.

You will love parts of Europe. I think you will like the little country I am in now. The people are good and very industrious. . . .

At the home where I have a room there is an adorable little Italian boy. He is a refugee whose mother works in Paris. He is the beautiful, precacious cameo type like the boy in *Death in Venice.* He is thirteen years old and speaks four languages well. He follows me everywhere and has about extracted all the knowledge I have of America. I wish I could bring him home for us to keep.

At this time my unit is resting and we hold our breath for it to last as long as possible. I am afraid it won't be very long. I feel that there are more horrendous battles ahead than Europe has yet seen.

In the café people were playing cards, and it was almost as though peacetime had already returned. "It is too bad that America doesn't allow herself an institution like the English pub or the Continental Cafe. Life is good to us here for the time being. The thing missed most is cigarettes — American. They just aren't to be had."

It worried him that he had had no word from Carson for days: the mail simply did not come. But a few weeks later, on November 8, eighteen letters arrived, almost all of them from Carson, the last of which was dated October 22. "Yesterday was one of the biggest events for me since D-day. I received a total of 18 letters. . . . Oh, Precious

Carson, your letters were so good, good. I have read them all over starting from the first."[30]

Carson was indeed writing almost every day, but many of her letters have been lost. All of them were addressed to "Lt. James Reeves McCullers 01301851. Company I 28th Infantry. 8th Division, A.P.O. 8, NY NY c/o Postmaster." She realized that the events of daily life that she was describing were "very remote" from Reeves, that they must all seem "extremely strange." But that was her small way of attempting to live once again with Reeves by her side. Anyway, for the moment nothing was happening in her own existence. There were only the waiting, a manuscript that would not budge, and the illnesses. She finally received a letter on November 12; it had taken more than a month to arrive. But in the other direction things were even worse. The letters she had written were not getting through at all, which made Carson doubly apprehensive that Reeves would feel abandoned and let his guard down when he needed to protect himself most:

> It distresses me to know that my letters to you are not reaching you. Oh I hope so much that by now you are hearing regularly from me.
>
> . . . I read every line [of the newspaper] hoping to come on some news of the 28th [Infantry] — or rather I fear, rather than hope, to read such a mention, for it would mean you are in combat. . . .
>
> It's a cold, bright Sunday here. . . .
>
> Dearest Reeves, please take care of yourself.[31]

Then on November 21, 1944:

> Reeves angel:
>
> This morning the first snow of the year has come. The whirling light wild flakes are at the window; the river is veiled and only a deserted brown little house with two red chimneys is there by the river's edge, looking more lonely than ever. . . . These are the times we loved together. . . . We always made a festival of our first snows. It is so lonely without you this First Snow.
>
> I still have no letter. I am grown sickeningly anxious. I wait and there's no word. The radio tell of the new offensive — and I hunt for some news of the 28th in all the newspapers. Perhaps there will be a letter on the afternoon mail.
>
> I spent the weekend in town [Carson speaks of an evening that she spent with the couple's writer friend Kay Boyle]. . . . We had

lobster and Sweedish food and quantities of some strong drink that was kept on the table in big pitchers. We sat down to the table at six and stayed there, except for changes of seats, until about two or three o'clock. I hadn't been to such a party for years — and I must say it was fun for a change. But I kept missing you and wishing for you. . . .

. . . If you were here we would have a cozy drink together and play a game of chess. The next First Snow, I feel that we can be together. This one I'll just try to ignore. I am worried and too sad.

If ever a letter was typical of a good war wife, this one is certainly it — and the expression is by no means pejorative; on the contrary, it highlights Carson's normalcy, though so many have delighted in calling her obnoxious, pathologically egocentric, and indifferent to everything other than her own notoriety. With no news of Reeves, Carson McCullers was worried sick. The first snowfall provided an occasion to remember happy moments shared with Reeves; yes, her evening had been pleasant, but how much more enjoyable it would have been for her if they had spent it alone together calmly playing chess. Next year, surely . . . In short, Carson said just enough not to feign that life had totally ground to a halt but to let Reeves know at the same time that his absence was unbearable. Why have some commentators found it so hard to imagine that Carson was *also,* especially at moments like these, a simple young American woman, twenty-seven years old, whose husband was fighting far away in Europe unaware perhaps of how much she was thinking about him? That particular anxiety at least disappeared:

Little darling Reeves! How happy I am today! The cable came yesterday, just as I was mailing that sad little letter about the first snow. And now *two* letters, the last written only November 8. My God, what a relief! But I almost cried when I read that for two months there had been no letters from me — and if you only got 18 letters, including those from others — then all my mail is *not* reaching you. It's the most maddening dreary feeling to suspect that my letters are lost or thrown away before they reach you.

I love all that you write about Luxemberg. But I think of that Hell of front line combat. No I won't and can't "accustom" myself to the thought that something might happen to you. My mind just can't work that way. You should not ask that. I have to *believe* in life — especially in your life. . . . Reeves, . . . I *know* you will survive — you have ahead of you so much richness, so many varied promises for the future. But, though I talk like this, I live always under this tension. . . .

Reeves, you *must* promise me, that when this European war is over and they [begin] shipping men to the Pacific you will take advantage of *all* your combat credits etc. — Yet I know I should not put it like this, as a personal demand. I never want to influence you in any vital decisions you might make. I want you to be on your own; we've talked about that before. Oh but it would be something to hold on to if I could believe that you can come home before summer. . . .

. . . Kanto [Alfred Kantorowicz] and Friedl [Kantorowicz] are coming out to share Thanksgiving dinner with us, and Louise Rainer is coming with them. I know, precious, that these gatherings and our little "teas with the Poors and Kay" that you mentioned are very remote from you. They are remote from me, too, Reeves. I write you about them because I wan't you to know everything that we do. . . . But, back to the Thanksgiving, we have read that every soldier is having turkey today — although I won't be too sure of it until you write to me.[32]

Carson followed with real attention the evolution of both the military situation, since it affected Reeves directly, and the global situation in Europe, as we see in her letter of December 5, 1944:

Reeves Precious:

It is late afternoon and I have been working and studying all day. First, I worked on my book all morning until about one thirty. Then this afternoon I plugged away with French idioms. . . .

The situation in the occupied countries seems to get more disturbing every day. Especially the Greek trouble is alarming. Why can't Winston Churchill keep his reactionary nose out of the internal affairs of other nations. . . . Why should the British Empire impose it's will on nations who want and need a democratic government. . . .

[There] is a jangling, eerie sounding piano out in the front hall and sometimes, late in the afternoon, I go out and play. The Bach preludes and fugues have an uncanny sound on the untuned piano in the empty hall. I miss my piano so much.

On December 9 Reeves was injured in Germany, the victim of "numerous shrapnel wounds in the body and a badly fractured hand" near Rötgen, where he had returned to the front on December 4.[33] When she found out, Carson would be more reassured than worried, for Reeves's life was not in danger but he had to be evacuated — and she hoped that he would not have to go back to the fighting. For the moment, however, she had not been informed and, plagued by uncertainty, Carson saw trouble or a frightening omen everywhere she turned:

> I tried to work, but this particular section I'm now on seemed so cumbersome and heavy when I read it today that I realize it will have to be done again — but first I'll finish it and then see what needs to be done. . . .
> Yesterday Mother and I went to the movie a few blocks up the street. It was a windy biting afternoon and I wore the knitted G.I. cap down over the ears. When we left the movie . . . the cap was dropped. . . . I burst out crying like a child. I have always been so careful of the cap you gave me, and it seemed somehow a dreadful thing that I should lose it. I cried all the way home and Mama was miserable. *But* when we got home we found that the lost cap was Rita's (I'd taken it by mistake) one that Frank gave her when he found she liked mine. . . .
> Today for some reason I can hardly see. I think I must have caught cold in my eye, for the right one is almost blind.[34]

It was no less frightening to listen to the news:

> The new German counter offensive has terrified me. I think you must be there where the worst of it goes on. I hang over the radio and walk the floor and wait and dread.
> Reeves precious, *please* don't go back to the line if you have hip reumatism. You can't fight properly when you are ailing like that. . . .
> You must excuse this odd, abrupt note. For the last days I have had some severe eye trouble, and am forbidden to look at a typewriter or to read a headline. It seems only to be a case of acute eye-

strain, and I'm taking care of it — wearing dark glasses and using poultices.[35]

Reeves did not receive that letter, written on December 18, 1944, since he had been wounded and hospitalized in the meantime. So it was returned to its sender — on March 2, 1945. Although it is certainly understandable that mail made its way slowly to soldiers in perpetual motion, people back home must have endured extreme psychological stress both from not knowing the fate of their loved ones for so long — at a time when, for six entire months, death could come at any moment — and from the pain of suspecting that the words of love and comfort, signs of life and harbingers of the future, were not reaching them.

No wonder Carson McCullers had a hard time making progress on her novel. Perhaps Carson, an admirer of Proust, shared the Proustian sentiment that to take one's mind off the other would imperil him, that such amnesia could place the person at physical risk. This might be one more reason why she did not escape her anguish by working on fiction. Some critics believe they pay homage to Reeves when they view Carson's creative "breakdown" as proof of his essential contribution to her work, but Reeves himself showed more intelligent generosity than his eventual supporters when he wrote, "I realize fully that it takes courage and great strength of mind to write and create in these times."[36]

Carson may have had an intuition of imminent danger, since she wrote three nearly identical letters over the course of two days:

Oh Reeves darling, — If only I could have some word from you today — but I don't mean a letter written two weeks ago, but word about you now. This new German offensive has me in the same state I was on D day. You see I *know* you are there where the most bitter fighting is. I can't seem to think about this offensive with any strategic perspective; over and over I am haunted by a picture of you, there in a ditch at the front line, when the German blitz attack came. You may even be taken prisoner now as I write this. It's almost more than I can stand — these next few days until more details come through.

For security reasons they are not giving us many details. We only know it is a desperate last ditch maneuver and the Nazis are putting everything into it. And I know you are there. Always before, you know darling, I have been able to think to myself that you are at some other part of the front, other than the place of the fiercest battles.

The only thread of comfort I have is the faint hope that the hip reumatism you wrote me about has grown worse and you were not directly on the front line when the attack came. I'm such a coward about you; I [hang] onto the most fantastic hopes.

Offensive fighting is so different from defensive war. In a retreat I am haunted by the thought of the wounded, and the probability that many may have to be left behind.

Write me, Reeves, the minute you get this letter.

I can't get my mind on anything else except those battles going on now. I keep the radio on, as on D. day.

. . .

I'm writing a v mail letter in the hopes it will reach you sooner than this. So I'll get busy with that one now.

Goodbye, darling Reeves. You know that my heart and mind is with you at every moment.[37]

"Fortunately," we may say at this moment when Carson was very near collapsing — which despite her fragile nerves she never did throughout Reeves's entire time in combat — she received the army telegram notifying her of his injury:

The War Dept. telegram has just come. After these last dreadful days it was an unspeakable relief to know you were "slightly injured" December 9. At the same time I remember how promptly you returned to combat the last time you were slightly wounded. . . .

I am so agitated I can hardly write. When the telegram came my eyes went blind and for a moment after the We Regret I could not read at all. Then when I knew what it was I burst out crying and laughing at the same time.

I try to picture you lying between clean warm sheets, with a good book and good meals brought on a tray, and with a wound in the foot that is not painful, not serious at all, but will take *some little time* to heal.

I am a little worried for fear the German Blitz might have caught up with your hospital. So don't fail to write me the *moment* you get this.

Reeves, listen to me carefully. While you are in hospital be sure to consult the doctors about your reumatism and the sinus trouble that has been plagueing you. This is very important.

The news that leaks through the security blackout is frightening. But somehow I believe we (We!) will be able to smash the Nazis, and turn this piece of desperation to our own advantage. I can't help but believe that Eisenhower and the other generals know what they are doing. amd forsaw the possibility of this attack all along.

. . . This is a grim, hazardous business. If we can't cope with it the war may go on and on.

. . . I'm drinking hot tea and not doing much. In fact, I haven't worked in about ten days, *and* the book is far from finished. I am discouraged sometimes. But it will be so much easier to work these next weeks knowing you were not the first shock of the German attack.[38]

On December 25 she wrote Reeves a long letter describing Christmas Day, a day dedicated to him, as it was in many families in which a husband or a son was at war.

You have been with us all through this day. We burned a special barberry candle for you that blazed on the central table and lasted all day. . . .

. . . It touches me to realize how kind people are and to realize how our friends love us. . . .

. . . If I hadn't got the war dept. cable saying you were slightly injured I doubt if I could have stood the suspense.

Finally, on December 27 a letter came from Paris. It was the sign that Reeves had been "saved": they were sending him to England, where he would stay until he was able to return to the United States. Carson would have liked to rush to his bedside or, better yet, to see Reeves repatriated. "Yet Reeves it is not so agonizing as the constant thought of the grisly miseries of a battlefield — the nightmarish dread for your very life. I know now that you are warm safe and cared for; now I ought to be able to sleep at night."[39] Carson and Reeves's friend the writer Kay Boyle was leaving for England on January 1, as she had planned to do for several months. So Kay would visit Reeves and bring him whatever he asked for. In all the letters written between December 25 and the early days of 1945, Carson rejoiced that the piece of mail containing Reeves's account of the worst moments of fighting in Germany had taken such a long time to reach her.

In one of the letters from December 28 Carson used the word *tranquillity* for the first time since Reeves's departure.

> Your letter written on Thanksgiving Eve, during the time of that ghastly fighting in Germany, came just after I had written you this afternoon. Never have I read a more terrible and moving letter. There is nothing for me to say. Thank God it comes to me only now, when I know you are out of battle — otherwise I wonder how I could have stood it. Reeves, my love, if ever anything happened to you the harmony of my life would be destroyed forever. Somehow I can't imagine a world without you in it anywhere. I won't write any more about this now; you know how I love you.
>
> I realize that the letters I write you now will have to go all the way to Belgium or Germany and then sent back to you in England. I'm so anxious to get the hospital address. Soon . . . I should have my precious letters from you. I read and read them and they are all quite ragged. . . .
>
> The news seems better today and yesterday. Patton's tanks seem to be slicing up through the German salient. But they say the losses have been very great. I think of all the wives whose husbands have been killed. . . .
>
> . . . I'm still in bed with this cold. I keep wishing you could be lying here close beside me. It's a clear bitter day outside. The sky is the palest blue, with a cold wintry yellow along the horizon. The river is iron gray and frozen on the shores. But here in the house it's cozy and there is the usual litter on the bed — a couple of volumes of Proust, several of your letters, *two* handsome boxes of Christmas candy, etc. It's just the time in the late afternoon when the lamps are being turned on. . . . I have the card table with the legs folded up on the bed with me as a base for the typewriter. I lie here and wonder how you are, if you are comfortable, if you have whiskey and plenty of cigarettes. . . .
>
> Mama has just come in to put a mustard plaster on my chest, and I'll be smelling like a ham sandwich all night.

In the early days of 1945, Carson's letters grew more and more lyrical, even passionate. She had obtained the address of the English hospital and thus believed that the mail would be somewhat less slow, or a little less erratic. Happily so, Carson having described "these days of limbo" spent waiting for Reeves's hospital address to arrive as "almost unbearable." On January 1, 1945, she wrote:

> My loved one, my husband and everlasting friend, I need you so. After the suffering of these last ghastly months, I know that no tenderness could be lavish enough; I feel that we must always be so gentle with each other. Always.
>
> . . .
>
> Kay leaves for England around the middle of the month (January). . . . She is bringing the marvelous poem, dedicated to us. . . . Kay and I tore up a two dollar bill, each keeping half until she returns.
>
> . . .
>
> This is the first day of the New Year. Mother is cooking black eyed peas — but she was unable to find any hog jowl; they seem never to have heard of it up here. But we will have the peas and white meat for the New Year's luck dinner. And I will be thinking of my darling with every pea.
>
> It's a ghostly, foggy morning. There is some sad looking porous snow on the ground and housetops. Beginning tomorrow I will make a great effort to work. . . . I must write some stories that will make you proud of me. I even must try to make some money — or at least finish what I have to do and then see if it won't bring me something. I feel I owe you a lot of money. But the main thing is to do work that I know is good. I believe that I can. I don't ever want you to be disappointed in me.

Nonetheless, she could think of nothing but Reeves's return and was counting the days since his injury — twenty-two, twenty-six . . . She simply could not concentrate well enough to get back to work. So she read short novels by Henry James, finding them "damn well worth while. One in particular I long to share with you."[40]

Carson assiduously continued to read Henry James, speaking of him often in later letters: "One is quite willing to stumble through pages of ambiguities for those sudden, exquisite lines, those almost unexpected revelations. I'd never realized how deeply he has influenced the present poets — Eliot, Auden etc. I want us to read the

Beast in the Jungle together," she wrote on January 8. And the next day she decided to get serious about settling down to work:

> I'm making a pact with myself to finish this monstrous story by March 15. This morning I worked several hours. But it's one of those works that the least slip can ruin. Some parts I have worked over and over as many as twenty times. I must finish it soon and get it out of my system — but at the same time it must be beautifully done. For, like a poem, there's not much excuse for it otherwise.
>
> The Henry James could be very discouraging at this point. Some of the nouvelles are among the best I have ever read. I gawk over them like a child watching the trapeze lady at the fair. They are really supreme achievements.[41]

On January 5 she got "the beautiful letter written Dec. 3, at the rest camp behind the lines":

> I have been reading it all during the day. But still I know no more about where you are *now*. Sometimes I picture you in an English hospital, without letters, with no boxes from me — and I weep. . . . I am still possessed, really possessed, with the fancy that you may be on the way home. Every time the telephone rings I tremble all over. . . . [42]

> I [have] lived with the fabulous thought that you would be sent home, that any instant I would open the door and my darling would be standing there, that I would hear your voice out in the hall. . . . [43]

> Reeves, my own darling, I have read many war book, letters, and stories. But your letters to me are the most powerful, suggestive pieces of writing about war I have ever read. I have showed a few of the letters, parts of them, to other people — and it has been suggested that they ought to be published. . . . Of course I know they were written with no such intention — they were written only to me, and they are the dearest treasure I possess. You may not like it that I read parts of these letters to anyone else, but I don't think you will be angry with me. . . .

I know my letters to you fail sometimes even to make sense. They are only the letters of a desperate woman, a little unbalanced sometimes by fear.[44]

Reeves clearly enjoyed telling stories, and he did have something of an eye, a knack for the quick sketch — Normandy bistros, Luxembourg peasants — but that wartime correspondence, whether from Reeves or even from Carson, has more value as a testament of the times than as a literary work. The conditions that brought it into being were hardly favorable to begin with, which explains in part why World War II did not give rise to the same epistolary literature that its predecessor generated in 1914–18. World War I was a more "tranquil" war, punctuated by moments of respite — albeit in the horror of the trenches — that most of the soldiers who landed in France on June 6, 1944, never knew. Reeves's letters thus, whatever Carson may have said out of emotion or affection, can plead neither for nor against his stature as an author. For both Reeves and Carson, the time of war unfolded in a place beyond literature.

✦　✦　✦

Despite her laborious resolutions and her relative tranquillity regarding Reeves, Carson still could not achieve a state of calm propitious to her writing. She grew more and more impatient. Why had Reeves not yet returned? It was almost as if he were dragging his feet. Though she softened her barrage with excuses here and there, Carson assailed Reeves with questions that he simply could not answer, penning letter after letter at a furious pace:

> You see, little darling, all the frantic letters I have been pouring out to you since the War Dept. cable came will have been sent all the way to Belgium and will very likely take months to reach you. But I had to write them and send them out, just as Noah sent out his doves. (Or was it ravens?) . . .
>
> I don't want to run you wild, with my insisting questions. But I must know the answers as soon as possible. (1) Is there any chance that you will be sent home to me? (2) Is it [at] all likely that you will be medically discharged? . . . (3) You mention that you do not expect to be in action again before March 15. But are you sure you will be returned to action? If a man's hand is stiff or weak it seems to me

he would be unable to handle a rifle properly, and so would not be send to the front. Tell me, my Reeves, isn't it likely that when your hand is well you will be transferred to some other unit other than as a combat infantryman? My darling heart, answer these questions *immediately.*

These last weeks, since the War. Dept. cable came, have been so unreal. . . . I *know,* my precious, I ought to be down on my knees this very minute and stay there all the time you are in hospital. I *am* grateful to God: The blissful relief of knowing you are safe in a hospital is more than I could ever write you. But at the same time this fantastic notion — that you were on your way home to me — dies hard this morning. Why is it that in *all* concerning you I make such monstous demands? From you and God I'm always asking *more,* and never satisfied. Why is that, darling?[45]

Now that I know you are safe and warm, after these unspeakable months, I can tell you I have nearly gone out of my mind with worry. If I could know that at the moment, the very instant, you were wounded or killed, I would be wounded or killed also — if that could be possible, then I could be brave. But as things are — I can't. . . .

I want to know everything about the hospital — the routine, the treatment etc. Do you have any whiskey? Can you get beer, darling? Does your hand pain you? I would give all that I have if I could be near you.[46]

Having learned that Reeves was not receiving her letters, Carson began sending telegrams almost every day to tell him she was waiting and to express her love. She nonetheless kept "piling on" letter after letter, imperturbably, recounting her days once again: she would talk about the weather, telling Reeves how cold the New York winter was, or complain that she was bored and often couldn't sleep.

This afternoon I read more Henry James, but otherwise the day was very unsatisfactory. Last night I was awake almost the whole night, and was so deadly tired today I couldn't work.

But for an hour or so last night I did sleep, and . . . dreamed that I waked up and you were lying there beside me. That was all — I didn't see or touch you in the dream, but I knew that you were there; the dream had no sense of war, and there was not the least surprise about your being there, it was all so beautifully natural. In the dream I felt only a contentment, knowing you were there, and (in the dream) turned over and went back to sleep again.[47]

Carson's "wild marvelous fantasies" about Reeves, induced by alcohol, were at the very most fanciful: "I imagine that you will be sent home to me. I think of a sudden wire sent from a hospital here — you have been flown over. I picture the scramble of packing a bag and getting the next train (or bus to N.Y. and then the train)."[48] The kind of lack evoked by this fantasy is purely childlike, devoid of all eroticism — a longing for the calm that would come from simply lying next to a body one loves. That said, if Carson was indeed suffering the consequences of some obscure kind of emotional deprivation, despite her mother's extreme (perhaps too extreme?) attention, her pain was no less intense for being that of a child. That may explain why this torrent of anxiety was unleashed precisely now, when Reeves was more or less out of danger and there was not so great a need for her to control its expression.

Until February 19, Carson's birthday and the date of her last letter before Reeves set foot again on American soil, she wrote missives that grew longer and longer, to the point of boredom (except perhaps for a wounded soldier at loose ends). She recited pleasant events — the carton of Camels sent by Edwin Peacock, who was still in the navy, though no one knew exactly where — and everyday annoyances. She commented on the music she was listening to and on the current military and political situation.

We heard the Mendelsohn E minor concerto, and it carried me back to that Sunday afternoon, so long ago, when we heard Yehudi Menuhin playing the same concerto in Charlotte on the Sell's radio — do you remember?

. . .

This morning I saw in the Times that 1,300 combat soldiers had been sent back to the states for a thirty day furlough. Do you think anything like that might happen to you? . . .

Reeves, do you know whether you will be sent to the Pacific after the war in Europe is over. Somehow I feel you won't. You have been wounded twice and have seen so much combat, and you are over thirty years old. If they would send you to the Pacific I don't think I could stand it.[49]

In almost every message she worried whether Reeves had enough whiskey and cigarettes, often adding personal reflections or anecdotes. "Speaking of cigarettes, I bought a little hand roller and some Bull Durham [a popular brand of rolling tobacco] this morning. Also, I got a pipe — and it promptly made me sick. . . . I feel constantly the guilt of living in a country that has not suffered in this war — excepting always, of course, the dreadful anxieties of those (and that means most of us) who have loved ones overseas. Sometimes I think it would be easier to stand this war if we had a bit more of the sense of deprivation."[50]

Whenever she discussed her work, the difficulties she was having with her manuscript, or the pact she had made with herself to reclaim her intellectual discipline, she always mentioned the books she was immersed in: after Henry James came Marcel Proust, whose works she was reading every afternoon at the end of January "after the postman comes." "Today I was thinking of the immense debt I owe to Proust," she wrote.

> It's not a matter of his "influencing my style" or anything like that — it's the rare good fortune of having always something to turn to, a great book that never tarnishes, never [becomes] dull from familiarity. [Of] course, part of this everlasting quality is due to sheer length; but only a part. This morning I was reading the parts about Swann and those early lovely Cambray scenes. — The copies, of course, are those you gave me years ago. It was books like these I wanted to send you to have while in the hospital.
>
> My dear one, I think about you constantly.[51]

On January 27, when she began with these words in capital letters, "MAY BE HOME SOON!" she knew that it was no longer a simple wish: she had received a telegram in which Reeves announced that he was coming home "soon." Obviously, she would have liked to know exactly what *soon* meant in this instance. "I am so excited. Mother and Skeet [a nickname for Carson's sister, Margarita] and I can talk of nothing else. I hold the cable and read it over and over. . . . I see myself cutting up your meat for you — or just gazing at you, and touching you lightly to see if you are real. — Reeves, let me know *immediately*, as soon as it's more settled. Until I know more I feel like somebody floating around in air. Excuse this crazy letter; under the circumstances, it's the best I can do." "This is the slowest month I have ever known," she wrote on February 8, 1945. "There is nothing for me to write. I work, and spend the rest of the time wondering when you will come."[52]

◆ ◆ ◆

Reeves finally left England on February 10. Carson met him on the twenty-fourth in New York, where his ship had just pulled into port. On March 19 — exactly one month after Carson's twenty-eighth birthday — the two remarried. On March 26 she wrote to Edwin Peacock, the friend from the 1930s who in 1937 had been the "master of ceremonies" at their first marriage, to ask if he would serve as a "witness" for the second, even though they were apart: "Reeves and I seek your blessing once again. This time we were legally married in New City [near Nyack, in Rockland County, where their friend Henry Varnum Poor, who painted a portrait of Carson that belongs today to Mary Mercer, lived with his family]. There was no Edwin to set up our Bach concerto on the gramophone: we were married in a courtroom by a judge dressed in a black robe. But no matter, we are happy once again."[53]

Oddly enough, in Carson McCullers's first novel, *The Heart Is a Lonely Hunter*, one of the main characters has the experience of remarrying the same man. It's Lucile, Biff Brannon's sister-in-law, mother of the spoiled child named Baby:

> You married this certain party when you were seventeen, and afterward there was just one racket between you after another. You divorced him. Then two years later you married him a second time. And now he's gone off again and you don't know where he is. It seems like those facts would show you one thing — you two are not suited to each other. And that's aside from the more personal side — the sort of man this certain party happens to be anyway.[54]

Later on, the play *The Square Root of Wonderful* would take up an identical situation but this time one directly inspired by the lives of Reeves and Carson. So the sort of fictional premonition at work with Lucile in *Heart* was not a factor in *Square Root*. Mollie marries Phillip

Lovejoy twice in this play, and the pitiful and disastrous story of Mollie and Phillip exploits Reeves and Carson's tragic destiny in an unmistakable way — Carson constantly attempts to justify herself. Mollie Lovejoy, for instance, cannot really say why she chose to marry Phillip for the second time. "I — I was under a spell — a strange spell."[55] "The first time with Phillip it was not against my will." The second time:

> I was under his spell. Love is very much like witches and ghosts, and childhood. When it speaks to you, you have to answer, and you have to go wherever it tells you to go. . . .

> Phillip — he struck me, he beat me up so many times. Once he tore off my nightgown and put me out of that front door . . .
>   (Points to door.)
> naked as a jaybird. And I stood it! . . .

> In spite of all Phillip's terrible failings he had a lot of charm. A redeeming charm, somebody once said.[56]

As for Reeves, whenever his friends asked him to explain this second marriage, he is said to have replied every time, "Because I think we are all drones — and Carson is the queen bee."[57]

Needless to say, the judgments people formed of this marriage, the attempts made by more or less well-intentioned friends to explain what a grave error it was came, of course, long after the fact. In the spring of 1945 Reeves had "miraculously" survived a war that in a sense had enhanced his relationship with Carson by giving it a heroic dimension. Why, then, is it forbidden to propose that Reeves and Carson might have wished to make their reunion official and might have done so joyously, out of desire? What other reason could they possibly have had to appear before "a judge dressed in a black robe" besides the wish to give their love — professed at length in so many letters — an official reality? Yet their choice to marry again — for worse, as the future would prove — has been treated with annoyance and sometimes even outrage, providing yet another excuse to criticize Carson. She had left Reeves once and did not like making love with him; now she was destroying his chance for a new life. Thanks to "his" war, Reeves finally existed. His decorations, which made Carson so proud, certified what he had accomplished: four battlefield commendations, the highly coveted Silver Star, three Bronze Stars, the Presidential Unit Citation, and several medals — among them the combat infantry badge and a Purple Heart, awarded to those who are wounded on the field of battle. But by becoming a civilian again, he risked turning back into "the husband of Carson McCullers." Remarrying Carson increased that risk. Because their remarriage ultimately was harmful to them both, many have felt compelled to unearth explanations — preferably sinister ones — for their reunion and to transform this sign of vitality and hope into an announcement of destruction and death. But remarry they nonetheless did, taking a step that cannot be reduced to any single interpretation, not even their own, or even the final one given by Carson in her memoirs:

> As soon as he returned to Nyack, he immediately started a barrage to make me marry him again.
>
> I said, "second marriages are so vulger."
>
> Naturally, I was happy to see him, but I said, "we're much better as friends, without marriage." Marriage, however, was his motive.
>
> I talked to Henry Varnum Poor, the great artist, and asked him his advice, and he said he could not give it to me. I also spoke with Dr. William Mayer, my Doctor and psychiatrist, and he could only say, "men don't change essentially because of a war."
>
> I had been hoping that there would be some sort of a miraculous change in Reeves because of his experiences. He was covered with campaign ribbons and when we walked down the street everyone looked at him. I, of course, was enormously impressed. He was so darn sweet that I forgot the reasons for my divorcing him in the first place.[58]

That they may have given in to the euphoria of the return, and to the image that each one had formed of the other — the valiant warrior, the loving woman who feared, hoped, and waited — in no way compromises their sincerity. They probably remarried out of mutual admiration: the admiration that Reeves had never stopped feeling for Carson and the entirely new admiration that Carson had for Reeves, the hero and the storyteller — at least for the Reeves who was finally revealing his desire to write and the pleasure he took in telling a tale.

Reeves seems also to have come to a better understanding of the pitfalls of the writer's trade during the war. On several occasions while he was in Europe, he told Carson how conscious he was of the difficulty involved in writing a successful book. He saw what strength it took, what courage and tenacity, to bring a work to fruition. A determination that causes everything else to become secondary — was he really capable of that? This question is important in light of the opinion that Carson supposedly killed the writer in her husband or put him to work writing for her — or both at once. John Brown, who saw a lot of Reeves and Carson in France, and who is not particularly well disposed toward Carson, calls this debate "ridiculous," stating categorically: "Reeves was a little American soldier. He was simply incapable of creating, of writing a book."[59] Still, John Brown's statement may be as simplistic as the belief that Reeves's guiding spirit was symbolically murdered by an odious, unscrupulous spouse. Reeves McCullers was intelligent and had a taste for literature; he "knew how to read" and wanted to write, and it is difficult to understand his love for Carson in the absence of that desire. Why, then, did he never write anything besides his letters from the war? Was it Carson's immediate success with her first novel that discouraged him? Did he actually sense that he was not capable of producing as fine a book as *The Heart Is a Lonely Hunter*? Was he simply fearful of measuring himself against Carson's reputation and winding up more bitter and frustrated?

The biographer most anxious to valorize Reeves is Jacques Tournier, who questioned Reeves's friends John Vincent Adams and David Diamond at length in the 1970s.[60] Adams, the companion of Reeves during his midtwenties, when his dreams of literary creation were at their height — the friend with whom he traveled north so that both men could become novelists — never read a single composition by Reeves. Adams "saw him writing," and that's all. He thought he remembered someone telling him that the *New Yorker* had bought three short stories by Reeves McCullers in 1947. They never appeared in the magazine, and there is no trace of them anywhere.

David Diamond, with whom Reeves lived for several months in Rochester around the time of his divorce, said he encouraged Reeves to write. "I know that he was working on a text inspired by the ninth chapter of *Moby-Dick*," Diamond confided to Tournier, "Father Mapple's sermon. He venerated *Moby-Dick*. It was his Bible." Diamond professed to be certain that Reeves had real talent as a writer, all the while acknowledging that every time he tried to read something he had written, Reeves, who could be "a tough customer," would burn it or tear it up. Why, then, was he so certain of Reeves's gifts? In order to blame Carson, evidently: "She did everything she could to discourage him." But what if a writer is precisely someone that you cannot so thoroughly discourage?

Tournier was clearly upset to find that no one had read anything written by Reeves, so he dug deeper and finally made a discovery. With utmost seriousness, Jacques Tournier recounts that one person had read some of Reeves McCullers's work — or, rather, had been present at a reading — and "still remembered it fifty years later." Her name was Ethlyn Massey. In 1928 at the high school in Jesup, Georgia, Massey sat next to Reeves in class. In a long article published in *The Issue,* a magazine based in Atlanta, she recalls that their teacher had asked the students "to write a short story" one day as a homework assignment. "Having judged Reeves's to be better than the others, he had read it aloud during the class. Ethlyn Massey had such a good memory — and the story had made such a strong impact — that she could still hear Reeves's sentences wafting through the classroom, bringing unexpected beauty to life with the help of the imagination's magic. 'It was a moment that will always be part of me,' she writes. 'A moment still intact in my memory, isolated and radiant. Reeves's style was strange and elegant. He knew how to play with words like no one else. Today I would call him avant-garde. At the time — I was in tenth grade — I simply thought he was superb.'" The dawn of genius, if you will. "A pupil more gifted than the others," comments Tournier, "a homework paper noticed by a teacher, a class that listened in silence and then broke into applause — perhaps these are the first symptoms of a devastating virus that John Vincent Adams quickly cured himself of but that got under Reeves's skin, filling him with bitterness and frustration and finally devouring him."[61] This fragment of a fifty-year-old memory is the strongest evidence that Tournier can offer concerning the suppression of Reeves McCullers's literary talent. We are not obliged to be fully convinced.

During the war in Europe, Reeves put part of his life down in writing. This experience should have given him a somewhat clearer idea of both his desire and his ability to write — an actual test of the pen. The war also transformed his position in life. No longer adrift and in conflict with Carson, he returned with a hero's prestige, which his wife liked to point out to all their friends. This life experience could have given him a boost in writing or another field, but his weak-willed side took over again extremely quickly. The possibility of a brighter future was soon squandered.

Reeves spent several months in various veterans hospitals — particularly the one in Utica, New York — receiving treatment for his injured hand. Doctors planned to do a bone graft but then abandoned the idea. Reeves would never be able to use his left hand the way he had before. Several doctors recommended that he be declared medically unfit for service and awarded a pension. In the end the military authorities decided to place him on "permanent limited service." The only plan that Reeves never renounced was the idea of returning to Europe. He tried to get into the American Military Government but was told they had already exceeded their quota of men for the European theater.

On a happier note, Carson and Reeves experienced one of their rare idyllic periods, acting like real newlyweds. She spent a whole week in Utica at his bedside. When Reeves got permission to leave the hospital, he would spend weekends in Nyack. Carson, furthermore, was writing him love letters regularly, like this one, dated April 2:

> My adored one, — I woke up at dawn this morning, wondering what sort of trip you had back. I'm afraid you were dreadfully tired. All day I have been with you. My Reeves, do you *know* my love? I want you to feel my tenderness for you every instant — I want you to feel it in each nerve and muscle and bone. I feel your love for me in that way. My love and safety in you — that is what keeps me going. We want to live and work, quietly and with some measure of serenity. We have so much ahead of us, so much to do.
>
> . . .
>
> My blessed Reeves. There are no words tender enough for me to call you. Take care of yourself. Drink very little, as I mean to do; too much drinking is very bad for both of us. Study and work. Our future, the chances of our being together these next few years, may depend on how much German and French you can learn these next months.
>
> This is just a love letter.

"You are with me always," she said a month later, on May 8, the day the Allies declared victory.

> After listening to the victory programs, I longed for us to have a quiet glass of wine. . . . I kept thinking of all those men who can

never come back. But you are back, and I can never thank God enough. . . . I am . . . greatly anxious to know about your chances of being released from the army. . . . And I am waiting for the telephone call about your wrist. Dear darling, I'm being very good. Only two jiggers of whiskey a day. Work. And I'll get out for a walk every day.

Reeves's mood darkened once again in July. As part of his permanent limited service, he was ordered to report to Camp Wheeler near Macon, Georgia. After the hardships of the war and the hopes raised upon his return — by his remarriage and the possibility of going abroad — it was unbearable to be sent back to the South, which he had spent twenty years trying to flee. This step backward weighed heavily on him, but he did not want to endanger his promotion to captain, which was then under way.

Carson did not succeed at finishing *The Member of the Wedding* by March 15, contrary to the promise she had made to herself and confided to Reeves. To complete it, she returned to Yaddo on June 26. Though it is true that Carson, who had been unable to finish her book, wrapped up the story in just a few weeks as soon as Reeves returned from the war, she did so at Yaddo, up north, and with Reeves far away down south in Georgia: it is difficult to see how he could have held her hand every day, as some people claim he had done for her first novels and subsequent writing.

As during the previous summer, there weren't many people at Yaddo, and Carson applied herself to her work with great rigor. She revised certain passages several times and had them read by Yaddo's director, Elizabeth Ames, to whom she was still very close. Ames encouraged her and helped her maintain the kind of discipline to which she had committed herself. Carson labored without letup for two months. Toward the end of August, on what for Elizabeth Ames was an unforgettable night, an exhausted Carson, seeming every bit as timid as she had when they first met in New York a few years earlier, dropped off her manuscript and said in a barely audible voice, "I have finished it."[62] Elizabeth Ames finished reading *The Member of the Wedding* late in the night, around two in the morning, and knew then that it was perfect, as she later recalled.

It would be several more months before the book was published in the spring of 1946. Carson's hesitation over which publisher to give the book to did not speed things along. Her editor, Robert Linscott, in whom she had genuine confidence, was now working for Random House. She wanted to follow him there but finally decided to remain at Houghton Mifflin. She believed that her work was back on track again, and that if she maintained her current level of discipline, she would complete all her literary projects.

If someone had told Carson that her life's work was drawing to a close, it might have been the end of her. And yet she had just finished her third book — *The Ballad of the Sad Café*, a long short story or short novel, would not appear until much later and was always published in a collection with other texts — and it would take her fifteen years to complete another one. At the very moment when she thought that her career was on a rapid upward swing, a sustained phase of creation, on the contrary, was coming to an end.

✦   ✦   ✦

Still, with the strength of her twenty-eight years, her finished manuscript, and her rediscovered love, Carson felt that she was at the height of her maturity, even to the point of becoming the "elder" who advises, supports, and encourages a young author. In the spring of 1945 a strange, short man of twenty-one came into the offices of *Mademoiselle* to submit a story. George Davis had refused it, but the story and the young man had made an impression on his assistant, Rita Smith, Carson's sister. Rita had seen this boy, whose pen name was Truman Capote, again and had decided that he should meet her sister. In believing that the two would get on well, Rita Smith was not mistaken. "Carson and Truman took to each other immediately, as well they should have," observes Gerald Clarke, Truman Capote's biographer, relating Capote's remarks about their first meeting: "The first time I saw her — a tall slender wand of a girl, slightly stooped and with a fascinating face that was simultaneously merry and melancholy — I remember thinking how beautiful her eyes were: the color of good clear coffee, or of a dark ale held to the firelight to warm. Her voice had the same quality, the same gentle heat, like a blissful summer afternoon that is slow but not sleepy."[63] Both writers had grown up in the South. "Even their writing was similar in substance, though not in style," Gerald Clarke goes on to note, "dwelling on loneliness and the perverse nature of love."

"I was very, very fond of Carson," Truman Capote always said. "She was a devil, but I respected her." Naturally, they had a falling out, but despite jealousy and even loathing, the respect would remain. It was a form of recognition of one writer by another and the instinctive complicity of Southerners. "She demanded a great deal from her friends, but Carson gave as much as she received, and she helped no other young writer as enthusiastically as she did Truman," Clarke stresses. "Together with Rita, she found him an agent, Marion Ives, and she wrote a warm letter of recommendation to Robert Linscott, a senior editor with Random House. . . . [O]n October 22, 1945, he signed Truman to a contract for *Other Voices, Other Rooms*."[64]

◆ ◆ ◆

When Carson left Yaddo on August 31 to return to Nyack, Reeves joined her, on leave from his army base in the South. But it would be several more months — almost until Christmas — before he could relocate permanently up north. He would leave the army then, having arranged a "medical discharge from active duty," which he obtained on March 16, 1946. "Settling down in Nyack" is no doubt a phrase that would have horrified Reeves McCullers. While Carson, in late 1945 and early 1946, was expressing a desire to "recharge her batteries in the South" — and did not go — Reeves could not content himself with having escaped the South by coming to Nyack. His sights were set on a more distant destination — Europe, to which he was determined to return. Reeves did not believe all hope of working in the American Military Government was lost. But this time he was clearly informed that only people with specialized skills — chemists, electrical engineers, and so on — were being recruited to help with European reconstruction.

So Reeves told himself that he should go back to school and, this time, finish what he started. Medicine held the most appeal for him, but everyone except Carson urged him to abandon that plan on account of his age — he was thirty-two. If his student days were over, then he would have to find work. But he couldn't. Every failure brought the same response: if only he could get to Europe, as if the mere fact of being somewhere else would solve every problem, reconcile every contradiction. In Europe, despite being constantly in danger, he had existed with tremendous intensity. But there, too, a man had to have work to survive — there especially, on a wounded continent where everything had to be rebuilt. There was no place for idle foreigners, even in those small villages of Luxembourg that Reeves still remembered so vividly.

Reeves had no desire to turn back into Mr. Carson McCullers. To avoid that fate, he would leave America behind and journey to a continent that only he knew. With Carson finally on his chosen turf, he would at least be the guide, if not the master. He would introduce Carson to the charming little ports of Brittany and to the strange magic of the French countryside, with its dozens of contrasting landscapes paradoxically assembled on a land mass smaller than the state of Texas. Captain James Reeves McCullers returning "with his wife" to the country he had liberated — now here was a prospect with appeal. He would mobilize all of his energy to transform that vision into reality. But Carson's desire, not Reeves's determination, brought him back to Europe. It was from Carson that everything sprang and to Carson that everything returned.

5

FRANKIE "THE EUROPEAN"

O N MARCH 19, 1946, after prior publication of part one
in the January issue of *Harper's Bazaar, The Member of the
Wedding* appeared, dedicated to Elizabeth Ames, the director
of Yaddo. In America this is the book most strongly identified with
Carson McCullers. Some commentators view the novel's depiction
of a closed Southern world in which an adolescent speaks her unease and loneliness over the course of a few months in 1944–45 as
McCullers's "masterpiece."[1]

The action itself, excepting the epilogue, covers only a few days in
late August 1944. "It happened that green and crazy summer when
Frankie was twelve years old," begins the novel. "She belonged to no
club and was a member of nothing in the world. Frankie had become
an unjoined person who hung around in doorways, and she was
afraid."[2] In an effort to close that empty space between others and herself, "to be part of" something, Frankie violently states her crazed desire "to be a member of the wedding" of her brother, Jarvis, and his
fiancée, Janice. "Here in the United States," says Carson's literary executor, Floria Lasky, "wanting to be a 'member of the wedding' has almost become a common expression used for people who passionately
want to belong — to a group or a community — to be accepted." In
French that unusual combination of words has never received a satis-
factory equivalent.

Frances Jasmine Addams, who calls herself alternatively Frankie or
F. Jasmine, is a "sister" of *The Heart Is a Lonely Hunter*'s Mick Kelly;

she is also a sister of Carson McCullers and of all adolescents fearfully becoming aware of their bodies' transformation and of time's inevitable march, which will force them to become adults. Like Mick and like Carson herself, Frankie resists, and she hates herself: "I wish I was somebody else except me."[3] She has the same dreams of snow and cold that Mick had and that Carson had during her childhood. She wants to see "the cold white gentle snow."[4] Like Mick and like Carson, "this summer she was grown so tall that she was almost a big freak, and her shoulders were narrow, her legs too long."[5]

> Frankie was too tall this summer to walk beneath the arbor as she had always done before. Other twelve-year-old people could still walk around inside, give shows, and have a good time. Even small grown ladies could walk underneath the arbor. And already Frankie was too big; this year she had to hang around and pick from the edges like the grown people. She stared into the tangle of dark vines, and there was the smell of crushed scuppernongs and dust. Standing beside the arbor, with dark coming on, Frankie was afraid. She did not know what caused this fear, but she was afraid.[6]

Frankie has two interlocutors: Berenice Sadie Brown, the black domestic, has been claiming to be thirty-five years old for several years now and has a bright blue glass eye, though the other eye is very dark. Frankie's cousin John Henry is a six-year-old kid who annoys her, though she loves him without realizing it. This is not the threesome of her dreams. She wants to form another one, with her brother and his fiancée — and she looks forward to the wedding as the moment when that union, the source of such anticipated happiness, will be established for everyone to see. "I never before in all my days heard of anybody falling in love with a wedding. I have knew many peculiar things, but I never heard of that before," says Berenice.[7]

Frankie has a father of whom we see little, and her mother is dead. This strange situation unfolds over several days that are every bit as strange (Frankie meets a soldier, the wedding takes place) and concludes in a postscript of sorts (F. Jasmine, now thirteen years old, takes back her original first name, Frances, and John Henry dies of meningitis). From it Carson McCullers composed an elliptical and poetic story that never descends into pathos, John Henry's death giving rise to no descriptive excess or sentimental commentary. The infamous wedding around which the whole plot — or lack thereof — revolves is dispensed with in one sentence, as was the eponymous event in Eudora Welty's novel *Delta Wedding,* which also came out in 1946 but was much less successful. Eudora Welty did not really have much taste for the novel and had trouble adapting the very dense, precise style of her short stories to the novel's longer distance.[8]

Music does not play as large a role here as it does in *The Heart Is a Lonely Hunter,* where Mick wants to be a musician, but a musical construction, as always in Carson McCullers, shapes and organizes the narrative. Oliver Evans has done the best job of describing the composition of *The Member of the Wedding,* which he sees as a musical score with a coda — "the short scene which, occurring several months after the main action, introduces us to the young lady whose name is Frances" — along with other musical elements: "The dialogue is full of strategic repetitions which suggest refrains in music, and the total effect is reminiscent of the group-singing of certain folk ballads in the South."[9]

Musical allusions are also present in the story. On the very first page we find the three main characters, Frankie, Berenice, and John Henry, sitting "at the kitchen table, saying the same things over and over, so that by August the words began to rhyme with each other and sound strange."[10] Berenice speaks with "a dark jazz voice that was like a song" of the South.[11] Sometimes instead of talking to each other, the three protagonists join together in singing a Christmas carol or a blues tune.

In his preface to the French translation of the novel, in 1949, the critic René Lalou presents Carson McCullers's Frankie in a highly pertinent manner:

> Reading the third novel, *The Member of the Wedding,* which she published in 1946, I got the impression that Carson McCullers had combined in that work the qualities we have admired in her two previous books. F. Jasmine Addams (whom you will come to cherish by the name of "Frankie") is obviously a sister of *Heart's* Mick Kelly. But her story is told with the same classic density we find in the text of *Reflections.* It is enclosed within forty-eight hours, between a Friday and a Sunday in late August. Most of it takes place in the stifling atmosphere of a Georgia kitchen: That is where the old black woman Berenice, haunted by the ghosts of four husbands,

tells the beads of her memories for Frankie and her cousin John Henry.

More essential here, however, than McCullers's adroit handling of space and time is the unity of action. What does the twelve-year-old Frankie so passionately seek from her brother's wedding? The right, by taking part in it, finally to escape the oppressive sense of being nothing other than herself. With what ardor she yearns to be included in the union of Jarvis and Janice! "*They are the we of me,*" she keeps saying on the eve of the ceremony. Right then and there her whole past becomes clear; what had tormented her up until that time was always having been reduced to saying and thinking "I." Now she was going to know the happiness shared by human beings when the kind of communication is established that allows them to belong to a "we."

The drama of her disillusionment is recounted by Carson McCullers with a delicacy defying any attempt at analysis. . . . The critic must confine himself to signaling the extent of Frankie's cruel experience. On the day before the wedding, the child convinced herself that she was "connected with all she saw"; with strangers seen on downtown streets she feels "a new unnamable connection, as though they were known to each other."[12] But, disappointed, she once again falls prey to the old obsessive fear: the world is separate from her and stands, a hostile mass, in her way. What that means she has well known for a long time. When Berenice maintains that all of us are "caught," Frankie asks her if it would not be more exact to say that all of us are "loose."[13]

In this novel Carson McCullers expresses Frankie's suffering, caused by a loneliness that has nothing in common with freedom, with particularly poignant force. There can be no doubt that she denounces here a kind of anxiety that many Americans experience, which is nothing for them to be ashamed of, for such distress may be the first stage of their spiritual salvation. But will we who have inherited a Europe in which centuries-old divisions have piled disaster upon ruin be so arrogant as to contemplate pharisaically the troubled souls evoked by this novelist from across the Atlantic? Can we boast of having better realized our solidarity with this world of which we are all particles? Must we not recognize, rather, that the call for human communion — Mick and Frankie's ingenious message, recorded by their elder sister, Carson McCullers — is in actuality addressed to the universal consciousness?[14]

René Lalou's description does great justice to the book's extraordinary qualities. It rightly expresses the idea that *The Member of the Wedding* is a very successful story of a troubled adolescence, an important book well within the logic of Carson McCullers's first two novels.

But readers who call *The Member of the Wedding* "the masterpiece of masterpieces" and Carson McCullers's best novel, far better than the rest, may be more concerned with matters biographical than they care to admit. Granted, this *is* the most patently autobiographical of Carson McCullers's works (aside from her play *The Square Root of Wonderful*). It is a spectacular affirmation of adolescence as a crucial turning point in life, a time of paroxysmal strangeness — and, at bottom, lucidity — that will never come again. Carson *was* Frankie. She experienced a similarly violent crisis just as intensely, probably when her piano teacher, Mary Tucker, left Fort Benning and the Columbus area. To little Carson that departure felt like an abandonment, a betrayal. Nevertheless, the overvaluation of *The Member of the Wedding* with respect to Carson McCullers's other three novels and other works is a way of diminishing the power of her oeuvre that undermines its singularity and destroys its perpetual mystery, a quality that makes people uneasy. The suffering, the anguish, the malaise that fill this novel can be described, analyzed, summarized, and made distant — a wrong-minded response, but a comforting one — if it is simply labeled "the story of an extreme adolescent crisis." Thus the reader can sympathize with the protagonist without feeling personally implicated in the social dynamics that cause her pain. The problems presented in *Reflections in a Golden Eye* or, later, *Clock Without Hands,* however, more directly target an adult audience's fears and lead readers to resist the idea that the tale tells us just as much about ourselves as it does about its author or characters.

The similarity between Carson and Frankie has been noted by many writers. Here is how Carson's sister Rita begins her introduction to *The Mortgaged Heart:* "Of all the characters in the work of Carson McCullers, the one who seemed to her family and friends most like the author herself was Frankie Addams: the vulnerable, exasperating and endearing adolescent of *The Member of the Wedding* who was looking for the 'we of me.'"[15] Oliver Evans also describes *Member* as a very autobiographical novel, with its portrait of an overly tall and self-conscious adolescent who sees herself as "abnormal" and its description of a "white, two-storey bungalow with a big, shady yard" that is exactly like the one at 1519 Starke Avenue in which Carson spent her adolescence.[16] Evans also believes that Carson freed herself, in this third book, of previous literary influences, that she was more successful here than in any other work "at fusing the realistic with the allegorical level: it is therefore, in this respect at least, the most nearly perfect of her works."[17] But unfortunately he doesn't comment on her ability to manipulate allegory or the liberation of what he apparently considers her once bridled imagination. Rather, he draws attention once again to autobiographical elements, noting that in the play based on this novel, in which unity of place becomes a factor in recasting the story, Jarvis and Janice's wedding, the cause of Frankie's mental disorder, takes place in the Addamses' living room, as the first wedding of Carson and Reeves took place at the Smiths' home in 1937.

The reviews were more favorable than those of *Reflections in a Golden Eye*. Some, like George Dangerfield's piece in the *Saturday Review* of March 30, 1946, were openly laudatory. In the eyes of this reviewer Carson McCullers was "unique."

> She is a suggestive rather than an eloquent writer, and often seems to present us less with a meaning than with a hint. And yet the lines of her work are clear and firm. . . . In fact, this book seems more and more to insist that it is, as it were, a monologue furnished with figures.
>
> For Carson McCullers's work has always seemed to me to be a form of self-dramatization. It is true that this can be said of most immature fiction. But Miss McCullers is both a mature and fine writer. She does not dramatize herself in the sense that she is merely autobiographical; but she does dramatize herself in the sense that she seems to invest the various sides of her personality with attributes skilfully collected from the outside world.
>
> The book avoids what T. E. Lawrence called "the kindergarten of the imagination" on the one hand; on the other hand, it never becomes a mere sequence of neurotic images. It steers a wonderful middle course between these two morasses. It is a work which reveals a strong, courageous, and independent imagination. There are other writers in the contemporary field who are of more importance than Carson McCullers. Of her it should be sufficient to say, once again, that she is unique.

The April 1, 1946, issue of *Time* magazine praised Carson's successful attempt "to recapture that elusive moment when childhood melts into adolescence," while Isa Kapp compared Carson McCullers to Thomas Wolfe in the *New York Times Book Review* of March 24, 1946, adding: "But rarely has emotional turbulence been so delicately conveyed. Carson McCullers's language has the freshness, quaintness and gentleness of a sensitive child." In short, everyone in his or her own way affirmed having been touched by "the perfume of childhood" emanating from *The Member of the Wedding,* which also imposed certain limits on the novel's literary success. Richard Match, for example, in the *New York Herald Tribune* of March 24, 1946, noted the depth and originality of this and other novels by Carson McCullers but deemed *The Member of the Wedding* to be "lacking [in] breadth" and saw everything that happens in the kitchen as too "static." Diana Trilling, of the *Nation,* thought the novel suffered from its author's overidentification with her characters, which sapped the book of vital energy. In her view Carson McCullers had not succeeded at placing the necessary distance between her and her memories, as Proust had done in *Swann's Way,* Mark Twain in *Huckleberry Finn,* or Elizabeth Bowen in *The Death of the Heart.*

These reservations were nothing, however, compared with the very bad reviews that greeted the book's publication some months later in Great Britain. Oliver Evans attributes the negative reaction of the English press to the impossibility of "transplanting" onto British soil the rhythm of Southern speech, which Carson McCullers so faithfully reproduced in this text, whose effect depends heavily on dialogue.[18] Certain accounts, like that of the March 15, 1947, *Times Literary Supplement,* opine that Carson McCullers's previous novels had received "disproportionate praise" — the expression is a commonplace of conformist criticism — and that her first two novels had been much too widely admired and celebrated in the United States as well as Europe. In the March 7 issue of the *Spectator,* D. S. Savage — the classic figure of a critic impressed with his own self-importance — has no qualms about the following assessment: "I wish I could say that this was a 'sensitive' study, but it appears to me remarkably insensitive, written in a clogged and turgid prose reminiscent of the worst of Faulkner and Gertrude Stein, with not a single clear visual image or pure emotional perception."

In the United States the harshest criticism, from the highly presti-gious Edmund Wilson for the March 30 *New Yorker,* was less preten-tious. For his part, Wilson allowed that he might be mistaken. Partic-ularly today, in the eyes of posterity, there is something incongruous about his review, beginning with the title, "Two Books That Leave You Blank: Carson McCullers, Siegfried Sassoon."[19] Wilson is careful to point out that Carson McCullers was a writer of talent and un-doubted sensibility but says she "seems to have difficulty in adjust-ing her abilities to a dramatically effective subject. Her last novel — "Reflections in a Golden Eye" — was dramatic but quite unreal. I do not mean merely that what occurred in it was fantastic but that it did not achieve the validity either of realistic fiction, supposed to take place in the actual world, or of the imaginative poem in prose which is true to psychological experience. Mrs. McCullers' new novel, 'The Member of the Wedding' (Houghton Mifflin), has no element of drama at all." After summarizing the book in an extremely banal way, Wilson concludes: "I hope that I am not being stupid about this book, which has left me feeling rather cheated."[20]

Stupid, Edmund Wilson surely never was, but a trifle conventional and inattentive, he may well have been. For instance, to prove that Carson McCullers had not told her tale coherently, he explains that af-ter the struggle between Frankie and the blue-eyed, red-haired soldier she met in a bar — whom she leaves lying unconscious after hitting him over the head with a glass pitcher — we are left with no idea about what happened to the soldier. "He lay there still, with the amazed expression on his freckled face that was now pale," wrote Car-son McCullers, "and a froth of blood showed on his mouth. But his head was not broken, or even cracked, and whether he was dead or not she did not know."[21] This incident occurs near the end of the novel's second part. Then the disastrous wedding takes place, and Frankie de-cides to run away from home and the town. En route she goes back to the Blue Moon, the bar where the incident with the soldier had taken place. A policeman there recognizes her: "'You're Royal Addams's daughter,' the Law said," telephoning headquarters to say she has been found. "The Law was a long time at the telephone, and, staring straight ahead of her, she watched two people leave a booth and, lean-ing close against each other, start to dance. A soldier banged the screen door and walked through the café, and only the distant stranger in her recognized him; when he had climbed up the stairs, she only thought slowly and with no feeling that a curly red head such as that one was like cement."[22] Thus the red-headed soldier is thoroughly alive, and Carson McCullers did not leave a thread of her plot dangling, asking readers to assume "that the man must have survived [because otherwise] something would have been heard about him."[23]

That error on Edmund Wilson's part did not console Carson McCullers, who had devoted five years of her life to the book. She was at Yaddo, having returned there on March 23, a few days after *Member*'s release — she stayed until May 31 — when she heard that Wilson's piece had come out in the *New Yorker*. She could not stop herself from breaking into tears several times, even in public. It was as if Wilson, because of his stature and reputation, had erased the others' praise. It was utterly unbearable, above all, that the book had left him "blank," as he said in his title. Yet in a letter from March 1946 another critic, whose name does not appear on the document, explained to Carson that reading so many bad novels for his job had made it hard for him to take pleasure in fiction unless it possessed a form of magic, real talent in the expression of emotions and feelings, and a style. "When that happens, it makes me so happy I could cry. Honestly, I have read only two or three novels these past five years as enchanting as *Member of the Wedding*. It is an exceptional success."

But it is probably difficult today to imagine what a comment by Edmund Wilson — who also published his famous *Memoirs of Hecate County* in 1946 — represented at the time for a novelist in New York.[24] Perhaps Michel Mohrt's lines from *Le Figaro littéraire*, published in 1966, will shed light on Carson's despair in March 1946:

F. Scott Fitzgerald would surely have been greatly surprised if someone had told him, shortly before his death [1940], that he would be famous in France around 1966 and that publishers would be fighting over his most mediocre short stories, while his Princeton friend Edmund Wilson would be known only to specialists in American literature. There was no man Scott Fitzgerald admired as much as "Bunny," as he commonly called him in his letters; no critic whose judgment mattered as much as his own. He admired him for his culture and his marvelous intelligence, which allowed him to assimilate a philosophical or economic theory, analyze a political situation, or detect the merits and flaws of a literary work. For Scott, as for most American writers of his time, Edmund Wilson was the most heeded and lucid of witnesses and guides. He was the Sainte-Beuve of his generation. Just as Sainte-Beuve identified with romanticism, trying his hand at all the genres in which he distinguished himself, sharing its hopes and espousing its quarrels, so, too, did Edmund Wilson, poet, critic, and storyteller, experience the enthusiasms, disappointments, and follies of the great "lost generation" of the 1920s.

Carson was deeply wounded by Edmund Wilson's reservations and promised herself never again to read what people wrote about her work — a promise that she obviously did not keep. She was not, however, one of those writers who reject all criticism. Regarding *The Member of the Wedding,* she had followed the advice of Kay Boyle, who in addition to her compliments had voiced a single objection, that the soldier was "evasive," as Carson reported in a letter to Newton Arvin — a comment not without relevance to Wilson's remarks, even if the latter were erroneous with regard to the facts.[25]

Truman Capote, who was not yet twenty-two years old, saw the work in a more positive light. He appreciated that the soldier remained on the margins of the main narrative. But Truman was not at Yaddo to comfort Carson after Edmund Wilson's article. Thanks to Carson he would spend time there, but he did not arrive until May 1 and left on July 17. He wrote a few juicy descriptions of his stay, which were scrupulously reported by his biographer, Gerald Clarke. Elizabeth Ames struck him as "a strange, creepy sort of woman." "Silent and sinister like Mrs. Danvers in *Rebecca.* She was always going around spying, seeing who was working and not working and what everybody was up to."[26]

So Carson and Truman Capote spent the month of May together at Yaddo, where they stirred things up a bit, behaving like brother and sister. "Whatever he had she wanted," Capote's biographer asserts, "she wore his clothes, even his shoes, and snatched his long-tailed white shirts whenever she could. Rummaging through his chest of drawers one day, she discovered a paper that carried his original name and threatened to inform everyone that he was an impostor, not Truman Capote at all but someone with the leaden name of Truman

Streckfus Persons. 'You go right ahead, honey chile,' he coolly told her, 'and I'll tell them your real name is Lula Smith.'"

To see them dancing together — "the tall partner, Carson, awkwardly jiggling up and down while the short one, Truman, was doing graceful little pirouettes of his own devising" — was an unforgettable spectacle that surprised even Katherine Anne Porter. Porter decided that she, too, would take a twirl with Truman, which earned her an unflattering comment in one of Truman's letters: "She must be about sixty," he said, "but oh how she can do the hootchy-cootchy. She tries to act like a Southern belle of sixteen or so. She is so unserious it is hard to believe she can write at all. She thinks I am a wonderful dancer, and makes me dance with her all the time: it is simply awful, because she hasn't the faintest notion of how to do the simplest steps."[27] (Katherine Anne Porter would later claim that Capote was a "career climber" who "latched on to" her because of her literary fame.)

Despite these escapades, which are particularly comical for having taken place at Yaddo, a hub of rivalries between young — and not so young — writers and artists, Carson's stay was a sad one. She was drinking more and more heavily. She did not feel well. She was obsessed, every day, by a fear of fainting in public. Other residents saw her as burdensome, even annoying; she constantly sought to be comforted, embraced, and loved in a way they judged invasive, indeed almost aggressive. Behaviors attributed to her illness and infirmity after she became paralyzed were already showing up in eyewitness accounts: Carson had a way of trying to get others to take care of her at the same time she insisted on remaining independent, a way of constantly seeking to make herself — "me the writer" — the center of attention. But this negative impression could be suddenly reversed by a burst of enthusiasm, an irresistible charm, an unfeigned tenderness, a disarming sincerity, or a gaze whose intensity was like a gift made to the person who received it.

It was time for Carson to get a change of scenery, to escape the universe of Yaddo and its conventlike protection as well as its perverse relationships and its confinement. When she found out, on April 15, that she had just been awarded a second Guggenheim fellowship, she knew that the money would allow her to return to Reeves — whose figure is remarkably absent from all of Carson's stays at Yaddo, including this one, even though it followed closely on the heels of their second marriage. Upon hearing the good news, reassured by that unexpected income, Reeves brought up the subject of Europe again. The old dream turned into a plan. He would show Europe to Carson, especially Paris. Better yet, they would live in Paris. Carson made the idea her own. They would be husband and wife again. Mr. and Mrs. McCullers would finally be leaving together, taking a boat for purposes of pleasure, not war, that would cross the Atlantic and deposit them in Europe. Mr. and Mrs. McCullers were going to make Paris their home.

♦ ♦ ♦

Meanwhile, no sooner had Carson gotten back to Nyack in early June than she left Reeves alone again. She was off to Nantucket to join Tennessee Williams, whom she had never met. It would be the start of a friendship that lasted until Carson's death and beyond. Tennessee Williams always stood up for Carson, writing articles and prefaces and even composing the foreword to Virginia Spencer Carr's biography so that, yet again, he could challenge the clichés about his friend and her illness.

In mid-May 1946 Tennessee Williams had come from New Orleans — with Pancho Rodriguez (Santo in his *Memoirs*) — to New York, where his drama *The Glass Menagerie* had been playing for several months with great success. It was in New York one night in May that he began reading the recently published *Member of the Wedding*. He was so enthusiastic that he immediately sent a congratulatory note to Carson. Here he was, a young, successful playwright, composing at the age of thirty-four his first fan letter to a writer — a letter in which the boy from Columbus, Mississippi, told the girl from Columbus, Georgia, how much he admired her work. He stressed what a pleasure it would be for him to make her acquaintance, adding that he had rented a house for the summer on Nantucket at 31 Pine Street.

"It must have been a persuasive letter," he wrote in his *Memoirs*, "for it was just a few days later that she came to Nantucket. She got off the ferry looking very tall and wearing slacks and a baseball cap and grinning her delightful crooked-toothed grin." Carson thought Rodriguez was "marvelous," especially after he made a violent scene in front of several proper old ladies at the beach when he was very drunk, as he was almost all day. "You are lucky to have him with you!" she told Tennessee Williams, who comments: "I was by no means convinced of this, but we went home and we set up housekeeping at 31 Pine Street. This was before Carson was ill. She was a good cook and she put the house in order while she prepared good meals."[28]

These recollections are at odds with the image of Carson in Charlotte or Fayetteville, but there is a big difference between occasionally tidying up or preparing little meals for friends in a vacation spot and looking after a house, or a "household," as they used to say, every day. Carson did more cooking during her month in Nantucket than she had done since her wedding.

Tennessee Williams has described that month on several occasions, with a few details changing from one remembrance to another. Pancho Rodriguez also told the story to Virginia Spencer Carr, somewhat grandiloquently. He remembered in particular Carson's playing "Bach, Schubert, and other favorite composers on the ancient upright piano in the living room," as well as popular songs that everyone could sing, and their purchase of "an old windup Victrola so that they could play some newly discovered records found stored in one of the unoccupied rooms."[29] In his essay "Praise to Assenting Angels," Tennessee Williams gives his most enjoyable, if not necessarily most accurate, account of that time.

> I should like to mention my first meeting with Carson McCullers. It occurred during the summer that I thought I was dying. I was performing a great many acts of piety that summer. I had rented a rather lopsided frame house on the island of Nantucket and had filled it with a remarkably random assortment of creatures animal and human. There was a young gentleman of Mexican-Indian extraction who was an angel of goodness except when he had a drink. The trouble was that he usually had a drink. Then there was a young lady studying for the opera and another young lady who painted various bits of refuse washed up by the sea. I remember they gave a rather cold and wet odor to the upper floor of the house where she arranged her still-lifes which she called arrangements. If the weather had been consistently bright and warm these arrangements would not have been so hard to take. But the weather was unrelentingly bleak so that the exceedingly dank climate of the arrangements did little to dispel my reflections upon things morbid. One night there was a great wind-storm. Promptly as if they had

been waiting all year to make this gesture, every window on the North side of the house crashed in, and we were at the mercy of the elements. The young lady who painted the wet arrangements, the opera singer and the naturally-good-humored Mexican all were driven South to that side of the house where I was attempting to write a play that involved the Angel of Eternity. At that time a pregnant cat came into the building and gave birth to five or six kittens on the bed in our downstairs guest-room. It was about this time, immediately after the wind-storm and the invasion of cats, that Carson McCullers arrived to pay me a visit on the island, in response to the first fan-letter that I had ever written to a writer, written after I had read her latest book, *The Member of the Wedding*.

The same morning that Carson arrived the two other female visitors, if my memory serves me accurately, took their departure, the one with her portfolio of arias and the other with several cases of moist canvases and wet arrangements, neither of them thanking me too convincingly for the hospitality of the house and as they departed, casting glances of veiled compassion upon the brand new arrival.

Carson was not dismayed by the state of the house. She had been in odd places before. She took an immediate fancy to the elated young Mexican and displayed considerable fondness for the cats and insisted that she would be comfortable in the downstairs bedroom where they were boarding. Almost immediately the summer weather improved. The sun came out with an air of permanence, the wind shifted to the South and it was suddenly warm enough for bathing. At the same time, almost immediately after Carson and the sun appeared on the island, I relinquished the romantic notion that I was a dying artist. My various psychosomatic symptoms were forgotten. There was warmth and light in the house, the odor of good cooking and the nearly-forgotten sight of clean dishes and silver. Also there was some coherent talk for a change. Long evening conversations over hot rum and tea, the reading of poetry aloud, bicycle rides and wanderings along moonlit dunes, and one night there was a marvelous display of the Aurora Borealis, great quivering sheets of white radiance sweeping over the island and the ghostly white fishermen's houses and fences. That night and that mysterious phenomenon of the sky will be always associated in my mind with the discovery of our friendship, or rather, more precisely, with the spirit of this new found friend, who seemed as curiously and beautifully unworldly as that night itself.[30]

That friendship was not universally welcomed, of course. Now that both parties have died — Tennessee Williams in 1983 — and can no longer speak for themselves, some people have forgotten the things they said about each other. Tennessee Williams, for instance, published a fine piece on September 23, 1961, in the *Saturday Review,* where he recalls: "From the moment of our first meeting, Carson, with her phenomenal understanding of another vulnerable being, felt nothing for me but that affectionate compassion that I needed so much and that she can give so freely, more freely than anyone else I know in the world of letters."[31] But some commentators prefer to emphasize Carson's jealousy toward Tennessee Williams, a better playwright than she, as well as other negative traits. For example, the French essayist Georges-Michel Sarotte accuses Carson of being "not very easygoing." "Emotional, egocentric, jealous of other writers, she always ended up falling out with them after throwing herself at their feet." To wrap things up, Sarotte calls on other great American writers:

> To read the biography of Carson McCullers, Tennessee Williams, or Truman Capote is to read the life of perpetual enfants terribles, big names, big deals, mired in their own contradictions, stuck in their egotistic, adolescent narcissism. It was not by mere chance that those giants Hemingway and Faulkner took care to avoid them.
>
> If a man does not march in step with his fellows, said Thoreau, it may be that he hears a different drummer. We must give McCullers and her group what they are due: In the 1940s and '50s they played a different tune and people heard it. Having suffered themselves for being different (they were homosexual or bisexual) during a time of dyed-in-the-wool conformity, they did succeed at reshaping American sensibilities, presaging from a long way off — at their own risk — not only the Beat Generation but also the racial, social, and moral explosion of the late 1960s. In their time it took a kind of courage that we can hardly imagine today to portray a homosexual captain, a homoerotic sportsman, or a pretty, effeminate adolescent. They earned the recognition of their fellow homosexuals the world over.[32]

These remarks are characteristic of the prevailing discourse regarding these writers, especially Carson: acknowledge their freedom — without ever uttering that positive word; stress their courage insofar as you can link it to your cause; but leave the reader with a perfectly unpleasant image of their personalities and their lives.

◆　　◆　　◆

Those two writers who were supposedly stuck in their narcissism, Tennessee Williams and Carson McCullers, nonetheless sat down to work every day at the same table, each at one end — "and for the first time," said Williams, "I found it completely comfortable to work in the same room with another writer."[33] Shortly after Carson arrived, Tennessee had suggested that she write an adaptation of *The Member of the Wedding* for the theater. For her it was a challenge, since some reviewers — Edmund Wilson in particular, in the *New Yorker* — had criticized her book for its lack of dramatic momentum. She had no experience at writing for the theater and could count on the fingers of one hand the number of times she had attended a play. But she was in a place where she could start working and benefit from the advice of a professional, while Tennessee Williams worked on finishing *Summer and Smoke*.

Predictably, people have not failed to suggest over the years that *The Member of the Wedding,* the play, owed a lot to the talent of Tennessee Williams. Here is what Williams himself had to say in an interview with Virginia Spencer Carr.

> In no sense of the word was I Carson's mentor. If she wanted to ask me something or read some lines aloud for my reaction, she would. But that was rare. Carson accepted almost no advice about how to adapt *The Member of the Wedding.* I did not suggest lines to her more than once or twice, and then she would usually have her own ideas and say, "Tenn, honey, thank you, but I know all I need to know." I was busy with my own script, and we sat there working very independently, you know. It was not until after Carson came to the island that I suggested she adapt her book as a play. And she pretty much finished the whole script while she was there.[34]

Carson's presence was very stimulating for Tennessee Williams. He liked her determination to write and her repeated urgings that he do so, too — as the two did every morning before mounting their bicycles to head for the beach. "Tennessee borrowed a typewriter for me and we settled down to the same dining table," Carson wrote in her preface to *The Square Root of Wonderful*. "We would work from ten to two and then go to the beach on sunny days or read poetry aloud when it rained. Tennessee and I have spent many ocean-summers since and our friendship is a continuing joy and inspiration to me."[35] When Tennessee was starting to despair of ever finishing his own manuscript, she restored his confidence: "When I told her that I thought my creative powers were exhausted, she said to me, wisely and truly, an artist always feels that dread, that terror, when he has completed a work to which his heart has been so totally committed that the finishing of it seems to have finished him too, that what he lives for is gone like yesterday's snow."[36]

◆　◆　◆

At the end of June, Carson returned to Nyack for a few days and invited Reeves to join her on Nantucket for the Fourth of July weekend. He stayed only a short time, quickly heading back to Nyack, and returned only to get Carson, in midsummer, when she had finished the adaptation of her play. "He was an ex-marine," remembers Williams in his *Memoirs*, "and I didn't particularly like him at that time. He was not good company. He seemed morose and introverted and so was I and he interrupted my happy companionship with Carson."[37]

Reeves drank sadly. But Carson did not wait for him to come before she began drinking too much, and not only with friends. Evenings, she would plop down on a stair with a bottle of whiskey she had purchased and spend part of the night there dreaming and drinking and making up stories of love — impossible ones, of course — with a young woman in the neighborhood whose primary interest was Tennessee. By the time she went to bed, the whiskey often was gone.

At summer's end, Carson had in hand the script of her first play, which she passed on to Ann Watkins, her agent since 1943, asking Watkins to find a producer. At the same time she received the money from her Guggenheim fellowship, and the plan for her European sojourn took shape. Thanks to George Davis, Carson met several Americans who were living in Paris. She saw John Brown again, whom she had known as an editor at Houghton Mifflin and who was now living in Paris with his French wife, Simone. He warned her that life in France so soon after the war was still difficult and that she should not expect either food or creature comforts comparable to those found in the United States. But he assured her that he would be there at the station to welcome her and Reeves if they went ahead with their travel plans. Reeves suddenly developed a taste for spending time with others, talking, discussing his hopes for the trip. It was a happy time, seeming to rejuvenate the man who boarded the ocean liner *Île-de-France* on November 22, 1946, in New York. On the bus that took them to the port, along with Carson's mother, her sister, and the couple's friends Truman Capote and Marguerite Young, Reeves noisily expressed his joy, celebrating their departure for Europe.

Six days later a punctual John Brown was at the Gare Saint-Lazare to meet Carson and Reeves's train from Le Havre. Brown had alerted members of the Parisian intellectual community who were interested in America and literature to the arrival of Carson McCullers, whose *The Heart Is a Lonely Hunter* and *Reflections in a Golden Eye* had just been translated into French. The little American prodigy was awaited by her editor, André Bay — who directed the collection of foreign works at Stock — and by her translators, her critics, and, already, her friends. Henri Cartier-Bresson, whom Carson had known for some time — he had come to photograph her in Nyack — introduced her to his sister Nicole: "They liked one another very much," remembers Cartier-Bresson. "My sister, like me, was very moved by Carson, by her sensitivity. They saw each other often. Nicole wrote poems, and they enjoyed discussing literature together. She invited Carson and Reeves to spend a few days at my parents' house in Sologne. I can't remember if I was there at the time. Perhaps not. But an anecdote about Carson's arrival is still famous in the family. She had brought a case of whiskey for my father, who had never drunk anything other than red wine and white wine. He put the case under his bed, and it stayed there a long time . . ."

"When I met Carson in the United States," he adds, "thanks to Mrs. Snow and George Davis, who got me working for *Harper's Bazaar* — I took some photos of George Davis and Carson on a beach — I immediately liked her adolescent side, at once fragile and strong, her finesse, and what you might call her translucence. I quickly perceived that there was something odd, even a bit dubious, about her relations with Reeves. Carson was sensitivity itself. The word that comes irresistibly to mind when I think of her is 'quivering.'"[38]

The American photographer Louise Dahl-Wolfe, who had taken some very fine photos of Carson back in 1940, also lived in Paris, as did Kay Boyle and her husband. Thanks to that community, Carson did not really feel that she was abroad. Janet Flanner, in 1972, remembered that "Carson burst like a tiny bottle of glass on Paris — melodramatic, a genius."[39] Carson herself dropped the name Janet Flanner — whom she also knew from the Middagh Street days — and always said that her life in Paris had been simplified by it, for "the name *Genêt* ["Janet" with a French accent] opened 'any literary door.'"[40]

In a postwar Paris where people attempted to forget the tragedy of war by dancing and going out a lot, Carson and Reeves were invited to more than enough parties to keep them up all night. They witnessed the infancy of "Saint-Germain-des-Prés," where artists and writers, particularly existentialists, gathered in now-famous cafés. Carson met some of the actresses and chanteuses associated with Saint-Germain-des-Prés: Juliette Gréco had not yet become its enigmatic symbol, a strange silhouette before becoming a singer and the incarnation of a myth, but the young Anne-Marie Cazalis was already there; Carson liked her a lot, and the feeling was mutual.

Sartre and Simone de Beauvoir passed this way, but Carson was never on close terms with them. As part of her biographical research, Virginia Spencer Carr sent someone to interview Simone de Beauvoir in 1972. Beauvoir spoke primarily of Carson McCullers's literary work, whose uniqueness and absence of moralism she appreciated, but could recall only one party at her apartment to which she had invited Carson — along with Richard Wright, who ended up moving to Paris — making clear that she and Carson had never been friends. It is easy to imagine the kind of annoyance that Simone de Beauvoir must have felt in the presence of that fragile perpetual adolescent who always looked a bit lost, who made no attempt to understand French, and who seemed every bit as "dependent" as Simone de Beauvoir was resolutely autonomous. By the same token, it is hard to imagine Carson McCullers reading *The Second Sex* — which Simone de Beauvoir was then in the process of writing — and recognizing herself in its pages. For any woman who, like Beauvoir, sought parity with men, the fragility displayed by Carson was a threat, an example that men would always put forth as proof that women needed to be helped, supported, even rescued.

The poet and novelist Claude Roy, for good reason, had no such fears. He was charmed by Carson — whom he had met through Cartier-Bresson in New York — as he recalls with great delicacy in *Nous* (We): "One of Cartier-Bresson's friends charmed and troubled me as much as the fine books of hers that we had just read: Carson McCullers, a pale cross between the flower called a sensitive plant and the greyhound in the Dame à la Licorne tapestries. Too sharp a glance, a slight rise in a person's tone of voice caused Carson, so easily terrified, to shy away, quivering."[41]

André Bay had observed Carson's sudden distress, her strange way of appearing "displaced," at his first, very curious, meeting with her. He had made a lunch date with Carson.

I had never had any direct contact with her until then. It was John Brown, who had been an editor at Houghton Mifflin before becoming a cultural attaché in Paris, that introduced me to her work. Since I had asked him what I should read in the line of young American literature, he had recommended Carson McCullers and Robert Penn Warren. I thought we should publish both of them. And we did. As for Carson McCullers, we translated *The Heart Is a Lonely Hunter* and *Reflections in a Golden Eye* in 1946. So when Carson arrived in France for her first visit, I asked if I could take her to lunch. She said yes, as always. She said yes to everything without really understanding what she was agreeing to and without making any effort to find out. At the appointed hour I went by to pick her up, as we had arranged, at the Hôtel de France et Choiseul on the rue du Faubourg-Saint-Honoré, where she was staying. They asked me to go up to her room.

What I found there was a woman with an oddly childlike air, dressed in a nightgown, still in bed, with a bottle of cognac next to her and a glass of cognac in her hand. I pointed out that it was past noon and that I had come to take her out to lunch. She did not seem to comprehend me very well. When she had understood, she explained that she could not go out, that she was having an attack of agoraphobia and was consequently incapable of taking two steps in the street. But I was hungry, and I was determined to go out. I decided to carry her after she had put on a coat, since she was not opposed to that plan. She was thin, but she was really quite tall and rather heavy all the same. We left the hotel in this curious fashion. I did not go far, stopping at the first bar. I got something to eat. She drank. We talked, as if the whole thing was utterly old hat. Still, she always seemed to be in something of a fog, as people who drink constantly from morning till night sometimes are. I think that was the day when I brought her a copy of *Reflections in a Golden Eye* in French. And I've kept it, because she signed it for me in a characteristic way — with handsome penmanship and a good, strong signature next to childish sketches like the ones drawn by very small children, of a fir tree and an almond-shaped eye.

That was only the first of any number of meetings, but she was obviously unforgettable. It is not every day that you encounter one of your authors in a nightgown, never mind picking one up in your arms! Perhaps it was that accidental intimacy that made me unreceptive to what people had to say about Carson McCullers's "boyish" side. On that particular day, in her nightgown in bed, she was really a woman. And the body that I carried in my arms was indeed the body of a woman.[42]

Carson got a great deal of attention in Paris, but Reeves was hardly neglected. Except at Carson's literary events, it was "the McCullerses" people wished to see. Whenever they learned that Reeves had landed in Normandy at dawn on June 6, 1944, they were quick to celebrate him as the hero he had been. Again he experienced the joy of his first contacts with the French two years earlier, the feeling of being a liberator. He told his war stories as he had in his letters to his wife. He talked as he would like to have written, and people listened with delight. He had learned a little French, and even though he could not hold a fluent conversation, he willingly expressed himself in that language, unlike Carson, who made no effort to learn even a few words. "That is precisely why it is entirely false to claim, as Reeves did in his letters to friends back in the United States, that 'the literary smart set in Paris had fallen at Carson's feet,'" says John Brown. "She arrived here preceded by a reputation as a good writer and a nonconformist, but her contacts with French intellectuals remained limited to those who were particularly interested in American literature and who spoke English well. She was not at all a follower of Camus, Sartre, or Malraux, and she was not touched in any way by the intellectual effervescence of France during the immediate postwar period."[43]

Reeves told anyone who would listen, and he said so in his letters, that returning to Europe was like being born a second time. He wanted to stay on that side of the Atlantic and find work there, at the United Nations or UNESCO. "That was all to a large extent fantastical," in John Brown's estimation. "In fact he talked a lot about the idea; Carson acquiesced and urged him on, but I doubt he ever really applied anywhere."[44] Reeves also wrote to Edwin Peacock that General Motors and American aid services in France had offered him jobs that he had to turn down because he would have been obliged to travel a great deal and did not wish to leave Paris. Still, in John Brown's view — and his hypothesis is entirely plausible — it was a way of keeping people from thinking Reeves was sponging off his wife and giving no thought whatsoever to earning any money of his own.

Despite his love for Paris and the delight he took in exploring the city almost street by street, with or without Carson, Reeves let boredom and idleness get the best of him, as he almost always did. He started drinking to excess again, and so did Carson. And yet the two had promised each other when they remarried that they would drink more moderately. Parisian cafés that were open until two in the morning, if not all night long, did nothing to promote their sobriety. The couple favored the Left Bank, where their friends had introduced them to the Café de Flore, the Deux-Magots, and a galaxy of small cafés in Saint-Germain-des-Prés that have since disappeared. On wilder nights they would go to the Tabou, the new temple of existentialism.

The child from Columbus, Georgia, did not understand very well what was going on in that minuscule corner of the French capital, what young people there were trying to affirm or to avoid with their new rhythms, their music, their parties that shocked the bourgeois world. She knew a bit more about it than others, however, thanks to Middagh Street, Klaus Mann, and Annemarie Schwarzenbach. She knew a bit more about it than Reeves, despite his firsthand experience of war. She vaguely saw that the Parisian youth of 1946 were both survivors and lost children, orphans of a Europe mourned by Annemarie and Klaus and Erika Mann. An earlier conception of Europe, of civilization, had died somewhere in the vicinity of Auschwitz and Dachau. Those young people dancing in the cabarets and nightclubs would need more than the lifetimes ahead of them to heal, and to rebuild, there being no way to repair the damage done.

Some evenings, Carson and Reeves would cross the Seine and make their way to the Lido or some other, less prestigious Right Bank cabaret. They loved going to music-hall shows. Carson was particularly fond of Edith Piaf; she was moved by her voice, by her acting, by the profound sense of tragedy within her. There was no need to understand the lyrics of her songs. But they quickly returned to the Left Bank, visiting the intellectual and artistic mecca Montparnasse, following in the footsteps of Ernest Hemingway. It is impossible to say if he would have enjoyed or carefully avoided meeting them, as Georges-Michel Sarotte claims: they were never in Paris at the same time.

The weather in that winter of 1946 and 1947 was typical for the Île-de-France: gray and rainy, dreary, just what it took to stimulate a craving for alcohol. Carson and Reeves drank as much as a whole bottle of cognac per day . . . apiece. Spring was magnificent, however, and Reeves recommenced his "lubricated" urban explorations, while Carson accepted an invitation from a couple she had met to spend a few days in the Italian Tyrol, where she was delighted to find herself surrounded by high mountains covered with deep snow. Meanwhile, in February 1947, an event that would be part of Carson's golden legend occurred. Carson described this "contretemps," to use her own term, in a 1950 article published in *Theater Arts* entitled "The Vision Shared":

> Soon after our arrival in Paris a charming gentleman came to see us and talked a good deal to me in French as rapid as a waterfall and equally intelligible to me. I understood nothing except that our caller wanted something rather urgently from me. So with amiability but little sense I spoke one of my few French words: "Oui." The caller pumped my hand and bowed out saying, "Ah, bon! Ah, bon!" He came twice again and the mysterious procedure was repeated. But things are strange in a new country and I didn't trouble myself until the day a friend came to our hotel and asked what in the world I was up to now. She took from her purse a card and I read it ten times and fell on the bed. The card was a nicely printed invitation to La Salle Richelieu at the Sorbonne to hear Carson McCullers lecture on a comparison between modern French and American literature. This was scheduled for the very next evening. My husband read the card and started packing. I telephoned an old friend from the American Embassy and he came to us. He laughed and I cried

and we all drank brandy for some hours. After rationalization he said, "Since you obviously cannot lecture in French at the Sorbonne tomorrow evening, try to think of what you *can* do?" I watched my husband packing, then I thought of a recently finished poem. Our friend, a former literary critic, heard the poem and thought that it would do. He wrote a little apology in French for me that began: "Je regrette beaucoup mais je ne parle pas français —" The next evening I went to La Salle Richelieu, said my poem and sat there on the platform, trying to look intelligent as two critics debated the aspects of the two literatures in a language I did not understand.[45]

The "American friend" called to the rescue was John Brown. Once again he saved the day by taking control and by summoning René Lalou. Lalou was meeting Carson McCullers for the first time, and the evening made such an impression on him that he described it in his preface to the first French edition of *The Member of the Wedding:*

> The working director of the "Today" club had organized a debate at the Sorbonne, in the comfortable Richelieu auditorium, on the attributes and accomplishments of the "new American literature." Many points of view were expressed — to begin with, regarding what was meant by that expression. At least they were not totally sterile, for they helped members of the audience avoid a dangerous oversimplification. The conclusion reached was that we French had contented ourselves for a good ten years, quite arbitrarily, with confining the title "young Americans" to a few novelists — such as Faulkner, Hemingway, Steinbeck, Caldwell — who were born between 1897 and 1900 . . .
>
> That was the point at which Georges-Albert Astre asked Carson McCullers to speak. As we looked on, a frail young woman then rose from her seat whom three fine novels, published before her twenty-sixth year, certainly entitled to speak for the much-renowned "new American literature." With a graceful awkwardness born of shy reserve, she apologized for being unable to express herself in our language and for having no theoretical formulas to dispense to us, even in her own. Quite simply, as a sign of goodwill, she proposed to offer us the last poem she had written, which she had since been carrying around in the pocket of her coat.
>
> Without striving for effect, she read those twelve lines in a steady voice and with contained fervor, as if sharing a confidence with a

friend. I don't think I was mistaken to take her tone of contempla-
tive intimacy as an encouragement to ask her for one of the two
copies of the composition that she was about to put back in her
pocket. For she very kindly consented, after replacing, with a pencil
stroke, a *goes* by a more expressive *runs* in the last line. I may be far
less inspired today in trying to translate that pure lyrical effusion,
but I can think of nothing that would orient us more faithfully:

> When we are lost what image tells?
> Nothing resembles nothing. Yet nothing
> Is not blank. It is configured Hell:
> Of noticed clocks on winter afternoons, malignant stars,
> Demanding furniture. All unrelated
> And with air between.
> The terror. Is it of Space, of Time?
> Or the joined trickery of both conceptions?
> To the lost, transfixed among the self-inflicted ruins,
> All that is non-air (if this indeed is not deception)
> Is agony immobilized. While Time,
> The endless idiot, runs screaming round the world.[46]

Obviously, I do not flatter myself for having discerned the various connections and nuances of this stream of images the first time
I heard the poem read aloud. But I had been particularly struck by
the end of the first verse, "All unrelated / And with air in between."
I had not read any of Carson McCullers's works at that time and
could judge them only according to what I had heard. Free of any
preconceived notions, I had a feeling that those eleven syllables
contained not only a painful observation and an appeal but perhaps
a key to her oeuvre.

That acknowledgment of isolation seemed to me uniquely pathetic but, above all, of a fierce lucidity.[47]

In April Carson went to Rome, without Reeves. As in Paris six
months earlier, she was celebrated. She met the country's important
writers, foremost among them Alberto Moravia, one of Italy's most
prominent post–World War II novelists, and she was introduced as
one of America's most promising young novelists. That year, the
American magazine *Quick* had chosen Carson McCullers as one of
America's best postwar novelists, and the British writer and critic Cyril

Connolly, reputed for his wit and for being rather hard on his contemporaries, wrote an extremely deferential letter to her on behalf of *Horizon* magazine:

> I was very sorry that you were not in America last winter when I visited New York, as I was greatly looking forward to making your acquaintance. I very much hope that we can meet another time. This letter is to ask you if you could let us have something for the special number of HORIZON devoted to the arts in America which I am bringing out this autumn. I would, of course, like a story that has not been published before, if that is possible, or [perhaps] a chapter of any novel on which you are working at the moment. We all very much hope that you can let us have something as we feel the number would be incomplete if it did not include you.[48]

Carson's neighbors in Columbus had been proved wrong. Carson was a "European" now, a famous and celebrated writer living in Paris. She even left her hotel, a place for "foreigners" in transit, to spend part of the summer in the country, at Rosay-en-Brie, in a small château on loan from friends before returning to a real house in the heart of the fifth arrondissement, at 53 rue Claude-Bernard, where Richard Wright had lived before moving to the rue Monsieur-le-Prince. She liked that little place with its small courtyard, even though it wasn't very comfortable. It seemed to her "so Parisian."

Carson McCullers was in Paris when she turned thirty. She did not know then that she was living her last springtime as a young woman whose health may long have been fragile but who did not look ill at first glance. A few months later everyone she met would immediately see that the person before them was physically impaired.

There are different versions of what led to that impairment. According to Constance Webb's biography of Richard Wright, Carson told Wright that the first incident, diagnosed as a stroke, occurred one midsummer night at Rosay-en-Brie.[49] Reeves was away at the American Hospital in Neuilly, being treated for an infected leg. Carson was sleeping alone and was abruptly awakened by a severe thirst. She got up but had taken only a few steps in her bedroom when she fell heavily to the floor and could not get up again, her left side refusing to move. Unable to speak, she could not call for help; she could not see well, either, but remained fully conscious throughout the eight hours

or so that she spent on the floor. Finally, Reeves came home and found
her, and she was taken to the American Hospital. Other accounts situ-
ate the attack later on in the summer — in the house on the rue
Claude-Bernard — and suggest that it was preceded by a somewhat
less serious incident. Carson's correspondence suggests that there were
indeed several "episodes." On July 28, 1947, Carson wrote to her
mother from 53 rue Claude-Bernard, "c/o Madame Vercoustre," and
said she was having trouble with one eye.

> Here we are in the new place. And I like it and find it [suitable].
> Our little shack overloods the vegetable garden and there are two
> trees on our doorstep. We can manage about the toilette bath etc,
> but these past days Paris has had the hottest weather of this genera-
> tion (Nearly 100) and I'd dearly love some ice or some place we
> could keep victuals cool.
> . . . We do miss you so. . . .
> I think I am better. My sight in the right eye seems to be coming
> back along the edges. All the doctors say it will pass without a trace.
> Quiet is the main thing and no worry. Otherwise I feel fine.
> It's a heavenly relief to be settled. To have a place where you can
> work and feel put.[50]

The attack described by Richard Wright — whenever and wherever it occurred — had much more serious and long-lasting consequences than what Carson mentioned in her letter: a vision problem
about which her doctors seemed optimistic. She spent several weeks at
the American Hospital. Upon her release she had firmly decided to
stay on in France; she rejoiced in the prospect of future encounters —
with "Sylvia Beach, James Joyce's friend and publisher," for example.
She had faith in the doctors who had taken over her care and wanted
to get back to some serious work on a new manuscript. But the doctors had absolutely forbidden her to drink, and Carson was unable to
abide that restriction. She drank beer all day long, switching to cognac
in the late afternoon.

In early November Carson was hospitalized once again, with a kidney infection. A day later she had another attack, worsening the paralysis on her left side. For three weeks the doctors tried, without success,
to combat both the terrible pain she was feeling in her paralyzed limbs
and the paralysis itself. They decided that Carson should return to the

United States to be treated at the Neurological Institute of Columbia Presbyterian Hospital in New York City.

◆   ◆   ◆

On December 1, 1947, Marguerite Smith was waiting for "her dear children" at the airport in New York. She was there when the plane landed, with two ambulances. In one they placed a stretcher bearing the paralyzed Carson and in the other a litter to which was strapped Reeves, who had suffered an attack of delirium tremens during the flight home. The "abusive mother" described by Janet Flanner now truly had her chance to reign supreme.

Carson's cousin Jordan Massee, however, defended Marguerite Smith.

> Of Bebe, what can I say that would not be wholly inadequate? I admired her more than I can express, and I loved her as much as I loved Carson. To those persons in Columbus, Georgia, who have suggested that many of Carson's problems in life were the result of an overindulgent mother, let me say only this, that without that mother, the genius of Carson McCullers could never have survived and flourished. It was a delicate plant indeed that she nourished, with a love that was equal to every demand. She moved from a narrow and provincial background into the broader sphere to which Carson as a free soul, and as a celebrated writer, had gravitated, and moved with a grace and an adaptability that still amaze me.[51]

Marguerite Smith's devotion, which was real, whatever its motivations, is of course also part of Carson's golden legend. But the order from some of Carson's Middagh Street friends to "free herself from her mother's clutches" — an order she never obeyed, instead calling her mother to the rescue every time she fell ill — was no longer even thinkable in late 1947. From that time on, Carson would need to be assisted.

◆   ◆   ◆

That year in France had been such a disaster that it is hard to imagine Carson and Reeves going back there one day. Carson left the country disabled, and her French contacts, intellectual and literary, do not seem to have decisively affected her career. Reeves's failure was greater still, if measured against his high hopes for the journey, hopes that he proved once again unable to transform into even the most modest reality. Nor is there any real evidence that Carson's unbearable demands were to blame.

Carson had done almost no work. What could she offer the people at the Guggenheim Foundation to prove that she had used her fellowship wisely? She had written only one ten-page story, called "The Sojourner." In it John Ferris returns to the United States from France to attend his father's funeral in Georgia. It is a flawlessly crafted and delicate tale, to be sure, in which a Bach prelude and fugue stir up "a wilderness of memory," and "a riot of past longings, conflicts, ambivalent desires. . . . '*L'improvisation de la vie humaine,*' [Ferris] said. 'There's nothing that makes you so aware of the improvisation of human existence as a song unfinished. Or an old address book.'" At the end of the story "Ferris was in a taxi crossing Paris. It was a clouded night and mist wreathed the lights of the Place de la Concorde. The midnight bistros gleamed on the wet pavements. As always after a transocean flight the change of continents was too sudden. New York at morning, this midnight Paris. Ferris glimpsed the disorder of his life: the succession of cities, of transitory loves; and time, the sinister glissando of the years, time always."[52] "The Sojourner" was published in the May 1950 issue of *Mademoiselle* magazine and reprinted the following year in the collection with *The Ballad of the Sad Café*. But however well written it may be, this short piece was a rather slim justification for a year-long fellowship.

What a godsend that "creative impasse" was, to use the expression of Virginia Spencer Carr, for those who sought to blame Carson McCullers for her infirmity. "Part of Carson's illness was perhaps unfairly attributed to the creative impasse she was then experiencing," writes her biographer. But Carr then goes on at length about "another factor that may have contributed to her various illnesses": "her distress over what had happened to her play *The Member of the Wedding*."[53] Ann Watkins, Carson McCullers's agent, had failed to find a producer for the work. When the Theatre Guild finally agreed to mount *The Member of the Wedding,* it did so only on condition that an experienced playwright revise the script.

That condition was profoundly distasteful, but tired of fighting a losing battle, Carson reluctantly agreed to it and signed a contract with Greer Johnson, who had been proposed — if not imposed — as coauthor. When she received the new manuscript in Paris in the fall of 1947, she thought it was dreadful. "Coincidental with her reading of the Johnson script," writes the ever neutral Virginia Spencer Carr, "Carson was stricken with a serious kidney infection. The next day she suffered a third stroke."[54]

In other words: Carson McCullers, a stillborn playwright and a broken-down novelist at thirty years of age, after three astonishing books, took refuge in an extremely disabling illness — another attack of which she constantly feared — to evade the cruel reality that her creative powers were extinguished. That opinion would be shared by certain people who had known Carson McCullers over the years, notably the playwright Lillian Hellman. The brilliant and caustic companion of the writer Dashiell Hammett, Hellman viewed Carson as a woman who enjoyed wallowing in her illness. She explained her impression of the younger writer in a few succinct sentences: "Carson burdened everyone who got close to her. If you wanted burdens, liked burdens, you accepted Carson and her affection. I don't like such burdens."[55] Lillian Hellman made no pretense of being objective. Her exasperation was entirely personal. Virginia Spencer Carr, by contrast, takes the stance of a detached investigator. She surely had the right, on a personal level, to share Hellman's repugnance for Carson's illness and her distaste for the way Carson used her weakness as a means to seize control over others. But her supposedly neutral presentation of Carson's illness tends to compel a certain reading. It leaves no room for compassion and progressively warps the image of the young novelist, arousing an unconscious antipathy that, in the end, asserts itself as "the truth" about Carson McCullers.

Marguerite Smith and her children Lula Carson (on the right) and Lamar Jr. (on the left).

Carson at sixteen, at Columbus High School.

Reeves and Carson in 1940 in Fayetteville, where she
completed *The Heart Is a Lonely Hunter.*

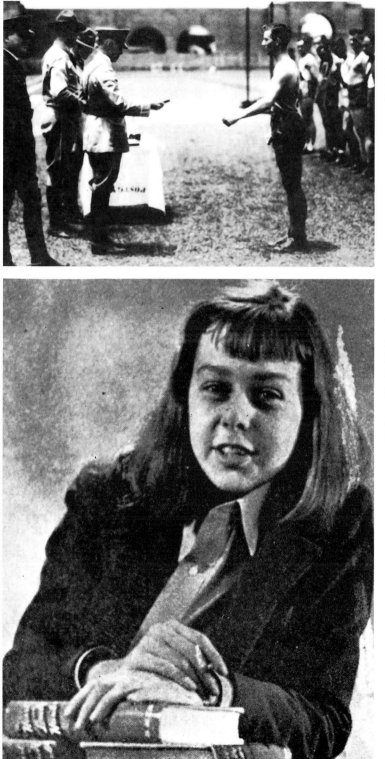

James Reeves McCullers at Fort Benning, around 1935.

The photograph of Carson chosen by Houghton Mifflin for the publication of *The Heart Is a Lonely Hunter* in 1940.

Carson and her sister, Rita, in Nyack in 1946, when Carson was twenty-nine. *Courtesy Henri Cartier-Bresson, Magnum Photos*

Carson working on *The Member of the Wedding* in Columbus,
Georgia (August 1943). *Courtesy* Columbus Ledger Enquirer

Annemarie Schwarzenbach, one of Carson's "imaginary friends,"
to whom the author dedicated *Reflections in a Golden Eye.*

Carson autographing one of her books in 1946. *Courtesy Henri Cartier-Bresson, Magnum Photos*

At the opening-night party for *The Member of the Wedding,* January 5, 1950. Left to right: Ethel Waters, who played Berenice, Carson, and Julie Harris, who played Frankie. Carson was thirty-three. *Copyright © Ruth Orkin, courtesy of Ruth Orkin Photo Archive*

Tennessee Williams in his apartment on Fifty-eighth Street in 1954. *Courtesy Phyllis Cerf Wagner*

Carson McCullers's house at 131 South Broadway, Nyack, New York,
to which she moved in 1945. Mary Mercer bought the house after Carson's death.

A Thanksgiving gathering in 1952 in Paris. Left to right:
Valentine Sherriff, Carson, Jack Fullilove, and Reeves.

A party at Carson's home in Nyack in May 1959. Left to right: *seated,*
Marilyn Monroe, Karen Blixen, and Carson; *standing,* Arthur Miller,
Felicia Geffen, Jordan Massee, and Clara Svendson.

Elizabeth Taylor
and Marlon
Brando in
*Reflections in a
Golden Eye,*
directed by John
Huston
in 1967.

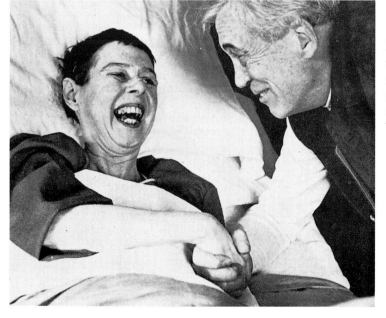

During Carson's
visit to Huston
in Ireland in the
spring of 1967.
Courtesy Irish
Times

Carson and Mary Mercer in 1959.

Carson McCullers's headstone
in the Nyack cemetery.

Carson McCullers and posterity: viewers at an exhibition of
photographs by Richard Avedon. *Courtesy Nicolas Guibert*

6

FIVE HUNDRED DAYS ON BROADWAY

As Christmas 1947 drew near, when Carson McCullers left the New York neurological hospital where she had spent the entire month of December, her physical state was hardly any better than it had been upon her arrival there. She returned to Nyack — where Marguerite Smith was caring for Reeves, still suffering attacks of delirium tremens — but could not get out of bed. It must have been the most terrible time of Carson's life. Granted, she would grow more and more solitary and sickly later on, in the 1950s and 1960s, and, barring rare periods of respite, her health would get progressively worse. It would probably be a mistake, however, to see the year 1948 as merely the beginning of a difficult existence in which the worst was yet to come. At that point, the worst difficulty undoubtedly involved accepting what had just happened: How could she bear, at thirty years of age, to abruptly become absolutely dependent? Was there a way to resist, or surmount, her disability? Or perhaps she would decide to give up, let someone else make the decisions, and lose herself in bitter resentment.

Carson was afraid of depending on others at the same time she wanted someone else to take charge. She contended time and time again with these conflicting impulses. During the summer of 1942 at Yaddo she confided to her companions that an obsessive fear haunted her both day and night: recurrently she dreamt that she was gravely ill, in need of constant assistance and attention for the rest of her life. Those nightmares filled her with terror that no one would be there to care for her. From the age of thirty, she did indeed require physical and practical assistance with almost every act of daily life — dressing, going up and down the stairs, cutting her food . . . Depending on others was no longer an option that attracted and repelled her; she now had no choice but to let others take charge. Carson knew that she had someone who would not abandon her. But that someone was her mother, and her mother's care inevitably conferred on her the status of a sick little girl.

Her mother, who was taking care of Reeves with identical devotion — even if she could not keep herself from holding him somewhat responsible for Carson's illness — tried to create for the two of them a real child's Christmas with lots of small, colorful packages, funny little gifts, music, and traditional dishes from the South. Nothing she did could lift their spirits. To make matters worse, 1947 bleakly ended with a record-breaking blizzard, and 1948 began the same way. Carson, who had always been subject to swings of emotion that could send her careening from elation to despair, from laughter to anger or sobs all in one day, now was uniformly, unremittingly sad. Even things that should have delighted her — public recognition of the quality of her literary work, for example — barely brought a smile to her lips or a tear to her eye. Nonetheless, it was an auspicious time professionally: After having been picked by the critics of five important newspapers as one of the six best writers in postwar America (at the instigation of *Quick* magazine),[1] she was chosen by *Mademoiselle* as one of "the ten most deserving young women in the United States."[2] She received a *Mademoiselle* Merit Award for "outstanding achievement by a young person in literature for the year 1947."[3]

While these pieces of good news failed to lift Carson out of her depression, they pushed Reeves even deeper into his own. He started looking for a job in mid-January 1948 but had little faith in his chances of finding a position that would showcase his talents. During "his" war he thought that he had become someone, without Carson and in a place where the two could never be compared. He now knew that his achievement had been only temporary and had occurred, precisely, in a universe from which Carson was absent.

After the anguish of battle, it had been touching to be asked if he were the author of *The Heart Is a Lonely Hunter*. In civilian life, Reeves had a harder time explaining his link to Carson McCullers. He now knew that he would never be a writer. The wound was more serious than it might have seemed, since no other calling could provide him a positive self-image once he had renounced his dream. Since leaving the army in 1946, Reeves had lived primarily on his wife's money — his military pension was far from sufficient for the kind of life he led, especially in Europe. When Reeves had been forced to admit, in 1945, that he was too old to embark on a career such as medicine, he understood that he would never practice one of those professions that establish a person socially, either. "My husband wanted to be a writer and his failure in that was one of the disappointments that led to his death," Carson wrote much later in her preface to *The Square Root of Wonderful.*[4]

Once again they separated — only a month after Carson's release from the hospital. Reeves took an apartment in Manhattan. One last time he was really going to try to become someone that he could respect: a man who did not drink, who worked, and who managed his own house. Did he still believe in the necessity of sharing daily life with Carson, as he had repeated since 1943? "We just have to live together five years straight," he wrote in August 1945, quickly going on to say: "This is it: *the great fear* (the only fear left in my soul; the others I have destroyed, or they have been destroyed for me) *that the imaginary friend would come between us to the extent that I would be destroyed this time.*"[5] It is worth noting that Reeves was speaking of destruction at that early date, as if he already had a premonition. As for "imaginary friends" — female ones especially — Carson and Reeves had invented that expression back in the early 1940s. It was a euphemistic way of referring to Carson's passions. All too often they totally took over her life and her mind for several weeks or several months, during which Carson used what she called her "beloved" as an excuse to refuse somewhat more peremptorily to let Reeves come close or touch her. That new separation — once again a temporary one — provides Virginia Spencer Carr an opportunity to revisit the couple's sexual problems, described by her as "due primarily to Carson's penchant for women." This "penchant" probably had very little to do with sex, though — Carson's brother, Lamar Jr., once said that he thought of Carson as being *asexual.*[6] In any event, during those first weeks of 1948 any question of the couple's sexual problems was secondary. Can anyone really imagine Carson McCullers, in a state of complete and constant pain for several months with one whole side of her body paralyzed, having sexual relations that winter?

To better grasp what Carson's infatuations with one person and another consisted of, we would do well to read a letter sent to Tennessee Williams in Italy on February 14, at a time when she was still very ill. Carson had left Paris believing she was pining with love for the doctor who had treated her there, Robert Myers. Tennessee Williams met Dr. Myers and wrote to Carson from Naples, saying that he didn't care one bit for the man. Carson wrote back the very day his letter arrived:

> May I tell you something very strange? No sooner did I read that you disliked Bob Myers, than my feelings for him utterly changed. The heartache that had eaten away at me for so long went away, and (miracle of miracles!) I realized I did not love Bob Myers, and never had really loved him. I saw that the sad state I was in was just another result of my illness — and my distressing "love life." I really should be able to rid myself of those complications on my own, you know. No matter, your letter helped me, dear Tenn. You are the being I admire most in the world, and if you have no affection whatsoever for Bob Myers, that helps me put things in perspective. Life seems much more bearable now that I have managed to stop peering through the eyes of a lover spurned. I'm enclosing the letter he wrote to me, after six weeks. Admit it, Tenn, it's like a tennis ball hit out of bounds, don't you think?[7]

It seems that Carson went to extremes to strip the objects of her passion of reality. They existed only as they fit into her mental universe at any given moment. All it took was a conflict between two emotional impulses for Carson to immediately reject, unconsciously but with a vital instinct, the disruptive element. Exit Dr. Myers.

For what was at stake early in the winter of 1948 was living, or staying alive, and the only desire that Carson clung to was the desire to write. Evidently, she chose Tennessee Williams as her confidant, knowing he alone would understand. In the same letter, Carson asked for his attention and advice. She had decided to revise her play *The Member of the Wedding* and to do everything she could to get it finally on stage. She wanted him to read the script. "I would like to write a collection of short stories, and I'd like to discuss it with you," she also confided. "Oh, dear Tenn, this is such a difficult time! Last week, I was in the deepest depths of hell. Dr. William couldn't make it here, for three whole weeks, because of the snowstorm. I was unable to sleep, unable to eat. I dreamed that I was swimming with you in the Mediterranean . . . If I didn't have this imaginary life, I would go mad. . . . I'm waiting for Dr. William, who will come this afternoon. His visit, your letter from Naples — yes, things are starting to improve . . . I am still very sick. There is almost no respite from the pain. Thinking of you in those moments means more to me than you can imagine."

But Tennessee was far away in Europe, where Carson feared she would never be able to return. Her days were long and full of suffering. How could she write when her mind was monopolized by pain? And the winter seemed endless. In early March Carson tried to kill herself by slashing her wrists. She was hospitalized at the Payne Whitney Psychiatric Clinic in Manhattan, and a month later her mother helped her leave that institution against doctors' orders. Carson detested her psychiatrist: his insistence on her refusal to accept her illness and infirmity proved, to her mind, that he was bent on destroying her. Fortunately, she was able to confide in another psychiatrist, a young man whom she had not yet met but who had written to her in February to express his admiration. The Payne Whitney doctor, Carson told him, was a narrow-minded fellow who rejected the one defense she had against her affliction — namely, forcing herself to keep on working. He considered writing itself a neurosis that she would do well to get over. Even at the height of her despondency and after a suicide attempt, Carson was not about to let anyone undermine her identity as a writer. The doctor's remarks — whether he actually made them or she believed that she could read his thoughts — made her leave that hospital as fast as she could.

During that spring Carson tried to persuade herself that her illness was psychosomatic — thereby feeding future rumors. Rather than accept being paralyzed for life, it was obviously preferable to think that the loss of mobility in her left arm and leg had psychological, not physical, roots. Master of her fate once again, Carson herself would cure Carson. And there was no need to fear that her condition would get worse or that she would fall prey to another attack. She was probably never entirely convinced that she had conquered her own impairments, however, for she lived in constant terror of an accident until she finally received a clinically precise explanation of her case in the late 1950s. Still, many insisted that Carson's illness was psychosomatic, that she was responsible for her condition. Were they trying to deflect their terror of such an affliction in a woman so young? Or were they jealous of someone with such talent, prey to the strange brand of resentment that artists so often incite? No doubt a little bit of both.

When working was so hard as to be nearly impossible, when Tennessee Williams was so far away and she too feeble to join him — although he had invited her to come to Rome — what comfort was left? Where could she turn to find the "we of me" equally desired by Carson and by her fictional creation Frankie Addams? Where else but toward Reeves? Reeves was the person Carson reached out for when she was lost, just as he reached out for her when he felt himself drifting. Reeves was the one, the only one, against whom she could never hold a grudge, no matter what wounds he inflicted on her. With others she was unyielding. Any act that in her eyes constituted a breach of friendship was an unpardonable wrong. That was why she fell out with Kay Boyle in Paris when Boyle and her family tried to move into the country house that had been promised to Carson and Reeves.

Exactly how the couple got back together this time is unclear, but sometime in the middle of the summer Reeves was once again received as a son by Marguerite Smith. He was always welcome in Nyack. He no longer drank and had joined Alcoholics Anonymous. He was now working as an accountant at the New York radio station WOR and expressed a childlike pride in having his own private secretary. One day he brought Carson an electric typewriter. Its keys were easier to strike and required less physical effort than her old manual. Still, Carson could not really type with both hands. She chose to dictate her revisions of *The Member of the Wedding*. At her request, Tennessee Williams encouraged and advised her, and this time she followed his advice. She hated Greer Johnson's work, and he was threatening to take her to court for refusing to grant him coauthorship of the work. In the end the two parties reached an arbitrated settlement.

Despite her courage, Reeves's attention, and Tennessee Williams's return to the United States, Carson felt that her physical condition was worsening. Her leg had grown stiffer and more painful; she could neither bend nor straighten her left arm; and her left elbow was oddly raised up away from her torso in a way that she could not control.

Carson published two pieces that September, but nothing could really console her for her sudden transformation into an invalid. And yet every confirmation of her existence — above all as a writer — was a victory. What had once been no more than an everyday event in her literary life had now become a proof of her survival. *Mademoiselle* had published her essay "How I Began to Write," and *New Directions in Prose and Poetry* had published two poems, "When We Are Lost" — the one she had read to the students at the Sorbonne — and "The Mortgaged Heart," which would later lend its title to a posthumous collection of stories, articles, and poems.[8]

In addition, Tennessee Williams convinced Carson to get out, to walk — she would use a cane from now on — and to adapt to what would have to become her normal life. At his side on October 6 she attended the Broadway premiere of *Summer and Smoke* — the play Williams had been working on when they first met on Nantucket, which he dedicated to her. It was not an easy evening. In his *Memoirs* Williams recalls the cocktail party that followed the performance and the moment when he said to Carson, "Let's get out of here."

"It was . . . a long and agonizing exit, everyone staring at us, the notices out . . . And those notices were not very good. I was living then in a Tony Smith designed apartment on East Fifty-eighth Street. When I woke in the morning, it was to a record of Mozart. Carson had already arrived in the apartment and put the record on to comfort my waking moments." He continued, "Well, I was not in the mood for comfort or for pity, which is really not comforting, much . . . so I told Frank Merlo (who . . . I lived with . . . for a long, long time) to cut the Mozart off and to see Carson to a cab before I got out of bed.

"I wanted to get back to work: alone, and right away."[9]

A few weeks later Williams invited Carson to spend the winter with him in Key West. She accepted joyously. Carson wrote to Edwin Peacock in Charleston that she would stop in for a visit on their drive down to Florida. But she never made the trip. Was Tennessee Williams afraid to set off on such a journey with a friend who was so fragile? Whatever the case may be, he abandoned the idea of spending the winter in Key West in favor of a trip to the Moroccan port city of Tangiers, where Paul and Jane Bowles had a house. Rather unrealistically, he asked Carson to go with him. She had no wish to. It would not be very wise, and above all, she explained to her friend, it was the South she yearned to see again, her native South into which she had to "plunge" from time to time "to renew her 'sense of horror.'"[10] Carson would have to wait several more months before returning to the South — and the greatest pleasure of 1948 would no doubt be seeing that year come to an end.

Nineteen forty-eight was also a presidential election year, and at the urging of Nobel Prize winner Sinclair Lewis, Carson, along with twenty-seven other writers, including Truman Capote, signed a statement of support for the Democrat Harry S. Truman, who carried the day. That declaration of faith, published in the *New York Times* on October 27, called on Americans to cast a "tactical vote": "We will not vote for what has traditionally been the party of reaction, nor will we contribute to the victory of that party by voting for minor candidates whose campaigns are quixotic or worse. . . . Harry Truman's stand in favor of civil rights, his constant advocacy of aid to Europe, his effective resistance to totalitarianism abroad and at home, . . . [t]hese are services to democracy that entitle him to the support of every liberal."[11]

Some who believe that Carson was entirely focused on her own physical and intellectual difficulties at the time have attributed this public stand solely to Reeves. Reeves McCullers was a man of progress, to be sure; and through his taste for ideological debate and his curiosity about politics during the 1930s, he doubtless had a great influence on the maturing young woman who became his wife. But there can be no doubt of Carson's personal commitment to political combat on the side of the most leftist forces. The fight for civil rights had always been close to her heart, and she was one of the few Southerners who relentlessly spoke up to demand that those rights be recognized and respected. At the height of her distress, in February 1948, Carson had dictated a letter to the editor of the *Columbus Ledger Enquirer* that denounced the unfairness of denying the black community access to the town's new municipal library.

> I believe that no one owes a greater debt to the Columbus Public Library than I. During my childhood and the formative years of my youth, our library was my spiritual base.
>
> I understand there has been some altercation about allowing all citizens, both white and Negro, the use of the new Columbus Public Library. I do not understand the concrete issues involved but I

understand too well the abstract ones. Always it has been an intolerable shame to me to know that Negroes are not accorded the same intellectual privileges as white citizens. As an author, represented in the library, I feel it is my duty to speak not only for myself but for the august dead who are represented on the shelves and to whom I owe an incalculable debt. I think of Tolstoy, Chekov, Abraham Lincoln and Thomas Paine.

I would like to go on record and like to say that we owe to these (the molders of the conscience of our civilization) the freedom of all citizens regardless of race, to benefit by their wisdom, which is our dearest inheritance.[12]

Carson's indignation — her letter was published in the newspaper, and a copy was sent to the director of the library — failed to sway the reactionary citizens of Columbus, and many years would go by before black citizens could use the library there.

Reeves was delighted, of course, by Carson's public support of the Democratic Party. He loved it when Carson was combative, defending their common ideals. But every time his wife made a spectacular gesture, he was forced to confront his own lack of a commanding personal image. He could not take a public stand without either having it rejected or exposing himself to reading that "the husband of Carson McCullers also thinks that we should vote for the left." By chance, during Harry Truman's campaign, Reeves was happy with Carson and not drinking, and so their public support brought the two closer. Once again they decided to move in together. Carson spent the whole month of January in Reeves's Manhattan apartment at 105 Thompson Street, two steps from Washington Square and their dear Brevoort Hotel. Reeves regularly attended meetings of Alcoholics Anonymous and still held his job at the radio station. Since his apartment was on the sixth floor, he had to carry Carson up and down the stairs. They must have laughed about it like two children.

And Carson began to believe that she could live happily with her disability. She wrote to tell Tennessee Williams how happy she was: "I am living in New York with Reeves. Just imagine — if you were here, too, we would see each other every day. Reeves is constantly gentle and kind with me. He takes marvelous care of me, cooking our meals, coming home every day for lunch, acting like a perfect mistress of the house. There is only one small problem: the apartment is on the sixth floor, and I can't go out alone. Reeves has to help me. We are right next to Washington Square. We're paying $18 a month. Reeves has fixed the place up and made it really comfortable."[13] She drew a diagram of the small three-room flat; discussed her doctor, who "thinks we have my illness completely under control, and that it is absolutely not weak blood vessels"; thanked Tennessee for giving her a ring that had belonged to his sister Rose, who had a serious mental illness and was constantly hospitalized; and detailed her new plans for life with Reeves. For a long time he had dreamed of owning a farm. "We are still thinking about putting some money aside, Reeves and I, to buy a farm — maybe one with an apple orchard. We intend to spend two or three months in Europe, every year. It would be marvelous, don't you think? An orchard, a comfortable house, a few animals, and a room reserved for 10. You can come back to the farm whenever the bright lights of the city start to pale."[14]

There is no evidence that Marguerite Smith approved of all this. Despite her affection for Reeves, she had harbored certain misgivings about him since the couple's return from Paris. More than ever she saw herself as *the* guardian of her daughter, the only guarantor of a possible improvement in Carson's existence. She urged Carson to come spend her thirty-second birthday, February 19, in Nyack, which both she and Reeves did. There was serious talk then of taking a trip south, as Carson had been wanting to do for several months. Reeves wrote to Edwin Peacock in South Carolina that he and Carson would be coming to Charleston, where Peacock ran a bookstore with his friend John Zeigler. Beforehand, Carson and her mother would travel to Columbus and then Macon, Georgia, to see Carson's distant cousin Jordan Massee.

Carson's return to Columbus was just as disappointing as her visit to Jordan Massee was decisive, forging an unbreakable link between the two cousins. Massee would love and support Carson for the rest of her life, and over the years since her death he has defended her memory with absolute fidelity. Of the dozens of people interviewed by Virginia Spencer Carr in the early 1970s, when nearly all of Carson's entourage was still living, Massee is the one who most steadfastly defends not only his cousin but the family, and particularly Carson's mother, Marguerite Smith, whom he always refers to as "Bebe."

Massee's unpublished journal follows the ups and downs of his relationship with his cousin over the years.

Carson had apparently been unaware that it might be unwise to retrace her footsteps to her childhood home. She had hardly stepped off the train, on March 13, when she realized that returning to Columbus was a bad idea. Carson spent four interminable days there before Jordan Massee came to take her to his home in Macon. No doubt her discomfort was heightened by her mother's presence, to say nothing of the way the people of Columbus regarded her. Her success meant they could no longer joke about the literary ambitions of "little Lula Carson, whose mother took her for a genius." But Carson's infirmity now often inspired a condescending sympathy that she found unbearable. So she did everything she could to avoid old acquaintances, refusing nearly all invitations. When she accepted one, she made no effort to be minimally courteous. The only pleasant memory Carson took away from those few days was that of reading Baudelaire's *Flowers of Evil* (in translation) and *Out of Africa* by Isak Dinesen (Karen Blixen), which she had reread every year since discovering the book in 1937.

For one of her worst memories — happily, one of little consequence — Carson was entirely responsible. On her last morning in Columbus, March 17, she decided to visit a beauty salon and get a "permanent wave," the latest fad in hairstyles. Not only did the overly feminine little curls make her look ridiculous, but the styling chemical caused an immediate allergic reaction. Her face swelled up and broke out in hives. When Jordan Massee arrived, Carson was deeply embarrassed by her appearance. Fearing the worst after hearing the story of her illness, Massee thought she looked better than he had anticipated. Marguerite Smith, on the other hand, "show[ed] the effects of the terrible strain under which she has lived these last two years,"[15] and quite possibly the effects of a more and more serious case of chronic alcoholism as well.

The week in Macon was very pleasant, although Carson joined her mother in drinking too much, especially beer. Carson never seemed drunk, her voice never changed, and she spoke at her usual — slow — pace in her customary thick Southern accent. Before turning in for the night, she ritually drank one last beer. "The doctors told Carson she could have two cans of beer every evening and one large drink — or two small ones," Jordan Massee comments. "Unfortunately, they didn't define 'large' or 'small.'"[16] In Macon Carson met with journalists, and everything went surprisingly well. With them, and with Jordan Massee's friends, she was smiling, at ease, simple, direct, as she seldom had managed to be since her paralysis.

While they played records in the living room, Carson told Jordan, whom she called "Boots," how unpleasant her return to Columbus had been, and she talked about the future, her plans, and her loves. On March 18 she spent the whole morning discussing her new novel with Boots, a work called *Clock Without Hands,* which was not published until twelve years later. She described the characters, and he suggested a few modifications — that she make such and such a character a lover of German lieder rather than Mozart, for example. Carson let him "play at constructing a novel," but she had "her own idea" firmly in hand. Carson "asked hundreds of questions about Klan activities in Macon . . . and about the attitudes of second and third generation Southerners after the Civil War."

She presented her friends in a series of vignettes, described an altercation between Truman Capote and Marguerite Smith, who had called the young author a "little crook" one evening in Nyack, and told Boots she thought that Truman was "following Tennessee" in Europe. On March 21 Carson got a letter from Reeves and read it aloud for all to hear: "Some of it was about the Southern senators who have defeated . . . President [Truman's] plans, how there is seldom any justice for such transgressions, but that someday perhaps these men will get the reward they deserve," noted Jordan in his journal. Carson then confided to her cousin "how necessary Reeves [was] to her, and how much she love[d] him," adding, "Boots, you know you and I are so much alike, but you are lucky that your loves have come to you successively, while mine came concurrently."[17]

Her love for Annemarie Schwarzenbach was still very much alive — likely rekindled by her friend's premature death, five years ago now. She told Boots that it had been an unforgettable experience, and Carson would speak of it throughout the rest of her life. Jordan knew how to listen, and he understood his cousin implicitly. She wrote to him a few weeks later when "the time of Annemarie" came back to her with such violent sadness — she had just learned from a newspaper article that Klaus Mann had killed himself in the city of Nice in southern France.

From Macon Carson was supposed to go directly to Charleston, to

Edwin Peacock's house. But on March 21 she got news that some writers who were regular residents at Yaddo were trying to force the resignation of the executive director she liked so well, Elizabeth Ames — to whom she had dedicated *The Member of the Wedding* — by accusing her of ties to the Communist Party. McCarthyism still was going strong. Despite the many challenges of traveling, Carson took the first train north. By the time she got to New York the affair had already been resolved and her friend "cleared."[18]

So Carson went back home to Nyack, eager to resume her tour of the South. She had to wait, though, until May 13, when Reeves began his first vacation since he had been hired by WOR. They left that very day, happy to be finally on their way to see the old friend from their youth who had arranged their first meeting in Columbus. They had planned to spend two whole weeks in Charleston, with Carson perhaps staying longer if she could work at Peacock's house — they had brought along her electric typewriter. Reeves was very attentive; he did no drinking, and he had never taken better care of Carson. As he had before, Peacock brought the two friends together. It could have been a dream vacation. And yet in one of the photographs taken during that stay Reeves has the grim, strained look that people noted in Paris three years later. Carson, meanwhile, who loved going to the beach, had to watch the others bathe every day and wait. She would never swim again. And, suddenly, Carson fell ill. Her temperature shot up, and she panicked and insisted on returning to Nyack right away. She had simply caught a cold, but every ailment, however benign, was now a source of anguish.

While she was still ill, Carson received a copy of the preface that Tennessee Williams had composed for a new edition of *Reflections in a Golden Eye*. She was so weak that she could not even write to thank him. Not until April did she get a letter off, in which she also recited to her friend Reeves's new plans. His weak-willed side had apparently gained the upper hand, and like an unrealistic child, Carson was sanctioning his various schemes. Having abandoned the bucolic dream of returning to life on a farm, Reeves was now hankering for army life again.

> All these last months, we've been contemplating, for Reeves, the possibility of rejoining the military. Which would mean that he would no longer receive his pension of $2,000 a year. But, as a cap-

tain, he could earn an equivalent salary, without having to work very hard — and he would still have time to read and enjoy himself. We would have a house of our own, and perhaps a car and a housekeeper. And (this would be especially for you), there are always swimming pools on military bases, and excellent libraries. The prospect appeals to me sometimes, because mama and Reeves don't always get along, which creates an underground tension that seems to get closer and closer to the surface. The problem first and foremost is: would you come see us in the Army? There would always be a room for you. You could make it your home base, fly off on personal safaris, then come back. I've have just finished writing nine and a half pages of my book by hand, and I'm exhausted.[19]

Future plans, dreams of happiness with Reeves, friendship, work . . . Carson was striving to fill up her daily existence in order to forget her physical pain. In her letters she sometimes complained, though she rarely went into detail — except for one day in June when Carson had heard that Tennessee Williams was returning from Europe and she wanted to see him. She described her plight coldly, without pathos, as she might have done in one of her books. Though Carson's letters are sometimes effusive, she is always tight-lipped about her physical condition and her health. The situation she describes nonetheless shows the extremity of her suffering. It is hard to imagine how she could have stood it much longer, either physically or psychologically, yet she had eighteen more years to live:

So you're coming home. Oh! dear, dear Tenn, can you understand what that means to me? I simply cannot tell you how difficult this past year has been. My health has gotten worse day by day. I can hardly walk once around the building. I can no longer play the piano, of course, or type. They no longer let me smoke — or drink, alas. And I have neuritis coming on. My nerves are so shot they never stop hurting and trembling. This summer, all the germs for miles around got together at 131 [South Broadway]. Dr. William is on vacation, and last week the Nyack doctor was away. I had a terrible migraine — accompanied by nausea and deep despondency. I was in agony for three days straight. Finally, a funny sort of doctor came. He gave me pills to make me vomit. A gland in my neck got infected, and, after such a long siege of ceaseless pain, I had sort of an attack of convulsions. The pain was so varied, so lugubrious, that one could almost have found it amusing, if it had been inflicted on someone like Isle Koch [a Nazi torturer]. But, Tenn, why must I suffer so? What have I done? I wanted to call for help, but no help was possible. And, what's worse than anything, I live in constant terror of a new catastrophe, constant terror that my health could deteriorate even further. Not of death, no, it's not death I am afraid of.

And yet, where my work is concerned, things have never looked so promising. I have envisioned my novel in its entirety. And everything related to the play is fascinating. Harold Clurman is directing it. Two days ago I made a very important change. I can't go any further, now, the play is finished. Clurman is requesting no more revisions. I like his director's sense of intuition. He immediately laid bare the main theme — the search for identity, the desire to be part of something — and he created a perfect array of voices in counterpoint around that theme. I hope you like the play. A radiance should emanate from it that resembles Mozart's rondo in A minor.

I so need to see you, dear Tenn. I have been in bed since nine o'clock this morning. I am waiting for the doctor.[20]

Any writer who is not an experienced playwright must expend an immense amount of energy to get a play successfully produced and staged. For the weakened, barely mobile, and suffering Carson, the task required phenomenal strength. Throughout the summer of 1949 and into early autumn, Carson followed step by step as *The Member of the Wedding* wended its way through the process of production, from the quest for a director — Harold Clurman turned out to be the one — to the search for a suitable cast. Approached to fill the role of Berenice Sadie Brown, the black actress Ethel Waters refused the part the first time around — she did not want to perform "in a play without God." She ended up accepting, on condition that one or two lines of religious inspiration be added to her role. The twelve-year-old Frankie would be played by an actress who at the age of twenty-three had an adolescent's face: Julie Harris. Harris's hair was cropped very short to enhance her youthful appearance. The day before opening night the director asked Harris to cut her own hair even shorter — and badly — as Frankie had done. When Carson saw the way she looked, it moved her deeply. To fill the part of John Henry they recruited a young boy who had never acted before — he hardly knew how to read — and he created a sensation: Brandon De Wilde, the son of actor Fritz De Wilde (who played Frankie's brother, Jarvis, the groom).

On November 28 everything was set, and Carson attended a first reading of the play by all the actors. Then rehearsals began. At the beginning she attended them almost every day. Reeves came, too — the play was dedicated to him — and he was fascinated by the work that went into the production, by the process of directing the actors, by the daily adjustments required to bring the project to fruition. Carson for her part did not really enjoy what she no doubt viewed as a trial-and-error process not unlike her own first drafts. She paid particular attention to Julie Harris. Listening to her, she sought "her" Frankie. Seeing the character portrayed allowed Carson to detach Frankie from herself. Frankie had ceased to be a double of the young Lula Carson, but she still had to reproduce the malaise of the lanky adolescent from Columbus.

On December 22 *The Member of the Wedding* was performed in Philadelphia, where the cast hoped to work out the kinks before it opened in New York. Of particular concern was how to shorten the four-hour play, much too long for a Broadway audience. Tennessee Williams, whom Carson had begged to make the trip north from Key West to support her — "I am waiting for you. I need you here with me" — was there along with other close friends.[21] At intermission they discovered Carson and Reeves dead drunk outside the entrance to the theater. Too fearful to attend the performance, they had gone into a bar across the street, where they sat drinking and waiting for the first act to end.

The Philadelphia run assured everyone that the play would be at least a critical success. Ten years after her much-noted appearance on the literary scene with *The Heart Is a Lonely Hunter,* Carson McCullers would once again move to center stage. She published two other pieces in December: "Home for Christmas," a remembrance of Carson's childhood Christmases, in *Mademoiselle* and "Loneliness . . . an American Malady" in the *New York Herald Tribune's This Week* magazine.[22] In this short essay Carson, whose entire work is marked by solitary, marginalized characters vainly attempting to escape their isolation, tries to grasp the specifically American quality of their loneliness. She speaks again of Frankie: "In *The Member of the Wedding* the lovely 12-year-old girl, Frankie Addams, articulates this universal need: 'The trouble with me is that for a long time I have just been an *I* person. All people belong to a *We* except me. Not to belong to a *We* makes you too lonesome.'"[23] According to Carson,

> The European, secure in his family ties and rigid class loyalties, knows little of the moral loneliness that is native to us Americans. While the European artists tend to form groups or aesthetic schools, the American artist is the eternal maverick — not only from society in the way of all creative minds, but within the orbit of his own art. . . . Whether in the pastoral joys of country life or in the labyrinthine city, we Americans are always seeking. We wander, question. But the answer waits in each separate heart — the answer of our own identity and the way by which we can master loneliness and feel that at last we belong.[24]

Directly following the Philadelphia performances, Carson spent several days in the hospital, where she had been admitted after a miscarriage. While she always refused to so much as allude to the episode, Carson provides a strange account of it in her autobiographical writings:

> The day after opening night I went home to Nyack immediately with my mother, who . . . commented that I looked peaked.
> "I feel like Hell," I said.
> "Don't use bad language, darling."
> "But I do," I said.
> So she called the doctor. He examined me, and after some tests at the hospital he told mother that I was pregnant.
> "But she can't be," Mother said.
> I was surprised but pleased. However, I fixed my attention on the scene between the doctor and my mother.
> "This is God's way of making up to her because of her ruined health," the doctor said.
> Mother's scorn was loud and voluble. "You don't know what it is to have a baby," she said, "it will kill my child."
> "Wouldn't you like to be a grandmother?"
> "A grandmother while my child is dead? No! Besides I have a

perfectly good grandson in Florida. I won't let Carson have this baby."

"What are you going to do about it?" The doctor asked.

"I'll do something" she screamed, "something. I know what it is to have babies and you don't."

The doctor who had delivered about five hundred babies let that pass.

"I'll do something," she said again, "in the meantime you're fired!"

Mother quickly called Dr. Mayer, my pshchiatrist, and he was as horrified as she was.

"Get her ready to go to the hospital immediately, I will make the arrangements."

That was on a Friday, and we had to wait until Monday for a room. The quarrel between Mamma and the doctor had upset me so, that I miscarried then and there. The miscarriage was not easy. Mother who had some outlandish fear that either they might put the baby back or do something that would kill me in the end, would not call another doctor. So I suffered until Monday, when a taxi took me to New York. The blood was all over the car by the time I got there, and Dr. Van Etten, the chief gynocologist at the Neurological Institute said to Reeves, "Why have you waited till now? Your wife is dying."[25]

Carson always said that she was very fond of children, though her infirmity frightened them. She never wanted children of her own, however, because they would have gotten in the way of her work.

On January 5, when *The Member of the Wedding* opened at the Empire Theatre on Broadway, Carson had left the hospital. When the players came out to greet the audience after the performance, the entire room rose to its feet. In the wee hours of the morning, when the party celebrating the premiere was winding down, the first reviews began appearing in the daily papers: all were good, and some were excellent. In the *New York Times* Brooks Atkinson spoke of the "grace" of both Carson McCullers and the actors, concluding: "In view of the rare quality of the writing and acting, the fact that 'The Member of the Wedding' has practically no dramatic movement does not seem to be very important. It may not be a play, but it is art. That is the important thing."[26] In the *New York World-Telegram* William Hawkins remarked that he had "never before heard what happened last night at the curtain calls for 'The Member of the Wedding' when hundreds cried out as if with one voice for Ethel Waters and Julie Harris . . . The two actresses are splendid beyond compare in this curious play about the tragedy of loneliness."[27] Of all the dailies only the *New York Herald Tribune* expressed reservations. Their critic, Howard Barnes, had a good word for the actors, but the play struck him as poorly constructed and "laggard."[28]

At the box office the play was an immediate smash, and it continued to sell out for months. *The Member of the Wedding* ran until March 17, 1951, for a total of 501 performances. That success assured the financial survival of Carson McCullers, who without that copious infusion of cash would have run into serious money problems during the 1950s.

In the periodicals the reception was no less enthusiastic. Most critics celebrated both the play — the work of Carson McCullers herself — and the production's perfect equilibrium: good direction, good actors, and so on. As in the novel, some reviewers lamented the play's lack of dramatic tension and the weakness of the action — if not its total absence. But the overall impression remained positive. "'The Member of the Wedding,' Carson McCullers' dramatization of her novel, is unquestionably the first serious new play of any consequence to reach Broadway this season," wrote Wolcott Gibbs, in the introduction to his *New Yorker* article. "It has a good many touching and rather difficult things to say; it often has a queer, fantastic wit . . . ; occasionally it reaches something very close to poetry; and it is illuminated by a magnificent performance by Ethel Waters and two remarkably spirited ones by Julie Harris and a seven-year-old boy named Brandon De Wilde."[29]

John Mason Brown's remarks, published in the *Saturday Review,* struck a similar note:

> Mrs. McCullers's study of the loneliness of an overimaginative young Georgian girl is no ordinary play. It is felt, observed, and phrased with exceptional sensitivity. It deals with the torturing dreams, the hungry egotism, and the heartbreak of childhood in a manner as rare as it is welcome. Quite aside from the magical performances its production includes, it has a magic of its own. The

script shines with an unmistakable luster. Plainly it is the work of an artist, of an author who does not stoop to the expected stencils and who sees people with her own eyes rather than through borrowed spectacles. . . . Common speech becomes uncommon in Mrs. McCullers's usage of it.[30]

At the end of his lengthy review, in which he cites Chekhov, Brown pays homage to the quality of the actors, and above all to Ethel Waters, who in the role of the black cook Berenice "demonstrates once again how exceptional are her gifts." As for the director, "Harold Clurman has never done a better job as a director than with 'The Member of the Wedding.' He has staged it with beauty, humor, and perception. He has not only assembled an excellent cast but has shown himself to be alert to every shading of an unusual script. The result is an evening as uncommon in its quality as it is radiant in its merits."[31] George Jean Nathan, the highly reactionary theater critic for *Esquire* magazine — who detested Tennessee Williams and was likely ill-disposed toward Carson McCullers for that reason — published a pure and simple panning. In his view what little action there was in the novel had entirely disappeared from the play, and he was bored stiff.[32]

Harold Clurman was exasperated by allegations, made even by people who enjoyed the performance, that the play lacked dramatic movement. He responded to the charges in a *New Republic* piece that came out in late January:

> It is impossible to direct a play that has no action. When a play is well acted, it means that a line of action has been found in it. It means that action was in it, however obscure it may have seemed at first sight. Without action, it would not *play.*
>
> The reason why Chekhov's "Seagull" did not seem to have action when it was first produced was that the original company had not found it. . . .
>
> . . . A renewal of faith in the sensitivity and awareness of our New York theatregoing public was perhaps the greatest lesson I learned from "The Member of the Wedding."[33]

An exchange of letters between Carson McCullers and the playwright John Van Druten echoes that stance. Until Van Druten's death, in 1957, the two writers maintained a distant but very admiring relationship. Unfortunately, only Carson's half of that exchange remains; in it she addresses several points probably raised by Van Druten:

> I have received many responses from people who have seen "The Member of the Wedding" but none has approached your uncanny perception and realization of what has been attempted in the play. This goes, too, for the professional observers, who, in the main, realized only the most visible aspects of it. I believe that the modern theatre-goer is unused to evaluating abstractions in the drama. As you say, it is an *inward* play and the conflicts are inward; the antagonist is not personified but is a human condition of life: the sense of moral isolation.
>
> Another abstract condition you noticed is that the play deals with the weight of time, the hazard of human existence, bolts of chance. The reaction of the characters to these unseen phenomena projects the movement of the play.
>
> Theatre Arts Magazine had asked me to write an article on "What is a Play?". I do hope that you don't mind that I used and enlarged your lucid evaluations of the play.
>
> I believe that the artist is the one in the most qualified position to understand the primary worth and intentions of another artist. So when an artist of your great stature writes me as you did I feel grateful and humble.[34]

The text referred to here by Carson, "The Vision Shared," appeared in April. In this highly personal essay Carson defends, not for the first time, the artist's singularity with acute sensitivity:

> I should rather say a poem now than write on the subject: "What is a Play?" For, first, I doubt the wisdom of arbitrary qualifications when an art form is concerned; and, secondly, my creative life has done nothing to equip me for formal aesthetic evaluations. For the writing of prose or poems — and I do not think there should be any immutable distinction between the two forms — this writing is a wandering creation. By that I mean that a given passage or paragraph draws astray the imagination with sensual allusions, nuances of feelings, vibrations of memory or desire. An aesthetic criticism has an opposite function. The attention of the reader should not be encouraged to wander or day dream, but should be fixed with lucid extroversion, cerebral and finite.
>
> The function of the artist is to execute his own indigenous vi-

sion, and having done that, to keep faith with this vision. (At the risk of sounding pontifical I use the words "artist" and "vision," because of the sake of accuracy and to differentiate between the professional writers who are concerned with different aims.) Unfortunately it must be recognized that the artist is threatened by multiple pressures in the commercial world of publishers, producers, editors of magazines. The publisher says this character must not die and the book should end on an "up beat," or the producer wants phony dramatics, or friends and onlookers suggest this or that alternative. The professional writer may accede to these demands and concentrate on the ball and the bleachers. But once a creative writer is convinced of his own intentions, he must protect his work from alien persuasion. It is often a solitary position. We are afraid when we feel ourselves alone. And there is another special fear that torments the creator when he is too long assailed. . . .

. . . I think of James Joyce's long, embattled years against publishers, prudery, and finally international piracy. Or we can think of Proust's Jovian patience and faith in the magnitude of his own labors. Sometimes communication comes too late for the part of the artist that is mortal. Poe died before he saw his vision shared. Before retreating into his madness Nietzsche cried out in a letter to Cosima Wagner, "If there were only two in the world to understand me!"[35]

Regarding *The Member of the Wedding,* Carson reiterated the remarks she had made in her letter to John Van Druten, sometimes almost word for word, before concluding:

I foresaw that this play had also another problem as a lyric tragicomedy. The funniness and the grief are often co-existent in a single line and I did not know how an audience would respond to this. But Ethel Waters, Julie Harris, and Brandon de Wilde, under the superb direction of Harold Clurman, brought to their fugue-like parts a dazzling precision and harmony.

Some observers have wondered if any drama as unconventional as this should be called a play. I cannot comment on that. I only know that *The Member of the Wedding* is a vision that a number of artists have realized with fidelity and love.[36]

Also in April, the New York Drama Critics' Circle named *The Member of the Wedding* best play of the season (April 1, 1949, through

March 31, 1950). Carson also received two other top honors, the Donaldson Award for the best first play by an author produced on Broadway and the Theatre Club's gold medal for the best dramatic author of the year. Once again, on her first foray into an unknown world, Carson achieved a spectacular triumph. Though she may have lacked technical mastery, she had a good feeling for contemporary drama. For American specialists her play became a symbol with historical significance. According to Gerald Weales in *American Drama Since World War II*, "a case might well be made for *The Member of the Wedding* as the most obvious structural innovation in the recent American theater," stretching as it did the traditional definition of dramatic action. The play also stood out as one of a small number of successful adaptations from a novel penned by the original author. "Seldom has an author, in adapting his own novel, been successful in creating a work that is both faithful to the original and an attractive play in its own right. Carson McCullers's *The Member of the Wedding* (1950), Alfred Hayes's *The Girl on the Via Flaminia* (1954), and Truman Capote's *The Grass Harp* (1952) are the only three examples that come to mind," asserts Weales. "*The Grass Harp,* to its disadvantage," Weales goes on to say [McCullers for her part simply accused Capote of plagiarizing her], "is full of echoes from Carson McCullers. . . . Capote's borrowings from Mrs. McCullers are not nearly as important as what he has not been able to borrow — a quality, a tone, a substance."[37]

◆　◆　◆

Carson McCullers's success could also be measured in dollars. A play that attracts a large audience earns a great deal more money for its author than does a novel, even a successful one. Carson and Reeves were thrilled. For the first time in thirteen chaotic years of life together, they had money. They even felt rich, however temporarily. As if to prove their good fortune, they moved into one of New York's most fashionable buildings, the famous Dakota on Central Park West, where it is every star's duty to reside at some point during his or her lifetime. In the end it is childlike, bohemian exploits like these — spontaneously yielded to whenever the pair were together — that make Carson and Reeves both so endearing. Another surprise came to Carson in the form of a letter from Mary Tucker, the piano teacher from Fort Benning whose departure had so deeply disturbed the young Carson and was probably linked to her eventual creation of *The Member of the Wedding*'s Frankie Addams. Tucker wrote to congratulate her former pupil, after fifteen years of silence. The two friends soon met again and never lost contact from then on. When she needed a rest, Carson sometimes took refuge in the Tuckers' home in Virginia, where she spent two weeks for the first time in the fall of that same year.

Having been gloriously rewarded for the enormous effort she had made to keep herself alive and active, Carson decided she should once again attempt to lead the life she might have had without the handicap created by her strokes. She continued to suffer, but, as Reeves repeatedly averred, Carson was "indestructible." The numerous trips she took, most often with his help, seem to confirm that sometimes wry observation.

She left alone, however, on May 20, for Ireland, where she had made plans to visit the novelist Elizabeth Bowen. Carson had just met Bowen in New York and had, said she — yet again — become infatuated with her. She had practically invited herself to Bowen's Court, the splendid Bowen family manor built in 1775, declaring it a propitious environment for work on her new manuscript, *Clock Without Hands*.

Carson's visit there got off to a rather bad start even before she left home: Miscalculating Ireland's time zone, Carson placed a telephone call to Bowen's Court in the middle of the night. A very British maître d'hôtel answered the phone, saying: "Madam, it is four o'clock in the morning. I suggest you call again later."[38] Carson delighted in the incident and laughed about it uproariously. But Miss Bowen and her majordomo probably did not find the faux pas, for which Carson never apologized, equally hilarious.

Carson was impressed by the magnificence of Bowen's Court, but she was like a displaced person there. She had no understanding of Elizabeth Bowen's reserve, her extreme but distant courtesy, her manners, or her perfect education, based on a tradition refined over many generations. Carson could not work and soon grew bored. She who had believed that she had something to share with Miss Bowen, artist to artist, realized that they had nothing in common. "Carson was a welcome visitor, but I must say a terrible 'handful,' to use that old-fashioned expression, once she'd arrived," Elizabeth Bowen admitted to Virginia Spencer Carr in 1971. That interview must have been a savory one, but it demonstrates above all a subtle understanding as well as a certain tenderness for the bewildering child that was Carson McCullers:

> I always felt Carson was a destroyer; for which reason I chose never to be closely involved with her. Affection for her I *did* feel, and she also gave off an aura of genius — unmistakable — which one had to respect. Possibly, some of the company she kept did her no good. . . . Therefore, hers and mine could not be described as a "close friendship" — in the sense that I rejoice in having a close friendship with that other great Deep-Southerner, Eudora Welty. . . . Carson remains in my mind as a child genius, though her art, as we know, was great, sombre, and above all, extremely mature. I remember her face, her being, her bearing with a pang of affection — and always shall.[39]

Carson sent Reeves a telegram, saying that she missed him and asking him to meet her in London. He had been waiting for just such a sign — it gave Reeves a "valid" reason for quitting his now tiresome job at the radio station. He joined Carson in London, and the two set off for Paris, a city that seemed to hold the same singular attraction for both of them. As soon as they arrived, they made plans to live there again permanently. They stayed first at the Hôtel de l'Université, then with their friend John Brown, who had always helped them out in any way he could. Tennessee Williams was also in Paris at the time and saw Carson and Reeves quite often. They had resumed their "Parisian life" — friends, cafés, cabarets. Reeves was supposed to drink only a small amount of wine, but for him as for Carson "a small amount" was an indefinite concept.

◆　◆　◆

Tennessee Williams had just written *The Rose Tattoo* for Anna Magnani, who fascinated him. Carson seems to have dined with the actress one night during June 1950, when she was out for the evening with Tennessee.[40] Although travel was not easy for Carson, in the space of a few weeks she went from London to Paris and from Paris back to London, then returned with Reeves to Bowen's Court, where they met the novelist Rosamond Lehmann, who charmed — and was moved by — the couple. Then they set off again for New York. On their return, in early August, they separated yet again. Reeves took a new apartment in Manhattan, and Carson went back home to her mother in Nyack after spending time with friends in New York and on Fire Island.

Reeves had clearly gone back to drinking, which was extremely upsetting to Carson. Only when her mother had again taken charge did Carson feel somewhat reassured. There were new discussions of divorce, but Reeves insisted he would straighten out. He returned to Alcoholics Anonymous and began looking for work. He found a less than inspiring office job at the Banker's Trust Company, and in October he resumed regular weekend visits to Nyack.

Jordan Massee went to Nyack that same month. He had not seen his cousin since her trip to Ireland. In his journal he describes those two days spent with "the Smith-McCullers clan."[41] Carson was doing quite well, even though she stayed in bed much of the time. As for Reeves, he had settled back into the role of the husband coming home from his job in the big city at week's end. It seems, though, that there had been some tension in the house before Jordan's arrival and that Carson was particularly pleased to have someone to create a diversion. Besides which, there was "an unpleasant argument after dinner." Carson retired to her room, inviting her cousin to come talk with her there. She was very upset: a friend had told Carson disagreeable things that had been said about her behind her back. Jordan wondered, rather naively, if unpleasant things had been said, why the "friend" had repeated them to Carson. But his private journal clearly conveys Jordan's tenderness for his cousin, his compassion, and his good sense: not once does he let Carson lure him onto the terrain of her fantasies. When she tells her cousin that she and he should have been married, for instance, that they would have understood each other and been happy together, Jordan writes: "She felt sure that if we had met sooner, before Reeves, we would have married. I was embarrassed because I knew it would never have worked, but she was so pleased with the idea that I left it at that."[42]

The following morning the house seemed calmer, and breakfast was spent discussing politics, in Carson's room. Reeves felt very much at ease with that subject, and he willingly held forth: "Reeves still believes that capitalism has failed and is 'cracking at every seam,' but he is certainly not pro-Russian. Just the reverse. We spoke of [the militant anarchist and feminist] Emma Goldman and the nobility of her disillusion. I told them what Isadora Duncan said to Ralph Lawton after her first return to Paris from the Soviet Union: 'They have embalmed the revolution in Red Square.'"[43]

A few days later Jordan and Carson were together again at a party in New York given by Tennessee Williams in honor of Dame Edith Sitwell. Dr. Sitwell's reputation both as a poet and as an eccentric British aristocrat had made Carson long to meet her. In an amusing journal entry dated October 31, 1950, Jordan describes Sitwell's highly colorful entrance:

> Dr. Sitwell arrived very dignified and very grand but with a natural grand manner, like genuine royalty, not a pose. Very grand and yet very simple, and that in spite of a topaz ring the size of a hen's egg. She wore a huge gold bracelet, oriental I think; English walking shoes with low heels; a long black dress and a long black cape, both to the floor, which she kept on, and a rather peculiar hat. She took her seat in the center of the sofa and we were presented. She was completely at ease and put us at ease immediately with her quiet charm and amusing stories. I had expected a kind of exotic epater le bourgeoise, but I think she simply dares be herself.
>
> Carson sat with Sitwell on the sofa and they talked for a long time. Dr. Sitwell treated her as gently as one treats a small nervous child and told Carson that when she returns to England she would send her all her volumes of poetry and would even copy out those poems that have not yet been published. Carson asked if she might send Dr. Sitwell some of her poems, and she replied, "M dear, I hope you will. How nice that would be." Carson told Dr. Sitwell not once but several times that I was her favorite cousin and Dr. Sitwell invited Carson and me to attend the rehearsal for her reading at the Museum of Modern Art. It's the only chance I'll have to hear her read since the Museum charged twenty five dollars a seat last year and probably will this year.[44]

Jordan and Carson were delighted to accept that invitation. With her thank-you letter Carson enclosed a copy of *The Heart Is a Lonely Hunter* and *The Member of the Wedding*. On November 21, after reading the two novels, Edith Sitwell wrote a long and lovely letter highlighting her admiration for Carson's talent as a writer — and touching on the kind of gap there was between the maturity of her work and her air of a perpetual child. "You are a transcendental writer," Edith Sitwell declared. "There cannot be the slightest doubt of that." *Heart*, she wrote, "is a masterpiece of compassion, of understanding, of writing. What a born writer you are." *The Member of the Wedding* she liked just as much if not more, so impressed was she by its poetic quality. "What a great poet's mind and eye and senses you have, together with a great pure writer's mind, sense of construction and character. . . . I have not been so excited by any books as by these for years. . . . May I send you love, which indeed I do, and my deepest admiration."[45] The two women would see each other on several occasions in the years to come. For Edith Sitwell such an emotion-filled reading experience was unforgettable, and like the person of impeccable gentility she was, Sitwell always welcomed Carson to her home in England with the utmost consideration.

♦   ♦   ♦

In early 1951 Carson sold the movie rights to *The Member of the Wedding* to Stanley Kramer. That new infusion of funds allowed her to purchase the Nyack house from her mother. Finally there was a place that she could call home. Adding to her comfort throughout the winter and spring were signs of her growing importance in American literature. A portrait of her and Tennessee Williams appeared in the April 15 *Vogue* magazine, emphasizing both her literary accomplishments and her immense success on Broadway. In May there were numerous — and favorable — reviews when Houghton Mifflin brought out an omnibus edition, *The Ballad of the Sad Café: The Novels and Stories of Carson McCullers*, containing the previously unpublished story "A Domestic Dilemma," a concentrated dose of the author's humor and methodical cruelty.[46]

Emily lives with her husband, near New York City, in a house with a view of the Hudson much like Carson's home in Nyack. Her husband, Martin, works in the city but is very careful to come home from work early on Thursdays, when the maid takes half the day off. For some time now his wife has been depressed and alcoholic, and he is afraid of what she might do to their two children — with good reason. On this particular Thursday "her kiss was strong with sherry," and she had made the children toast that was sprinkled with cayenne pepper, which she had mistaken for cinnamon. As in "Instant of the Hour After," Carson describes alcoholism, creeping dependency, the way alcoholics try to hide their affliction, with great intelligence. And she keeps that question, which concerns her as much as Reeves, at enough of a remove to ensure that the story never resembles a complaint or a confession.

> As he busied himself with the dinner downstairs he was lost in the familiar question as to how this problem had come upon his home. He himself had always enjoyed a good drink. When they were still living in Alabama they had served long drinks or cocktails as a matter of course. For years they had drunk one or two — possibly three drinks before dinner, and at bedtime a long nightcap. Evenings before holidays they might get a buzz on, might even become a little tight. But alcohol had never seemed a problem to him, only a bothersome expense that with the increase in the family they could scarcely afford. It was only after his company had transferred him to New York that Martin was aware that certainly his wife was drinking too much. She was tippling, he noticed, during the day.
>   The problem acknowledged, he tried to analyze the source. The change from Alabama to New York had somehow disturbed her.[47]

Too austere and not sufficiently convivial, life in the North weighs on Emily. She is homesick for Paris, the city she loves — Paris City, Alabama, that is. Domestic quarrels between Emily and Martin are dreadful: "His youth was being frittered away by a drunkard's waste, his very manhood subtly undermined."[48] But emotion resurfaces as Martin contemplates his sleeping wife, and the story concludes with this image: "His hand sought the adjacent flesh and sorrow paralleled desire in the immense complexity of love."[49]

◆   ◆   ◆

The reviews of Houghton Mifflin's new volume were superb, and the book sold well. The *New York Times* expressed thanks that America was the country of Carson McCullers and William Faulkner.[50] Lacking Faulkner's power — but she was only thirty-four years old, and who can say how her oeuvre might have evolved had it not been for her illness? — Carson McCullers, like Faulkner, knew how to create atmospheres, unforgettable characters, and a network of endlessly evocative symbols. The situations she describes have a curious way of lodging themselves in memory. Oliver Evans, in discussing *The Ballad of the Sad Café*, draws parallels between Carson McCullers's fascinating Miss Amelia and the title character of Faulkner's "A Rose for Emily," who is shut up in her home, where no one except a black servant has set foot for ten years. Both are independent women proclaiming their strength with no fear of being marginalized. Both are viewed as somewhat crazy by their neighbors. The two stories give rise to the same readerly discomfort and prompt the same admiration for their fine craftsmanship. "It is condensed and disciplined and brilliant writing," writes Coleman Rosenberger about *Ballad* in the *New York Herald Tribune* of June 10, 1951, "which carries the reader along so easily on the wave of the story that he may not at first be aware how completely he has been saturated with symbolism."[51]

Time magazine declared that Carson McCullers was unquestionably one of America's dozen most important contemporary writers.[52] The following year, when the new collection was released in the United Kingdom, the *Times Literary Supplement*, constantly unfavorable to Carson in the past, now placed her "in the front rank of the younger American writers."[53] But most important was V. S. Pritchett's praise in the British *New Statesman and Nation:*

> What we look for is the occasional American genius — the Faulkner, for example — who will build his own original, imaginative or intellectual structures. . . .
> Such a genius is Miss Carson McCullers, the most remarkable novelist, I think, to come out of America for a generation. . . . She is a regional writer from the South, but behind her lies that classical and melancholy authority, that indifference to shock, which seem more European than American. She knows her own original, fearless and compassionate mind. The short novels and two or three stories now published in *The Ballad of the Sad Café* . . . make an impact which recalls the impression made by such very different writers as Maupassant and D. H. Lawrence. What she has, before anything else, is a courageous imagination; that is to say one that is bold enough to consider the terrible in human nature without loss of nerve, calm, dignity or love. She has the fearless "golden eye" of the title of one of her stories. . . . It may be objected that the very strangeness of the characters in a story like *The Ballad of the Sad Café* is that of regional gossip and, in fact, turns these characters

into minor figures from some American Powys-land [referring to the British Powys brothers, all writers with a rural focus]. They become the bywords of a local ballad. But the compassion of the author gives them their Homeric moment in a universal tragedy. There is a point at which they become "great." A more exact definition of the range of her genius would be to say that human destiny is watched by her in the heart alone . . . Miss McCullers is a writer of the highest class because of her great literary gifts; but underlying these, and not less important, is her sense of the completeness of human experience at any moment.[54]

Carson greatly needed these new successes, this recognition, the confirmation of her place among the era's great writers — early in 1952 she would be elected to the National Institute of Arts and Letters — to help her bear up under new blows. On the one hand, in late 1950, after consulting several physicians, Carson's suspicions were revealed to be true: she would never regain mobility in her paralyzed limbs. On the other hand, Reeves had left Banker's Trust for another detoxification treatment. Between two hospital stays he was welcomed in Nyack, where Carson organized a few dinner parties. Some of those who harshly criticized her after her death, first and foremost Lillian Hellman, willingly traveled to the small New York town to attend.

The Member of the Wedding's five hundred performances at the Empire were likely not unrelated to the sudden upsurge of interest in Carson. David Diamond, who had more or less lost sight of her and Reeves, came to one of Carson's parties in June — and what he wrote in his journal about Carson's alcoholism struck Virginia Spencer Carr as so important that she devoted more space to it than to the critical reception of *The Ballad of the Sad Café*. The young man, who had had a brief affair with Reeves when the two lived together in Rochester during the early 1940s, came up from New York with him on the evening of June 26, 1951. In his view Carson had never been so sickly, so fragile, so anguished and withdrawn, though her paralysis seemed less disabling than he had feared (Diamond had not seen Carson since her attack). He underlines that when he arrived, Carson was drinking whiskey as if it were orangeade and that she lived in an almost constant alcoholic haze — which is certainly true enough. However, he also states unequivocally that Carson did not realize the extent of her drinking, a surmise that is less certain.

If Diamond had read "A Domestic Dilemma," he would no doubt have been less unequivocal. Not once does he seem to consider Carson's feats of writing, achieved despite physical impairment and her drinking habit. His comments are little more than biographical anecdotes and romantic or sexual speculations. And his recollection of that particular evening in 1951 has an unpleasant tone, perhaps because Diamond found it distressing to recollect his younger days with Carson and Reeves and their common alcoholic failings. He delighted in seeing Reeves dry out and "become someone who's enjoyable to talk to." He declared that even Carson's mother had stopped drinking and was getting along better with her son-in-law because of it — an observation contradicted by Lillian Hellman. Having spent the night in Nyack, she found Marguerite Smith dead drunk in the kitchen at six o'clock in the morning.

◆ ◆ ◆

Just a month later, on July 28, Carson embarked for England on the *Queen Elizabeth.* Reeves was to return to the hospital to resume his detoxification treatment. That crossing was one of the most fantastic episodes in the couple's shared life, a scene that might have leapt off the screen of a delicious 1950s comedy into real life. At least that's the impression Carson's account conjures up.[55]

But whatever literary flourishes may have been added, one undeniable fact remains: Reeves McCullers stowed away on this ship as if playing a child's game writ large. Carson speaks of spotting someone who looked strangely like Reeves in a passageway. After the third such "encounter," she was so intrigued by the resemblance that she decided to consult the ship's passenger list, but the name James Reeves McCullers was nowhere to be found. On day three of the crossing, a cabin boy supposedly brought Carson a note signed by Reeves indicating that he was on board and needed her assistance. Carson claims to have sent him back a message saying, "That's nice. Are you free for lunch, by chance?" — a good punch line, though probably a writerly embellishment.[56] More likely, not having eaten since the ship had set sail, Reeves simply came out of hiding. Carson had to straighten matters out and pay his passage. When the *Queen Elizabeth* arrived in port, British authorities refused to let Reeves disembark, since he had no passport. A U.S. consul was called on board, and the embassy had to be called to vouch for his identity.

Then the comedy turned foul: Reeves obtained permission for a two-week stay, but everything went badly. He accompanied Carson to parties to which she had been invited. At Edith Sitwell's he got so drunk he wound up rolling on the floor. More than once he was found collapsed in a corner. Carson's British hosts, with characteristic composure, seem to have taken it in stride, but Carson was relieved when Reeves left. Once again out of work, he returned to Nyack, where, alone with Marguerite Smith, he waited for his wife to come back home.

His wait lasted three months. Carson's literary friends in England, foremost among them David Garnett — who considered her one of the only American writers worthy of respect — David Gascoyne, Rosamond Lehmann, and a few others, were willing and generous hosts who graciously welcomed fellow artists into their homes for a few days.

But Carson was no easy houseguest. She visited each friend for only a short time, except for David Gascoyne, her host for most of her stay. While there she worked on a long poem begun on board the *Queen Elizabeth*, "The Dual Angel: A Meditation on Origin and Choice." She would not finish it, though, until December in Nyack after falling ill in London. The illness sparked a new romantic adventure. Through David Gascogne she had met Katherine Cohen, the psychiatrist wife of her English editor. Cohen was immediately interested in Carson's clinical case and asked the author to allow her to treat her. Carson, thoroughly charmed by Dr. Cohen, said yes.

In her letters to Reeves, most of them undated and handwritten in pencil, Carson has a great deal to say about that new "imaginary friend," who "only started her studies at the age of 37 — she is now 46. And she had had to stop high school at 14 to earn a living."[57] Carson went into the hospital for tests. According to Katherine Cohen, the results all showed that nothing was organically wrong with Carson. Her paralysis was not due to a stroke; rather, its roots were psychological. She could be treated — and cured.

Today, in light of the correct diagnosis that Carson had suffered an untreated bout of rheumatic fever as a child, we can take the full measure of how cruel that error — and the wild hopes it engendered — was. Katherine Cohen proposed treating Carson through hypnosis, and Carson enthusiastically agreed, convinced that movement would soon be restored to her left arm and leg.

In her letters she expressed total faith that the hypnosis treatment would succeed. With a revival of attention and tenderness for Reeves, she said time and again how much she missed him. She worried about him, urged him to take heart: "You have just left and I miss you beyond telling. Darling, you must fight to get well — and stay well. I believe in you and trust you. And I know in my soul you *will NOT* fail me."[58] "I wonder what you think of the ambition you once had — to be a doctor," said she in another letter. "You have a pure and scientific mind. And such great love, humanity."[59] Writing to Reeves was an urgent need that Carson gave in to even when she was feeling unwell. Her longest letter, undated, reached Nyack on August 25. In it Carson tried to explain how ill she had been. In addition to a "brain convulsed by images of despair," she had been unable either to sleep or to walk for three days:

> Then there was a miracle. Do you remember that periscope [actually a kaleidoscope] that the Poors [Henry Varnum Poor was Carson's painter friend] gave me that first long year of illness — remember I used to marvel at it so many hours. Well, as the periscope shifts color and form at the flick of the wrist, then in some mysterious way the images and agonies that had assaulted me were transfigured — not diminished or anesthetized, but simply changed. . . . So obscurity became radiance, discord the most lucid harmony. . . . At this time I called [Katherine] Cohen. Remember I wrote you about her — the wife of Dennis Cohen of Crosset Press (pub). She and I had become friends. (I can see you now — leaning back and drinking a ginger beer — saying to yourself that now after all this the drama is going to commence — you can laugh if you want to — it's all quite clear and gay — I *don't* mean that in the campy way. She is a doctor and the first real doctor I have ever known, the only one, however loving, who did not go away, leaving me alone with sickness. I realized I had never felt such affinity for anyone — you know by now that she is my imaginary friend — but she is real. You have said many times that you dreaded the time when I would meet my imaginary friend. You feared you might be excluded. Now Reeves, that will *not* be. There is no one who knows more about the sorrow of seperation than [Katherine], and that will not happen — that is, unless you will it yourself — as you have done so many times. I am going to be well, in body and spirit, and that will make

me a better friend — altogether a lot nicer to have around the house.

You know, Reeves, I had sometimes dreaded to find my imaginary friend. For instance, I never expected her to look like much. If she had been ugly as homemade sin, blind in one eye and crippled with 6 strokes, if she had been like that [I] could have accepted her I suppose — although I would have been disappointed. But, darling, [Katherine] is the loveliest creature I ever saw. Her beauty will for a moment stop your breath.

There is so much to say and I have a torrent of images. . . .

One more thing, darling. I want to thank you for your understanding — your wisdom of heart that allows me to write you this letter. I am somehow exalted. Of course this won't last long. This illumination will go away — but it will come back — again and again. . . . In a few days [Katherine] is going to Amsterdam. No, I'm not plotting to stowaway in the fan belt of the plane (what *is* a fan belt?). Something of her will remain with me and she will return. I have felt that your frenzy about geographical seperation (my flying off to Europe and other places by myself) is due to a failure of your love for me — a failure of understanding that love and trust are one.[60]

Reeves, too, wanted to believe in Cohen's treatment, as he repeatedly wanted to believe that his relations with Carson would grow calmer. In fact, that is what constantly recurred, however provisionally: the two would separate in order to find each other again, then split up and reunite anew.

In London, alas, as might have been expected, the hypnosis treatment failed totally. Carson was in such despair that she believed her condition had taken a turn for the worse: her limbs were even stiffer and more painful than before. At the very least she wanted Katherine Cohen to console her with a shower of affection. Cohen, likely humiliated by her mistake, became instead more and more distant, cold, "professional." At the end of October Carson went back to Nyack. She was extremely depressed. To "take her mind off her troubles," Reeves suggested a trip to New Orleans, where she immediately developed a violent fever. The two travelers came home as soon as they could and went directly to the hospital, where Carson was treated for bronchial pneumonia and pleurisy. In the wake of that new scare both

Reeves and Carson finally decided to stop running away from each other, or fleeing together to providential places where they expected to smooth out their relationship. They told their friends that for a good, long time, they planned to stay in the United States and learn to live together again.

A vain promise — a commitment "for life" that lasted at most a few weeks.

7

"TOMORROW I'M GOING WEST"

L IKE UNSTABLE ADOLESCENTS, Carson and Reeves began
the year 1952 by doing exactly the opposite of what they had
just pledged to do: they left for Europe. First they would travel
to Rome, where their friend David Diamond was living. After that
they would see where the spirit moved them. Before departing, Carson spent the whole month of January working on a part of *Clock
Without Hands* called "The Pestle" (which appeared the following year
in *Mademoiselle* and in the Italian magazine *Botteghe Oscure*) and reading the screenplay for the film based on *The Member of the Wedding*.

Though her visitors may have thought that she lived in a perpetual
alcoholic haze, as David Diamond had observed several months earlier, Carson was utterly precise when it came to her work. She knew
that the real means of her survival resided in her writing; nothing and
no one — including herself — would take that away from her. Carson wrote a long letter to Fred Zinnemann, director of the film, saying
that the script seemed weak, totally devoid of the tense atmosphere essential to the drama: "For one thing, the basic theme of the play is
missing, that is, the will to belong. Frankie wants to be a part of the
wedding because it is her own particular symbol of togetherness. I believe that the soldier should be used as he again is someone who is desperately longing to belong . . . The script lacks cohesion and any sense
of form."[1]

Carson analyzed the screenplay almost scene by scene, and her remarks are all very perceptive. She acknowledged that the script was
only a first draft, saying she looked forward to a more polished ver-

sion. Carson asked Zinnemann to write to her in Rome, at David Diamond's, and made a date to meet him in Paris in the fall. He agreed with her remarks, and the two began a sustained correspondence devoted to perfecting the scenario that would last throughout the year.

On January 30 Carson, Reeves, and their boxer, Kristin, boarded the ocean liner *Constitution* en route to Naples. From there they went by car to Rome, where they stayed at the Hotel Inghilterra before moving into an apartment in Castel Gandolfo, a small city not far from Rome and known for being the pope's summer residence. Fortunately, the attorney Floria Lasky had taken charge of Carson's financial interests. She dispatched monthly allotments, which forced Reeves and Carson to keep track of their expenditures: they had to live on Reeves's pension and Floria Lasky's monthly remittance. The three months spent in Italy were rather chaotic and marked the end of their friendship with the composer David Diamond. Long gone were the days when they had come together in an amorous and creative threesome, during which Diamond dedicated to them, in 1941, his ballet *The Dream of Audubon.*

It is probably true that Reeves was sullen and demoralized, that Carson drowned her own ill humor in hard liquor and was impossible to bear. She was ill at ease in Italy, and she did not like the apartment they had rented in Castel Gandolfo. Still, she could not make up her mind to leave. Frankly, she did not know exactly where she wished to go. Reeves tagged along. It is easy enough to imagine that the couple had lost much of their former appeal, especially for someone who had known them ten years earlier. Nonetheless, the fact remains that, here again, there is something unpleasant about David Diamond's account. It seems somewhat odd that when Virginia Spencer Carr questioned him nearly twenty years after the fact, he was unable to examine his past from that temporal distance, preferring instead to hand over, to a biographer, fragments of his personal journal. In that journal Diamond meticulously listed what he believed to be "the facts of their visit," that is, all the petty affronts, the clichés, the mediocre thoughts that occur in the course of a day. To comment ironically on Carson McCullers's immaturity, then imperturbably assert that Reeves must have been thinking, "At last David has what I could not give him," is, to say the least, piquant.

Several of Carson's old friends were in Rome that spring as well, among them Wystan Auden. He no longer showed any great desire to see her, however. She spent more time with Truman Capote, who was also very fond of Reeves, but quarrels between her and Capote grew more and more frequent and violent. Two "brilliant terrors" — not to mention literary rivals — together in a room: it's not hard to imagine the explosions that such a combination could set off. Gore Vidal, also in Rome, would willingly have spent the night running around the Coliseum had that been the only way to avoid Carson McCullers. But since she hated Vidal just as vehemently, chances were good that they would steer clear of each other.

Carson received invitations to social gatherings from the Italians she had met during her first visit in the spring of 1947, including Alberto Moravia. More and more, she neglected to tell Reeves that he, too, had been invited to such gatherings. There is no point in dwelling on what shape Carson was in when she came home from these affairs — or what shape she found Reeves in on returning. It seems they started beating each other, which had never happened before. Reeves denied it, then conceded that he might have "shaken" Carson a bit. She claimed that he struck her with great violence. And on several occasions he threatened to kill her, once attempting to throw her out a window. André Bay, who tried to look after his author throughout her stay in Europe, remembers "various stories circulating about how Reeves supposedly tried to put Carson out the window in Rome. According to one, Carson, always fearing she would once again fall ill, is rumored to have said, 'If I ever have another stroke, please don't leave me that way — promise me you'll throw me out the window.' So one evening in Rome, the story goes, she was severely unwell, had again lost her ability to speak, and found it nearly impossible to get across to Reeves, who was dutifully carrying out his promise, that she had no desire to be thrown out the window."[2] True or false, the incident is "in the same key" as the overall experience of those two children suffering the effects of alcohol and desperation in Rome.

But, where her work was concerned, Carson always did what had to be done. Thanks to her literary connections, she published "The Dual Angel" in *Botteghe Oscure,* which would publish several of her pieces for the first time in Europe. Nor did she forget to stop and see her publisher in Milan when, toward the end of April, she and Reeves traveled to Paris by car with their dog and their trunks — trunks packed within a few hours when they abruptly decided that they had had enough of Italy.

Almost six years had passed since their first stay in France. Much had changed since the triumphant arrival of the little American prodigy, an exceptional novelist, who had been so endearing in her white cotton socks. (Carson still wore white socks.) No one was expecting the McCullerses in Paris, and the pair had no place to stay. As usual, John Brown came to the rescue, generously offering to help. The house that he, his wife, and their two little boys occupied in Brunoy, in Essonne, was very large. Why didn't Carson and Reeves come stay there?

Brown quickly realized, though a little too late, that his invitation had been extremely rash. Even in a very big house, life in the vicinity of Carson and Reeves was difficult. The painful memory of this visit would definitively alter the Brown family's relationship with Carson. They never saw one another again after Carson left Europe. "It was quite simply impossible," John Brown recalls:

> There is no point today in dredging up all the sordid details, and there were plenty. We could not live under the same roof with those two, whatever feelings of friendship we may have had: there was too much drinking, too much screaming, too many scenes, too many fights between people so drunk they were no longer in control of themselves. Reeves spent his time trying to stop drinking. Carson had ordered him to, though she herself drank all day long. Alcohol arrived by the case, and seeing my look of dismay, she would say with all the charm she could muster: "Don't worry, dear John, it's only wine." She couldn't make head nor tail of the mess her life was in, her very disabling illness, her desire to write, her impossible life with Reeves, her dependence on alcohol — and it's hard to know how much she even knew she was dependent. Carson would invite friends over, for example. Then, inexplicably, something would go wrong. She refused to make the slightest preparations and would not even leave her room to go greet them. Reeves was at a loss. So he got drunk. Those two had an abominable, cannibalistic relationship. But she was the vampire. With him she threw tantrums. She wanted him to wait on her, to attend to her every need. She had a colossal power of destruction.[3]

After a few weeks, furious and fearful that this pitiful spectacle would harm their young sons, the Browns asked the McCullerses to move out. It was a salutary decision for everyone concerned. Carson and Reeves began looking for a house in the country and, once they'd found one, were happy for a time. Their dream of having their own farm became almost a reality, even if the property that they acquired was not a farm but the former presbytery of a little village in Vexin called Bachivillers, about an hour outside of Paris and rather far for anyone liking lots of company. But for the moment Reeves and Carson gave the matter no thought, excited as they were about having their own place — and a garden — to arrange as they saw fit. There was a bit more than an acre of land, and the orchard was resplendent with apple, peach, and pear trees. Not long after they arrived, their alcohol consumption diminished, and they fought far less. Reeves was very good with his hands. He liked to make his living space comfortable and pleasant, as he had done on Thompson Street in Manhattan in 1949. At the post exchange, where his former military service entitled him to shop, Reeves filled the trunk of his car not only with bottles of alcohol — which had formerly taken up all the room — but also with nails, lumber to be turned into shelves, paint, brushes, and various other tools.

When Carson wrote to her friends in America, she cheerily informed them that, for the moment, she was working to the sound of pounding hammers. She sang the praises of the house, where life was very pleasant not only thanks to Reeves's abilities and taste but also because the dwelling had central heating and a bathroom, not yet common in France at the time. She urged her correspondents to visit this little corner of rural France that they would find so exotic. In addition, Madame Joffre, who took care of the house, was a very good cook; she would make nice little French meals for them. Reeves for his part talked about his kitchen garden, his fine vegetables, which, along with fruits from the orchard, allowed them to live quite inexpensively. Reeves also had an ornamental garden, for he liked flowers, as did Carson. But his greatest pleasure was planting the seeds, caring for the plants, watching them grow and bloom. As for the dwelling itself, Carson retained an equally fond memory of it many years later:

> The property was the most beautiful piece of land I've ever seen. It was called "L'Ancienne Presbyter," and was the place where the former [curé] used to live. . . . The orchard had plums, pears, peaches, figs, green gage plums, and even small walnut trees which rattle in the wind. The house even had central heating of a sort, as an Amer-

ican had restored it and had lived there. We had a very good French couple to look after the household and a gardener. There was a fire place in every room and our dogs, we had five boxers at the time, loved to doze before the fire, between swift sorties to investigate other smells from Madame Joffer's kitchen. In true French fashion, the Joffers fed us enormously. First soup, then a souffle, then meat and salad, and a fruit dessert. I've tried to find the recipe for Madame Joffer's vegetable soup, the world over, but without success. It was a small house, but Reeves and I had separate bedrooms and there was a guest room.[4]

Few friends would make the journey, however, whether from the United States or even Paris. An hour by car from the capital, Bachivillers was too far to drive just for a drink. And it was extremely difficult to arrange a get-together with Carson in advance: you could never be sure what mood she might be in at the appointed time, if she would really feel like seeing someone then, if she would be in a state to receive her guests properly, if Reeves would or would not be there to help her. One of her first visitors was Tennessee Williams, on his way to Italy with his companion Frank Merlo. The always impeccably faithful Tennessee came to share in his friends' fantasies, reconfirming what Carson had written to him when she was so gravely ill: "No matter where we are, there will always be room for you. You will come, won't you?"[5] Tennessee Williams the writer felt admiration for Carson, who was probably an even more mysteriously gifted writer than himself; "Tenn" the friend — whose first name Carson sometimes wrote as "10⁶" ("ten *et six*")[6] — felt compassion for the McCullerses, who never really found a way to live together but could not find a way to separate, either.

At Éditions Stock, André Bay decided to have everything that Carson McCullers wrote translated into French. An attentive and considerate editor, he, too, worried about how things might be going in Bachivillers. The house, which he found charming, and its occupants made "a rather favorable impression" on him:

I have good memories of Bachivillers, but it is true that I did not go there "in the latter days." Early on, the "team" appeared to be functioning well. Better than it had during their previous stay in France, despite the difficulties caused by Carson's infirmity. Reeves would type what Carson wrote. His left hand was damaged, too — less so than Carson's, of course. His wrist had been wounded during the war. They were trying to straighten themselves out, to "start fresh." But it didn't last. They were probably too isolated up there. And the tensions between them resurfaced. Too many of them.[7]

First, there were that summer's calamities. In the Austin archives there is a bill from the American Hospital in Neuilly for a two-day stay. No first name is given, so we can't tell whether Carson or Reeves was the patient, both spouses being "regular customers" of the establishment. Also in July, back home in Nyack, Carson's mother had a heart attack. Carson and Reeves took the first plane home. Once she was out of danger, they returned, after making her promise to visit them in Bachivillers. But a few weeks later she was hospitalized once again for a pulmonary embolism. This time Carson traveled to Nyack alone — now it was her turn to rush to Bebe's bedside rather than the other way around. There could no longer be any possibility that Marguerite Smith would make the journey to France; those two serious blows would leave her health permanently weakened. This misfortune also cost Carson the maternal tower of strength that for so many years had been her first and last resort in times of trouble.

In September Carson and Reeves moved back to Rome for two months. Carson was to work with the director Vittorio De Sica and the producer David O. Selznick on the movie *Terminal Station* — yet another disastrous episode. Convinced that nothing should stand in his way, Selznick was determined to make his wife, Jennifer Jones, the star of a European superproduction. Toward that end he decided to "treat himself" to Vittorio De Sica, though he himself kept a close eye on the project — if for no other reason than to superimpose on Italian neo-realism the Hollywood effects that would destroy the film's coherence. In addition to Carson, Selznick put a team of screenwriters to work. He had initially contacted Truman Capote, who refused the job because, first and foremost, he had to "get on with [his] own work." But as his biographer, Gerald Clarke, notes, "Writers, particularly those with empty bank accounts, should not be bound by such rash promises of artistic purity." Only a few weeks went by before Truman Capote agreed to replace Carson, who had just been fired.[8]

The prospect of humiliating Carson by filling a position in which she had just failed may have held considerable appeal for Truman Capote. The two former friends could not stand each other now. They were no longer on speaking terms. In one of those savory postscripts that he loved adding to his (already very funny and malicious) letters, Capote penned a vitriolic description of Carson and Reeves — which, sadly, is likely quite accurate: "Heaven knows there are enough old acquaintances about — I am going to buy a heavy veil to wear in the streets. Sister (the famous Carson McCullers, you remember *her*?) and Mr. Sister are frequently to be observed *staggering* along the Via Veneto, where they are now established members of the movie crowd (she is writing a movie for David Selznick); but of course Sister and Mr. Sister are too exalted, and usually too drunk, to recognize my poor presence."[9]

Capote was not mistaken. Reeves had taken to his bed as soon as the McCullerses arrived in Rome: it took him two days to recover from what he had drunk on the plane. He and Carson attempted to resume their "teamwork" mode of writing — she dictated, he typed — but things were not functioning properly. And Selznick's growing dissatisfaction only made matters worse. They held on to the idea that they were earning a good deal of money — and that they needed it. But it did no good. Reeves was taking sleeping pills. Their effect, combined with that of alcohol, sunk him into depression. He began to talk about killing himself. When Selznick told Carson that her work was not acceptable, that he would have to let her go, she gave in to mounting exhaustion, fell ill, and had to spend several days in an Italian clinic before heading back to France.

◆　◆　◆

The McCullerses' return to Bachivillers in October marked the start of a disastrous and irreversible course of events, a long descent into solitude and alcoholic isolation that would end in tragedy. Even Tennessee Williams stayed away, so depressing was it to see the state the couple were in. Doctors at the American Hospital, in particular Jack Fullilove, who had befriended the McCullerses, tried to help, attempting to extract them from their self-imposed confinement. Reeves and Carson both went into the hospital during this period for several short stays. They seem to have found some degree of comfort there.

A photograph taken on Thanksgiving Day in 1952 shows how

much energy it must have taken to spend an evening with the pair: Jack Fullilove, young and smiling, gazes tenderly at a pouting, demoralized Carson. Another friend, Valentine Sherriff — who was a great help to Reeves a few months later, though she failed to save him — is also doing her best to put up a good front. Reeves is in the right-hand corner of the snapshot and only partially visible. He is looking off to his left, essentially unrecognizable. Even though the autobiographical account that Carson wrote at the end of her life is particularly bitter — indeed, excessively so — her description of her relations with Reeves during that period speaks volumes:

> At this time Reeves said he was writing a book, which delighted me, so I built him a studio in one of the "Dependence [that is, in an outbuilding]." Every day he would go faithfully "to work" in his studio. I realized he was always rather tight at lunch, but didn't wonder too narrowly until I also realized that his studio was right over the wine and liquor cellar, which meant he only had to walk down a flight of stairs and bring up a jug whenever he wanted to. There was a further disappointment. I must say that in all of his talk of wanting to be a writer, I never saw one single line he'd ever written except his letters. Reeves' temper became more violent, and one night I felt his hands around my neck and I knew he was going to choke me. I bit him on his thumb with such violence that the blood spurted out and he let me go.[10]

Carson hung on because she had her work. But where was Reeves to find a reason to endure such an existence? Still, Carson's letters — often typed by Reeves — give the impression that things were taking their normal course. In November, for instance, Carson answered a letter from India, agreeing on behalf of her husband and herself to travel there in September or October of the following year. She also responded to mail from her German, Danish, and other publishers with meticulous precision.

In December she met with Otto Frank, Anne Frank's father, regarding a possible theatrical adaptation of the young girl's famous *Diary* — a job done in the end by Albert Hackett. Carson said again and again how much she was moved by her meeting with Frank. The two wrote back and forth for a time, but Carson finally decided against adapting Anne Frank's story. In his last letter Otto Frank said that her decision had been wise and that he hoped she would keep him informed of her progress on her novel.[11] And in fact Carson was soon writing to her agent, Audrey Wood, that she was devoting all of her energy to her new novel.[12]

In early January 1953 Fred Zinnemann wrote Carson a splendid long letter full of news about *The Member of the Wedding*. No sooner had the movie come out than it gave rise to radically opposed views among both critics and the general public. Certain periodicals, such as *Time* magazine, called it one of the ten best films of 1952; others found it vastly inferior to the play, which it transposed too literally, even using the same actors. "At any rate," added Zinnemann,

> I would like to tell you that it has been a great joy and privilege for me to make the picture, and to be associated — even in an indirect way — with the people who created the play. Personally, I am satisfied that this was a reasonably good and honest job of film-making, even though I still think that the film should have been made on the basis of the novel.
>
> In conclusion, I would like to express my very deep gratitude to you for the faith you had in me. Also, I sincerely hope that our paths will cross in the not-too-distant future, even though at the moment I am snowed under, trying to start a new picture — "From Here to Eternity." All my best to you.[13]

Carson answered him warmly on January 27, thanking him for his loyalty and for his movie — she still had not seen it since she was in France, but she had heard many good things about it.[14] Carson also wrote a few words about her new novel but still believed she might have to interrupt her work to adapt Anne Frank's *Diary*. She also touched on her unpleasant experience with Selznick and acknowledged that in fact it probably would have been better to adapt the cinematic version of *The Member of the Wedding* from the novel rather than the play.

In other words, Carson's letters are intellectually rigorous and full of common sense. The impression they give is of a perfectly organized, mature writer juggling film adaptations, work in the theater, a new novel, magazine articles, and so on, with faultless precision.

An engaging interview conducted by Hans de Vaal at the Hôtel Castiglione in Paris and published in the April 1953 issue of the Dutch magazine *Litterair Passport* gives the same impression. Carson started off by saying that she had never visited the Netherlands but that she was very interested in this country, especially after having read Anne Frank's *Diary*. When asked why several of her main characters are children, she responded: "There is so much truth in children and so little selfconsciousness. . . . It always strikes me that they are so capable of losing and finding themselves and also losing and finding those things they feel close to." To the remark "You probably know that your work has been judged in terms of 'spiritual isolation of the individual,'" she answers, "No, I think that is a wrong interpretation. I do believe that any body who makes his own life is to be lonely and I think this loniless implies a condition of moral isolation."

"Do you consider moral isolation to be universal?" the interviewer queried.

"Yes," Carson McCullers affirmed, adding, "although I think it is more prevalent in the United States than in Europe. Many times I have stated, in France, the more conscious feeling of belonging to a family."

A question regarding the different critical interpretations of her books and her reaction to them elicited this succinct response: "I think some people are wrong. For instance," she went on, "Singer, in *The Heart Is a Lonely Hunter,* is taken by some critics to be a person who pretends to understand all the people who come to visit him and talk to him. But Singer doesn't understand a thing and doesn't pretend to understand a thing; only all the people in the novel *think* — or *believe* — Singer understands them. And that is something quite different. He is really an emotional catalyst for all the other characters."

Carson also offered this explanation of her presence in Europe: "Both Reeves and I love France. We have many friends here, very many friends. And you know, it is less expensive here than in America. We'd always been poor until the play *The Member of the Wedding* brought us some money, and the movie version, too." Regarding writers who interested her, Carson said, unsurprisingly: "I like Faulkner, yes, specially Faulkner, in particular *The Sound and the Fury.*"

Vaal's political questions — notably, about the race problem — reveal no change in Carson's positions: "One cannot be revolutionary enough about that. When I say revolutionary I don't mean in the communistic way, of course. I believe that people ought to be made [aware] of new ideas. It is like art. What value has a creation that cannot be shared? All this, of course, is dependent on time. Many people find it very difficult to accept something they are not used to." Does she have plans for the future? Of course. "Reeves and I want to go to India. We're interested in that country. We will probably go next year."[15]

◆ ◆ ◆

Behind the image of Carson McCullers the great American novelist fresh from a huge theatrical success, steadfast in her aesthetic and political positions, sure of her marriage and its future — "Both Reeves and I love France," "Reeves and I want to go to India" — there lay another figure. Each one had its element of truth, and there is no way to make the two harmonize perfectly. Behind the first image — or beside it, for by no means did Carson try to hide her darker side — there was "Sister," a thirty-six-year-old, half-paralyzed, alcoholic woman who called her husband "Brother." And there the two of them were, in a pretty little house in a very French village, yelling too loud and too late at night, in English. This was also the time in France when "U.S. go home" was scrawled everywhere on walls and on roads and on the parapets of bridges . . .

Suddenly, in the early days of 1953, there came a lull in their fighting, as if that year's abundant snow, soft and white as in the dreams of little Lula Carson Smith back in Columbus, had muffled their cries. The winter in their region was unusually severe, and for nearly two weeks the couple was snowbound at the Ancien Presbytère. Carson wrote every day and declared she was progressing once again on her manuscript. Reeves helped her do the typing and wrote a few letters. He spoke amusingly of being "snowed in" so close to Paris and offered news of Kristin, the dog he was so fond of: she had had six puppies, four of which they sold. The other two, Nicky and Automne, they decided to keep. Finally, Reeves described the "ulcer diet" he was following and said that he was feeling a great deal better on account of it.

That bright spell would be their last. When the weeks of snow came to an end, predictably enough, they were ill. Carson wrote in March to her sister, Rita: "We have both been a little ill but now with spring here and some sun we are feeling better. Flowers are coming up and the garden will soon be lovely." And in response to a question posed by Rita, she furnished the following details about J. T. Malone, the protagonist of *Clock Without Hands:*

> Malone is engaged in a struggle with his soul which is more important than his physical disease. There are times when he seems lost in hatred, prejudice and cruelty but in the end his soul turns to goodness although his body dies.
>
> (Incidentally before deciding on leukemia I talked with four doctors and consulted several case histories so the medical data is correct.)
>
> What are symbols? To me they are personal cyphers to the solution of a work. Why one symbol comes instead of another, I don't know.
>
> More narrowly the symbol of the white blood cells in the case of leukemia crowding out the dark ones is peculiarly a symbol of the South. . . .
>
> This book, a long one, is about good and evil, prejudice and the affirmation of the dignity of life. Malone's disease, with the attendant moral agony, quickens and intensifies these conflicting emotions.[16]

Later in the year Carson's British publisher, Dennis Cohen, expressed to her his admiration for the beginning of *Clock Without Hands,* which he had just read:

> I want very definitely to congratulate you on a brilliant and encouraging start to your novel. It has all the power and quality of the stories in THE [BALLAD] and the compassion of THE HEART IS A LONELY HUNTER. It is the beginning of another great book and I do beg of you to do your utmost to continue it. God, or whoever it is, made you a great writer, and rare gifts such as these must not be neglected.[17]

◆   ◆   ◆

In Bachivillers spring may well have arrived, but those who made their way to the Ancien Presbytère found two people adrift. Andrée Chédid, the soul of discretion and delicacy, did not dwell on any negative impression she might have gotten when she stopped by the McCullers home. In the letter that she sent to Carson on March 4, after her visit, she simply said that they had not really had time to talk "the other day . . . but your wonderful books are an invisible and strong bond between yourself and those who love them."

Of all modern novels that I have read "The Member of the Wedding" and "The Heart is a lonely Hunter" are those that have touched me the most deeply.

I should be very glad to meet you again and if you and your husband come down to Paris let us know and come see us.

I am sending you two books of mine. One is poetry and the other my first novel. I have heard that you wrote poems, have you had any published? I would love to read them.

Please give my kindest regards to your husband and let me tell you again what a joy it was for us to meet you both.

Croyez, chère Carson McCullers, à mon amitié et à mon admiration profunde [I send to you, dear Carson, my friendship and profound admiration].[18]

Sometimes Carson would not say a single word to her guests. It was as if she were completely overwhelmed. Reeves was less absent, less lost in public than she was, which is probably why a more positive image of him appears in various memoirs. But when they were alone, he was frightening, and Carson got scared.

Fortunately, the persistent myth of "poor tender and devoted Reeves, the 'blocked' writer devoured by a man-eating Carson" is challenged by Janet Flanner, whom Virginia Spencer Carr met in 1972. A few years later Jacques Tournier also visited the distinguished *New Yorker* columnist, but by then her memory was gone. Janet Flanner did not see Reeves and Carson much during the Bachivillers period, despite their friendship, because she was too old, she said, to go for weekend jaunts in the country — and far too worldly-wise to take the risk of being the houseguest of such hosts. Nonetheless, she traveled to the Ancien Presbytère one afternoon, during which Reeves drank several glasses of what she at first thought was spring water — it turned out to be straight gin: "I was very fond of Reeves," she remembered. "Of course, he was a liar and thief, unreliable — especially a liar. . . .

And Carson? Ah, she was a sharp persuader if ever I met one. One couldn't possibly know Carson and not realize that she also created her own truths. Part of her fictions became part of her truths. Reeves was a storyteller, too, but he was not gifted. And that was the great difference . . . one of the many great differences between them that was apparent. Yet Reeves was a very courageous man, a very brave man. And he was simply splendid when he went overseas to serve his country during the war — the country that he so loved. But together they were not good for each other.[19]

A great reader, a person of culture who had been around artists and writers all her life, Janet Flanner told a simple truth: Reeves was not gifted, he had no talent. He could not have been a writer. But this truth continued to be fiercely contested more than forty years after Reeves's death — and more than thirty years after that of Carson. Some people may never stop believing that Carson, the recognized writer, constructed her works on a foundation of fakery, compromise, and broken promises, whereas the man whose compositions dazzled tenth-graders and who never wrote another word must have endured some sort of personal or social oppression that erased any chance of success. And when a couple is made up of a woman who creates and a man who cannot, specters of castration and phantom bloodsuckers are often found abroad in the land.

But as Janet Flanner observed, Carson and Reeves probably were not good for each other. It is certain that each ceaselessly wounded the other, that their relationship alternated between brief intervals of unrealistic euphoria and long-lasting disasters that were all too real. Perhaps they would not place well on any measure of conjugal bliss, but that is not the sole standard of intensity in living. Their respective offenses could be aired until the end of time — but they pertain to their personal life, not to literary creation. And on this point the record is indisputable. If indeed a writer is someone who writes no matter what, then Carson McCullers, the sickly, paralyzed, alcoholic, and depressed Carson McCullers, was a writer, and Reeves was not.

◆　◆　◆

Reeves threatened suicide more and more frequently. Even as early as 1941, when he and Carson divorced, Reeves had spent an evening telling David Diamond that suicide seemed to him the only way out and that sooner or later he knew he would end up killing himself. For a long time friends did not take his suicidal threats seriously. When he threatened to jump out a window, people thought it was the alcohol talking. They calmed him down, and he eventually let them talk him out of it. In his *Memoirs* Tennessee Williams speaks of witnessing one of those scenes at the Hôtel du Pont Royal in Paris, where he had come to attend the Parisian premiere of a film starring Anna Magnani. Reeves and Carson were there, too. Carson phoned Williams in his room:

> "Oh, Tenn, darling, we've had to move from the fifth floor to the second because Reeves is threatening to jump out the window. Please come at once and try to dissuade him."
>
> ... [S]o I rushed to their room.
>
> "What's this about suicide, Reeves? You can't be serious about it!"
>
> "Yes, completely."
>
> "But why?"
>
> "I've discovered that I am homosexual."
>
> Not foreseeing, of course, that he was really going to kill himself a year or two later, I burst out laughing.
>
> "Reeves, the last thing I'd do is jump out a window because I'm homosexual, not unless I was forced to be otherwise."
>
> Both the McCullerses were amused by this, and Reeves's suicidal threat was put aside for a time. [20]

Legend has it that in the spring and summer of 1953, Reeves suggested to Carson that the two commit suicide together. Some have absolutely refused to explore this hypothesis. Jacques Tournier, for example, calls "the idea that Reeves had hidden two ropes in the trunk of his car before dragging Carson deep into the forest one night to hang himself with her on a good, solid branch" an "absurd episode of the golden legend."[21] Tennessee Williams, conversely, presents it as incontestable truth. At the Ancien Presbytère, writes Williams, "there was a cherry tree which Reeves kept suggesting to Carson that they should hang themselves from."

> He even had two ropes for the purpose. But Carson was not intrigued by this proposition.
>
> One of her relentless illnesses forced her to return to Paris for medical treatment.

Reeves drove her in, but on the way he produced the two ropes and again exhorted her to hang herself with him.

She pretended to acquiesce, but she persuaded him to stop at a roadside tavern and get them a bottle of wine to fortify themselves for the act.

Soon as he entered the tavern, Carson clambered out of the car and hitchhiked a ride to the American Hospital in a suburb of Paris.

She never saw poor Reeves alive again. He killed himself, some months later, with a bottle of barbiturates and booze.

How lightly I write of these dreadful remembrances!

How else could I present them to you, so few of whom have known Carson and Reeves?[22]

It is not so much the tone of his account that is light — its emotion and decency are evident — as the story itself: it is difficult to picture the handicapped Carson McCullers escaping Reeves's clutches in the middle of the night somewhere in the French countryside and then hitching a ride to the American Hospital. Still, she was well and truly terrified. And it is equally light to contend, with just as little proof, that she calmly departed for the United States, telling Reeves to pack their bags and come along.

Gone forever were the days when the two of them could plan a common future, try to live another life, embark on one of their famous "fresh starts." Carson could no longer live under the same roof with Reeves, especially far from the city. After exactly sixteen years of a strange life together, two marriages, countless scenes, many illnesses, and more or less sheer madness — but also laughter, shared dreams, the renewed desire to come together again — something had broken in two, and no one can say with any certainty how.

Late that summer Carson flew back to Nyack alone. She had brought almost no luggage, perhaps because she left in haste, perhaps because the indispensable Marguerite Smith, likely too easily fatigued to fulfill her former stewardship functions, would not be there to meet her. Once again, Carson asked John and Simone Brown to help her. They saw to sending her the trunk that Reeves had packed. Above all, Carson wanted her books and records back. And her silverware. She wrote to the Browns and to others who she thought might assist her in getting her things shipped back to the United States. About Reeves she said not a word. Despondent, he had stayed on alone at the Ancien Presbytère with the dogs. Carson apparently had left him no money. He was penniless. Then he wrecked the car, which left him with no transportation. He was deeply depressed, did not eat, and lost a lot of weight. His telephone service was cut off.

Carson was growing impatient because none of the possessions she was waiting for had arrived in New York. Still she made no reference to Reeves. She wanted what belonged to her, that's all. And yet Simone Brown had warned her that things were going very badly at Bachivillers:

> I am sorry of the delay in sending your things, but, I am doing my outmost. Reeves was here for a few days and we have packed one trunk containing your clothes and the silverware. I am now waiting for Reeves' phone call since he was to handle the business with the American Express. . . . Mme Joffre . . . and her husband are quite desperate and alarmed. . . . Reeves is drinking quite heavily these days and that is also a cause of distress for your couple.[23]

A few weeks earlier Madame Joffre, who must have liked Carson and Reeves — why else would she not have promptly quit looking after that incredible household? — had written a letter to Carson in which she attempted to mask her anxiety. It was the touching letter of a simple woman, written in French:

> Mr. Price asked me to send some more things to Brunoy [where the Brown family lived], but Monsieur has not given me permission to send them. Mr. Price told us that you were in good health and very calm. My husband has not yet recovered from his accident. Your little pups are superb. Please say hello to your family for me. Mr. McCullers is well, but he is quite sad to be separated from you. If you would be so kind, Madame, please let me know what you decide, whether you will be staying where you are or intend to return to Bachivillers.
> Henri and I send our sincere kind regards and love.
> Love from Mr. McCullers.[24]

"I feel that there is so much before us," Reeves had said a few months after their second marriage. "We are in the full growth and maturity of our lives. However, I have no intention of allowing us ever really to grow old."[25] Eight years had passed since then, and there was nothing "before them" that fall, no future for the two of them together. Adults they did not become; but they did grow old. Indeed, they were a very old couple who had consumed and cannibalized and destroyed one another. "And nothing I do or feel is good unless I can share it with you," Reeves went on to say in that same letter from 1945. Nothing must in that case have been good, for there truly was nothing left to share.

Since the telephone was down at the Ancien Presbytère, Jack Fullilove and Valentine Sherriff decided to go there in person one day in late October. Reeves was in a daze and had lost more than twenty pounds. Valentine Sherriff persuaded him to come to Paris, to the Hôtel Château-Frontenac in the eighth arrondissement at 54 rue Pierre-Charron, where she herself was staying. She paid for his room and gave him a little spending money. Reeves started eating again and going out here and there in town. Almost every evening he had dinner with her and Jack Fullilove. But during the day he just hung around, bored and feeling useless. "Frankly, neither Valentine nor I had any idea that he was in such deep despair," Jack Fullilove confided much later.[26]

On the morning of November 19, a maid found Reeves's inanimate body, covered with vomit, in his bed. He was dead. He had taken a very large dose of barbiturates with an enormous quantity of alcohol. That combination made him vomit when he was already nearly unconscious, and he suffocated. His friends could not understand what had happened, although they knew of Reeves's suicidal tendencies. He had called several of them the day before — the Browns, for example, and Jack Fullilove — to announce that he was returning to the United States. Or at any rate that is what they thought he meant when he said, "Tomorrow I'm going west." But in fact he was telling them that he was going to die. Reeves knew that the expression "going west" had been used in the past, particularly during World War I, by soldiers who believed the end was near. Some of his friends probably knew it as well, but, out of context, they had paid no attention, perceiving Reeves's adieu as no more than a simple goodbye. After all, for an American in Paris who had decided to go home, "Tomorrow I'm going west" was not such an unusual remark.

On November 18 Reeves McCullers had also sent a telegram to his wife: "Going west — trunks on the way." He had sent flowers to Janet Flanner and a curious message to Truman Capote — as if to issue one last provocation, to allow a final chance that someone might understand what he was going to do and try to stop him.

Janet Flanner offered two versions of the incident. To Oliver Evans she said she had received a magnificent bouquet sent by Reeves on November 18. She had called him to say what an extravagance it was, and he had made jokes along the lines of "Don't worry — it's my funeral."[27] In the account she gave Virginia Spencer Carr a few years later, the flowers were still as abundant and beautiful; indeed, there had even been several bouquets over the course of the last week of Reeves's life. The last one arrived the day after his death with a calling card bearing this phrase: "From the man across the Styx."[28]

These words are exactly the same ones that Truman Capote recalled, as his biographer reports:

> In November Truman received a call from Carson's husband, Reeves McCullers. "This is your friend from across the River Styx," said Reeves — a bit of black humor that Truman did not fully appreciate until a few days later. Carson had angrily left for America, refusing to advance Reeves any more money, and Truman invited him to his hotel for dinner that night. Reeves never appeared, and it was that night, apparently, that he committed suicide. "Carson treated him very, very badly," said Truman afterward. "There was nothing wrong with Reeves except her. He should have been running a gasoline station in Georgia, and he would have been perfectly happy.

At Carson's insistence, Reeves's ashes were buried in France, rather than Georgia, as his family wanted, and Truman, much shaken, was one of only a handful who attended his funeral in early December. "My youth is gone," he lamented to one of the other mourners.[29]

The young Truman Capote — he was twenty-nine years old — was there that day in early December 1953 in front of the American Legion mausoleum at the new cemetery in Neuilly. He and not many others. A few servicemen were present to pay the final honors to one of their own and to fly the American flag next to the mortal remains of Captain James Reeves McCullers, who had landed one morning in June 1944 on a Normandy beach to liberate France and had died nine years later, at forty years of age, in a hotel room in that same country, drunk, alone, and desperate.

There was also a group of Reeves's friends, fifteen people perhaps — and one whose absence loomed huge. Carson McCullers had remained across the Atlantic, where day was barely dawning.

Janet Flanner had made several promises to Carson, among them that she would give her friend back home a detailed description of the funeral ceremony. "Darling Carson, many friends came, to think of Reeves + you at the service in the American church. John Brown read the 23rd Psalm with his delicate pronunction + musical voice, after the minister had announced that you had requested it," she wrote in her December 5 letter. Flanner observed that "the Bach was decently played by the organist" and described the flowers, among them her own: "The flowers I had sent for Natalia & me behaved disgracefully, the bouquet falling apart as it lay against the flag-draped box." She then gave an almost exhaustive list of those present at the cemetery, where a "most touching ceremony" was held.

> We all then threw flowers in, one by one. I threw in narcissus with my left hand & then with my right threw a great red rose saying, "This is goodbye from Carson, darling Reeves. She wanted me to kiss you goodbye," & turned away crying. We were all weeping. Truman had been weeping & I took him by the hand & we walked out toward the gate. In Odette's car he told how he could not forget that he had been with you two when you had first started for Europe, in the bus that took you to New York & Reeves kept saying to the other passengers, "You think this is just a New York bus for me? Oh no, this bus is starting me off to Paris, do you hear me? I am going to Paris, that is where we're going," all this said in his joy to go there.[30]

On the back of Flanner's letter was a handwritten note: "There was a photographer at the cemetery and his pictures will set for you the final scene."

It had taken more than ten days to organize Reeves McCullers's burial. Dr. Robert Myers, the couple's physician at the American Hospital, had written to Carson: "As we have explained, in as much as he was discovered in the hotel some hours later, there is always the question of determining the exact cause of death. We can do nothing about final services until then."[31] The cause of death was determined to be asphyxiation, as Jack Fullilove had observed, but various rumors circulated on the subject at the time. The military authorities attributed Reeves's death to natural causes, which allowed his widow to continue getting part of his pension. The *New York Times* obituary mentioned the automobile accident Reeves had in fact been in — weeks earlier — wondering if his death might have been related to the crash. Once the investigation into the cause of death was completed, a decision had to be made regarding whether or not to ship the body back home to America. That question gave rise to one of those sordid family arguments that can crop up at the most tragic times.

It was the wife's place to decide where her husband's body would be laid to rest. Carson thought that Reeves should be buried in Paris — that his body should remain in the city he had loved so much, that his name should join those of the soldiers who fell to rid Europe of Nazism. That kind of symbolism was beyond the understanding of Reeves's family, who were staunchly opposed to the idea. They maintained that Carson was being stingy, that she wanted to leave Reeves's body in France on account of the high cost of repatriation. The producer and agent Cheryl Crawford tried to raise the necessary funds to bring Reeves back to the United States. She called Lillian Hellman, among others, and asked her to make a donation. Hellman did so, thinking Carson's conduct intolerable. That incident only fueled Hellman's exasperation with what she perceived as Carson's greed, which contrasted so sharply with Reeves's great generosity. She failed to mention, however, that if Reeves was generous, it was with Carson's money, since she had long been the couple's sole source of financial support. Besides which, all those people who wanted to repatriate Reeves's body had only the vaguest idea of conditions in Europe during World War II and understood nothing about Reeves's passionate relationship to that continent — which he had tried to pass on to Carson without really succeeding. At least she herself understood what caused him to be so attached to Europe — to begin with, the feeling of having existed in his own right as a soldier there without her.

The disagreement might have been less likely to degenerate into a sinister settling of scores if Carson had been in Nyack when the news of Reeves's suicide arrived and had made her decision right away. But she was traveling in Georgia, the state of her birth, collecting information and memories with a view to writing an article on her native region. So on November 19, 1953, Carson was in Clayton at the home of the novelist Lillian Smith and her friend Paula Snelling when her sister, Rita, called to tell her Reeves had died. Rita did not have the courage to speak to Carson directly and asked Lillian Smith to break the news herself. As Carson had had quite a bit to drink, Smith preferred to wait until the following morning and entrusted the delicate task to Paula Snelling. Indeed, it was Snelling who provided her version of the facts to Virginia Spencer Carr in 1970, in such a way as to make Carson look nearly indifferent to her husband's demise.[32] Her account goes no further than Carson's visible reactions, from which she draws conclusions that betray first and foremost the conventionality of Paula Snelling. For her, there is clearly a "good way" — along with several bad ways — to react to the death of a loved one.

Carson did not know the good way. She did not say a word when she was told of Reeves's death. Then she asked for a drink. After a first glass she began phoning various people, among them her mother, her sister, her lawyer, and her agent. Over the course of that day, according to Mrs. Snelling, Carson supposedly forgot she was paralyzed, using her formerly nonfunctional arm to pick up the telephone and open doors before losing mobility again the next day. The episode struck Mary Mercer, Carson McCullers's last doctor, as totally far-fetched — as even a shocking mistruth. Mrs. Snelling's version of events is probably reliable, however, where Carson's consumption of alcohol is concerned: she downed a whole bottle of whiskey that day.

Not feeling able to return directly to Nyack, Carson called one of her acquaintances in Augusta, Georgia (about a hundred miles from Clayton), Dr. Cleckley, a psychiatrist whom she had met in 1948 when she was deeply depressed. She then went to Augusta for three days and did not head back up north until November 25 to arrange with authorities in France all the practical details of Reeves's funeral. The dispute over Reeves's burial place began at this time. Dr. Cleckley, too, said that Carson did not give him the impression of being in distress or of feeling guilty with regard to the death of her husband.[33] Interesting choice of words, from a psychiatrist. Is he implying that she should have felt that way?

Carson McCullers was indeed urged to feel guilty about this suicide or at least to let it be known that she believed herself to be. Not once did she do so. She even declared loudly and firmly that she was in no way to blame. Despite these denials, another psychiatrist, Dr. Ernst

Hammerschlag — who sent her several years later to Mary Mercer, thereby saving her life — nonetheless believed that she was overwhelmed with guilt over Reeves's tragic and solitary death. Taking one side or the other is of no great interest here; but, though only Carson knew what she was feeling — despair, guilt, hatred, resentment, or whatever else — it would be absurd to think that she could have been utterly indifferent to Reeves's death.

Tiresome bromides about suicide colored the accounts of Reeves's death, both at the time and long afterward. The letters of condolence contain every conceivable platitude, along with some surprises. Comments run the gamut from the classical "I can't believe it's true" or "How can we tell you how much we loved that man?" to "I have just now read the news in the *New York Times,* and it has left me speechless" to the astonishing letter from Natalia Danesi Murray, who worked in Italy for Mondadori publishers and had known Carson since 1947:

> In the disappeance of Reeves there is a measure of greatness because it has been the supreme act of deliverance of liberation from a destructiveness that was engulfing you both. Whether it was fate or the act of will, it must be looked at as the one important and positive gesture of a weak soul; as the one positive, support, the supreme gift, to a genious: you. Do not regret it. Reeves has found his peace and with his peace he will have given you your peace, in life — for you greatness is in living. Bless you Natalia.[34]

Nearly twenty years after Reeves's death, when Virginia Spencer Carr conducted her research, the comments made about this suicide were still every bit as contradictory, every bit as passionate, indeed, every bit as vicious. Reeves's friends had completely forgotten all the problems he had had, problems mentioned in a letter Dr. Myers wrote to Carson right after her husband's death: "All of us here feel badly about the whole matter, in spite of the troubles Reeves gave this year. Don't forget, they were real problems to him, too. He was [mentally] sick, and we must all look back at it from that angle."[35]

But in the memories of those who idealized him, Reeves was perfectly normal, easy to talk to, with a keen and lively sense of humor. In short, he was the best thing that ever happened to Carson McCullers, and she destroyed him. Some came very close to accusing her of push-

ing Reeves to suicide. Tennessee Williams himself told Carr —
"Reeves died, ultimately, out of great love for Carson. His was a desperate loneliness. Without her, he was an empty shell." He then
launched into what for him is a surprisingly banal attempt to explain
Carson's reaction: "The only thing Carson ever did that I did not like
was casting off Reeves as she did and showing no feeling for him or his
memory after he was dead. She spoke of him in the most unkind
terms, and it always upset me. Reeves died for her, yet she refused to
admit it."[36]

It's startling to find Tennessee Williams contending that people kill
themselves for someone else or something else rather than because
they can't live with themselves any longer. It is much less surprising,
however, to hear Virginia Spencer Carr claim that "Carson . . . suffered less from Reeves's death than did her mother or sister."[37] Jordan
Massee, for his part, as always, took Carson's side. With no apparent
scores to settle, he concludes: "For one to expect compassion from
Carson at that moment revealed, also, a lack of compassion for *her.*"[38]

Curiously, few have attempted to see things from Carson McCullers's point of view. Why has it been crucial to so many that she
shoulder the entire responsibility for her husband's death, that she
even be seen as having wanted Reeves to die? Why make her into a
monster? Isn't that asking her to pay a steep price for her success, or,
even more to the point, for her resolve to keep on writing in spite
of her illness, in spite of Reeves's death, and then in spite of her loneliness?

Other than Jordan Massee, the people who defend Carson are
the ones who understand her work as a writer. Whit Burnett, for example, as a professor and a magazine editor, had been there when she
first started out: "With Carson, compassion transcended talent. Her
creative and life drives were based on compassion. She never took
advantage of anyone — or anything."[39] Or Francis Price, who worked
for Doubleday publishers in Paris in the early 1950s: "Most people who knew Carson *well* loved her until the day she died, and love
her still."[40]

About suicide, feelings of guilt, loneliness — Reeves's death made
her dependent once again on her mother, now weak and unwell —
Carson expressed herself in books rather than in face-to-face conversations, which inevitably fall short. Can she really be criticized for it? In

the excellent short story "The Haunted Boy," a youngster named Hugh, returning home and not finding his mother there, is overcome by anguish, remembering "the other time" his mother disappeared. He had found her, finally, bathed in her own blood after a suicide attempt. "Hugh could . . . tell no one of the empty house and the horror of the time before." Increasingly terrified of the deserted house and its hostile- or deformed-looking objects, Hugh feels a kind of hatred welling up both for his friend John, whom he detains for fear of being left alone — "He hated John, as you hate people you have to need so badly" — and for his mother, who has simply gone out shopping for clothes.[41]

Some years later Carson wrote *The Square Root of Wonderful,* a play that in many ways is an exorcism of Reeves's death. Mollie, *Square Root's* female protagonist, has married her husband twice and has recently separated from him: "When I was a child," Mollie says, "I could still live with you. You could beat me and I could still love you the next day. We have been like children, Phillip, primitive like children. Sexy, sure, but primitive like children."[42] After Phillip's suicide Mollie wonders why she never managed to help him: "If I had truly helped him, he would be alive today. But I was responsible and so were you. I nursed him, I lived with him, I loved him, for fifteen years, so let me alone, leave me to my grief."[43]

In the preface to that same play, Carson writes, as if in passing, "Certainly I have always felt alone."[44] To escape that loneliness, which frightened her when she was not writing, Carson had habitually gone in search of Reeves. Together they resumed — always temporarily — their strange, still largely unexplainable relationship: that of two aged children who wished to get along but never quite managed to do so, no more than they succeeded at living together. This odd alliance she had formed with the "first boy who kissed her" was nonetheless in the end what had oriented, organized — and disorganized — her life for more than sixteen years, nearly half of her existence.

When Reeves decided not to be there anymore, Carson was only thirty-six years old. Not only was Carson's youth coming to an end, as Truman Capote had said about his own at Reeves's funeral, but an entire way of relating to the world was becoming impossible. The wild plans — changing every three days — to journey to Europe, then press on as far as India, to stay in the United States and live on a farm, to take a flat in Manhattan's Dakota because she had just earned a little money, or to share an apartment on the sixth floor of a building with no lift when Carson could no longer climb stairs — all of that was well and truly over, forever. The time had come to see reality otherwise and to learn the difference between "feeling alone" and "being alone."

8

SOMETHING FROM TENNESSEE

THE STATE OF Georgia loomed large in Carson's life. It is where Lula Carson Smith was born; where she got to know James Reeves McCullers; where, by marrying him in the living room of the house where she had spent her adolescence, she became Carson McCullers; where she was staying when she learned that Reeves had just died; and where she went in late 1953, after her aunt died in Columbus, to complete the trip interrupted by Reeves's suicide.

Carson would never see Columbus or Georgia again after that. Except for brief visits to the faithful Edwin Peacock in Charleston, she saw little of the South from then on. She had always said that she was not at all fond of Columbus, even though that city, with its stifling heat and its oppressive social mores, never ceased to nourish her imagination and sharpen her thinking. But in the article that she had been composing for the magazine *Holiday* at the very moment when Reeves was killing himself in Paris, she allowed herself to wax a bit nostalgic. Written during the weeks after Reeves's death, Carson's essay was rejected by *Holiday* — they were looking for a lighter, more descriptive, less personal piece. One version of the essay, preserved in her archives in Austin, is called "Untitled Article on Georgia." The undated manuscript consists of thirty-seven pages and begins, "After many years in Europe I visited my home state, Georgia. Until that time I did not realize that I was homesick, homesick for Georgia countryside, Georgia voices, Georgia ways. I wanted to go back and restore my contact with the state and see old friends."[1]

The essay combines certain didactic inclinations, its historical overview of the state's founding, for example, with recollections of Carson's reunion with Lillian Smith, who "feels passionately about the problems of the Negro." Carson McCullers — and these are the best parts of the manuscript — was carried away by the joy of rediscovering simple things such as Georgia breakfasts, complete with "fish roe and grits or at least eggs or maybe country sausage." "I have never gotten over this orange juice, coffee breakfast they have up north," she confides. She took great pleasure in the intimacy shared by people from the South. "Georgia people are so much more intimate than Northerners." "A great many girl children are called 'Sister,' — not only by the family but by other people in the town."

> It is nostalgic to go back to one's hometown, remembering place and childhood events. It is emotionally disturbing, too. I was sad when I saw that the old timey Victorian house where I was born had been razed and rebuilt into a brick grocery store. The house we moved to when I was ten years old used to be near the city limits of the town and there was a sense of country and space. Now it is surrounded with a settlement of cottages with picture windows, all just alike, and the air smells of exhaust and filling stations.[2]

"It is in Columbus that I feel most strongly the continuity of the past," she observes before recalling that the novelist Julien Green, whose family was also from the South, and his wife, Anne, "had rice every day at their table even after twenty years in France." That sparks an elaborate description of the special features and delights of Southern cuisine. She then describes the military installation at Fort Benning:

> Fort Benning played a big part in Columbus people's lives. . . . Many Columbus girls marry young officers. . . . It was at Fort Benning that I spent the happiest years of my childhood. For to my great fortune I had lessons there with the most musical musician I have ever known. Mary Tucker was the wife of a colonel at Fort Benning and a devoted teacher and friend. . . . The Tuckers have now retired to a Virginia farm where I still run to when I am in trouble or when I need a vacation. . . .
> . . . I met Edwin Peacock who had driven with the Tuckers and

me to a Rachmaninoff concert in Atlanta when I was 14 and there began a friendship and devotion that has lasted ever since.

. . .

I did not visit my father's store for I had heard that it had changed. . . . [H]e would never be there again.[3]

In Atlanta she spent an entire day with Ralph McGill, the editor in chief of the *Atlanta Constitution* and "one of the most distinguished writers and journalists in this country." "Georgians are mighty proud of him," she adds, "although they often disagree with his views and occasionally there is a strained silence around his name when racial matters are discussed." McGill introduced her to a young woman lawyer who told Carson that legislation had been passed that day giving women the right to serve on juries. Carson describes an "old cracker's" reaction: "'Well, if they make us put the niggers in the jury box I guess we'll have to let the women too,' and he spat in the cuspidor of the courthouse." Like all whites in the region, she had to accept her Confederate heritage, the family memory of the Civil War, the arrival of the Yankees, and the death of Bobby Carson, her great-grandmother's son, who had fallen during a fruitless battle while trying to retrieve a Confederate flag. "Southern white children during the Civil War thought of the Yankees as mythical people — perhaps with horns and tails, but the Negroes awaited them as their deliverers."[4] Carson highlights the beauty of the South and of Savannah — in her view one of the most magnificent cities in the world — and the aristocratic character eternally bound to the land. Such a burst of Southern sentiment was hardly typical of her, but it seems to have been a way of saying she "belonged" to that place.

What the first weeks of a life without Reeves were like for Carson McCullers, there is no way to imagine. She herself never discussed them. The people close to her — notably, Margarita Smith — refused to cooperate with her biographer, Virginia Spencer Carr, and since then many have died. Surely Carson must have been painfully aware that her solitude now placed her in an unconditional state of dependency, and she may have become hostile toward those caring for her, namely, her mother and her sister. The only detailed information available is peripheral, financial, or practical. Floria Lasky took money matters even more firmly in hand than before, which saved Carson from falling into poverty. She was utterly incapable of dealing with finances herself. In early 1954 Carson began giving a series of lectures, mostly on university campuses. Many American writers choose this expedient to supplement their income or to avoid having to pursue a second occupation — Eudora Welty for one, among numerous others. For Carson, who still enjoyed relative financial security at this time thanks to her theater and cinema royalties, lecturing was first and foremost a sign of life and of personal independence. It was also, at least in the beginning, something that she forced herself to do, since speaking in public was extremely painful for her.

Overcoming her discomfort, if not her panic, was very difficult for Carson, but what she had to say about her work, about literature, about her position as a writer in society was generally fascinating. With her faltering voice, her slow delivery, her long silences, she knew how to make herself heard, to make people pay attention. Many thank-you letters she received after her appearances show how greatly she could move and disturb her audience. In the posthumous collection *The Mortgaged Heart*, her sister, introducing her poems, remembers a touching anecdote: "About her poetry, I remember best one evening at a university lecture. After she had recited 'Stone Is Not Stone' in her gentle Southern voice, there was a long silence. Then suddenly a young student stood up and said, 'Mrs. McCullers, I love you.'"[5]

When he could be, Tennessee Williams was there to lend support and read some of her work. Tennessee did his best to keep Carson calm, urging her to take more lightly a subject he believed she was preoccupied with: almost obsessively, and sometimes in the middle of her lectures, Carson had begun accusing Truman Capote of plagiarizing her. Having been a friend of the young Truman, she had stayed out of this old quarrel when it first erupted. Why revive the matter now? In 1948, explains Capote's biographer, Gore Vidal and Capote had fallen out, and Vidal had accused Capote of getting all his plots from Carson McCullers and Eudora Welty.[6] At the same time, when Capote's first book, *Other Voices, Other Rooms*, appeared, Elizabeth Hardwick wrote in the *Partisan Review* that Capote's work was "a minor imitation of a very talented minor writer, Carson McCullers" — which was not very pleasant for anyone.[7] In the early 1960s, when Oliver Evans wrote his book on Carson, he wholeheartedly agreed. In one of his letters, dated

August 1, 1963, Evans says he was "appalled to discover how much of it has been copied, by Truman Capote."[8] He provides some examples:

1. The snow symbolism in *Heart*. Just as Mick yearns again and again for the snow she has never seen, so does Joel on pages 57 through 59, of *Other Voices, Other Rooms*.

2. The incident of Bubber's shooting Baby doll is the obvious source of Capote's story, "Children on their Birthdays," which I believe won an O'Henry Memorial award. The little girl in that story is exactly like Baby, and even the incident about Bubber's hidding in the tree-house is imitated in that story. . . . Miss Roberta and her Princely Place are obviously modeled after Miss Amelia and her café. I don't think that the Negress, Missouri Fever, could have existed without the example of Portia [in *The Heart Is a Lonely Hunter*] — and perhaps Berenice [in *The Member of the Wedding*] as well. The opening paragraphs of *Other Voices*, which describe the monotony and boredom of the small Southern town remind me irresistibly of the *Ballad*. These are just a few random instances by which I have happened to be struck; doubtless others will already have occurred to you. (That said, I like Capote very much. . . . I don't know him personally, so there is no malice in these observations.)[9]

Similarities do indeed exist. But small Southern cities resemble one another. Their inertia and oppressiveness were exactly the same for the young Carson as they were for the adolescent Truman. Carson McCullers had no need to accuse her talented junior of plagiarism, but who knows what she did need to defend herself against? Who knows how many battles Carson fought in an attempt to forget she was no longer the creator she wanted to be? Being forced to write and type with only one hand, suffering every single minute, must surely have been torture for her.

When he met Virginia Spencer Carr in 1972, Truman Capote elegantly professed to have no recollection whatsoever of the whole affair.[10] He could not even remember if he really had or had not been present on the day in 1954 when Carson, believing that she spotted him in the audience at one of her lectures, had done everything she could to tell the man she thought was Truman that she considered him a cheater. He admitted seeing little of Carson in the last years of her life but didn't think that implied that there had been serious problems between the two writers, much less that he had been professionally jealous of his Southern compatriot.

Capote could afford to be generous; he had won the battle. His work had not experienced the vicissitudes that Carson's had. There was therefore no point in hunting high and low for proof that Truman Capote thoroughly detested Carson. Carr failed to discern the complicated dynamics that characterize relationships among artists — the respect, the envy, the bitter resentment artists often feel for one another. Even less does Carr perceive the anxiety, the uncertainties, the extraordinary wager artists make when they decide to create a work of art. Carr's insistence on Carson McCullers's jealousy toward her contemporaries is naive, not only where Truman Capote was concerned but also Flannery O'Connor — who was only too happy to return her fellow Southerner's hostility. A few years later O'Connor would say that she had never read anything as bad as McCullers's last novel, *Clock Without Hands*. And even Tennessee Williams supposedly confided that, without ever daring to tell Carson so, he did not think his friend an extraordinary author of plays and believed that she was jealous of his talent as a playwright — which is merely to say that Carson was a person of good sense.

Carson kept fighting; she knew no other way to live — and to remain alive right up to the end. Others, not surprisingly, were resentful of Carson or exasperated by her behavior. In the spring of 1954, before returning to Yaddo for the first time in eight years, Carson spent some time in Charleston at Edwin Peacock's home. Peacock gave her all the attention and tenderness he had displayed since their youth. Probably hoping to distract her, he invited their friends Robert Walden and Edward Newberry, who lived in Charlotte, to spend a weekend. The group had not been together since the evening of the New York premiere of *The Member of the Wedding* four years earlier, and they came up with a plan to make *The Ballad of the Sad Café* into a musical.

Walden and Newberry asked Carson to spend some time with them in Charlotte. She enthusiastically accepted — but things did not go well: she behaved rudely toward her hosts and, worse still, toward several of their friends. Walden nonetheless admired Carson and made no attempt to hide the strong impression she had made on him one night when she spoke of the Bible. He was surprised by her intimate knowledge of biblical texts. They decided to read a few passages together every evening, which Carson always chose with perfect discernment.

Beyond that, however, Robert Walden apparently had a very hard time putting up with Carson that spring, to the point of asking Rita to come up with a pretext for calling Carson back up north earlier than planned. In his interview with Virginia Spencer Carr, Walden, who initially takes care to acknowledge Carson's positive attributes and culture, eventually indulges in a few less kindly comments. According to him, Carson should not be

> depicted biographically for posterity cloaked in white or wearing a halo. She was a bitch, and I don't want her coming out looking like an angel. Although what *she* wanted to be was always most important to her, she also could be exactly what *you* wanted her to be. If she wanted to please you, she would suddenly decide "I'm going to be charming," and charming she was — like a princess. But she was still a bitch.[11]

Carson could no doubt be unbearable. But to insist that posterity should know her first and foremost as a bitch does little to ennoble the author of these comments.

◆　　◆　　◆

Unaware of Walden's role in cutting short her visit, Carson left Charlotte for Yaddo on April 20. There she stayed till the end of the summer, leaving occasionally for a few days to give one of her lectures or visit some friends. Elizabeth Ames had not seen her friend since the attack that had left her paralyzed, and Ames was shocked by what Carson had become, an invalid who moved about only with the aid of her cane. In addition, Carson was extremely pale and somewhat bloated. It was not so much that the author had aged; she had fallen into ruin.

Watching how she lived only confirmed Ames's first impression. Carson was drinking even more than before. She smoked so much, from morning till night, that Elizabeth feared she would set her room on fire. Not only had the strokes affected her physical appearance, they had also changed her behavior. With Elizabeth Ames, for whom she felt great affection, Carson was as warm as ever, but toward other residents, especially during the summer when the group was larger, she could be very disagreeable, even cutting. She had grown much more nervous and, when she drank, irascible. Tragically, Carson had come to resemble her own description of Alison Langdon: "She was very ill and she looked it. Not only was this illness physical, but she had been tortured to the bone by grief and anxiety so that now she was on the verge of actual lunacy."[12]

The French critic René Micha, too, was struck that same year by Carson's physical appearance:

> I visited Carson McCullers one time. It was toward the end of 1954. Nyack, where she lives, is a small town gently sloping toward the Hudson. . . . I found Carson McCullers ill and almost disabled: her left hand, partially paralyzed, rested on another hand made out of metal. Although I had seen several photos of her, her little-girlishness surprised me. Her head seemed too heavy for her body: perhaps I got that impression from her eyes, which were unusually prominent. I remembered that someone had called her a mixture of Garbo and Slim Summerville. She was pale. I got the sense of a genius cramped by fragile appendages. Her mother lived with her. And an old black nanny, who, as someone once wrote, had the dark color of wisteria and eyes bathed in milk. We lunched at a large iron table on foods that were pretty to look at and delicious. We listened to music from Georgia — and music of Satie. . . . She spoke in a timid, faraway voice — with a Southern accent. . . . When I compared one of her heroes, Biff, to the widowed Charles Bovary, she said, "You could pay me no greater compliment," and gave me her hand to kiss (her hand was lost in lace).[13]

The first thing people felt when they saw her that summer at Yaddo was compassion. Carson seemed too ill to be an "artist in residence." She was treated as a privileged guest of Elizabeth Ames, an already accomplished writer being helped through a difficult period. The few who dared to push their relations with Carson a bit further could not help but be charmed "in spite of everything." Leon Edel, for example, the magnificent biographer of Henry James, speaks of the ambivalent feelings she elicited from people, including both tenderness and irritation in the face of her childish side, disapproval of the way she was apt to rebuke conversational partners, condemnation of her harshness and sometimes even vulgarity. "Carson had a great deal of warmth," remembers Edel,

> and a picturesque mind — a mind in which its fancies leaped and plunged and offered always the unexpected. . . . she could be, in a group, very lively and witty. But also like the little girl she could be attention-demanding, and there was a certain pathos in her pleading look, those large liquid eyes that asked the world for love and in the way of the little girl in *The Member of the Wedding,* found such fanciful logic in the asking. . . . I do remember that her inventions were always startling and often delightful, like some surrealist painting. . . .
>
> I valued knowing her, even so briefly. I saw in her always a parade of the grotesque, the morbid, the joyous and the free, and I suspect it is the merging of these opposites that gives her work its peculiar color and its eerie fascination. One always felt the burden she carried — a kind of sense of doom which she eased with the comedy of her mind and her devotion to her art. She shaped and reshaped her fancies, and her "case" — a little case — is poignant in its accomplishment, in the face of her life-denying demons.[14]

The insightful comments of Leon Edel offer a more coherent picture of Carson than does Robert Walden's blunt assertion of her bitchiness. But it must be conceded that Walden had to tend to Carson's needs night and day within the confines of a private home rather than simply cross her path at his convenience in the collective environment of Yaddo. That experience may well have tested his patience.

Leaving Yaddo at the end of the summer, the residents of 1954 thought that they would never see Carson McCullers again. Weekend visitors — some of them old friends of Carson's such as Granville Hicks, with whom she had traveled to Quebec in August 1941 — got the same impression, convinced that Carson would only briefly outlive Reeves, who had been wrong to believe her "indestructible." They were mistaken. Obviously, Reeves had known her better than they. Carson's relationship to life was much more complex than they thought. She was not an intellectual in the sense that many of her fellow residents were, and the exact nature of her relationship to the world, to reality, to literature remained unclear to many of her contemporaries. Her capacity to "live" — to get around, to be alone in a house or a hotel, to run errands, to keep herself nourished — was considerably diminished, but her life force was immense.

Moreover, at Yaddo Carson finished the first draft of her play *The Square Root of Wonderful* — whose hero, a failed writer, commits suicide — and made at least some progress on *Clock Without Hands.* Before returning home — she would divide her time that fall and winter between the house in Nyack, where her mother was recovering with difficulty from a broken hip, and the apartments of friends in New York — she went to Roslyn Harbor on Long Island to meet Gabriela Mistral, the Chilean Nobel Prize winner in literature for 1945. Carson, who had cultured, multilingual friends, was familiar with her poems even though she knew no Spanish (Gabriela Mistral's work was not translated into English until after her death in 1957). Having moved to the United States only in 1953, Mistral did not know English well enough to read Carson McCullers's novels, but she had read about her visitor and considered her a writer of quality. Carson's enduring adolescence, surviving even her illness, captivated the Chilean poet. Carson for her part developed an immediate fondness for that woman pacified by age.

The two writers were marked by another similarity: each had lost a man in her life to suicide. In any event the Nobel Prize was enough to make one dream, especially in that era when the award still bore some relation to literary talent. Did Gabriela Mistral give Carson the impression she would nominate her for that prize, or did Carson willfully infer as much from the attention paid to her by the former prize winner? Whatever the case may be, for several months she fantasized about that prestigious distinction, though declaring herself unworthy of it, as her letter to Newton Arvin reveals. Was this the dream of a sick and devastated woman who had nothing left as a rampart against death except her status as an artist? No doubt. But that does not stop Virginia Spencer Carr from portraying Carson's "illusions about the Nobel Prize" as simply one more illustration of her intolerable sense of self-importance.

And yet she "hung on." In Nyack that fall Carson's mother hired Ida Reeder, who would be much more than a domestic employee or a housekeeper for Carson throughout her remaining years. That gracious black woman was like an incarnation of certain important characters in Carson's books, a benevolent Portia — the servant in *The Heart Is a Lonely Hunter* — and a self-assured cook à la Berenice in *The Member of the Wedding*. Ida would be there till the very last day, a comforting presence imported from the South, from childhood — and from literature, too. The two women called each other "Sister." Ida tried to make Carson forget that she was growing more and more fragile and dependent. Ida carried her, consoled her, went with her everywhere she had to go — even on a final journey to Europe.

Over the course of fall and winter 1954–55, Carson tried not to stay home for too long, probably to keep from feeling isolated. She shuttled back and forth between New York and Nyack. During that time she was introduced to the producer Arnold Saint Subber, who offered to produce her play *The Square Root of Wonderful*. Their attraction and fascination were mutual. The two were born on the same day in the same year and felt spontaneously close to each other. That new friendship, along with theatrical plans and frequent changes of scenery, reenergized Carson. When she took off in April for Key West, Florida, to join Tennessee Williams, Carson was eager to get down to work. He had to finish *Cat on a Hot Tin Roof* with all possible speed, and she had three manuscripts in progress: the stage adaptation of *The Ballad of the Sad Café*, inspired by Carson's springtime conversations with Robert Walden; *The Square Root of Wonderful*; and *Clock Without Hands*.

To Key West the two friends invited a very young woman arriving from France, where she had published, at the age of nineteen, a short novel, *Bonjour Tristesse* (Hello sadness), that caused a scandal. Françoise Sagan, in all her interviews with the American press, had expressed her admiration for Tennessee Williams. Touched by her remarks, Williams invited Sagan to visit him in Florida. She accepted immediately. Thirty years later Françoise Sagan, who professed her admiration with extreme elegance and delicacy, described that encounter at length in one of her finest books, *With Fondest Regards:*

> At 6:30 we were told Tennessee Williams had arrived. A short man with blond hair and a gleam of amusement in his blue eyes made his appearance. Since the death of Whitman, he had been for me — and still remains — America's greatest poet. He was followed by a cheerful-looking, dark-haired man, perhaps the most charming

man in America and Europe put together, whose name was Franco. He was a complete unknown and never became anything else. Behind them came a tall thin woman wearing shorts; she had eyes that were pools of blue. With one hand gripping a wooden support, she looked a little lost. In my view this woman was the best, certainly the most sensitive, writer in America at that time: Carson McCullers. Franco linked arms with these two people of genius, two loners, and enabled them to laugh together, to endure together the life of the outcast and pariah, the life of the scapegoat and misfit, a life familiar at that time to every American artist and nonconformist.

Tennessee Williams preferred the company of men in his bed to that of women. Carson's husband had committed suicide not long before, and she was half-paralyzed. Franco liked both men and women, but he preferred Tennessee. And he also loved poor, sick, tired Carson very dearly. All the poetry, all the suns of the world proved incapable of lighting up her blue eyes, of animating her heavy eyelids and gaunt body. But she kept her laugh, the laugh of a child forever lost. I saw how these two men, whom people would then refer to with a kind of prudish distaste as "pederasts" and who nowadays would be described as "gay" (as if they should somehow be cheerful when they are despised by every Tom, Dick and Harry for loving the way they do), I saw how they took care of this woman, putting her to bed, getting her up, dressing her, entertaining her, warming her, loving her — in short, giving her all that friendship and understanding and attentiveness can offer to someone who is too sensitive, who has seen too much and learned too much from what she has seen, and perhaps written too much about it, to be able to bear it or endure it any longer.

Carson was to die ten years later, and Franco not long afterwards. As for Tennessee — by then the writer perhaps most hated by puritans, but most acclaimed by the public and by critics — the author of *A Streetcar Named Desire, Cat on a Hot Tin Roof, The Night of the Iguana,* and many other plays died a miserable death in a hotel room in New York which he left wide open, rain or shine. . . .

So we spent a torrid and riotous two weeks in Key West, which was deserted at that time of year. This was twenty-five years ago. More than twenty-five years ago. In the morning we would meet on the beach. Carson and Tennessee used to drink tumblers full of water — or what I took for such until I finally swallowed a large mouthful and realized it was straight gin. We went swimming, we hired little rowboats, we tried in vain to catch big fish. The men drank, and the women too, only a little less. We had truly awful picnics. And after these really memorable outings we would go home tired, sometimes happy, sometimes sad, but happy or sad together.

I can still see Carson in those incredible Bermuda shorts that were too long for her, with her long arms, her little bowed head and short hair, and her eyes such a pale blue they made her look a child once more. I can see Tennessee's profile as he read the paper, laughing occasionally — because otherwise, he used to say, it would have made him weep (at that time I took very little interest in politics). I can see Franco making his way along the beach, coming down the steps, going to fetch glasses, running from one to the other, laughing; Italian, well-built, not handsome but charming, Franco was light-hearted, droll, good, full of imagination. . . .

Two or three years later I came across Tennessee again. It was the day of a presidential election and so the blue laws were in force. We sat once more at the bar in the Hotel Pierre, where he very coolly ordered two glasses, ice and a bottle of lemonade, then took out of his back pocket a flask of strong whisky from which he poured me a typically generous measure. His latest play was doing very well, but he did not mention it. He was sad, because Carson was sad; because Carson had had to return for a while to a hospital — for "the highly strung," as he put it — and he said this with the utmost conviction. He was sad because Carson had then left this institution, supposedly recovered, but now she was staying in the large house where she had spent her childhood, to be with her mother, who was dying of cancer. She was pleased to hear I was in New York, and Tennessee had promised that we would drive out and see her the following day. . . .

We were . . . singing when we arrived at the home of Carson McCullers, author of masterpieces such as *The Heart Is a Lonely Hunter, Reflections in a Golden Eye,* works that have only gradually become known in France. It was an old porticoed house with three steps and all the doors were open because of the heat. Sitting on a divan was a very old, anemic-looking lady, ravaged by suffering or something else which set her apart and made her almost disdainful of our presence. And then there was Carson, wearing a brown dress thrown on any old way; Carson, grown even thinner and paler, but who still had those eyes, those extraordinary eyes, and that childlike laugh.

We set about opening bottles, and Carson's mother made a show of consenting to have a drop only after being pressed to do so. We drank a lot. The weather had become really cold by the time we drove back and the return journey in the car was a sad one, despite the fact that we were heading for that galaxy of a city, that enormous place where every city dweller knew their names by heart, yet knew nothing of their souls. Unfortunately, as it turned out, it was not even a month later, just a week, in fact, before Carson had to go back to that place where they look after the highly strung. Neither Tennessee nor even Franco could raise a smile after that . . .

. . . Whether I think of the fair-haired, sun-tanned man with blue eyes and a blond moustache who carried Carson McCullers up to her bedroom, laid her against her two pillows like a child, sat at the foot of her bed and held her hand until she fell asleep because she was afraid of nightmares; or the gray-faced wreck of Tennessee, drained of life by the irrevocable loss of Franco; or the Tennessee who so kindly came such a long way and probably thought our staging of his play to be like some pantomime in a village hall but nevertheless had the goodness and gallantry to say the opposite — I shall always miss the unvarying directness of his gaze, his unvarying strength, tenderness, vulnerability.[15]

Tennessee Williams, too, was charmed by the young French novelist. He wrote an article in *Harper's Bazaar* saying how highly he thought of her and discussing his hopes for her future: "Perhaps she doesn't have, now, at this moment in her development, the alarming, deeply disturbing, visionary quality of her literary idol, Raymond Radiguet [French novelist and poet], who died so young after a little great work, nor has she yet written anything comparable to Carson McCullers' *Ballad of the Sad Café*, but I have a feeling that if I had met Mme. Colette at twenty I would have noticed about her the same cool detachment and warm sensibility that I observed in the gold-freckled eyes of Mlle. Sagan."[16]

Surrounded by Tennessee Williams and his friend Frank Merlo and amused by the diversion created by the presence of Françoise Sagan, Carson went about her work. On May 25 she completed the short story "Who Has Seen the Wind?"[17] It is the last story in the posthumous collection *The Mortgaged Heart,* about the disintegration of a successful writer who can no longer write, and the implosion of a couple. It contains a theme developed later in *The Square Root of Wonderful* — creative impotence leading to suicide. Like the play that Carson was still in the process of writing in 1955, the story is one of mourning, a sort of death song for Reeves. In it are his dreams of owning a farm — "He had dreamed of manual labor and an apple farm. If he could just go for long walks on the moors then the light of creation would come again — but where are the moors of New York?"[18] — and his war:

> The war had come as a relief to Ken. He was glad to abandon the book that was going badly, relieved to turn from his "phantom rock" to the general experience of those days — for surely the war was the great experience of his generation. He was graduated from Officers' Training School and when Marian saw him in his uniform she cried and loved him and there was no further talk of divorce. On his last leave they made love often as they used to do in the first months of marriage. It rained every day in England and once he was invited by a lord to his castle. He crossed on D-Day and his battalion went all the way to Schmitz. In a cellar in a ruined town he saw a cat sniffing the face of a corpse. He was afraid, but it was not the blank terror of the cafeteria or the anxiety of a white page on the typewriter. Something was always happening — he found three Westphalian hams in the chimney of a peasant's house and he broke his arm in an automobile accident. . . . to a writer every day was automatically of value because it was the war. But when it was over what was there to write about — the calm cat and the corpse, the lord in England, the broken arm?

But Ken Harris is also a figure of Carson and her terror that she would from now on be a shadow of the writer she had been, her pain in knowing that her powers were diminished:

> The paper was still blank and the white page blanched his spirit. Yet there was a time (how long ago?) when a song at the corner, a voice from childhood, and the panorama of memory condensed the past

so that the random and actual were transfigured into a novel, a story — there was a time when the empty page summoned and sorted memory and he felt that ghostly mastery of his art. A time, in short, when he was a writer and writing almost every day. Working hard, he carefully broke the backs of sentences, *x*'d out offending phrases and changed repeated words. Now he sat there hunched and somehow fearful, a blond man in his late thirties, with circles under his oyster blue eyes and a full, pale mouth.[19]

Making Ken Harris, like Phillip Lovejoy in *The Square Root of Wonderful,* not someone who had never succeeded at writing but a writer who had become impotent allowed Carson to play on both Reeves's and her own destiny in a single character. It gave her one last way, perhaps, to join "Sister" and "Brother." Exposing herself only minimally, she could speak of her personal wound by hiding it "in Reeves's camp." When Ken Harris arrives at a party, for example, does he not feel, as Carson almost always did, like a "displaced person"?

"Nowadays when I enter a crowded party I think of that last party of the Duc de Guermantes."

"What?" asked Esther.

"You remember when Proust — the I, the narrator — looked at all the familiar faces and brooded about the alterations of time? Magnificent passage — I read it every year."

Esther looked disturbed. "There's so much noise. Is your wife coming?". . .

"When I find myself at a party like this it's always almost exactly the same. Yet there is the awful difference. As though the key lowered, shifted. The awful difference of years that are passing, the trickery and terror of time, Proust . . ."

But his hostess had gone and he was left standing alone in the crowded party room. . . . There was a change — thirteen years ago when he published *The Night of Darkness* Esther would have fairly eaten him up and never left him alone at the fringe of a room.[20]

As if the fates had conspired to stop Carson McCullers from triumphing over her terrors, the bad dreams she had both night and day, and her writing difficulties, her mother died suddenly on June 10, 1955, of a heart attack. She was sixty-five years old. Carson was visiting friends in New York when Jordan Massee brought her the news. Carson remembered her mother's death a dozen years later in her autobiographical essay:

> I had slept with my mother in twin beds for all the years that she had been delicate, but one day I was invited by my friends, Hilda and Robert Marks, to spend the night with them. Mother insisted that I should not call Ida and she said she'd be perfectly all right. With misgiving I acquieced to her, and Ida, of course, would be there first thing in the morning.
>
> "You've been confined to the house so long, darling," she said, "go out and enjoy yourself."
>
> I still worried about her in the evening and called and she said she was fine. Then early next day my cousin came. He embraced me tenderly and said, "I have some bad news for you, darling."
>
> My sister had been in the hospital with an appendicitis operation and my first thought was to her. "Rita?" I asked.
>
> "No, darling, not Rita, it's your mother."
>
> I said, "Is she dead?"
>
> My cousin patted my hand and embraced me again.
>
> I could only say, "What can I do?" But even as I heard my own voice, I knew the question was a foolish one. I called Ida at the house, and although she was crying she did say firmly, "Come home immediately, the funeral people are already arriving."
>
> Ida had come to work very early and told mother she would bring her breakfast immediately.
>
> "I'm hungry," my mother said, "And cold."
>
> "Wait just a jiffy," Ida said, "while the stove heats up."
>
> She came in with my mother while she was waiting and suddenly, very suddenly mother began to vomit blood. She died in Ida's arms.
>
> Mother was only able to gasp, "Thank goodness Sister isn't here," and with her last breath she added, "it would be too much for her."
>
> It was too much, almost too much.[21]

Carson did not want to return to Nyack, as her mother had not wished to return to Starke Avenue after the death of her husband eleven years earlier. With her friends' help she organized the funeral. Afterward, everyone came back to Nyack to help Carson "gain a foothold" in the house once again. But several days later the reading of

Marguerite Smith's will sparked a conflict among her three children that was not resolved quickly — if ever. Marguerite Smith had written her will in 1949 at a time when Carson, already ill, had been in a more precarious financial situation than her brother and sister, both of whom had jobs that paid a decent salary. So their mother had left a larger share of her estate to her elder daughter. In the meantime Carson had become a successful dramatic author and now enjoyed greater financial security than either Rita or Lamar Jr. Carson's attorney, Floria Lasky, at once friendly and smart, took charge.

The death of Marguerite Smith left Carson completely on her own — no longer was she anyone's child — and gave her one inescapable choice: either abandon herself to her illness, perhaps even die, or fight to remain Carson McCullers, a writer who would keep on publishing. If giving up had ever really been an option, she would already have done so. Nonetheless, the shock was so severe that 1956 was like a year-long battle between the two alternatives. On the one hand, she was almost constantly sick, her left arm causing her to suffer more and more intensely. On the other hand, as soon as she was able, Carson worked every day with Saint Subber, revising the whole script of her play, though the two collaborators had decided to postpone production for one year. During those long months Saint Subber was an indispensable source of support. Carson declared that they were living a magnificent love story, sometimes even that she was going to marry him. Observers were more skeptical. Some believed that Carson and Saint Subber greatly exaggerated their relationship as well as the importance of their work together.

They had a falling out after the failure of the play, but when Arnold Saint Subber talked to Virginia Spencer Carr by telephone long afterward, in 1970, he spoke of Carson McCullers in an ardent, passionate, and hyperbolic manner: "There is nothing I could say about her that someone else could not contradict and also be true. Carson was the most innocent angel in the entire world and also the reddest, most bitchy devil." According to Saint Subber, she was contradiction itself, delicate and refined on the one hand and swearing like a trooper on the other.

No two people ever gulped life as we did, ever ate as much as we did together, smoked as much, cursed as much, believed in God as much, read the Bible as much as we did together. . . . She clung to life and believed only in one thing: life.

. . . She was a powerhouse. There was nobody stronger in the world. She was enormous. She staggered the imagination. She was the iron butterfly.[22]

Nineteen fifty-seven would bring a new confrontation with the public — and all the anxieties and hopes that went along with it. The year got off to a promising start for Carson far from home in London, where *The Member of the Wedding* was performed at the Royal Court Theatre by the English Stage Company with Geraldine McEwan. Across the Atlantic, Carson and company were working hard to get *The Square Root of Wonderful* under way. But nothing went as planned, and one problem after another eventually led to the play's failure. Nonetheless, Anne Baxter had been chosen to play Mollie, a woman twice married to a writer who has lost his inspiration, Phillip Lovejoy. At the time of the play's action, the couple is separated again, and Phillip is going to kill himself. Anne Baxter was a great admirer of Carson's novels, and she had a passion for the character Mollie. Still, Baxter thought the play needed further adjustment and rewriting before it could go into rehearsal, as it was scheduled to do in September. Carson, said Baxter, was not up to the job.

That was not at all the opinion of Albert Marre, the successful thirty-one-year-old director who had been approached to produce *Square Root.* In his view Carson would have been perfectly capable of completing the needed revisions if she had been allowed to establish her own rhythm and given a certain amount of liberty, which she was not. Marre told Virginia Spencer Carr that he enjoyed working with Carson, whose complex personality and sense of humor he appreciated.[23]

But Marre eventually bowed out of the project. Scheduling conflicts left him no choice, he later said. Carson bore a grudge against him for it, even though she got on well with his successor, José Quintero, with whom she may have drunk a bit too much. When Quintero in his turn quit the play, right before its pre-Broadway opening performance at Princeton University, Carson was less shattered than she had been by Marre's departure. She and Quintero remained on good terms. The actors all decided to stand by Carson, who took over as director despite never having directed a play before. She was finally relieved by George Keathley. But everyone already knew that, barring a miracle, they were headed for catastrophe. The ten-day pre-Broadway run at Princeton was less than brilliant. *The Square Root of Wonderful* opened on Broadway on October 30 at the National Theatre. It closed December 7 after forty-five performances. Years later Anne Baxter, who, like everyone else involved in that production, was hurt by its failure, nonetheless said that if given the chance to do the play again exactly as Carson conceived it, she would take the part.

Carson turned a lucid gaze, not devoid of humor, on what she herself called a "disaster":

In 1954 I began to write a disaster not on purpose, God knows, but day by day, inch by inch I was falling into chaos. It is easy to blame Saint Subber, but I won't. He was the one who insisted I write the "Square Root of Wonderful" . . . [and] he was the most insistent and persevering man I'd ever known in my professional life. Every day he would come to 131 South Broadway, Nyack. I could see him with a whip in his hand all ready to shove me on. The play was about a writer who had married a foolish woman, and since my mother was failing in health and I wanted to preserve and recognize her most charming foolishnesses, which is fine in real life, but deadly on the stage, I had tried to capture her innocence. But the innocence turned out to be just dumbness and the unsuccessful writer was an extension of all my own fears of fallowness and failure. I was particularly hard on him as I sometimes get very hard on myself. He combined all the most unloving traits that were in me. My selfishness, my tending to gloom and suicide. . . . Why I wrote this crap is hard to realize; of course, I had no idea it was so bad.

Not until the horrifying first night of the try-out in Philadelphia. Then like an angry hen defending it's young I tried fiendishly to do something about it. Saint Subber was trying too, so that we had a change of six directors in all, one worse than the other. Nobody seemed to realize it was just a bad play and so all the frenzied hiring and firing went on. It went on till the opening in New York.

As I don't go to openings, I certainly made no exception with this one. I skulked around the theatre waiting fearfully for news. I was wearing my beautiful two thousand year old, this is the truth, chinese robe, and as I passed the theatre I did not even have the nerve to pray.

A couple who had walked out on the show said,"I wonder if *she's* a member of the play?"

When we went to the party given by the co-producer it was so painful I forget his name, Saint cried, the co-producer cried, and when the reviews were read from the New York Times, they all cried double.

But me, I just sat there stoney and crying inwardly, but never with a sob or a tear. At the risk of seeming to defend this utter failure, I must say the play read better than it acted. Finally after forty-five performances the play painfully expired on December 4, 1957.[24]

Of the era's seven New York dailies, only one, the *World-Telegram and Sun,* published a favorable review. The others were devastating. John Chapman's piece in the *New York Daily News* is fairly representative of the most widely shared reaction: "'The Square Root of Wonderful,' which was handsomely and intelligently presented at the National Theatre last evening, might be described as a trauma in three acts. Watching and hearing it, I had the odd and uneasy feeling that I was a reluctant psychiatrist listening to the confidence of strangers. Since I did not know or particularly care for these strangers, I was uncomfortable."[25]

Then the weekly magazines had their turn. Wolcott Gibbs was very negative in the *New Yorker,* though he did put in a good word for Carson McCullers. After citing a particularly mediocre dialogue, he adds: "For one reason and another, I decline to believe that Mrs. McCullers wrote these horrid lines herself, preferring to attribute them to some skulking littérateur in the ranks of the management. Nevertheless, they are delivered loud and clear on the stage of the National, and with each of them the poor play collapses more helplessly into absurdity."[26]

Brooks Atkinson, too, did her best to be gentle with Carson McCullers, recalling her brilliant past: "After 'The Member of the Wedding' Carson McCullers' second play seems commonplace. . . . Especially at the end, there are passages of the precise though allusive prose with which Mrs. McCullers can weave golden sentiments and wistful dreams out of common material. But most of 'The Square Root of Wonderful' remains earthbound. The characters are hardly distinguishable from inhabitants of the conventional comedy of manners."[27]

The coup de grâce was delivered by Harold Clurman, the much-celebrated director of *The Member of the Wedding*. In the November 23 issue of the *Nation* he wrote that the play was "a dud," calling it a bad script with bad direction and bad acting: "The characters often fall out of focus, and it is one of the mistakes of the play's composition that the author felt constrained to make her story straightforward so that it might appear logical to the prosaic mind. The script might have been better if it had had the faults natural to its author's genius."[28]

"It was a logical failure, unfortunately," Floria Lasky comments soberly, "because *The Square Root of Wonderful* was a failed play. The theater is unforgiving. Obviously, for Carson, it was not simply a play, it was a posthumous argument with Reeves. That may have been its fatal flaw."[29]

It is worth noting that Carson's description of her project, written, admittedly, many years after the fact, contains no allusion to Reeves, which says a great deal about Carson's ambivalence regarding him in her final writings.

After the critics and the public, theater specialists and essayists were also extremely severe. Louis Kronenberger, in his work on the plays of the 1957–58 theater season, salvages nothing from the wreck:

> The author of *The Member of the Wedding* this time wrote on a variety of themes, in a variety of tones, at a variety of tempos. A work containing enough material for several plays emerged, for lack of integration, no play at all. The parts were not only greater than the whole; they destroyed the whole.
>
> . . . Jangling with false notes, *Square Root* could not mate humor with horror, or get its varied themes to coalesce; and in the attempt, Miss McCullers' genuine individuality and special feeling for life became sadly blurred. What emerged was a square root in a round hole.[30]

While he readily acknowledged the problems the play had when it was performed in 1957, the first director, Albert Marre, believed its

failure was due not only to "good reasons" but also to a disparity between what Carson McCullers had created and the expectations and
conventions of the time. It is possible that all the elements simply did
not "hold together" on stage, but it would not be correct to say the
script itself was poor. Besides, when *The Square Root of Wonderful* was
published as a book, in 1958, it got much better reviews. "Although
this play was a Broadway failure," wrote George Freedley in the June 1,
1958, *Library Journal,* "Mrs. McCullers has filled it with lovable and
most attractively written characters."[31] And the May 1, 1958, issue of
Kirkus said, "While the Broadway record of this second of Carson
McCullers' plays was not impressive, the quality of the writing makes
the play in book form worth reading."[32] But the manuscript was reworked for its release in book form, Carson McCullers having quite
rightly been furious with what someone had seen fit to rewrite instead
of respecting her work. She discussed the matter in a foreword entitled
"A Personal Preface":

> I have learned this in my work in the theatre: the author must work
> alone until the intentions of his play are fulfilled — until the play
> is as finished as the author can make it. Once a play is in rehearsal,
> a playwright must write under unaccustomed pressure, and alas,
> what he had in mind is often compromised. This may be due to the
> actors, the producer, the director — the whole prism of the theatri-
> cal production.
>
> And so begins a transmutation that sometimes to the author's
> dismay ends in the play being almost unrecognizable to the creator.
>
> That is why of the five or six evolutions this play went through I
> prefer to publish the one which follows. It is the last one I wrote be-
> fore the production was set in motion and is the most nearly the
> truth of what I want to say in *The Square Root of Wonderful.*
>
> Many novelists have been attracted to the theatre — Fitzgerald,
> Wolfe, James and Joyce. Perhaps this is because of the loneliness
> of a writer's life — the unaccustomed joy of participating cre-
> atively with others is marvelous to a writer. It is rare that a writer
> is equally skilled as a novelist and a playwright. I don't want to
> open this can of beans, but I would say simply that the writer is
> compelled to write, and the form is determined by some veiled
> inward need that perhaps the writer himself does not fully under-
> stand.[33]

As always, in putting pen to paper Carson was apparently able to face up to anything, dispassionately learning the lesson from what had happened and starting over. But this time it was too much for her. The forty-year-old writer, who had put everything she had into that theatrical venture — in the hope that its success would once again bring her happiness, respite from physical suffering, and attention from others — seemed to have expended all the strength she had left. In his memoirs Tennessee Williams remembers the night *The Square Root of Wonderful* opened, calling it one of the three "longest" and "most agonizing exits" of his life — for each of which Carson and he had been together. The first one had occurred at a birthday party given for Dylan Thomas by his publisher. Thomas had said to Williams when they were introduced, "How does it feel to make all that Hollywood money?"

> In retrospect it [Dylan Thomas's question] was thoroughly understandable and excusable, but then it stung me badly. Carson he simply ignored. After a few moments, she said, "Tenn, honey, take me out of here!" — This was after her stroke, and as I led her out of the birthday celebration, she trembled in my supporting arm and the exit seemed to be everlasting.
>
> Another exit was more painful.
>
> Carson had made the mistake of attending the opening night party of her play, *The Square Root of Wonderful* and the greater mistake of remaining there till the reviews came out.
>
> They were simply awful.
>
> Carson again said to me, "Tenn, help me out of here." And it was an even longer and more agonizing exit.[34]

It was no help at all to remember that, though he had encouraged her to write for the theater, Tennessee Williams had warned her of the dangers — saying, with his famous laugh she found so reassuring, "It takes a tough old bird to work in the theatre" — still, Carson simply could not rise above that failure.[35] She was now totally bereft, the very figure of despair. Like an oyster without a shell, her friends said. As Frankie puts it in *The Member of the Wedding*, "I feel just exactly like somebody has peeled all the skin off me."[36] Right down to the bone.

9

THE ULTIMATE REBELLION

IF CARSON MCCULLERS could no longer write, what was the point of enduring so much physical suffering? There wasn't one, as far as she could see. Carson sensed that she would not be granted time to grow old; yet when she turned forty-one on February 19, 1958, she had already been walking with the aid of a cane, her body subject to constant pain, for ten years. Like Flannery O'Connor, she had been forced to write from inside that pain, and in spite of it.

Flannery and Carson did not care for each other, as all their friends confirmed. And since each knew that the other was a good writer, their hostility could not simply be transformed into scorn or indifference. There were too many strange similarities between the two women anyway. Flannery was born eight years later but also in Carson's home state of Georgia — in Savannah, the city that Carson found so beautiful during her last tour of the South in 1953. Unlike Carson, Flannery had hardly budged, except to attend college. When she was separated from her mother, the two had exchanged letters every day, as had Carson and Marguerite Smith. Just as Lula Carson had one day decided to call herself only Carson, Mary Flannery had opted to become simply Flannery. One woman could no longer walk without a cane, the other got around on enormous crutches. "I have decided I must be a pretty pathetic sight with these crutches," wrote Flannery O'Connor on November 10, 1955.

> I was in Atlanta the other day in Davisons. An old lady got on the
> elevator behind me and as soon as I turned around she fixed me

with a moist gleaming eye and said in a loud voice, "Bless you, darling!" I felt exactly like the Misfit and I gave her a weakly lethal look, whereupon greatly encouraged, she grabbed my arm and whispered (very loud) in my ear, "Remember what they said to John at the gate, darling!" It was not my floor but I got off and I suppose the old lady was astounded at how quick I could get away on crutches. I have a one-legged friend and I asked her what they said to John at the gate. She said she reckoned they said, "The lame shall enter first." This may be because the lame will be able to knock everybody else aside with their crutches.[1]

Carson McCullers would live three years longer than Flannery O'Connor, who died in 1964. Both women managed to retain a sense of humor and to build their writer's work.

At the beginning of 1958 Carson had no hope, no projects, no prospects; she could not imagine how she would make it through the winter. And her friends couldn't, either. Since she never complained, they had no real way of knowing how unbearable her illness was. During this terrible winter her voice was sometimes altered on the telephone. When a friend expressed concern, she said simply, "I am in such pain I can hardly talk."[2] Nothing more. The writer Dorothy Salisbury Davis, her neighbor, recalls even today a conversation in which the intensity of Carson's suffering came to the surface. Carson had asked Dorothy Davis if she believed in God. When she said no, Carson added: "I don't either, or I could say, 'God, take this pain away,' and if he did exist, I think he would do it."[3]

Following Flannery O'Connor's example, Carson hated to complain — and could not stand having people feel sorry for her. She was not interested in anyone's pity, with its retinue of mawkish, often feigned emotions. Did her friends finally come to have a better understanding of Carson's sometimes irritating ways, of those times at parties when she went off by herself, clammed up, and drank in silence? Probably. Certainly, they hated feeling totally powerless to help her. This time Carson was just too far gone.

Fortunately, one of her psychiatrist friends, Dr. Ernst Hammerschlag, succeeded at convincing her that regular psychotherapy treatments from a practitioner not far from her home would be infinitely helpful to her. The memory of her 1948 experience at Payne Whitney and the doctor who had tried to convince her that writing in itself was a neurosis was hardly likely to encourage her. She consented nonetheless, probably to give herself "one last chance." Dr. Hammerschlag sent her to Dr. Mary Mercer, who had been living in Nyack since 1956 with her husband, Ray Trussell. The couple divorced in 1961.

Carson recalled that decisive meeting in her unpublished memoir "Illumination and Night Glare." Though her account may be a reconstruction after the fact, it gives an accurate idea of first the reticence and then the enthusiasm with which Carson threw herself into the analytic adventure:

I went professionally to Mary Mercer because I was despondent. My mother had died, . . . and I was ill, badly crippled. Several psychiatrists who are social friends of mine, Ernst Hammerschlag (?) and Hilda Bruck and others had suggested strongly that I go to see Mary Mercer. I resisted just as strongly; not only was the horror of Payne Whitney Hospital still fresh to me, . . . but I resisted psychiatry itself, as I did not accept it as a medical science. The last thing left me, I argued, was my mind, and I was not going to let anyone fiddle with it.

Dr. Mercer lived in the county and was a specialist for children I was told. That seemed to let me out. Ida was a firm ally with me. She knew that my sister had been more than a dozen years in psychiatry. Tennessee was in psychiatry and he was all for it. So between Ida and Tennessee I did not sleep very well for many nights.

I had expected that Dr. Mercer would be ugly, bossy and try to invade my soul's particular territories. I would have to call her to make an appointment Hilda and Ernst had said. That was one telephone call I delayed and suffered over. Walking with my crutch to the living room, picking up the receiver, putting it down, and going through all the motions except actually calling. Finally, I did call, and in a low, pleasant voice Dr. Mercer made an appointment for me.

The day before I went to see her I was awake at three o'clock in the morning, and was getting dressed by nine for an eleven o'clock appointment. Ida had tears in her eyes, "Why you're not crazy, Sister, you're just depressed because so many awful things have happened these days."

So, well before the appointed hour, I was waiting at Dr. Mercer's office. The screen door was hard for me to manage and almost knocked me down. I was breathless by the time I actually faced Dr. Mercer. She was and is the most beautiful woman I've ever seen. Her hair is dark, her eyes gray-blue and her skin very fair. She is always impeccably dressed and her slim figure radiates health and grace. She always wears one strand of pearls. Most of all, her face reflects the inner beauty of her noble and dedicated mind.

I not only liked Dr. Mercer immediately, I loved her, and just as important, I knew I could trust her with my very soul. There was no difficulty in talking to her. All the rebellion and frustration of my life I handed over to her, for I knew that she knew what she was touching. When the fifty minute session was over, she asked me what I was going to do then.

"Go home and think things over."

"It's my lunch time," she said, and to my great surprise and unbounded delight, she asked, "Would you like to join me for lunch?"

We never mentioned psychiatry at lunch time. We talked of books, but mostly we ate in silence. She had said in our first fifty minute session, "I love words, but I tell you Mrs. McCullers, I'm not going to be seduced by your words. I've seen your play, 'Member of the Wedding,' but I've not read any of your books. I want it to stay that way, and will not read them until our therapy is finished." Thereafter after every session we had lunch together, and that was the solace and high point of my day.

Therapy went marvelously well, and in less than a year, she discharged me as a patient. We have become devoted friends, and I cannot imagine life without our love and friendship.[4]

Anyone familiar with psychoanalytic practices may find certain parts of this narrative disconcerting, particularly the surprising postsession luncheon. It seems that the barrier between therapeutic and personal relations is much more porous among Anglo-Saxon practitioners than among their French counterparts — Samuel Beckett's English psychoanalyst, Bion, for example, invited Beckett to attend a Jung conference with him . . .[5] Nor is the extremely short duration of treatment — one year — exceptional for the period. But the strange thing, as Mary Mercer admits, was what took place during Carson's sessions. "I'm quite sure that I did not even know that Carson McCullers lived here," says Mary Mercer today. "Or someone may have mentioned it, and I paid no attention. I had in fact seen her play *The Member of the Wedding* and found it remarkable. That's all. In other words, not very much. She came to see me because she was in urgent need of help. She thought that she would never write again. I agreed to take her on as a patient. But our therapeutic relationship lasted only one year. Afterward we remained friends."[6]

This is certainly a modest description of a daily relationship that held Carson McCullers together, that allowed her to transform a painful process of surviving into a new lease on life, to do more traveling, and especially to write — and that undoubtedly counted a great deal for Mary Mercer. Though she has little to say, it suffices to see the way she speaks of Carson, how she contains her emotion — and sometimes fails to contain it, when she thinks that one is mistaken or not understanding something properly, or when one brings up disagreeable comments that others have made about her friend. Mary Mercer was the most important figure in Carson McCullers's latter years. Thanks to her, Carson was able to finish and publish her novel *Clock Without Hands,* and the few months people once had given her to live were transformed into nearly ten years.

Some of Carson's friends, brilliant artists and creative thinkers, saw Mary Mercer — and continue to see her — as a prosaic woman, very much the figure of smartly dressed conventionality. Photographs from the period do not contradict them. Mercer thoroughly annoyed Janet Flanner, who accused her of trying to cut Carson off from all her old friends. When we met, Mary Mercer was an eighty-four-year-old woman of great distinction, as elegant in her manner of expression as in her appearance. What she said about Carson McCullers is not really conventional at all. Mary Mercer is one of those people who, without uttering a word, immediately discourages a person from asking any question that might be too personal, a quality that makes her extremely appealing. Needless to say, the opinions of people who knew her over time more than thirty years ago cannot be discredited on the basis of a single, brief meeting. Still, after talking with her, after reading the letters and other documents, it is not easy to picture Mary Mercer as yet another person whom Carson charmed and "used."

"It has been stated that I refused to talk about Carson McCullers to people who were doing research on her," Mercer says. "That is not entirely accurate. After all, I'm discussing her with you. But these interviews are very hard for me. For what is analysis if not work on biographical material? Relating biographical information borders on betraying what we did in analysis. But I feel a bit freer now, knowing that Carson herself revealed details in the papers preserved at the University of Texas at Austin, which are essentially open to the public."[7]

She may also have believed that nearly thirty years after her death, Carson McCullers was passing from "memory" into "history," and that that history had to be written. She possesses some exceptional documentation, the tape recordings of Carson's therapy sessions. After Carson's death, when the family, Floria Lasky, and her agent, Robert Lantz, were looking for an authorized biographer, Lantz spoke of these recordings in a letter to Mary Mercer:

> Carson told me that her first session or sessions with you were completely unhelpful to her because she wouldn't talk. Then you had the inspiration to tell her to treat the sessions as "literature," gave her a dictaphone, had transcribed the tapes that she recorded.
>
> It was those pages of transcription which she had in her nighttable drawer and from which she eventually pulled those single sentence statements which were published in Esquire under the heading THE FLOWERING DREAM. As a matter of fact she planned to publish a great deal of that transcript under that title and develop it into a full fledged autobiography.[8]

It is true that "The Flowering Dream" contains elements found on the pages catalogued as "Transcriptions of Meditations During Analysis," but only two of the tapes are in the Austin archive. Moreover, Mercer's version of the facts is somewhat different from Robert Lantz's, and probably more accurate. "Carson did not have much money," she recounts.

> We had decided on a payment of ten dollars per session. One day she arrived in a very gay mood. She had "had an idea." "What do you think about us taping our sessions so I can make a book out of them later?" I told her that in my opinion she was the only patient who would ever come up with such an idea. Besides which, it couldn't be done. It was contrary to the therapeutic "contract." Nonetheless, against all reason and against all the rules of my profession, I agreed to make the tapes — one copy for her and one copy for me — clearly stipulating that this material was not to be

made public in its original form and would constitute only a resource for this book she planned to write. We were in perfect agreement on these terms.

After a few weeks went by, some of my colleagues started calling to express their surprise and disapproval. They had heard that I was "recording cassettes with Carson McCullers that she was playing for anyone and everyone." I, too, was rather shocked. At our very next session I said, "For goodness' sake, Mrs. McCullers, we agreed that those tapes were something we would keep between the two of us." More than private. Secret. She admitted as much. By no means had she played the tapes to embarrass or harm me in any way. She simply did not see why it posed a problem. So she brought me back all her copies — excepting most likely the two that are now in Austin.

"I have them still," adds Mary Mercer, undoubtedly knowing full well how much frustration her remark will engender, "every one."[9]

◆   ◆   ◆

In addition to the passages appearing in "The Flowering Dream," a few snatches from those recordings have been transcribed on paper. They are at once ordinary and strangely touching. Carson's anxiety at the prospect of "really" talking to Mary Mercer comes across in her helpless, disconnected, simultaneously confident and panic-stricken speech.

In the transcription dated April 2, 1958, Carson remembers Annemarie Schwarzenbach, then changes the subject:

That does it I had always thought of Psychiatry as a flat, colorless science, shapeless and rigid. I had the feeling it was simply based on the cliche of how the twig is bent so shall it grow, which may be true enough so far as it goes but is on the dull side. . . . I am beginning to comprehend the beauty and prsmatic wonder and immagination involved. . . . In effect, I'm saying that [for] the first time I understand the use of symbolic logic and the truly musical structure of PYS — damned if I'll struggle with that word again) in which invention of musical figures both re-emphise the original theme and give to the composition variety and warmth.

I am trying to say that as a writer I have always only [understood] from intuition and one [peculiar] aspect of such [instinctive] work is that I never understood what I had written until it was done

— and sometimes not even believe that still, I'm not sure that will change even if you analyse to death.[10]

On April 11, 1958, she speaks of Baudelaire's "My Heart Laid Bare," then questions Dr. Mercer:

Oh, by the way have you been seeing through the bones of my forehead Have you been reading my mind? Dr. Mercer? . . . All my life I have felt that the longer I . . . ["wrote"(?) — noted as "inaudible" in the transcription] the further I went into my own work, the longer I live with the work I love, the more I was aware of the dream and the logical God. . . . and then I met you, Dr. Mercer, and it evolved further than that. (Confusion, association) . . .

I'm thinking of Van Gogh's doctor who . . . you must realize that Van Gogh never sold a single painting in his life and gave them to his doctor. . . . I'm thinking also . . . of schizophrenia . . . and fearing it. . . . Van Gogh killed himself. Nijinski, the great flying angel of the dance, is broken. He's dead now. I'm thinking even of Von Braun and Robert Oppenheimer. . . . V.B. was a Nazi, you know, Hitler's great pal. . . . Oppenheimer is an angel and a poet . . .

. . . If I am going to get an advance from my publisher . . . I have to have some kind of . . . humor and fun . . . or else he will never give me an advance. This leads to Gypsy Rose Lee . . . and Mr. Wechsler. Now Mr. Wechsler . . . When I was living at Gypsy's . . . would come often. We laughed a lot.

I was afraid last night . . . of having a stroke and I even had these false symptoms of a stroke . . . and I was very much afraid. . . . And therefore I called you up at five o'clock. . . . And god bless you. . . .

In the old days I would have just drunk a whole bottle and smoked. . . . I had just one drink. . . . A half a drink really. . . . I would have slept, I think, if I had a couple. . . . I would have in the old days have smoked two packs of cigarettes. . . . (I hardly ever drink anymore when I'm with people.)

I was terribly afraid of yielding to you my childhood, my youth, my fun, my laughter. . . . I didn't know. . . . But never having reached it (maturity) I didn't. . . .

Do you know how I used to suffer over writing letters to friends? Because I yearn to communicate.[11]

It is easy to imagine from this sample how interesting the rest of Carson's taped therapy sessions must be, "every one" of which remains in Mary Mercer's possession. Here, the reference to Van Gogh, who never sold a painting in his lifetime — no more than Reeves ever published a book — or the mention of Nijinski, who after "flying" was "broken," as her own body was, obviously gives one pause, as does the surprising association between the Nazi and the poet, then Carson's remark about requesting an advance from her publisher, which suddenly brings to mind a memory of Gypsy Rose Lee and Mr. Wechsler — the striptease artist from the Brooklyn Heights house and her gangster friend who had left a thousand dollars on the carpet in front of her room.

The transcriptions also show the rebirth of hope and the newly spawned creative plans to which Carson's analytic sessions gave rise:

> This morning I woke up very early, eager to get here, and suddenly I had the most magnificant idea . . . that is that Anna Magnani should play Miss Amelia in the Ballad of the Sad Cafe and [Carol] Reed should direct it. C[arol] R[eed] I just met him once . . . He came to Nyack to see me . . . and he gave me this beautiful cigarette case . . . A wonderful man . . . We talked the whole afternoon. . . . He wanted to do Reflections in the Golden Eye and I said I didn't think it could be done . . . But I'm not sure, You see . . . But I know the Ballad would be magnificent with Magnani with him directing, Don't you think? One we'll have it done in England and he's fabulous and we'll have Orson Welles do some of the sets, You know. He's worked with Orson and Tennessee to write it . . . the film script, see.[12]

The following month she did in fact write a letter to Sir Carol Reed, the British director, to this effect, a letter in which, as was often the case during the last years of her life, Carson sounds bereft. Building pitiful castles in the air, she seems to dream as a way to bear the real, to keep on going:

> After that enchanting afternoon we had together, I began to write a letter to you. It was a long letter. I tried to explain the hazards and the safety of my work. I tried to explain that I felt that your idea was wonderful about having reflections [*Reflections in a Golden Eye*] set. First, it is because I think that an English production will be less bothered by censorship and also by that golden haze of Hollywood and money.

The Heart Is a Lonely Hunter is a natural and I don't think you would have any problems there. It ought to be filmed on location.

That was about the substance of the letter, but also I was telling you in the letter how much I loved you. How much fun we had together and hoping that we would see more of each other. I would adore working with you because you are the most distinguished and beautiful director in the world.

When I did Member of the Wedding, Harold Clurman was there and I was working with Ethel Waters and Julie Harris. It was a real work of art. All of us were there and that would be the way it would be with you and me.

Now, Sir [Carol], I certainly have had a brain wave. I want to do The Ballad of the Sad Cafe. I want you to direct it. I want Anna Magnani to play it. Orson Welles, if we can possibly afford him, to be there for three days — as he was for the Third Man. He told me that. Tennessee Williams and I will do it together, so it will be a beautiful script, you know, with professional advice.

. . .

Now, Sir [Carol], I also sent you my favorite book Out of Africa, which I sent you just as a love gift.[13]

Several times in that long letter she asks her correspondent to answer her quickly. She describes one of her young friends. He was nineteen years old and in love with her,

as a 19 year old boy is in love with an older woman. He reads Finnegan's Wake to me, he reads Yeats to me. He started to read Henry James and I said, "No, I don't want that." He reads Eliot. He is a wonderful reader. . . . He is a lovely boy but when I gave him the letter to read and to correct the spelling, he said he was going to mail it. But he was furious and said, "How could you write a letter like that to a man you only saw once?" So I think he didn't mail it — he kept it for himself.

She speaks again of a possible cast for the film based on *Ballad,* as she had in her psychotherapy session: "Our ideas of casting are as follows, Anna Magnani (Amelia), Marlon Brando (Marvin Macy), Truman Capote (Cousin Lymon)."[14] Truman Capote in the role of the little hunchback loved by Amelia in spite of his deformity — now there's an entertaining idea! And one that shows precisely what Truman and

Carson's relations would never cease to entail: a desire to pull the other down, but also respect and, at bottom, a certain kind of affection.

◆   ◆   ◆

The tone of the letter is fervid, and there is no question but that 1958 was a profoundly unsettling year for Carson. After having believed herself to be "finished," "dried up," literarily impotent, she was beginning, thanks to her sessions with Mary Mercer, to work again. Later on she spoke of having been in such good form intellectually on certain days that she would compose several pages in her head and concentrate on them until her secretary came to write them down. "In addition, something crucial had happened with respect to her illness," Mary Mercer points out:

> To reach my house, Carson had to navigate a sloping walkway, then climb the stairs. I had never given it a thought. One day when she got home from an appointment, she fell ill. She was taken first to Nyack hospital, and eventually to Harkness Pavilion in New York. Normally, I don't concern myself with my patients' physical health. That's another doctor's province, not mine. But I made an exception. I referred Carson to the doctors at Harkness. Their prognosis was very pessimistic. I wanted to find out what was really going on with Carson's physical health, and I asked them to examine her thoroughly, and to take a complete "medical history," starting from scratch. That's how we discovered the cause of her strokes, which are highly unusual in such a young woman. She had had rheumatic fever as a child that went undiagnosed and untreated. It had done irreparable damage.[15]

That was a crucial piece of information not only for the doctors but for Carson herself. For the first time, after ten years of ambiguous anxieties, she finally had a name for her affliction. She no longer had to live in constant terror of "mysterious attacks that could erupt at any moment without anyone knowing what caused them." It would be false, of course, to think that Carson's fear was the sole reason for her excessive consumption of alcohol, but it was certainly an aggravating factor. Remaining in a kind of alcoholic haze was a way of masking her alarm.[16]

After these comprehensive examinations, the doctors decided, in concert with Mary Mercer and Carson McCullers herself, to undertake a series of operations — which should have been performed long before, according to Mary Mercer — to partially restore the mobility of Carson's left arm and hand and, above all, to diminish her suffering. They took place in 1958 and 1961. The list of Carson's various hospitalizations, composed later by Mary Mercer, is pitiful in its very terseness. For 1958 alone we find:

Feb. 19, 1958
Nyack Hospital Acute Left Heart Failure and pneumonia.
May 18 to 30, 1958
Harkness, 3 Reconstruction of left elbow muscles + tendons.
Sept 24–Oct. 14, 1958
Harkness, Reconstruction of left wrist.[17]

Despite everything, in the early spring of 1958, Carson went to New York to take part in an MGM recording that would feature William Faulkner and herself reading their own work, Sir Ralph Richardson reading Joseph Conrad, and Sir Alec Guinness reading Jonathan Swift. Almost impossible to find today, the album has become a collector's item because of Faulkner and Carson McCullers, whose reading of a passage from *The Member of the Wedding* is extremely moving: "She stood in the corner of the bride's room, wanting to say: I love the two of you so much and you are the we of me. Please take me with you from the wedding, for we belong to be together."[18]

When the record was released, in May, the *New York Times* was justifiably somewhat reserved — why choose such brief excerpts of important works? — underlining nonetheless the emotion one felt when listening to Faulkner and Carson McCullers read: "Mrs. McCullers' recording stands apart from the others, for it is not so much an introduction to her work as it is to the lady herself. Her occasional waywardness with the text, her emotional involvement in what she is reading, the break in her voice in certain passages — all these give this recording its own special quality though it is not always a literary one. Mrs. McCullers reads from 'The Member of the Wedding,' 'The Heart Is a Lonely Hunter,' 'The Ballad of the Sad Café,' and three of her poems. The poetry was a good idea, since it is a side of her art not so well known."[19]

Once again Carson had surmounted the obstacle, the failure, the pain, to defend her literary identity and her place as an American writer. In July she gave a conference at Columbia University in New York and wrote the preface to *The Square Root of Wonderful,* which Houghton Mifflin was to publish. On August 19 she took part in a television program on the theater, but most of her time was spent working on what she called "a new manuscript," "The Flowering Dream." The full manuscript, dated August 23, 1958, can be found in the Austin archives. A shortened and revised version appeared the following year in *Esquire* magazine with the subtitle "Notes on Writing." Although born of autobiographical preoccupations, it gives Carson's general reflections on writing and literature. Here again is the intellectual firmness that Carson McCullers has shown before on these subjects:

> A writer's main asset is intuition; too many facts impede intuition. A writer needs to know so many things, but there are so many things he doesn't need to know — he needs to know human things even if they aren't "wholesome," as they call it. . . .
>
> When someone asks me who has influenced my work, I point to O'Neill, the Russians, Faulkner, Flaubert. *Madame Bovary* seems to be written with divine economy. It is one of the most painfully written novels, and one of the most painfully considered, of any age. *Madame Bovary* is a composite of the realistic voice of Flaubert's century, of the realism versus the romantic mind of his times. In its lucidity and faultless grace, it seems to have flown straight from Flaubert's pen without an interruption in thought. For the first time, he was dealing with his truth as a writer. . . .
>
> Few Southern writers are truly cosmopolitan. When Faulkner writes about the R.A.F. and France, he is somehow not convincing — while I'm convinced in almost every line about Yoknapatawpha County. Indeed, to me *The Sound and the Fury* is probably the greatest American novel. It has an authenticity, a grandeur and, most of all, a tenderness that stems from the combination of reality and the dream that is the divine collusion.
>
> Hemingway, on the contrary, is the most cosmopolitan of all the American writers. He is at home in Paris, in Spain, in America, the Indian stories of his childhood. Perhaps it is his style, which is a delivery, a beautifully worked out form of expression. As expert as Hemingway is at producing and convincing the reader of his vari-

ous outlooks, emotionally he is a wanderer. In Hemingway's style some things are masked in the emotional content of his work. If I prefer Faulkner to Hemingway, it's because I am more touched by the familiar — the writing that reminds me of my own childhood and sets a standard for a remembering of the language. Hemingway seems to me to use language as a style of writing. . . .

The writer's work is predicated not only on his personality but by the region in which he was born. I wonder sometimes if what they call the "Gothic" school of Southern writing, in which the grotesque is paralleled with the sublime, is not due largely to the cheapness of human life in the South. The Russians are like the Southern writers in that respect. In my childhood, the South was almost a feudal society. But the South is complicated by the racial problem more severely than the Russian society. To many a poor Southerner, the only pride that he has is the fact that he is white, and when one's self-pride is so pitiably debased, how can one learn to love? Above all, love is the main generator of all good writing. Love, passion, compassion are all welded together.[20]

Part of that summer and fall were taken up by a dispute with Carson's French editor, André Bay, regarding the French adaptation of *The Member of the Wedding* for the stage. Composed by Bay, the script had originally been approved by Carson. Now she was suddenly dissatisfied with it. The play was finally produced in Paris, at the Alliance Française, in an adaptation by André Bay and William Hope, a young American also born in Georgia who had a passion for the writing of Carson McCullers, under the direction of the same William Hope. But the play's venue and extremely brief run garnered only critical rather than popular acclaim. Gabriel Marcel's review in *Les Nouvelles littéraires* highlights the originality of Carson McCullers's work: "People have spoken of Chekhov with regard to Carson McCullers and *The Member of the Wedding*. I do not deny the connection. But we are in the presence here of an indisputably authentic work of art."[21]

The conflict put an end to the congenial relations between André Bay and Carson. Carson was not mistaken to say that French translations of her novels were poor and thus gave her good reason to be cautious; and Bay had every reason to be upset that she had originally approved his adaptation, only to call everything to a halt as the play was going into production. But the incident is fascinating for what it reveals about Carson's recaptured pugnacity. Telegrams and letters to André Bay — and Bay's astonished responses — follow one upon the other that June.[22] Carson, for her part, wrote notably:

> I have no recollection of having approved this translation — or a similar one — in 1954. Since I neither read nor understand French well enough for such a purpose, I really don't see how it could have been reported to you that I had "heard" the French text and approved of it. . . .
>
> I arrived at my decision to withhold approval of the present text after having it read by a French girl who is a close friend of mine, who is quite familiar with all my work and who is a successful artist in her own right. Her opinion was that the translation was too literal and that it was lacking in poetry and grace. She checked this with a qualified friend of hers who agreed that such was the case.
>
> . . .
>
> Two qualified persons, one of them Janet Flanner, have pointed to the dialogue of both Frankie and Berenice as being lacking in the poetry which stems from their special language. . . . We are not objecting to the faithfulness of the translation, but to the spirit of the translation.
>
> . . .
>
> Finally, I regret that you did not consult me about either Mr. Hope or the cast. But these are things of the past; and the problem, now, is one of the future. Thus I shall earnestly hope that you will keep me posted on all further developments because of my devotion to this play and my desire to arrive at an amicable resolution.

Meanwhile Audrey Wood, Carson McCullers's agent at the time, had gotten in touch with the person who handled Carson's interests in France. Having been assured of Bay's and young Bill Hope's good intentions, Wood reported to Carson that the two men "had never seen this project as a mere commercial venture but had worked in a real spirit of devotion to [her], as a person and an artist."[23]

On July 19 Carson sent a final letter to André Bay, written in French, to seal the peace, but, with touching firmness, she insisted on reiterating that she had been right, so strong a sense of dispossession, indeed annihilation, did she have — as would any writer but all the more so someone who, like her, had to fight to stay alive — when, rightly or wrongly, she felt herself excluded from her own work: "I do not understand how the objections of a writer who values the integrity of his oeuvre, of which he alone can judge, can be deemed unjustified or incomprehensible."

The Frenchwoman mentioned in one of the letters, "a successful artist in her own right," was Marielle Bancou. Beautiful, refined, about thirty years old, she had a great deal of charm. She was also one of the people who made Carson McCullers's life bearable, and sometimes gay, during her last years. Since 1953 Marielle had lived in the apartment house next door to 131 Broadway. After that building burned down in January 1959, she stayed for several months in Carson's large house, where she lived on the ground floor. In "Illumination and Night Glare" Carson speaks of their meeting on a Nyack–New York bus, Marielle's distress after the fire, and the Frenchwoman's devoted friendship even after she moved out:

> When she moved away I missed her terribly, but she still managed to come for Sunday supper. . . . She would tell me all about her work as a fabric designer and show me her lovely prints. . . . The fire didn't finish her or even slow her down very much. Gracious, and with the beauty of spirit I've seldom encountered, funny, witty and profound, she's my oldest and along with Mary Mercer my best friend.[24]

When Carson wished to write in French to André Bay, Marielle translated for her. As she did at the time, Marielle still believes today that "it must have taken a miracle, and all the power and magic of Carson's oeuvre, for the French public to be able to appreciate her writing despite such really mediocre translations. I hear that new ones have been done, and I'm glad. They could only be an improvement."[25]

Marielle Bancou, whom Carson called "Snowflakes" or "Little Color Combination," was a fashion designer and designed numerous articles of clothing for Carson, who had developed a passion for costly, diaphanous fabrics, particularly white ones. Much later, after Carson's death, Marielle Bancou created "painted books" linking text with visual artistic expression; several of her pieces are tributes to the oeuvre of Carson McCullers and were exhibited at the La Hune gallery in Paris in 1992.

A very strong friendship existed between the two women, who

shared a deep affection and a love of laughing together. In Carson's universe Marielle was vitality and youth; she was fantasy, while Mary Mercer stood on the side of reason. The two friends were necessarily antagonists. Marielle Bancou can be counted among those who saw Mary Mercer as "a very traditional person," and her description of the relationship between Carson and her doctor, a highly personal portrait that makes no claim whatsoever to being objective, is amusing:

> Mary Mercer was a child psychiatrist. Conventional and traditional, she had the kindness and compassion of a country doctor. Plus a certain curiosity about the very famous person Carson still was at the time. Plus an amorous attraction, cultivated by Carson, who had snared a new victim she could easily suck the lifeblood from. Mary Mercer was clearly no match for her patient. Carson wished to undergo analysis because she was no longer able to write — which is the problem of the hero in her play that had just failed, *The Square Root of Wonderful.* It was much more convenient to have an analyst in Nyack, and that's where Mary Mercer entered the picture. Carson already had a hard time getting around, and taking a taxi up the hill in Nyack was easier for her.
>
> Not so easy were Carson's Machiavellian preparations for every therapy session. She was constantly making up cock-and-bull stories about an imaginary past that she intended to recount, then she would try them out on me to see how someone might react. My response was always: "It doesn't shock me; try it on Mary."
>
> "What about this one? Do you think it will shock her?" Carson would persist, coming up with yet another fabulous tale.
>
> That said, Mary was a very organized person with a practical mind, and she put some order into Carson's chaotic existence, her parade of nurses, secretaries, and so on. Carson was very dependent. She needed almost constant assistance even for the seemingly simplest things, which her paralysis made it impossible for her to do alone.[26]

Marielle Bancou's account minimizes Mary Mercer's role or at least her closeness to Carson and the affection Carson surely had for her. But what Bancou says about Carson's duplicity, how she tried not to submit to the psychiatrist and her techniques, how she claimed to be manipulating her and taking control of the analysis, can be seen as a sign of vitality. Nothing indicates, though, that Mary Mercer was duped by Carson's deliberate fabrications, supposing she was ever exposed to them. On the one hand, Carson's "boasts" in front of others clearly served as a means of denial and were rarely repeated within the analytic relationship; on the other, while the therapy sessions that we have on tape contain flagrant departures from reality — particularly concerning Reeves — there is nothing that stems from a deliberate desire to "shock" anyone.

Carson needed Marielle Bancou, who made her feel young, as she would still have been — at forty-two — had it not been for her illness. When Marielle went away to France in the autumn of 1959, Carson was disconsolate and wrote letters asking her to come home soon, in time for Thanksgiving. Similarly, for Marielle, Carson "was America."[27] Her attachment to the United States, where she still resides, dividing her time between New York and Paris, was forged by her relationship with Carson. Marielle Bancou paints the liveliest imaginable portrait of her friend, vividly remembering her with humor. Marielle conjures up the image of a feisty Carson McCullers who was very much alive, who may have called her friends "those sugary Southern names like 'Precious,'" but who well knew how to impose her will.

◆　◆　◆

She would put that will to use once again to bring to Nyack one of her heroines, Karen Blixen. On January 28, 1959, Carson traveled to New York to attend a lecture by the author of *Out of Africa,* Isak Dinesen, the Baroness Blixen, and the dinner party given in her honor by the American Academy of Arts and Letters. Carson, who had reread *Out of Africa* every year since 1937 and gotten all her friends to read it too, possessed an unconditional admiration for its author. She had written an article on her that appeared in 1943 in the *New Republic* and an essay, "Isak Dinesen: In Praise of Radiance," which came out in the *Saturday Review* in 1963:

> With [Dinesen's] simplicity and "unequalled nobility" I realized that this was one of the most radiant books of my life.
>
> The burning deserts, the jungles, the hills opened my heart to Africa. Open to my heart, also, were the animals and that radiant being, Isak Dinesen. Farmer, doctor, lion hunter, if need be. Be-

cause of *Out of Africa,* I loved Isak Dinesen. When she would ride through a maise grassland, I would ride with her. Her dogs, her farm, "Lulu," became my friends, and the natives for whom she had such great affection — Farsh, Kamante, and all the people on the farm — I loved also. I had read *Out of Africa* so much and with so much love that the author had become my imaginary friend. Although I never wrote to her or sought to meet her, she was there in her stillness, her serenity, and her great wisdom to comfort me. In this book, shining with her humanity, of that great and tragic continent, her people became my people and her landscape my landscape.

Naturally, I wanted to read her other works, and the next book I read was *Seven Gothic Tales.* Instead of the radiance of *Out of Africa,* the *Tales* have a quite different quality. They are brilliant, controlled, and each gives the air of a deliberate work of artistry. One realizes that the author is writing in a foreign language because of the strange, archaic quality of her beautiful prose. They had the quality of a luminous, sulphuric glow. When I was ill or out of sorts with the world, I would turn to *Out of Africa,* which never failed to comfort and support me — and when I wanted to be lifted out of my life, I would read *Seven Gothic Tales* or *Winter's Tales* or, much later, *The Last Tales.*[28]

Karen Blixen's biographer, Judith Thurman, devotes a long passage to Carson's meeting with Isak Dinesen:

At the dinner that followed [the presentation at the American Academy of Arts and Letters], Isak Dinesen sat next to one of her most distinguished fans, Carson McCullers. It was something of an epiphany for both women, for Dinesen had admired *The Heart Is a Lonely Hunter* and had reread it many times, while McCullers had "fallen in love with Isak Dinesen twenty years before, after reading *Out of Africa.*" Despite her own extreme frailty, she had come to the dinner hoping to wangle an introduction to her "African heroine."

When McCullers learned that Isak Dinesen longed to meet Marilyn Monroe, she eagerly volunteered to arrange it. Arthur Miller, an old friend, was sitting at the next table; he came over, and the party — a luncheon — was set for February 5. The Millers were to call for the Baroness and Clara in their car, and they arrived with the unpunctuality Marilyn was famous for. She had just finished *Some Like It Hot* and her beauty was at its ripest. Dressed in a black sheath with a deep décolletage and a fur collar, incredibly fair, radiant, and rather shy, she looked — Clara thought — "fifteen years old." Isak Dinesen, wearing the gray ensemble she called "Sober Truth," had a different kind of radiance; "her face was lit like a candle in an old church."

A meal that included oysters, white grapes, champagne, and a soufflé was laid on Carson McCullers's black marble table. Marilyn told the party an amusing story about her own culinary adventures. She had tried to make pasta for her husband and some guests, using her mother-in-law's recipe. But it got a little late, the company was arriving, and the pasta wasn't ready, so she had tried to finish it off with a hair dryer. Everyone laughed, but Clara was a little shocked. She found it odd that a goddess would spend her time cooking macaroni. Arthur Miller, in the meantime, questioned the Baroness about her eating habits. Was it wise, he asked, for someone so frail to eat nothing but grapes, oysters, and champagne? She brushed him off by saying: "I am an old woman and I eat what agrees with me."

"Carson," writes her biographer, "always performed best in small groups in which she could be assured control as the center of attention. Yet this day [she] happily relinquished the stage to her guest." Isak Dinesen told "Barua a Soldani" and went on talking about her life "with such warmth that her listeners didn't have to try to interrupt her marvelous conversation." Later, she sought out her hostess's black housekeeper, Ida Reeder, and had a long talk with her, explaining that she "missed her black friends." Toward the end of the afternoon, so the story goes, McCullers put a record on the phonograph and invited Marilyn and the Baroness to dance with her on the marble table, and they took a few steps in each other's arms. Other members of the party (including Miller) "doubt" that this took place, but the hostess loved to retell it. This was "the best" and most "frivolous" party she had ever given, and she expressed "childlike pleasure and wonderment at the love which her guests seemed to express . . . for each other."[29]

Whether or not they danced together, it is difficult to picture a more poignant or fantastic couple than Dinesen and Monroe. They died in the same year, and Glenway Wescott imagined that "the same boat carried them across the Styx." Dinesen "loved" Carson McCullers and enjoyed meeting Arthur Miller, but it was Marilyn who made the real impression. "It is not that she is pretty," she told Fleur Cowles, "although of course she is almost incredibly pretty — but that she radiates at the same time unbounded vitality and a kind of unbelievable innocence. I have met the same in a lion cub that my native servants in Africa brought me. I would not keep her."[30]

When his opportunity came to speak about that day, Arthur Miller told Virginia Spencer Carr that Marilyn had probably never read anything by Carson.[31] At best she had seen *The Member of the Wedding* in the theater, but there had been a kind of spontaneous sympathy between the two women. About Miller himself Carson had written in 1949 to Tennessee Williams that she had been "very impressed" by *Death of a Salesman.*[32]

Today Arthur Miller claims to have only a vague memory of that luncheon. He nonetheless remembers the year, almost the month, and the presence of another guest, even though he says he had forgotten that it was Karen Blixen: "Marilyn was the one that Carson especially wanted to meet. She seemed very ill, she was almost an invalid, paralyzed, her muscles shriveled. And contrary to the legend, she did not start dancing on the table. She simply would not have been capable of it."[33]

It is Carson herself, in her essay, who describes the alleged dance — but she does not say they danced on the table. Carson speaks of calling Isak Dinesen "Baroness" "until we were on a first-name basis and she asked me to call her Tanya, which is her English name."

Tanya ate only oysters and drank only champagne. At the luncheon we had many oysters and for the big eaters several large soufflés. Arthur asked what doctor put her on that diet of nothing but oysters and champagne. She looked at him and said rather sharply, "Doctor? The doctors are horrified by my diet but I love champagne and I love oysters and they agree with me." Then she added, "It is sad, though, when oysters are not in season, for then I have to turn back to asparagus in those dreary months." Arthur mentioned something about protein and Tanya said, "I don't know anything about that but I am old and I eat what I want and what agrees with me." Then she went back to her reminiscences of friends in Africa.

It was a great delight for her to be with colored people. Ida, my housekeeper, is colored, and so are my yardmen, Jesse and Sam. After lunch everybody danced and sang. A friend of Ida's had brought in a motion picture camera, and there were pictures of Tanya dancing with Marilyn, me dancing with Arthur, and a great round of general dancing. I love to remember this for I never met Tanya again. Since writers seldom write to each other, our communication was infrequent but not vague. She sent me flowers when I was ill and lovely pictures of her cows and her darling dog in Rungsted Kyst.[34]

Miller is right that she could not have danced, and certainly not on a table. That detail was probably added by someone or other to make the story more improbable. But when Carson wrote — even what was supposedly just facts — she was compelled to tell the story according to her own desires, the way she would have wanted it if she had never been ill. "Carson saw her life one way and those intimate with her often perceived it differently," recalls her sister. "Besides, she simply liked a good story and frequently embellished the more amusing ones of her life."[35]

"I no longer remember the conversation — if there was one, that is," adds Arthur Miller. "She wrote works of loneliness and isolation. Very moving. I liked some of them. But in the grand scheme of things, I think she was a minor author. Though her oeuvre may simply have been 'broken,' precociously interrupted because she fell ill at such a young age and then died at the height of her maturity."

Carson would have been seventy-eight years old in 1995. Arthur Miller was eighty. His determination to portray her as "a minor author" — shared with many survivors from that era — is interesting. Miller would even have us believe that he could not name a single one of her books, while he remembered his visit to her home, contenting himself with a vague "I was very fond of . . . one or two of the stories she wrote." He seems greatly preoccupied by posterity, by the possibility of sudden oblivion to which almost all once-famous people succumb. One almost gets the impression that although he himself was still among the living, Arthur Miller wanted to make certain that Carson McCullers would not literarily outlast him.

Though he may have understood that the matter was already settled — for the readers of Carson McCullers around the world, not vast in number, form a club of devotees whose membership is constantly renewed. Every adolescent who loves reading sooner or later opens up *The Heart Is a Lonely Hunter* and shares the emotion and interest of his or her elders. Carson McCullers's oeuvre is admittedly limited in its breadth as well as its themes, and it can be called minor for those reasons. But it does not age, which is rare for minor works. It is as if the premature death of its author, far from dimming the brilliance of her work, provided a form of protection.

◆　◆　◆

Toward the end of August 1959, Carson rejoiced at having finished composing a libretto so that *The Ballad of the Sad Café* could be made into a musical and, above all, at having passed the halfway point in *Clock Without Hands.* She was working, however, in conditions that she formerly would have deemed impossible, conditions that compelled her to reassess her own conception of what it meant to be a writer, what it meant to create. Dictating was difficult for her. Back in Reeves's day, at least he had been able to sit down at the typewriter whenever Carson felt the urge to compose, making it possible for her to go faster than she could have alone with only one good hand and shaky spelling. Now, when her inclination to work did not coincide with her secretary's scheduled hours, she did her best to jot down points of reference on a sheet of paper or, more often, memorize them. She had to find the right words, remember the precise sentence, preserve its rhythm . . . It became an obsession, and indeed it created a psychological stress that is difficult to measure — mentally formulating the sentence, outlining new approaches to it, modifying this or that in her head, attempting to etch the definitive form of it all in memory — and fearing that some new thought might come along and blot out or modify its traces.

And yet the book advanced, to Carson's own amazement. She was feeling better than she had in a very long time, as she wrote to several friends, including Edith Sitwell. Yes, indeed, a novel was taking shape. And what a novel meant was absolute victory, formal proof — in all senses of the word *formal* — that Carson was a writer again. Mary Mercer had been right at their first meeting. Carson McCullers had not lost her soul or her intelligence or her creative genius. "Mary saved my life," said her grateful patient. Or, rather, Mary had made it possible for Carson to save *her own* life, to reject yet again a death she ceaselessly defied, though it never ceased trying to snatch her. Her suffering had not disappeared for all that. But it again became possible to make it take a backseat to the pleasure of writing.

And reading. Carson even began to enjoy reading newspapers again. She preferred the *Daily News* to the *New York Times*, the news-in-brief column and stories about crime, dysfunction, or the down-and-out to global politico-economic analyses, human-interest pieces to historical material. "Every day, I read the New York *Daily News*, and very soberly," she wrote in "The Flowering Dream."

> It is interesting to know the name of the lover's lane where the stabbing took place, and the circumstances which the *New York Times* never reports. In that unsolved murder in Staten Island, it is interesting to know that the doctor and his wife, when they were stabbed, were wearing Mormon nightgowns, three-quarter length. Lizzie Borden's breakfast, on the sweltering summer day she killed her father, was mutton soup. Always details provoke more ideas than any generality could furnish. When Christ was pierced in His *left* side, it is more moving and evocative than if He were just pierced.[36]

Her imagination had come back to life. Carson was watching, comparing, storing up ideas for new stories. She even made new plans to ensure — materially — that she could carry them out. On August 23, a novelist in search of funds, Carson wrote to one of her peers, Thornton Wilder:

> This may sound like the department of mutual admiration but for years I've been telling you how much I love your work. Two or three weeks ago I received a letter from the Ford Foundation offering fellowships to stimulate interest in the theatre among poets and novelists. Your interest in the theatre has already well stimulated the whole world, but at this point I need a little stimulation myself. I am hoping that you will be willing to recommend me to the Ford Foundation.
>
> Since it would be the grossest nepotism for me to recommend myself, I am inclosing the blank in hopes that you will be willing to lend me your support. . . .
>
> Gratefully, and with much love,
> Carson[37]

Whatever Wilder's reaction to the playfully ironic letter was, the fellowship application itself got "lost in the sands." Carson came up empty, too, when she tried for a Guggenheim the following year; her application was denied on the grounds that she had already received the award twice.

Above all Carson did not want to break her rhythm and stop writing. When she felt unable to progress on her novel manuscript, she tried writing poetry for children. At least that is what she told Mary Tucker when her old music teacher came to see her, a visit during which Mary Tucker met Mary Mercer. As it happened, the two women liked each other — probably because they both were "well established," as Carson's artist friends would no doubt say.

Dear Darling Mary [Tucker]:
I think I cannot remember any more beautiful afternoon and evening than we spent together. Mary, Trussel loved you, and to see my two mayors together was an unutterable delight. . . . I still haven't found a composer and have to wait until I myself know the way the Ballad is going. As a composer is the prime essential, from now on, as you know, I still have much work to be done but am going to put it aside temporarily, work on CLOCK WITHOUT HANDS, until the right composer materializes.[38]

No composer seems to have "materialized," but in July 1960 the playwright Edward Albee (who would achieve international success in 1962 with his play *Who's Afraid of Virginia Woolf?*) staked his interest in adapting *The Ballad of the Sad Café* for the stage.

Also in 1960 the young Democratic senator John Fitzgerald Kennedy was elected president. Like all "leftist intellectuals," Carson had been disappointed when the Democratic convention failed to nominate the highly cultured and elegant Adlai Stevenson as that party's candidate for the White House. But the young senator from Massachusetts had an intriguing charisma and eventually won her over. Once he was chosen by the Democratic Party, she supported his candidacy with passion. And for that Carson was invited to attend the presidential inauguration in Washington. She very much wanted to be present at that event but let her friends convince her that she was too weak to make the trip. So Carson stayed in Nyack and on December 1, 1960, was able to proclaim that she had won a victory against substantial odds: she had finished *Clock Without Hands*. It had taken her ten years of fierce determination to reach the finish line. Carson's last great novel, *The Member of the Wedding*, had come out in 1946, just before her health had taken its disastrous turn.

✦ ✦ ✦

Clock Without Hands was to be published in the fall of 1961 by Houghton Mifflin. That spring Carson, accompanied by Mary Mercer, had gone to see Edward Albee on Shelter Island to work with him on the adaptation of *The Ballad of the Sad Café*. On June 20, as planned, Carson had a second operation on her left hand. The surgery left her very weak. From that time on, she would spend most hours when she was out of bed — which were not very many — in a wheelchair. During her hospitalization Carson got a letter from Tennessee Williams, to whom she had sent her manuscript. He believed that when she felt better, she should do some more work on Chapter 4, and he suggested changes pertaining for the most part to the young black rebel Sherman Pew.

The letter was not given to Carson while she was ill, and Jordan Massee's journal reflects the various points of view held by her friends. Robert Lantz, her agent, felt that publication should not be postponed: it was too late to make changes at that point — supposing that Carson would agree to any. Jordan Massee, for his part, thought that Tennessee Williams's remarks were probably relevant but that the playwright did not realize how sick Carson was "nor how important the publication of *Clock Without Hands* is to her pulling through." Besides which, he doubted that Carson would agree to a single correction despite her high regard for Tennessee's opinion. "It was difficult enough to get her to agree to corrections in spelling, punctuation, and grammar back in February when changes were still feasible."[39]

Massee's journal from that period — or at least the excerpts from it that he has shared with others — shows how some of Carson's friends reacted to her new book. Jordan Massee's father, for example, claimed that he was deeply hurt to find stories reiterated there that he had once delightedly told Carson: there were, in his opinion, "things in the book that a woman just ought not to be writing about." His son suspected, rather, that the elder Massee may have recognized himself somewhat in the figure of Judge Clane, a backward-looking, elderly Southerner, and had little taste for the comparison.

◆　◆　◆

No sooner did Carson's new novel, dedicated to Mary Mercer, reach bookstore shelves, on September 18, 1961, than it revealed the level of the public's anticipation and the author's intact reputation: *Clock Without Hands* immediately appeared on the bestseller list, at number six — and it stayed there for six months. Set in a small Southern town, the story involves a confrontation between an old segregationist Southerner, his grandson, a young black boy who has blue eyes and wonders if he might be of mixed race, and a man who is dying of leukemia at forty years of age.

Carson had not visited the South for a a long while, but having been born there, she could never really leave: "The locale of my books might always be Southern, and the South always my homeland."[40] Also in 1961, Carson, having become a celebrity in Columbus, Georgia, received a request that she entrust her manuscripts to that city's public library. She refused on the grounds that the library — to which Carson had already sent an open letter of protest and indignation — was still reserved for whites only:

> In response to your letter of some months ago, I immediately began a search of my archives and have, I am delighted to report, come up with a large collection of manuscripts. Then the thought occurred to me: "How can I, in all good conscience, deposit these works of love in a place where all mankind is not permitted to read, enjoy and use them?"
>
> And so, before I send along the papers in which you are so kindly interested, I must inquire whether or not the Columbus Public Library is truly a public one. . . . I believe now, as I have believed all my life, that God created all men. And my idea of God precludes the possibility of His having created men to be anything but equal in His sight.
>
> Since I am pleased and flattered that you want my manuscripts, I shall look forward to hearing from you further; and to their eventual transfer from me to you.[41]

Carson could simply have sent them her novel. It contains her entire response, as Granville Hicks perceptively noted in the piece he wrote for the *Saturday Review:* "In an important sense this is a novel about the race problem. . . . But Mrs. McCullers is not trying to underline the obvious fact that there is a problem, nor has she a solution she wants to thrust upon us; her purpose is to show the problem at the deepest possible level, as it penetrates the secret recesses of human souls."[42]

In the fall of 1961 *Clock Without Hands* was the novel that no periodical could overlook. Never had a book by Carson McCullers received so many reviews. In Great Britain all responses were extremely favorable, but in the United States opinions were divided. *Time* magazine, on September 22, offered one of the harshest, even though the article begins by paying homage to the talent of certain Southerners, among them Carson McCullers:

Violence colors the surface of Southern writing, but its core is a sense of violation. In Southern historical memory, the great act of violation was, of course, the Civil War and its aftermath. Put as baldly and inartistically as Margaret Mitchell put it, the lament of the South in *Gone with the Wind* was: a rape — of a people as well as a person — is a rape. Among greatly talented Southern writers, the theme of violation is indirectly stated but pervades the whole texture of life. In Faulkner, the social order is violated, debasing the semifeudal values of a landed gentry. In Tennessee Williams, what is violated is love and a kind of vagrant individuality. In Carson McCullers, there is the violation of innocence. At its best, this mixture of grief and grievance is poetic, at its worst, bathetic. As craftsmen, the Southern writers are generally sloppy; they represent the triumph of mood over matter.

. . . What happens when the mood fails is sadly apparent in *Clock Without Hands,* a novel without direction or much visible point except as a tame foray into race relations. Novelist McCullers drops story threads and comes close to losing the entire narrative spool. . . . Motivations are inept and mystifying. Her people are all of a piece or all in pieces. What redeems some of these flaws is the special McCullers gift, the moment of high emotion when a lonely soul rapping on the wall of his imprisoned self hears an answering knock.

. . . Death is admittedly the theme Novelist McCullers chose for her novel, but its dark and powerful presence is not felt. Instead, there is only death's counterfeit, the absence of life.

Whitney Balliett's short review in the September 23, 1961, issue of the *New Yorker* is more negative still. Balliett's piece exemplifies hateful, reactionary criticism whose heavy-handed attempts at humor do not wear well over time:

> Carson McCullers' "Clock Without Hands" (Houghton Mifflin) is about three resolutely grotesque symbols who live in a small, baking Southern town. The largest of them is eighty-five-year-old Judge Clane (the Old South), who, diseased, mad, and sunk in past glories, shares a rambling house with his squeamish grandson, a teenager. Symbol No. 2 is Sherman Pew (the New, or Negro, South), a young, blue-eyed Negro who becomes a companion to the Judge. Pew is nasty and effeminate, and the Judge's grandson falls in love with him. After drinking up a lot of the Judge's liquor and sassing him, Pew quits his job and rents a house in the run-down white section of town. Poor white trash, organized by the addled Judge, bomb the house and kill Pew. The third symbol, a gaunt forty-year-old druggist and an admirer of the Judge, is J. T. Malone (the Conscience of the South). He discovers at the start of the book that he has leukemia, wastes slowly away, and dies on the last page. He refuses to have any part in the bombing. Mrs. McCullers' prose, rumpled and gossipy, gives the peculiar impression of having been slept in.[43]

Less devastating reviews also pointed to what the *New Republic* of November 13, 1961, called "weaknesses of structure and conception" or, like John Gross's piece in the *New Statesman* of October 27, called the work Carson McCullers's "weakest book to date." Catherine Hughes's long article in the October 13 *Commonweal* wrote that this highly ambitious novel failed to rise to the level of its pretensions, though she thought Carson was one of the rare American writers capable of mastering important and difficult topics.

Happily, Jean Martin of the *Nation* saw things in a better light: "From the standpoint of its author, *Clock Without Hands* is a step forward, a success, for it eschews the pointed and labored allegory of her earlier works and the frequently trumped-up Southern characters have now been blended happily into a believable story level. . . . *Clock Without Hands* is warm, funny and readable; its point may not quite click, but the writing is quietly superb."[44] The novel also had its share of unconditional and enthusiastic defenders, prominent among them Rumer Godden, whose article appeared in the Books section of the *New York Herald Tribune* the day before *Clock Without Hands* was released, on September 17. "For me not a word could be added or taken away from this marvel of a novel by Carson McCullers," Godden wrote.

> Her talent is extraordinary; the name of her first book "The Heart Is a Lonely Hunter" might be a description of it: the steady life-giving beat that is the core of every book; the pursuit of the quarry she sees and would catch and hold for us, often something so fleeting and ephemeral that most authors would quail at trying to catch it in words — and Mrs. McCullers' words are the coin of every day, plain, frank, slangy, unemotional.[45]

On October 20 the British *Times Literary Supplement* was very positive:

> Novels of the south have at the moment a sharply topical relevance. The problems of race which they naturally explore confront us all in one shape or another; and the sense of a large, expectant audience is a temptation to melodrama and exaggeration. It is vastly to Miss McCullers's credit that she avoids such pitfalls, while subtly presenting the moral issues and analysing the psychology of the distressing situation. She has been able by dint of honesty as much as by technical skill to write a good and moving book which comes up to all the demands raised by her reputation.

Even Gore Vidal, who was hardly inclined to indulgence toward Carson, wrote: "Technically, it is breath-taking to watch her set a scene and then dart from character to character, opening up in a phrase, a line, a life," he writes, adding, "McCullers writes in exact prose closer to the Flaubert of *Un Coeur simple* [A simple heart] than to [the Faulkner of] *Absalom, Absalom!* . . . There is never a false note. . . . [McCullers's] genius for prose remains one of the few satisfying achievements of our second-rate culture."[46]

Bolstered by scholarly essays, the enduring opinion has been that the negative reviews got it right and that *Clock Without Hands* should be treated, at worst, as a second-rate effort, at best, as Carson McCullers's least worthy novel. Could this be because Tennessee Wil-

liams suggested that changes be made and supposedly said, in addition, that this text did not "rise to the level of Carson McCullers"?
Could it be because Flannery O'Connor detested it, contending that
for her the novel represented total disintegration?[47] Could it be because it is Carson McCullers's most committed novel on the racial
question? Or could it be, more simply still, because it is strictly unacceptable that a writer should meet success with a book that was half
written, half dictated, abandoned, salvaged, thrown out, and resumed
— while nonetheless retaining, by some mysterious means, its charm,
its originality, its intimate music? All these things probably played
their part, since the tired clichés about this "failed" work persist.

Like *The Heart Is a Lonely Hunter,* like *Reflections in a Golden Eye,*
and like *The Member of the Wedding, Clock Without Hands* is pure
Carson McCullers right from the start:

> Death is always the same, but each man dies in his own way. For
> J. T. Malone it began in such a simple ordinary way that for a time
> he confused the end of life with the beginning of a new season. The
> winter of his fortieth year was an unusually cold one for the South-
> ern town — with icy, pastel days and radiant nights. The spring
> came violently in middle March in that year of 1953, and Malone
> was lazy and peaked during those days of early blossoms and windy
> skies. He was a pharmacist and, diagnosing spring fever, he pre-
> scribed for himself a liver and iron tonic. Although he tired easily,
> he kept to his usual routine.[48]

Oliver Evans was the first, in his discussion of Carson McCullers,
to initiate a reappraisal of this book:

> Doubtless it is still too early for a critic to evaluate *Clock Without
> Hands* with the proper degree of perspective. My own feeling is:
> granted that the book is uneven stylistically, that it suffers from a
> division of narrative purpose, and that its themes do not combine
> so smoothly as one might wish, Mrs McCullers's latest novel is, af-
> ter *The Member of the Wedding,* the best of her full-length works. (I
> am excluding, of course, since it is a novella, *The Ballad of the Sad
> Café.*) It is less ambiguous in its implications than the first novel, its
> psychology is subtler and more complex, its compassion is more au-
> thentic and all-embracing, its form is firmer, and its style is gener-
> ally more impressive. It lacks the high polish and the formal perfec-

tion of *Reflections in a Golden Eye,* but it is a much maturer work, and infinitely more difficult of achievement. . . . [T]o my mind Mrs McCullers's greatest defect is a defect of *form,* of the vehicle or medium by means of which she chooses to communicate her meaning. When, as in *The Ballad of the Sad Café,* the medium is uniformly abstract, the result is high art. When, as in *The Member of the Wedding,* the medium is an almost perfect compromise or adjustment between the abstract and the concrete, the symbolic and the realistic, the result is, again, high art. On the other hand, when the medium is uncertain, when realism struggles with allegory, and the concrete alternates and is made to compete with the abstract, the result is a hybrid. *The Heart Is a Lonely Hunter* is such a hybrid; so also, I think, is *Clock Without Hands.* And both are among the most interesting American novels of the last quarter century.[49]

Margaret B. McDowell's essay — the most intelligent writing on Carson McCullers that has appeared in print — also urges reconsideration of the dominant view of this book. "More than most of McCullers' fiction, it now stands in need of new reading, interpretation, and evaluation."[50] McDowell questions first the range, then the diversity, of critical opinions regarding *Clock Without Hands:*

Positive reviews tended generally to praise the novel but to find it less good than one or more of McCullers' earlier works. The most common weaknesses mentioned were a lack of controlled organization, a carelessness in style, or a dependence on flat or stereotypical characterization. Several concluded that McCullers at less than her best was still one of the most interesting of American writers. . . .

The range and complexity of disagreement and the strongly emotional tone of the reviewers — ranging from disappointment and anger to excitement, enthusiasm, and even joy — cannot be explained by study of the book alone. They surely reflect the facts that McCullers' early work had made an unforgettable impression on thousands of readers, that she had written no novel for fifteen years, that her recent attempt at drama had failed, and that no critic could be unaware that she, like her main character, J. T. Malone, faced death.

The social and intellectual climate of the early 1960s must also be considered in evaluating the outpouring of critical response to *Clock Without Hands.* That the book remained one of the top ten best-sellers for many months indicates, perhaps, that between the time which the book ostensibly elucidates (1953–54) and when it was published (1961), racism had become fully recognized as a national and international problem and also as one which reached back to the beginning of history. McCullers' social satire presented the milieu of 1953 and 1954 with a comic detachment and a bitter nostalgia to which readers in 1961 could respond. The incidents of racial violence, ironically stylized to exaggerate the impassiveness of white bystanders and curiosity-seekers, would, in 1961 in any part of the United States, have produced riots.[51]

Margaret McDowell analyzes the book at length, as always with great delicacy, stressing that a new way of treating the South appears here in the fiction of Carson McCullers:

> McCullers, to a greater degree than in her earlier novels, focused in this last book upon the economic, political, and ideological aspects of the South as it was undergoing, or else resisting, change. Although she experimented with techniques of political satire, the exploiting of stereotype for ironic effect, and a stylized comedy of manners, her greatest talent remained where it had always been — in her dramatization of internal conflict in her characters. Racial antagonism, political controversy, class differences, and the barriers between generations are all issues explored in this novel, primarily as realities which magnify loneliness, isolation, and internal conflict.[52]

She concludes with a noteworthy sense of proportion and nuance:

> The balance and symmetry, the inevitability of the action, and the naturalness of the dialogue of the best of McCullers' earlier fiction are all qualities, unfortunately, that are less evident in this last novel. Nevertheless, the precision that marked the height of McCullers' artistry in *The Ballad of the Sad Café* and *The Member of the Wedding* still occasionally appears as she evokes the intensity of a dramatic moment or as she sharply portrays a character through a single gesture, look, or exclamation. If the book is not consistently controlled and so lacks the highest degree of artistry, the poignancy and irony of certain events or words are impressive and suggest that the book might have become a master work.[53]

The critics of 1961 having preferred excess — of invective or praise — to analysis, Carson McCullers had decided that she, too, would take a radical position: she simply would not read any unfavorable reviews. Apparently, she stuck to it. She did not, however, withdraw from the game and agreed to receive several journalists. What they found often was a woman wearing tennis shoes and a long cotton gown or a white silk negligee who was a great deal more frail than they had imagined — she scarcely weighed a hundred pounds despite her five-foot-nine-inch frame. But Carson made the effort to rise from her wheelchair to greet them, proffering a glass of bourbon with the Southern phrase "A little toddy for the body?"

One of the mostly fondly recollected interviews for both participants was no doubt Carson's meeting with Rex Reed, a formidable critic who had had a passion for Carson McCullers since attending the theatrical production of *The Member of the Wedding* in 1950. He had written Carson a letter at the time, which she immediately answered. The two had corresponded since that time but had never met. Rex Reed made the trip to Nyack, as he would again a few years later. He was the last person to interview Carson McCullers, publishing an article entitled "'Frankie Addams' at 50" in the April 16, 1967, edition of the *New York Times*.[54]

For the moment "Frankie" was only forty-four — the age of maturity for many writers. She would never know what it felt like to be in full possession of her creative capacities or to watch the contours of her oeuvre become clear over time to a creator beginning to master them. Carson was merely doing her best to gauge the time she had left.

10

"THE DOUR DESIRE TO ENDURE"

"**B**UT HIS LIVINGNESS was leaving him, and in dying, living assumed order and a simplicity that Malone had never known before," wrote Carson McCullers at the end of *Clock Without Hands.*[1] She herself must surely have been thinking, at least secretly, that "livingness" was leaving her as well, despite all the battles won, all the years salvaged from the wreck, all the obstacles surmounted so that she might see piling up in bookstores new volumes that bore the name Carson McCullers.

But she had chosen to keep on. She was not J. T. Malone, for whom "the pulse, the vigor was not there and not wanted."[2]

At the end of 1961, on December 28 to be exact, she had insisted on attending the premiere of a new play by Tennessee Williams, *The Night of the Iguana,* on Broadway. Jordan Massee wrote a crisply factual account of the event in his journal, which takes on a certain poignancy today:

> Carson arrived at 6:00 P.M. We had a bite to eat, then met Rita and Jack Dobbin at the Royal Theatre for the opening of Tennessee's new play, *Night Of The Iguana.* Saw Judy Garland arrive. Talked to Mrs. Williams (Tenn's mother), who sat with us. Lillian Gish and Helen Hayes were there together.
>
> After the performance, Tennessee took Rita and me backstage to meet Margaret Leighton and Bette Davis. Carson couldn't manage the backstage stairs. Margaret Leighton gave a magnificent perfor-

mance. . . . Bette Davis was badly miscast and had no end of trouble with her voice. When we entered her dressing room, she kicked Tennessee in the seat of his pants and said, "Look what you've done to me, you son of a bitch," in mock anger. Tennessee howled with laughter and replied, "You look better than you did in Chicago," with particular reference to the orange fright-wig Miss Davis wore. It was hard to believe that she looked worse in Chicago.

Before the curtain went up on the first act, Eleanor Roosevelt got up from her seat and crossed the aisle to speck to Carson, a tribute that meant more to Carson than the Pulitzer Prize, and a moment that I shall never forget. A great woman and a great lady. . . .

Then we all went to Tennessee's apartment to wait for the reviews. Miss Davis didn't join us there but telephoned Chuck Bowden every half hour to inquire about the reviews. When, finally, he was able to tell her that we had the New York Times review, she told him not to read it to her, just to tell her whether the Times said she was bad. She evidently felt reassured by what Chuck told her of the Times review and said she was going to sleep and would read all the reviews when she got up the next morning.

It was after three when Carson and I got home but we talked for another hour before going to bed.[3]

Carson wrote little during 1962. Rather than blame it on the state of her health, she preferred to say that she was working on a long-term project. In February, accompanied by Mary Mercer, she visited Mary Tucker in Virginia. While there she took advantage of the chance to meet with Edward Albee, a professor at the University of Virginia, and continue their discussion of adapting *The Ballad of the Sad Café* for the theater.

Two months later she learned that William Faulkner had been invited to lecture at West Point, the United States Military Academy, where he would be staying on April 19 and 20 — it turned out to be one of Faulkner's last journeys, as he died on July 6. West Point was not far from Nyack, and Carson decided to attend. Frederick Karl recounts the visit in his biography of Faulkner:

Faulkner was asked to West Point, for April 19–20, under the invitation of General William C. Westmoreland, superintendent before his appointment to lead American forces in Vietnam. The air force sent a plane for the Faulkners, who were the immediate guests of Major Joseph L. Fant. Fant and Robert Ashley would put together a book, *Faulkner at West Point,* based on the visit. The treatment of the writer was that afforded a visiting dignitary or head of state: private plane, presidential suite at the local Hotel Thayer, consideration for his every need. . . .

. . . [T]he main event was not military or political, but [Faulkner's] reading of a segment of *The Reivers,* the amusing passage about the horse race. The moment was enlivened by the photographs of Henri Cartier-Bresson. The stay was celebratory, and the reading itself went well, bringing forth a standing ovation. The next day in the class meetings Faulkner spoke of his admiration for aspects of the military, its sense of valor and courage, but attacked war and especially those old generals who decide the fate of young men without jeopardizing themselves. At mess, he was given "thunderous applause." Having apparently become weary of the whole thing and uninterested in a sight-seeing tour of the Point, Faulkner was now ready to leave.[4]

Frederick Karl makes no mention of Carson McCullers, but Oliver Evans recalls that

when another writer whom she greatly admired, William Faulkner, was visiting the Military Academy at West Point (where Carson's cousin, Major Simeon Smith, is an English instructor), she was able to attend the dinner given in his honour: when Faulkner, during cocktails, saw her standing in the distance and learned who she was, he deserted the circle of "top brass" which surrounded him and crossed the room to join Carson and her cousin, an incident which caused some of the officers' wives to raise their brows.[5]

Henri Cartier-Bresson well remembers that moment at West Point, "not only because I was taking the photographs," he recalls, "but because Faulkner died three months later. I even remember a question asked by a student-officer: 'What relationship is there between servicemen and literature?' and Faulkner's response: 'If there were a relationship, there would be no literature.' Too late I learned that at the back of the room, while I was listening to Faulkner and photographing him, a very sickly Carson sat taking in the scene."[6] Somewhere it was written that Henri Cartier-Bresson should not behold a paralyzed, defeated Carson and that for him she should forever remain the woman-child he so marvelously photographed in the mid-1940s.

◆ ◆ ◆

On Friday, June 8, Carson underwent another operation. She had breast cancer. "The doctors performed the originally scheduled operation on her hand [an eight-hour operation on all the tendons of the hand]," wrote Jordan Massee "and, in addition, removed the right breast, when it was determined that the growth was malignant." When he saw her the following Wednesday, he was shocked: "How indescribably frail my poor child looks. It is as though only the eyes and the spirit remain."[7]

By August, however, she was sufficiently recovered to be able, accompanied by Mary Mercer, to spend a week with Edward Albee on Fire Island, where the two writers resumed their work on the stage adaptation of *The Ballad of the Sad Café*. Better still, in October Carson flew alone to England, where she took part in a symposium on love at the Cheltenham Literary Festival: she had been invited by the British novelist Elizabeth Jane Howard, artistic director of the festival and wife of the writer Kingsley Amis. A plaster cast immobilized Carson's left arm, and a nurse followed her everywhere. On October 4 she spoke, reading an excerpt from *The Ballad of the Sad Café* as part of a session on "the relationship between the lover and the beloved." On the panel were the Frenchman Romain Gary, the Englishman Kingsley Amis, and the American Joseph Heller. In the October 12, 1962, *Spectator* the writer Frank Tuohy, reporting on the Cheltenham festival, noted that "there was the strange and suffering presence of Carson McCullers to remind us that the creation of art can still be a tragic and desperate endeavour, worthy of the last resources of the human spirit. At Cheltenham, an enjoyable British occasion, it was very easy to forget this."[8]

Participants in the festival, among them Joseph Heller, remembered that Carson spoke with difficulty and that her already drowsy Southern speech had grown sleepier still. She nonetheless granted a long television interview to Jane Howard, which aired November 28, 1962, on the BBC's *Bookstand* program. She talked about her work, reiterating many of the comments she had previously made in writing and in other interviews. Jane Howard asked her to speak about the

South: "Well, I'm American, naturally, and I'm a Southerner," Carson McCullers replied. "And in that order, I guess."

McCULLERS: I think that every writer writes of her own — of his own childhood scenes. I think when you are about fifteen you really have — your impressions have already been set.

HOWARD: You've soaked everything up — you write in fact about the exact country you knew as a child?

McCULLERS: Not at all, . . . not the country . . . I mean the towns are always small, as in — Columbus was much smaller now than — than it was then — it's much larger now than it was then — excuse me. And I don't really have any special localities. Just in general. It is a Southern scene usually.

HOWARD: Well that's very noticeable, I think, about scenes, and not only scene — in all the openings of your novels, the thing that strikes one very much is that they catch you from the very first sentence, one is absolutely riveted to what it is you're going to say. Do you try very hard about the beginnings of books?

McCULLERS: Oh, very, very hard. For instance "Member of the Wedding," I struggled for a whole year before I got the first paragraph.⁹

Carson once again explained how the characters of *The Heart Is a Lonely Hunter* came into being, how one day while she was taking a walk, through a mysterious process she had never really understood, it suddenly became clear to her that the main character of the novel had to be a deaf-mute.

McCULLERS: For *Ballad of the Sad Café* it was a different story. . . . I went to a bar in Brooklyn, you see, in this — on the waterfront of Brooklyn, you see, with W. H. Auden and George Davis and there came in this woman they called "Submarine Mary" with this little hunchback and I was just looking at them and I just — and then I forgot completely, you know. Then I went back to Georgia. I was hearing that beautiful Berlioz March to the Scaffold, when just suddenly to the music, the hunchback and Submarine Mary's great big hulking form came together and I was able to begin *Ballad of the Sad Café* — why, I don't know. . . .

HOWARD: Yes, I see, but musically . . .

McCULLERS: is what Henry James always used to call the Precious Particle and which I call illumination.

HOWARD: What — these sparkes of something suddenly coming to you without thought apparently?

McCULLERS: Without any thought . . .

HOWARD: Yes . . .

McCULLERS: Or any notion.

HOWARD: Yes — and you can't choose when that is.

McCULLERS: No — and, therefore, writings so perilous. Such a perilous occupation because you never can discern whether you're worried about this or worried about that.

HOWARD: What was that you said Thomas Mann said about that?

McCULLERS: Yes — Thomas Mann said that a writer is a person to whom writing is very hard — comes very hard and that's me!

. . .

McCULLERS: Yes, when I was a child — and my own — my chief interest in life was music. . . .

HOWARD: And music has gone on mattering to you even though you've stopped.

McCULLERS: Well, yes — because I can't play the piano now because of my bad arms but . . . I love to hear music and hear it at home every day.

HOWARD: But this . . .

McCULLERS: . . . But I miss — I used to start the day with a Prelude and Fugue every day of Bach.

. . .

McCULLERS: and that would set the whole tone of my day you know, that Bach, you know.

HOWARD: He's actually useful for writing, is he?

McCULLERS: Yes.

HOWARD: Very curious that — but when you're writing — it's fascinating. It seems to me as if you — the way in which you write is like poetry. I mean, it has all this feeling of colour and sound about it.

McCULLERS: Well, thank you very much Jane because that is the thing I prize most in writing — is the full sense of one's senses and things.

. . .

HOWARD: In your books you do have some odd people, a hunchback, cripples, deafmutes and so on. Do they stand for more than themselves?

McCULLERS: Well, I think there is a kind of allegory between — a kind of symbolism rather — as I said, of man's isolation to each other and the terrible need to try to communicate, and not to be able to communicate.

HOWARD: And so that really this is another thing about your work, which one feels very much, that you are writing about one idea, in many different ways, and to me it seems that you are writing about this agony of loving without being loved. This not knowing — the other person doesn't even know what you feel and can't respond even if they want to, they can't. This is what you mean by moral isolation is it — part of it?

McCULLERS: Yes — I think that's it Jane, but I think that nearly always writers tend to write more or less in the same way, although all my books are quite different. . . .

To Howard's question regarding her characters, Carson responded: "You're asking if I'm a happy person in my characters. Well, I think sometimes yes, I'm very wildly happy, especially when work goes well but when it goes badly and I'm blocked I'm wildly unhappy, just suicidally unhappy but usually I'm just — I enjoy life very much and am happy — and praise God for being in this world."[10]

After the festival she extended her stay, which ended up lasting two weeks. The trip exhausted her physically but made her feel alive again: one more time she had triumphed over illness — cancer in this instance, which had appended itself to all the maladies already assailing her. She attended the party that Edith Sitwell gave for her own seventy-fifth birthday; Marielle Bancou, who was in Paris at the time, flew to London to see her, bringing beauty and youth; she saw Cecil Beaton, David Garnett, and V. S. Pritchett again. These occasions made it seem as if illness no longer hung over her like a dark cloud, as if it were still possible to "live with it." Mary Mercer wrote to her in England, offering support and encouragement: a few brief letters with the little childish drawings that Carson enjoyed, revealing on the part of Mary Mercer a discreet and violent tenderness.

Carson left England with regret but probably out of necessity: she was on the verge of collapsing from exhaustion. England, which had newly welcomed her first books, was now a country in which she felt recognized, admired. Even *The Square Root of Wonderful,* produced in Glasgow in March 1963, got good reviews. That same spring Jane

Howard wrote to Carson on behalf of all her English friends to wish her better health and to remind her of the great success of their televised interview: "Many people talked about it afterwards."

◆　◆　◆

In 1963 the theater was a central preoccupation in Carson's life. She had to finish adapting *The Ballad of the Sad Café* with Edward Albee — which she did that summer on Fire Island — as the play was to be launched on Broadway that fall. Carson gave the young Albee a great deal of freedom for this project. She admired his talent, his sensitivity, his love of nature. In an article in the January issue of *Harper's Bazaar*, Carson recalled the nighttime walks she had taken with her collaborator on Fire Island and listening "like a rapt child" as he talked about the stars.[11] Albee, for his part, was struck by Carson's adolescent air, coupled with a great professional rigor and a level of maturity belied by superficial appearances or conversations. He was dazzled by Carson's strength and by the joy that she managed to express against a background of constant pain.[12]

When rehearsals began in late summer, they discovered that the play was three hours long. Albee made cuts that trimmed an hour off the running time. Carson attended only a few rehearsals. The premiere had originally been scheduled for October 14 — the anniversary of the opening of *Who's Afraid of Virginia Woolf?* (which had made Edward Albee famous and which remains a Broadway favorite) — but it had to be postponed for two weeks.

The reviews for the most part were good, stressing the quality of the original text. Some noted Albee's deft contribution. But very few commented on the play's direction (by Alan Schneider) or its cast (Michael Dunn as Cousin Lymon and Colleen Dewhurst as Miss Amelia), never a very good sign in the theater. *The Ballad of the Sad Café* closed on February 15, 1964, after 123 performances — a relative failure, especially at a time when every play that made it to Broadway was in theory on the schedule for at least a full season. *Who's Afraid of Virginia Woolf?* (Albee's original creation) was still being performed after *Ballad*'s run ended — certainly no comfort to Carson. Naturally, she had to blame someone — in this case, Albee — and she did so, with moderation. Where could she have found the strength to take the burden entirely on her own shoulders? Virginia Spencer Carr accuses Carson McCullers of "immodesty" for making the following statement to Marjory Rutherford, a reporter from the *Atlanta Constitution* who wrote a piece entitled "New Broadway Hit for Carson McCullers?": "I believe his adaptation will be interesting and compelling and add a new and beautiful dimension to an already beautiful work."[13]

Carson answered Marjory Rutherford's questions in writing. And there is nothing arrogant about the general tone of her responses — unless it is immodest, given the state of Carson's health, to be making plans like those described here:

> 5. I have found my association with Edward Albee a most pleasant and rewarding experience. My work with the *Ballad* was finished about twenty years ago, and his adaptation of the play is his own. In the course of our relations about this play, I have made little or few suggestions, so he is quite free to create his own adaptation. I believe that his adaptation will . . . add a new beauty to an already beautiful work. . . .
>
> . . .
>
> 7. Yes, right now I have very little emotional room for *Ballad* which I had finished a long time ago, because of a new work which I am just starting.
>
> . . .
>
> 14. I do not wish to comment on it [the new book] because "obscurity is the privilege of all young things."[14]

In addition to this book — or even several books whose subjects would be specified in the future — Carson had other plans: during the spring of 1963 the producer Ray Stark took an option for the rights to a film adaptation of *Reflections in a Golden Eye;* filming did not begin, however, under the direction of John Huston, until 1966.

Carson also seemed a bit nostalgic for her past. In several letters to a Swiss reporter who had written an article on her, Carson remembered Annemarie Schwarzenbach.[15] She also said how much she would like to shorten Nyack's long winter by another European sojourn, emphasizing with regret how difficult it was for her to travel now.

♦   ♦   ♦

She did not go to Europe. But on April 12 she flew to Charleston with Mary Mercer. For four days they visited Edwin Peacock and John

Zeigler. Edwin was probably the oldest friend Carson had left, since they had met during the 1930s. While she was there, Carson became acquainted with a curious young man, Gordon Langley Hall. He was the cousin of an American painter, Isabel Lydia Whitney, and also the adoptive son of the English actress Margaret Rutherford. This complex character — who underwent a sex change to become Dawn Pepita Hall — claimed that Carson, with whom he remained friendly, immediately saw that he was "a little girl" and that she was the first person to tell him so directly.

In 1971 Dawn Pepita — whose married name by then was Simmons — told Virginia Spencer Carr: "Years later — after Carson had 'discovered' me — Dr. Elliott Phipps, the eminent Harley Street gynecologist was to pronounce me as having always been a woman, wrongly sexed at birth, and capable of having children." "Carson, her senses sharpened by her own affliction," he added, "saw me for what I was in a moment of truth and her heart went out to me. I was a freak, yes, a freak, like one of her own characters in *The Ballad of the Sad Café.*"[16]

We don't know if Carson and the one she called "Gordan" corresponded for a long time, but for the year 1963 fifteen letters from Carson, most of them very long, are preserved in the Austin archive.[17] Written between June 12 and August 19, they are brimming with details about her daily life and about the early stages of her work with Oliver Evans, a professor friend of Tennessee Williams who had decided to undertake a biographical essay on Carson — *The Ballad of Carson McCullers*, which was first published in England in 1965 and came out the following year in the United States. We learn from those letters, for example, that Carson was "reading *War and Peace* again for about the 'dozenth' time," and that Montgomery Clift had been approached, as she had hoped, to act in the film version of *The Heart Is a Lonely Hunter*. "Let me tell you a funny thing that happened," she wrote.

A week or so ago Monty [Clift] was coming for the first time to talk with me. (He is going to play Singer in the Heart Is A Lonely Hunter.) As you know, I have tenants in my house. All of them very nice. All of them work except the tenant on the top floor who is very well supported by her navy officer husband, so she just looks out of the window and dreams, and goes downstairs to gossip with

Ida, etc. When Ida told her that Monty [Clift] was coming, she blushed and said she had adored him a.t.c. So she was waiting at the window when they arrived and then came downstairs just in time to look at the great man. Ida, you must realize, has two beautiful black eyes and in the back of her head she has one round cyclops eye so that she sees backwards and forwards as a natural course! When she was seating Mr. Cliff and his agent and my agent, etc., in a rather complicated procedure, she saw in the back of her eye, Joyce, the girl upstairs, going upstairs to primp up more. She was already primped up to begin with. Then she tripped downstairs and came back with Mr. Cliff's chauffeur. They went upstairs together and according to Ida they stayed one hour. Oh! but that girl is a sucker for uniforms. Knowing of Ida's visual speciality, she had to explain when she came downstairs with the chauffeur, and said what a nice man he was, "he helped me move so many things."[18]

Despite these "tableaux of daily life," sketched with humor, Carson waged a combat every single day to keep writing, to create, to stay in contact with those who made her feel she was still part of the world's rhythm. On June 23, 1963, she wrote, "Gordon, it is very hard for me to type with one hand which I have been reduced to doing. My letters come out absolutely illiterate. My spelling is never good but with one hand it is grotesque sometimes. When I type like that I always have to have a secretary to redo the letter before anybody can make much sense of it, but I do wonder if I could write to you on my typewriter and when you see everything all higgely-piggely, you will know that I am not crazy but just trying to type under very unfavorable circumstances."[19]

While Carson waged battle with her body and the distorted image of her being created by her writing — the very writing that had founded her power and authority — her cherished Tennessee was waging his own battle against other demons:

July 2, 1963

As soon as I got home, there were several telephone calls from Tennessee. . . . So, as soon as I came home I knew that Tennessee was in trouble, so I called him. His doctor had said he was on the verge of cirrhosis of the liver and should not drink alcohol. I told him that if he would stop alcohol completely, I would stop also in a kind of AA Club together, calling up each other every day. But Tennessee said that he could not stop.

Always, he said, there was a trinity in his life — work, sex and alcohol. He said that he could not work without alcohol and he begged me to go to talk with him this summer. His best friend, Frank, has cancer of the lung. and I am afraid that it will kill him. I have just recovered from cancer of the breast and thanks to Mary and the other doctors, they made a radical operation and they do not think it will ever come again.

Mary does not like Tennessee — not him, but the company he keeps. Frank I love, but I cannot stand the people he goes with. They are terribly vulgar, and I think you might understand what I mean when I say that. I want to help, but I cannot go to Nantucket.

Tennessee is so distressed about cutting out alcohol that he told me that he was going to start smoking marijuana cigarettes which he said had the same effect as alcohol. You can imagine how distressed I was. Immediately I began to speak cross with him. (One of my dearest friends, Annemarie, to whom I dedicated affection, died eventually of dope addition.) Then, Tennessee said he would go on to hashich (a strong drug) among other things. What can I do now to help Tennessee?[20]

Oliver Evans arrived. He was very pleasant and cultured, though he tended to exhaust her with his endless questions, which the scholar's partial deafness rendered particularly thunderous. On July 8, 1963, Carson wrote,

All week Oliver Evans has been interviewing me. It is a mistake to have someone who is interviewing you stay in the house as he did. Although I am very fond of Oliver, as an interviewer he never gave me any peace. . . . Mary reads the Bible every day and usually goes to the seven o'clock Episcopal service on Sunday, here in Nyack or in the city. It is a great comfort to me to know that she prays for me, and she *lives* the prayer I love most: "Take my mind, speak to it; take my heart, make it kind; take my body, use it."

Oliver found the original manuscripts of BALLAD OF THE SAD CAFE and MEMBER OF THE WEDDING, and many other valuable papers. They were rotting away in the basement. He also found literally thousands of letters which I do not dare to read — letters from Reeves, my husband, who is now dead, and from

[Annemarie Schwarzenbach], a Swiss poet whom I dearly loved, and who is dead also. I will have to wait and read them with Mary because it is just too much of the past to face by myself.[21]

Between Mary's prayers and Oliver's research there was still room for Carson's current projects:

Tommy Ryan came Friday and read the HEART. It is the most beautiful movie script I have ever read. Everyone who has read it thinks so, too — creative, yet true to the heart. The great trouble is about Monty. No one will insure him because he is mad. While he was doing Freud, budgeted for eight million dollars, he met someone in a bar and went with him to Africa without letting anyone know where he was. It took two months to find him costing two million dollars. So forth and so on. . . . He might walk off on location and run away. I will feel like Faulkner — just give me the money and don't make me see the film, but Tommy's script is such a beautiful work of art that I cannot feel that way now.[22]

Curiously, 1963 is among the years from which the largest number of Carson's letters are preserved at Austin. One of them, which she typed herself, in capital letters and with many typographical and spelling errors, is particularly moving. It is addressed to Carson's friend and former tenant Marielle Bancou, who was in Paris at the time. There is no date on the letter, but it was written several days after the assassination of President John F. Kennedy. In one clumsily typed sentence Carson McCullers sums up the situation perfectly: "THE SHOCK OF THE PRESIDENTS ASSINATION AND THE FOLLOWING MURDER [of Lee Harvey Oswald by Jack Ruby] HAS MADE THESE PAST DAYS UNREAL, LIKE SOMETHING SEEN UNDER WATER."[23]

Holding that letter in one's hands creates a strange emotion, so palpable is Carson's desire to say more about that tragic event, to share what she was feeling in the wake of the violent death of that young president whose charisma had touched her, a death that left the country in a state of shock. There can be no doubt that Carson McCullers had forceful things to say about Kennedy's assassination. But that must have been a day without a secretary — and Ida Reeder, who had faithfully remained at Carson's side for nearly ten years now, at once housekeeper, cook, confidant, and companion, could neither read nor write. So all we have left are those few chaotic, erratically typed words, each character a poignant victory of communication's urgency over the body's immobility.

Prohibited, physically, from writing, how is it exactly that a writer exists?

♦   ♦   ♦

Dating from 1963, there is also abundant correspondence — dictated this time — with Oliver Evans, who was planning to finish his book before the end of that year, though he didn't succeed. In one of her letters to Evans, on August 12, Carson provided some specifics on the "book of memories" she wanted to write. She announced her intention to call the book *The Flowering Dream* — often confused with the essay of the same name published in the posthumous collection *The Mortgaged Heart.* She would compose only fragments of this "memory book." Two autobiographical texts are preserved in the Austin archives, "Illumination and Night Glare" and "Illuminations Until Now."[24] "Oliver, I have a lovely idea," wrote Carson McCullers on August 12. "Soon I will be writing my book, *The Flowering Dream.* This is a book about my life and, therefore, I think it will feed into your book beautifully so that they will nourish each other. . . . This is a book about which I have been thinking for a long time."[25]

From that time on, all of Carson McCullers's writing energies would be devoted to this autobiographical project. What deep desire was she attempting to fulfill? Was she trying to recapture an existence that she may have felt partially escaped her while she was living it? Was she attempting to integrate — be it at the cost of one or two distortions of reality — the chaotic events of a life that had lurched from moments of illusory euphoria toward all too certain disasters? Was it a way of returning to a time when her body had functioned as it should without her even knowing that it was a threatened gift, a time of bicycling with Reeves, of swimming in the "brown river," a time when fleet fingers flew over the typewriter keyboard?

No doubt she felt a cluster of desires — yet few pages appear to have been written before the final months of Carson's life.

But those pages are extremely useful to anyone who hopes to grasp what Carson McCullers's childhood was like, or parts of her relationship with Reeves. A list of Carson's hospitalizations since her stroke in 1947, compiled by Mary Mercer in 1970, reveals in what incredible conditions those autobiographical fragments were composed during the 1960s. After 1958 hospital stays for various afflictions were clearly on the increase, creating the terrible impression that everything in Carson's body was breaking down.

Dec. 11, 1947
Admitted to Neurological Institute after "stroke" in France.
Mar. 14, 1948
Payne Whitney Clinic.
Feb. 19, 1958
Nyack Hospital Acute Left Heart Failure and pneumonia.
May 18 to 30, 1958
Harkness, 3 Reconstruction of left elbow muscles + tendons.
Sept. 24–Oct. 14, 1958
Harkness, Reconstruction of left wrist.
June 18–30, 1961
Harkness, Beginning of reconstruction of fingers and of left hand.
June 6–20, 1962
Harkness, Cancer of right breast + radical mastectomy and final reconstruction surgical repair of fingers and left hand.
Sept. 11–17, 1963.
D+C. Cancer of cervix feared. Not clear cut. To be watched.
Feb. 11–18, 1964
St. Lukes Pneumonia. Decompensating heart function.
May 15–June 18, 1964.
Harkness, Fractured left hip. Pneumonia. Pulmonary smbolus.
Dec. 1964 to Jan. 25, 1965.
Rehabilitation Clinic at Neurological for physio therapy. Left leg.
June 28, 1965
Readmitted to Rehabilitation Clinic for opinion re rt left leg.
July 11, 1965
Transferred to Harkness. Dr. McElroy to operate — transplanting tendons on left leg.
July 15, 1965
Operated. Complications of pneumonia and cardiac failure.
Oct. 13, 1965
Discharged — Miss Miranda for full time nursing care.

Aug. 15, 1967
  Nyack Hospital. Stroke right side.
Sept. 29, 1967
  Carson died at 9:30 A.M.[26]

The year 1964 was particularly difficult from a medical point of view: after a week-long hospitalization for pneumonia that winter, Carson spent nearly a month in the hospital with a broken hip in the spring. She had developed the habit of telephoning Mary Mercer every time she had to get up in the night and then calling her again to say she'd gotten back to bed. On that particular night, Carson did not call a second time. Mary found her on the floor, unable to move.

The next year was even worse: Carson's hip, intolerably painful, had to be operated on again. Complications set in and Carson almost died. She spent three months in the hospital, and when she was released a full-time nurse went home with her.

Faced with this disaster of the body, this invasion of existence by illness, a biographer has to make a choice: Give in to morbidity; launch into the litany of hospitals, suffering, relapses, voicelessness; describe that woman sentenced to death who now weighed less than ninety pounds. Or else side with Carson McCullers and try to grasp the miracle that kept her alive — her will to keep writing. In 1964 a short book of poems for children appeared, *Sweet as a Pickle, Clean as a Pig.*[27] And newspaper articles affirmed, "Carson McCullers is alive, and she is publishing books."

"Indestructible," Reeves had always said, though it began to seem likely he was wrong. But indomitable, definitely.

◆　◆　◆

During the horrible year 1965, Carson received a small word of encouragement from Richard Burton. At that time Burton was married to Elizabeth Taylor, who was slated to play Leonora Penderton, the captain's wife, in John Huston's film version of *Reflections in a Golden Eye.* Carson's agent, Robert Lantz, had told Burton that Carson was in the hospital that summer:

> We have never met, but through your work (and Robby Lantz) we feel very close to you.
> Please get well soon. We shall look forward to seeing you on the

set of "Reflections in a Golden Eye" this fall. I'm sure it will be a great success.[28]

Filming did not in fact begin until the fall of the following year, 1966, first on Long Island, then in Rome. In connection with this film — and thanks to John Huston's friendship, marvelous warmth, and generosity — Carson experienced an ultimate pleasure, a final act of real life, in the form of a 1967 trip to Ireland.

The mere act of conceiving such a plan seems like madness, every bit as unreal as the long list of projects Carson McCullers hoped to take on — and in part managed to complete in her two last years. First, work was done with Mary Rodgers on transforming *The Member of the Wedding* into a musical — the piece was staged in May of 1971, though in Theodore Mann's adaptation, and performed only twenty times off Broadway. She aimed to finish two books, *Illumination and Night Glare,* her memoir, and something she referred to as *In Spite Of,* which Carson described, delighting in her use of the cliché, as a work about personalities "who have triumphed over adversity." It should come as no surprise that she placed Sarah Bernhardt, who had had a leg amputated and continued to appear on stage, at the top of the list, because Carson herself was in danger of losing a leg to amputation: "I want to be able to write whether in sickness or in health, for indeed, my health depends almost completely on my writing," she declared.

"This has been a time of waiting for me," she wrote.

> The doctors have all decided that my crippled leg must be amputated. They cannot do it right away because the hospitals are so full, and I must wait for my own team of doctors at Harkness Pavilion. So in the nights of glare I just cuss out the doctors for making me wait, and cuss out my leg for hurting so. I have read Sarah Bernhardt and her superb gallantry and courage have comforted me. They are going to chop off the leg so I can have more mobility and can get from the bed to the wheel-chair more easily.[29]

Carson spoke of Sarah Bernhardt and her elegance several times throughout her memoir, viewing the actress as a kind of model:

> I have thought many times about Bernhardt, and other people who have lost their legs, but a friend told me about a young man who in

a fit of despair, jumped under a train. He lost a leg and an arm. I am not despairing, and don't like to dwell on that story, but rather think of Bernhardt who in World War One visited the trenches and encouraged the soldiers to such a point that the German High Command put an enormously high reward for her capture. Finally she was drawn back from points of danger by the Allied Command who also feared her capture.[30]

Mary Mercer herself remembers obsessing about the prospect of the amputation, "while Carson appeared able, psychologically, to go through it. The trip to Ireland was extremely important in restoring her confidence. And then there was the manuscript in progress." Carson wanted to write. She was no longer stuck as she had been ten years earlier, when, distraught, she had first come to Mary Mercer. "At that time, on the contrary, everything was going well, and the autobiography would have gone quickly had it not been for the practical questions, the material and physical difficulties she had trying to write."[31]

♦   ♦   ♦

This journey to Ireland was madness — marvelous madness — that John Huston and Mary Mercer wanted Carson to experience. Both of them strongly suspected that it would be her last major trip, no matter what the chances that she would survive the amputation of her left leg.

Between Carson McCullers and John Huston there had been immediate complicity and mutual admiration. Given how hard it is to care for a person who is totally dependent on others, the mere fact of Huston's asking Carson to come see him in Ireland stands as ample proof of his affection.

In her autobiography Carson gives her version of the meeting with Huston:

When Ray Stark, the producer of "Reflections In a Golden Eye," called in Mr. Huston to direct it, John said "This film could be done in two ways; one, it could be a low budget art film; two, it could be a film using the best talent available. I'm not interested in a shoe-string art film, and I don't think Mrs. McCullers is either. I can only direct it with the finest actors. Ray Stark agreed and the contracts were drawn up. John meant what he said when he said the best talent available: Marlon Brando, Julie Harris, Elizabeth Taylor, Brian Keith. . . . Then John came to see me, and immediately I felt his seriousness, and charm and wit. I gave him carte blanche and never felt the least hesitancy. He was in control and I was glad.

The more he discussed his conception of "Reflections" the surer I was that he was the right man for the job. He not only was the director; he, Gladys Hill and Mortimer? had written an excellent script in which they followed the novel very faithfully.

Also at our first meeting John said, "Why don't you come to Ireland to visit me?"

Since I've been in bed for three years, it seemed a little fantastic, but said,"Are you serious?"

"As serious as I can get. You know there are always airplanes."

So at Christmas John sent Ida and me round trip first class tickets to Ireland, via Irish Airlines.[32]

Marlon Brando, who starred in the film with Elizabeth Taylor (he played Captain Penderton), was also touched by Carson McCullers. In a *New York Times* interview on October 17, 1966, between one provocative remark and another, Brando made a point of mentioning her name when he was asked why he had taken the part: "Seven hundred fifty thousand dollars plus 7 and $\frac{1}{2}$ per cent of the gross receipts if we break even. That's the main attraction . . . plus the fact that it's a book by Carson McCullers."[33]

To Carson herself Brando wrote:

John [Huston] often speaks about you with what seems to be an odd kind of pride and deep affection. He was so pleased to [hear] in your last letter how utterly determined you are to get out of that damn bed and get to Ireland. I thought you would care to know how much you inspire John to do his best in making this film truly reflect the spirit and qualities of your brave and beautiful book.

Although its been a long time since we've met at your apartment I've remembered the feeling of you very well and you made me feel at home and accepted but mostly understood in spite of clumsy words. I send you my love Carson and warm rememberances. Marlon[34]

On January 5, 1967, John Huston sent a telegram: "Carson dear, come as quickly as you can, and be sure I'll be here. Love, John."[35]

"As quickly as you can" was April 1. Carson was entirely absorbed in preparations for the journey. Marielle Bancou designed dresses for her to take along — and Carson wanted infinitely more of them than would be needed for the short stay of a person who could hardly leave her bed.

Mary Mercer tried to sort out innumerable practical details, sending Huston lists of prescriptions and recommendations, all the while worrying whether they would or could be followed. In John Huston's handsome residence near Galway, St. Clerans, Carson would require a room on the ground floor. She was strictly forbidden to climb even one stair — people should keep that in mind when planning any possible outings. The trip from the airport in Shannon, where Carson's plane would land, more than an hour's drive from Huston's estate, also posed several problems. Even with Carson lying down in an ambulance, it would be a very long trip. John Huston proposed renting a helicopter, a prospect Carson relished, believing this mode of transportation to be reserved for very important people, chiefs of state, for example. But when the time came, more prosaically, Carson began her Irish sojourn in an ambulance.

Ireland gave her one week of true happiness. Carson was treated like a star, with people anticipating her every desire. Her room was taken over by flowers — on day two of her stay the Irish public learned that the famous American novelist was Huston's guest, and bouquets poured in, as did requests for interviews.

Carson received few visitors, sustained conversation having grown extremely difficult for her, as was noted by a reporter for the *Irish Times*.[36] She preferred to save what breath she had left for John Huston. The two friends talked at length about James Joyce, and Carson confided to her host that "The Dead," the last story in *Dubliners,* was one of her favorite pieces of writing. It was also one of the ones she knew best, since she and her mother had read it together every year at Christmastime. (Whether by coincidence or more profound "correspondence," the last film that John Huston directed before his death in 1987, *Dubliners* — in which his own daughter, Angelica Huston, performed — was an adaptation of none other than "The Dead.")

Ida, too, Carson's housekeeper, was treated as never before in this country where some of the people she encountered were meeting a black person for the first time. All the servants did their best to make her work easier for her. Children, who viewed Ida with astonishment, sought her out and wanted to talk with her. John Huston well knew that without her, this journey would have been impossible to arrange. Who else would have taken the risk of such a long airplane ride with someone whose health was so fragile?

Carson, too, knew how much she owed to Ida:

Ida Reeder is the backbone of my house. She was my mother's housekeeper, and she is among my most faithful and beautiful friends. She does everything almost to perfection — even flower arrangements which my mother taught her to do. Since I have tenants in the house, the job is one that demands a great deal of tact, judgement and diplomacy. Thanks to Ida I've never had a bad tenant in all those years. She is a superb cook, and John Huston just called all the way from Ireland, to say that he wanted her fried chicken and potato salad the day he arrives.

She and John get along marvelously, and when we left Ireland everybody wept: John, Ida, the whole staff. She endeared herself completely to the Irish at St. Clerans, as she does to everybody else.

Since my mother's death, she has taken her place for me, and calls me her foster child.

. . . [A]mong her other duties she is my social secretary. She alone remembers the comings and goings of people. She is the one who regulates my daily habits, such as reading and working. Other people come and go, but Ida always remains, and I thank the good Lord for her.[37]

On returning to Nyack, Carson had a new treat in store: Rex Reed's friendly interview-portrait, "'Frankie Addams' at 50," which appeared in the April 16 *New York Times.*

"Everyone," says one of her friends, "has someone — a husband, a wife or a lover. But Carson lives strictly on the will to survive." . . .

Carson sat up in bed, thin and frail, like a quivering bird, with dark, brilliant eyes and an aura of other-worldliness about her: Frankie Addams grown up, sipping a bourbon toddy from a silver goblet, smoking endless cigarettes, talking cheerfully and admiring the chrysanthemums and anemones sent by her friends. "On February 19 I was half a century old," she said. "Ida made a pineapple tree out of toothpicks, cocktail onions, cheeses and cherries and there were so many flowers — it looked like somebody had been laid out. Mercy me, far from it. . . .

. . . "I don't know what I'd do without my friends. They are the 'we' of me. I can't get out of bed at all now. I broke my leg and can no longer walk. . . . Sometimes I think God got me mixed up with Job. But Job never cursed God and neither have I. I carry on. . . . There are awful days when the pain is so intense I can't write. . . ."

With long, elegant hands turned out like ivory carvings, she described her house in Nyack, a Southern Gothic Victorian building the color of vanilla ice cream right across the street from the Methodist church, where she greets her guests in long white nightgowns and tennis shoes. . . .

Her next books, she says, will be a collection of stories about Negroes she has known in the South ("The speech and feeling of one's childhood are always inherent to me as an author and Negro speech is so beautiful") and, eventually, a journal about her life, her books and why she wrote them. "I think it is important for future generations of students to know why I did certain things, but it is also important for myself. I became an established literary figure overnight, and I was much too young to understand what happened to me or the responsibility it entailed. I was a bit of a holy terror. That, combined with all my illnesses, nearly destroyed me. . . ."

And that is where I left her, surrounded by clouds of pillows and lost in her own memories, fortified by no-cal orange soda and a bedside apothecary shop of assorted rainbow-colored pills, like Easter eggs on a white table.[38]

That year, 1967, seemed to Carson much less lonely than the previous one. Even the president of the United States was concerned about her:

The President and Mrs. Johnson have just learned that it was necessary for you to be hospitalized and they send their warm best wishes that your hospitalization is in every way successful and of short duration.

They hope that by the time this message reaches you, you will be in happy spirits and well on your way to recovery.

Please know you will be remembered in their thoughts and prayers.[39]

As in the past, returning from Europe gave Carson a pronounced burst of energy and a new desire to be on the move. "It irks me terribly to know that I can no longer travel with anonymity and ease," she wrote. "When you have to get from one place to another by ambulance and stretcher, it takes a lot of doing. My friends usually have to come and see me, but after the amputation I hope I will be more mobile."[40]

Nonetheless, she made a point of keeping scrupulous track of outings or trips she was planning — from the most inconsequential to the most improbable, as if writing them down gave them an existence that reality could not fail to verify:

> I've already made out a round of travels. First, to my doctor's home, Dr. Mary Mercer, with my faithful Ida Reeder who always accompanys me. Since I had such a grand time at Mr. John Huston's estate in Ireland this spring of 1967, and since he's invited me to come whenever I like, I am planning to visit him again as soon as my leg is healed. I just plan trips in my mind, and every single person whom I've broached about staying with them have been delighted. So after three years in bed, I will be able to travel again. . . .
>
> Although I've been bedridden for the last three years, my life is not without excitement. In June, of 1967, "The Heart Is A Lonely Hunter," will be filmed. [In fact filming would not begin until after Carson's death, on October 2.] Joseph Strick who so brilliantly directed "Ulysses" will direct it. . . . In July of this year I'm expecting to see the first showing of "Reflections In A Golden Eye." Meanwhile I'M waiting eagerly to hear Mary and Marshall's work on "Member Of The Wedding."
>
> When John Huston invited me to go to Ireland this year I joyfully accepted, and the visit was one of the happiest times of my life. John was the first person I told about the leg operation and he was the first to advise my following the doctor's orders in respect to the amputation.
>
> "You'll move about so much easier," he said, "and it will be a blessing to be rid of all that useless pain."[41]

John Huston's support, the film that he was then engaged in crafting, the proof of friendship constituted by his invitation to Ireland, and above all her own autobiographical writing — everything led Carson to believe that she was entering a new phase of her life, much less dismal than the one she would be leaving behind. After all, she was moving a book toward publication, the only thing that gave meaning to her painful days; once again she would inscribe her name upon the literary firmament. And was that lofty realm not officially recognized as hers when, on April 30, she received the 1966 Henry Bellamann Award for her "outstanding contribution to literature"?[42]

◆　◆　◆

In her July 31, 1967, letter to John Huston — no doubt one of the last ones she dictated — she returned to the subject of Joyce, lamenting that, as Virginia Spencer Carr reports, "Joyce's theme of sterility and moral blindness in Dublin over fifty years ago seemed so like the condition in the United States today."[43] Her autobiographical manuscript, too, evoked Joyce and *Dubliners,* in a passage introducing Carson McCullers's ultimate thoughts about literature:

> This week I've been rereading "Dubliners." How such a spasm of poetry could have come out of the grimy Dublin streets of that time is miraculous to me. . . .
> Sylvia Beach of Paris, published Joyce, and softened his hard life. He and his children were able to live in comfort.
> I wish I could say the same for another lesser writer who is also dear to me. Scott Fitzgerald, always in debt to his agent; with a wife that was mad and confined to institutions. Scott, extravagant, loveable, playful and impossible. His genius flourished, and he wrote "Tender Is The Night," in the most appalling psychological situation.
> I have been reading "Papa Hemingway." I turn from one book to another. . . . I'm not a Hemingway admirer, but for the first time I really realize him as a man, as an alive and suffering person. Fundamentally, he had been joyful, fun-loving, generous and a precious friend. I want to go over Hemingway again now after the Hotchner book. He also was a language path-finder. His short, terse sentences are a heritage to the American prose writer. But what I deplore is his sentimentality, and fake toughness.
> I read everything; books on house decorations; catalogues on flowers; cook books, which I especially enjoy, and like the New York Times, everything that's fit to print.[44]

But everything came to a halt on August 15, when Carson fell victim to a new, and massive, stroke. It affected the right side of her body, which had previously been her good side. Unconscious, she was transported to the hospital in Nyack.

◆ ◆ ◆

Exactly when did Carson dictate what, by virtue of her stroke, became the end of "Illumination and Night Glare"? How long before her attack? At that moment, when her conscious life would soon come to a close, she was discussing her first two books and Reeves, who in that distant past, in their first years together, had been so kind, so loving, so eager to help. She was responding to a question posed by Mary Mercer about her relationship with Reeves: "But you must of had happy times," Mercer had said, in Carson's transcription.

> "Yes," I said. "I remember one night we climbed up on the mansard roof of our house just to see the moon. We had good times, and that's what made it so difficult. If he had been all bad, it would have been such a relief because I would have been able to leave him without so much struggle. And don't forget, he was of enormous value to me at the time I wrote 'Heart' and 'Reflections.' I was completely absorbed in my work, and if the food burned up he never chided me. More important, he read and criticized each chapter as it was being done. Once I asked him if he thought 'Heart' was any good." He reflected for a long time, and then he said, 'No, it's not good, it's great.'"[45]

"Great" was therefore Carson McCullers's last written word. It pertained to her oeuvre and was uttered by Reeves. Is there ever really such a thing as chance in the life of a writer?

◆ ◆ ◆

When he learned that Carson McCullers was gravely ill and in the hospital, John Huston had just finished editing his film. He was starting to make the preparations for Carson's trip to New York — every excursion, no matter how near the destination, was complicated to arrange — but Huston wanted Carson finally to see the results of his work as much as she did.

Huston inquired daily about the evolving state of Carson's health. He quickly realized that she would not regain consciousness. Robert

Lantz wrote to him on August 31 that though Carson was still in a coma, her face appeared relaxed, at peace. As if she were sleeping.

◆　◆　◆

On September 27, with great sadness, Lantz and Huston attended a showing of *Reflections in a Golden Eye,* which would be released on October 11. The auditorium was rudely invaded by priests and members of the National Legion of Decency. The film was magnificent, one of Huston's great works. Without a hint of sentimentalism, it was tense, elliptical, secretly violent. Brando was at his peak.

◆　◆　◆

Two days later, on September 29, 1967, at nine-thirty in the morning, after forty-seven days in a coma, Carson McCullers died at Nyack Hospital.

A religious service was held on October 3 at St. James Episcopal Church on Madison Avenue in New York. The music of Bach was played, of course, as on the day of Carson's first marriage with Reeves in the living room of her parents' home in Columbus. Friends from the past came back one last time, from Wystan Auden, Gypsy Rose Lee, and Janet Flanner to Truman Capote — who now could say that if his youth had come to an end in France with Reeves at the cemetery in Neuilly, his old age was beginning right there in New York City. Only a few mourners then went on to Nyack, where Carson McCullers was buried at the top of a hill in the cemetery next to her mother.

◆　◆　◆

Twelve days later John Huston's film *Reflections in a Golden Eye* was in American theaters. And like the short novel by a twenty-three-year-old woman published twenty-seven years earlier, it caused an immediate scandal.

Carson McCullers, the writer, was saved: Self-righteous detractors would never cease pursuing her. Her lucid liberty would distress them forever.

EPILOGUE:

"SHE WAS AGELESS, CARSON WAS"

I hope that with increasing study of Carson McCullers it will be recognized, generally, that despite the early onset of her many illnesses, she was, in her spirit, a person of rare and luminous health.

— Tennessee Williams, February 1974, Foreword to
The Lonely Hunter, by Virginia Spencer Carr

I AM LOOKING for a small cemetery-garden. Near the Hudson perhaps. Or next to a church.

"No, don't go toward the church. Follow the signs for Nyack Hospital. It's just across the way."

Not a very comforting sight for the patients . . . The cemetery is a large park, but despite the trees and flowers the gravestones are still clearly visible.

"There are some twenty-one thousand graves. The cemetery covers a huge area, and the deer come in and do a bit of damage," says the caretaker, a forty-year-old hippie who doesn't really know how he ended up keeping watch over a cemetery.

"Yes, Carson McCullers is one of the most popular graves. You'll have to go by car. It's a long way from the entrance. There's a beautiful view from up there. I'll give you directions — I'm used to it. People come to see her all the time. But we also have the painter Edward Hopper and a few local celebrities and . . ."

Carson McCullers's grave is almost at the top of the hill — "her perennial passion to dominate," as spiteful gossips have long claimed. A small brown marble stele on the lawn — no headstone like the ones usually found in American cemeteries — with the simplest inscription:

Carson McCullers
February 19, 1917
September 29, 1967

Right beside it an identical marker indicates her mother's grave:

Marguerite Waters
Wife of Lamar Smith
June 4, 1890
June 10, 1955

A red azalea is flowering. It is hard to tell whether it is planted beside the grave or on top of it. Near Carson's stone there is another plant, purslane perhaps. Someone looks after these graves, that's for certain, taking care that they never look neglected. I do not dare ask Mary Mercer if it is she.

Mary Mercer has purchased Carson McCullers's house at 131 South Broadway across from the Methodist church. In the entryway hangs a copy of a portrait of Carson — a drawing by Vertès; the original belongs to Marielle Bancou. Mary explains,

> I can only show you this, and the yard sloping toward the Hudson because the house is divided up into apartments I rent out. Carson's bedroom was down here on this floor on the left. We tried to arrange it so that she could reach as many things as possible from her bed: the typewriter, pencils, paper, etc. The living room was over there on the right. The upstairs apartments were already rented when Carson was here, since she could not climb the stairs. I wanted to turn this place into a small museum. But it was very complicated. Then I became extremely ill. Now I am eighty-four years old. So I ended up renting to artists. I believe that Carson would have liked to see her house occupied by other artists.

Dr. Mercer is an unusual woman: tall, thin, elegant — and intimidating. She has very blue eyes behind large glasses with delicate frames, long hands concealed by supple black leather gloves. She does not volunteer information. She observes. She listens to questions and answers them briefly. She does not want me to record her comments

— she will not even let me take notes: "I am talking to you, and it's my job to know with whom I am talking," says she as we sit parked in front of Carson McCullers's house in her car. She manifests no visible intention to pursue the conversation further somewhere else. "I have no doubt that you are capable of remembering everything I say. You want to take notes for reassurance. You have absolutely no need to."

Then, suddenly, she stops answering my questions, and her previously compact responses give way to what she wants to say — which she may have been keeping to herself for a long time. She talks about Carson, describing the author in detail. Rather than a series of facts or ideas, she would like me to take away an image of the writer. Once or twice Mary Mercer interrupts herself to say: "I must let you ask the questions. That is why you came . . ." But the details that biographers attempt to track down do not interest her, understandably. How tiresome their endless efforts are to verify this or that particular: "Was it indeed in February that you met her?" "How long did you have her in treatment?" "Did she try to commit suicide?" "Did she talk with you about Annemarie?"

Are all these the things that matter?

"It is rare in a life to meet someone like Carson McCullers, who was profoundly honest, who so violently wanted to live," says Mary Mercer. "Some people have described her as envious, jealous, mean. That is false and ridiculous. The truth is that many things were of no interest to her, that she did not have time for them. Or, rather, she had time for nothing but the truth. And she had a reason for everything she did — a good reason." It is surprising to hear Mary Mercer use exactly the same words as those spoken by one of the witnesses interviewed by Virginia Spencer Carr, Terry Murray, a New York City merchant who was also a talented pianist and friend of Carson's during the last third of her life: "Carson never did anyone 'dirty.' She had a reason for everything she did."[1]

I think that she and Reeves, whom I did not know, loved each other deeply. But how could you not love that woman? I think that she fascinated him, that she fascinated him enduringly. He certainly suffered when he understood that she was a writer and he wasn't. They were very fine people, the two of them — exceptional beings. But they never managed to "function" together. More often than not they damaged one another.

She was ageless, Carson was. All she had was a mad desire to stay alive. To live and to write. To live in order to write. That is what I would like to have people recognize and retain about her: her immense and fundamental will to live. I would like people to remember her humor, her sense of play, of the farcical. Not just her will to live but her joy in living. At the height of her distress she maintained her taste for practical jokes, she held on to the shield of laughter.

Carson loved to laugh — including at my expense. She invented her own little plays, as she did one day when she had the whole neighborhood in a panic. Once a week the Nyack Volunteer Ambulance took her to the Nyack Hospital for physiotherapy. On the return trip that day she asked the ambulance drivers, whom she knew well — for good reason — if they would give her a lift to my house. She asked them for "the works" — high speed, squealing tires, sirens. They liked her, and they admired her courage. They immediately agreed, even though it was absolutely forbidden and knowing that, to please Carson, they were taking a risk.

My black housekeeper, her face ashen with fear, informed me that an ambulance, making a terrible racket, was in the driveway. It had been traveling so fast that the bus bringing children home from school had had to pull off the road into the woods across the way to let the ambulance pass. I ran out, panic-stricken . . . to find Carson laughing her head off and thanking the ambulance drivers. The mischievous little girl from Columbus was still inside her. And she was secretly proud of having kept her alive. I admired her for that strength.

Fifteen minutes later I received a telephone call from my closest neighbor, who wanted to know if I was all right. Her seven-year-old daughter had been on the school bus, and she had come home saying: "An ambulance just arrived at Dr. Mercer's house with its sirens on and going as fast as it could. She must be dying."

◆　　◆　　◆

Mary Mercer laughs, as if seeing the scene all over again in her mind's eye — her own fear, the maid's terror, the ambulance drivers happily serving as Carson's accomplices. And Carson's childlike joy, the pleasure of having staged such a prank — to have turned illness into a game.

Then Mary Mercer's voice, usually so controlled, takes on a sudden intensity: "How can I put it? Carson was the exact opposite of sui-cidal. The opposite of plaintive. She was . . . yes . . . a magnificent writer and, I was going to say 'obviously,' a magnificent being. A natu-ral. A person.

"That is what people must see."[2]

NOTES

WORKS ABOUT
CARSON McCULLERS

INDEX

NOTES

Introduction

1. Author's interview with John Brown, May 1993.

2. Raphaëlle Rérolle's interview with Arthur Miller, June 1995.

3. Author's interview with André Bay, July 1995.

4. Tennessee Williams, "Some Words Before," in *The Lonely Hunter: A Biography of Carson McCullers,* by Virginia Spencer Carr (New York: Doubleday, 1975; reprint, New York: Carroll and Graf, 1985), xviii (page citation is to the reprint edition).

5. Carr, *Lonely Hunter.*

6. Jacques Tournier, *Retour à Nayack: À la recherche de Carson McCullers* (Return to Nyack: In search of Carson McCullers) (Paris: Seuil, 1979). The spelling "Nayack" transcribes the way "Nyack" is pronounced.

7. Carr, *Lonely Hunter,* 469.

Mary

1. Author's interview with Dr. Mary Mercer, Nyack, May 1995.

1. Columbus, Georgia, 1917

1. Carson McCullers, *The Heart Is a Lonely Hunter* (Boston: Houghton Mifflin, 1940), 3–4.

2. Carlos Lee Barney Dews, "The Unfinished Autobiography of Carson McCullers," 2 vols. (Ph.D. diss., University of Minnesota, 1994), 2:466. Describing the manuscript "Illuminations Until Now," Dews states: "This 50-page

manuscript is written entirely in pencil in Carson McCullers's hand. The manuscript is progressively less legible" (2:458).

The manuscripts and letters of Carson McCullers, as well as those of other writers quoted in this book, sometimes include spelling and other mechanical errors. Those errors have been corrected only where they affect readability. Corrected spellings are enclosed in brackets.

3. McCullers, "Illuminations Until Now," transcribed in Dews, "Unfinished Autobiography," 2:466. The two-volume manuscript was published by the University of Wisconsin Press in 1999 as *Illuminations and Night Glare: The Unfinished Autobiography of Carson McCullers.*

4. Carson McCullers, "Illumination and Night Glare," transcribed in Dews, "Unfinished Autobiography," 1:61; McCullers, "Illuminations Until Now," ibid., 2:465.

5. McCullers, "Illumination and Night Glare," transcribed in Dews, "Unfinished Autobiography," 1:57.

6. Ibid., 57–58.

7. Carson McCullers, "Author's Outline of 'The Mute,'" in *The Mortgaged Heart,* edited by Margarita G. Smith (Boston: Houghton Mifflin, 1971), 147–48. This outline was published for the first time in the critical biography *The Ballad of Carson McCullers,* by Oliver Evans (New York: Coward McCann, 1966), 195–215.

8. McCullers, "Illumination and Night Glare," transcribed in Dews, "Unfinished Autobiography," 2:469.

9. Ibid., 471.

10. Virginia Spencer Carr, *The Lonely Hunter: A Biography of Carson McCullers* (New York: Doubleday, 1975; reprint, New York: Carroll and Graf, 1985), 19 (page citation is to the reprint edition).

11. McCullers, "Illumination and Night Glare," transcribed in Dews, "Unfinished Autobiography," 1:58–59.

12. Ibid., 2:471–72.

13. Carson McCullers, *The Member of the Wedding,* in *Collected Stories of Carson McCullers* (Boston: Houghton Mifflin, 1987), 264.

14. Carr, *Lonely Hunter,* 15, 23.

15. McCullers, "Illumination and Night Glare," transcribed in Dews, "Unfinished Autobiography," 1:147–48.

16. Carson McCullers, "Books I Remember," *Harper's Bazaar,* April 1941, 82.

17. McCullers, "Illumination and Night Glare," transcribed in Dews, "Unfinished Autobiography," 1:58.

18. Carson McCullers, *The Ballad of the Sad Café,* in *Collected Stories,* 197–98.

19. Ibid., 252–53.

20. Carson McCullers, "The Russian Realists and Southern Literature," in *The Mortgaged Heart,* 253–54. This text was first published in *Decision* (a magazine founded and published by Klaus Mann), July 1941, 15–19.

21. McCullers, "Illumination and Night Glare," transcribed in Dews, "Unfinished Autobiography," 1:139–42.

22. Margarita G. Smith, editor's note in McCullers, *The Mortgaged Heart*, 205–6.

23. Carson McCullers, "Home for Christmas," in *The Mortgaged Heart*, 235–37. This text was first published in *Mademoiselle*, December 1949.

24. Carson McCullers, "The Discovery of Christmas," in *The Mortgaged Heart*, 243.

25. McCullers, "Illumination and Night Glare," transcribed in Dews, "Unfinished Autobiography," 1:190 n. 85.

2. I Was Eighteen Years Old, and This Was My First Love

1. Carson McCullers, "Illumination and Night Glare," transcribed in "The Unfinished Autobiography of Carson McCullers," 2 vols., by Carlos Lee Barney Dews (Ph.D. diss., University of Minnesota, 1994), 1:190 n. 85.

2. Ibid.

3. Ibid.

4. Carson McCullers, *The Heart Is a Lonely Hunter* (Boston: Houghton Mifflin, 1940), 14, 17.

5. Ibid.

6. McCullers, "Illumination and Night Glare," transcribed in Dews, "Unfinished Autobiography," 1:138.

7. Carson McCullers, "Books I Remember," *Harper's Bazaar*, April 1941, 122.

8. Ibid.

9. McCullers, "Illumination and Night Glare," transcribed in Dews, "Unfinished Autobiography," 1:138.

10. Carson McCullers, "How I Began to Write," in *The Mortgaged Heart*, edited by Margarita G. Smith (Boston: Houghton Mifflin, 1971), 249–50.

11. Carson McCullers, "Sucker," in *The Mortgaged Heart*, 17–18.

12. Ibid., 18.

13. McCullers, "Illumination and Night Glare," transcribed in Dews, "Unfinished Autobiography," 1:59–60.

14. Stanley J. Kunitz and Howard Haycraft, *Twentieth-Century Authors: A Biographical Dictionary of Modern Literature* (New York: H. W. Wilson, 1942), 868–69.

15. McCullers, "Illumination and Night Glare," transcribed in Dews, "Unfinished Autobiography," 1:61–62.

16. Tennessee Williams, "Praise to Assenting Angels," quoted in introduction, by Margarita G. Smith, to McCullers, *The Mortgaged Heart*, xii–xiii.

17. McCullers, "Illumination and Night Glare," transcribed in Dews, "Unfinished Autobiography," 1:62–63.

18. Ibid., 63–64.

19. "Court in the West Eighties" first appeared in the posthumous collection edited by Margarita G. Smith, *The Mortgaged Heart.*

20. McCullers, "Illumination and Night Glare," transcribed in Dews, "Unfinished Autobiography," 1:64.

21. Virginia Spencer Carr uses the title *Columbus Ledger;* Oliver Evans calls the paper the *Columbus Enquirer* in *The Ballad of Carson McCullers* (New York: Coward McCann, 1966), 28.

22. Evans, *Ballad,* 28.

23. Virginia Spencer Carr, *The Lonely Hunter: A Biography of Carson McCullers* (New York: Doubleday, 1975; reprint, New York: Carroll and Graf, 1985), 59 (page citation is to the reprint edition).

24. McCullers, "Illumination and Night Glare," transcribed in Dews, "Unfinished Autobiography," 1:65. Carson McCullers seems to be confusing 1935 and 1936 here and there in her account.

25. Evans, *Ballad,* 33.

26. McCullers, "Illumination and Night Glare," transcribed in Dews, "Unfinished Autobiography," 1:66.

27. Linda Lê, *Les Évangiles du crime* (The four Gospels of crime) (Paris: Julliard, 1992), 23, 25–26.

28. McCullers, "Illumination and Night Glare," transcribed in Dews, "Unfinished Autobiography," 1:66–67.

29. The comments of Sylvia Chatfield Bates follow the last paragraph of "Poldi," in McCullers, *The Mortgaged Heart,* 37–38.

30. The comments of Sylvia Chatfield Bates follow the last paragraph of "Instant of the Hour After," in McCullers, *The Mortgaged Heart,* 62.

31. Ibid.

32. Evans, *Ballad,* 34.

33. Carson McCullers, "The Flowering Dream: Notes on Writing," in *The Mortgaged Heart,* 275.

3. The Birth of Carson McCullers

1. Mrs. George Woodruff, interview, January 3, 1970, in Columbus, Georgia. In *The Lonely Hunter: A Biography of Carson McCullers,* by Virginia Spencer Carr (New York: Doubleday, 1975; reprint, New York: Carroll and Graf, 1985), 71–72 (page citation is to the reprint edition).

2. Oliver Evans, *The Ballad of Carson McCullers* (New York: Coward McCann, 1966), 35.

3. Carson McCullers, *The Square Root of Wonderful* (Boston: Houghton Mifflin, 1958), 16.

4. Carson McCullers, *The Heart Is a Lonely Hunter* (Boston: Houghton Mifflin, 1940), 234–35.

5. Margarita G. Smith, introduction to *The Mortgaged Heart*, by Carson McCullers (Boston: Houghton Mifflin, 1971), xi.

6. Carson McCullers, *The Member of the Wedding*, in *Collected Stories of Carson McCullers* (Boston: Houghton Mifflin, 1987), 268.

7. Carson McCullers, "Illumination and Night Glare," transcribed in Dews, "The Unfinished Autobiography of Carson McCullers" (Ph.D. diss., University of Minnesota, 1994), 1:70–71.

8. Linda Lê, "Reeves C.," in *Les Évangiles du crime* (The four Gospels of crime) (Paris: Julliard, 1992), 22.

9. Ibid., 27.

10. Carson McCullers, "Instant of the Hour After," in *The Mortgaged Heart*, 42–47.

11. Carson McCullers, "Author's Outline of 'The Mute,'" in *The Mortgaged Heart*, 124–49.

12. Ibid., 124–25.

13. See William Sharp (Fiona MacLeod), *Poems and Dramas* (New York: Duffield and Company, 1914), 14.

14. The title *Reflections in a Golden Eye*, suggested to Carson by her publisher, comes from a line in a poem by T. S. Eliot, "Lines for an Old Man."

15. Unpublished radio interview with Tennessee Williams, 1948, Harry Ransom Humanities Research Center, University of Texas, Austin (hereafter cited as HRHRC).

16. Carr, *Lonely Hunter*, 105.

17. Geraldine Mavor of Maxim Lieber, authors' representative, to Carson, November 10, 1939, transcribed in McCullers, *The Mortgaged Heart*, 29–30.

18. Unpublished radio interview with Tennessee Williams, 1948.

19. McCullers, *Heart*, 17.

20. Klaus Mann, *Le Tournant: Histoire d'une vie*, translated into French by Nicole Roche (Alençon: Malakoff Solin, 1984), 530. The English version of this text, *The Turning Point: Thirty-Five Years in This Century* (New York: Marcus Wiener Publishing, 1984), does not contain all of the material appearing in the German *Der Wendepunkt*, on which Roche's translation is based. Notably absent from *The Turning Point* are the June 26 entry quoted from here and the specific passage cited below from June 2, 1941. Those passages can be found in *Le Tournant* on pages 530 and 561.

21. Carr, *Lonely Hunter*, 100.

22. McCullers, "Illumination and Night Glare," transcribed in Dews, "Unfinished Autobiography," 1:73–74.

23. Mann, *The Turning Point*, 187.

24. Mann, *Le Tournant*, 318–19.

25. Carson McCullers, "Annemarie Schwarzenbach," unpublished, untitled essay, n.d., HRHRC.

26. Carr, *Lonely Hunter,* 105.

27. McCullers, *Heart,* 113.

28. McCullers, "Illumination and Night Glare," transcribed in Dews, "Unfinished Autobiography," 1:98.

29. Alfred Kazin, *Bright Book of Life: American Novelists and Storytellers from Hemingway to Mailer* (Boston: Little, Brown, 1971), 52–53.

30. Carson McCullers, *The Ballad of the Sad Café,* in *Collected Stories,* 221.

31. Ibid., 216.

32. Jean-Pierre Joecker, "Carson ou les amours non partagées" (Carson, or unrequited loves), *Masques,* no. 21 (spring 1984): 35–37.

33. Anaïs Nin, *The Diary of Anaïs Nin: 1939–1944,* ed. Gunther Stuhlmann (New York: Harcourt, Brace and World, 1969), 270.

34. McCullers, "Annemarie Schwarzenbach."

35. Carr, *Lonely Hunter,* 110–11.

36. Annemarie Schwarzenbach to Klaus Mann, July 23, 1940, in *L'Ange inconsolable: Une Biographie d'Annemarie Schwarzenbach* (The inconsolable angel: A biography of Annemarie Schwarzenbach), by Dominique Grente and Nicole Müller (Paris: Lieu Commun, 1989), 224–25.

37. Annemarie Schwarzenbach to Robert Linscott, August 23, 1940, *L'Ange inconsolable,* 225.

38. Carson McCullers, "Meditations During Analysis," HRHRC, quoted in Dews, "Unfinished Autobiography," 1:12.

39. McCullers, "Meditations During Analysis."

40. Denis de Rougemont, preface to *Le Coeur est un chasseur solitaire* (The Heart Is a Lonely Hunter) (Paris: Club des Libraries de France, 1946), n.p., quoted, with the exception of the final sentence, from Carr, *Lonely Hunter,* 125.

41. Carson McCullers, "Brooklyn Is My Neighbourhood," in *The Mortgaged Heart,* 216–19. This essay first appeared in *Vogue,* March 1941.

42. Carson McCullers, "Look Homeward, Americans," in *The Mortgaged Heart,* 209. This essay first appeared in *Vogue,* December 1940.

43. Unpublished radio interview with Tennessee Williams, 1948.

44. Carr, *Lonely Hunter,* 344.

45. Smith, introduction to McCullers, *The Mortgaged Heart,* xii.

46. Carson McCullers, "Night Watch over Freedom," in *The Mortgaged Heart,* 214–15.

47. Carson McCullers, *Reflections in a Golden Eye* (Boston: Houghton Mifflin, 1941), 3.

48. Rose Feld, review of *Reflections in a Golden Eye,* by Carson McCullers, *New York Herald Tribune,* February 16, 1941, 8.

49. Carson McCullers, "The Flowering Dream: Notes on Writing," in *The Mortgaged Heart,* 276–77. The text was first published in *Esquire,* December 1959.

50. Carson McCullers, "Some Notes About *Reflections in a Golden Eye,* 1967," HRHRC.

51. See Margaret B. McDowell, *Carson McCullers* (Boston: Twayne, 1980).

52. Otis Ferguson, review of *Reflections in a Golden Eye,* by Carson McCullers, *New Republic,* March 3, 1941, 317.

53. Tennessee Williams, preface to *Reflections in a Golden Eye* (New York: New Directions, 1950), xix, xviii, xvii–xviii.

54. Unpublished radio interview with Tennessee Williams, 1948.

55. Evans, *Ballad,* 87.

56. Jacques Tournier, *À la recherche de Carson McCullers: Retour à Nyack* (Paris: Éditions Complexe, 1990), 86.

57. Carr, *Lonely Hunter,* 7.

58. Tournier, *À la recherche* (1990 ed.), 126–27.

59. Ibid., 132–33.

60. See Deirdre Bair, *Simone de Beauvoir: A Biography* (New York: Summit Books, 1990).

61. John Fuegi, *Brecht and Company: Sex, Politics, and the Making of the Modern Drama* (New York: Grove Press, 1994).

62. See D. H. Lawrence, "The Prussian Officer," in *The Prussian Officer and Other Stories,* ed. John Worthen (New York: Cambridge University Press, 1983), and Evans, *Ballad,* 60.

63. McCullers, "Books I Remember," in *The Mortgaged Heart,* 125.

64. Carr, *Lonely Hunter,* 142.

65. Andrew Field-Nabokov, *Djuna: The Life and Times of Djuna Barnes* (Austin: University of Texas Press, 1985), 233.

66. Carr, *Lonely Hunter,* 155.

67. Ibid., 156.

68. Ibid., 161.

69. Ibid., 162.

70. Ibid., 144.

71. Gore Vidal, quoted in *Capote: A Biography,* by Gerald Clarke (New York: Simon and Schuster, 1988), 97.

72. Carson McCullers, "The Jockey," in *Collected Stories,* 104–9. This story was first published in the *New Yorker,* August 23, 1941.

73. Carson McCullers, "Madame Zilensky and the King of Finland," in *Collected Stories,* 110–18, and "Correspondence," in *Collected Stories,* 119–24. "Madame Zilensky" was first published in the *New Yorker,* December 20, 1941, and "Correspondence" in the same magazine, February 7, 1942.

74. Carson McCullers, "We Carried Our Banners — We Were Pacifists, Too," *Vogue,* July 15, 1941, 42–43, reprinted in *The Mortgaged Heart,* 221–26; "The Twisted Trinity," *Decision,* no. 4 (November 1941): 30.

75. Carson McCullers, "The Russian Realists and Southern Literature," in *The Mortgaged Heart,* 251, 257–58.

76. Carr, *Lonely Hunter,* 152.

77. Ibid., 153.

78. A few months earlier Muriel Rukeyser had dedicated to Carson and Reeves a poem, according to Virginia Spencer Carr, that "revealed much of the ambivalence and dichotomy of the young couple's troubled relationship and of Miss Rukeyser's tender attitude toward each" (Carr, *Lonely Hunter,* 182).

79. Lê, *Les Évangiles du crime,* n.p.

80. Annemarie Schwarzenbach to Carson, October 3, 1941, written in Leopoldville, HRHRC.

81. Annemarie Schwarzenbach to Carson, December 29, 1941, written in Thysville, HRHRC.

82. See Evans, *Ballad,* 88.

83. Carson McCullers, "A Tree. A Rock. A Cloud," in *Collected Stories,* 131. This story was published in November 1942 in the magazine *Harper's Bazaar.* It was adapted for the screen by Christine Van de Putte in 1981 with Rufus.

84. Mann, *Le Tournant,* 656.

4. A War Wife

1. Anaïs Nin, *Diary of Anaïs Nin, 1939–1944,* ed. Gunther Stuhlman (New York: Harcourt, Brace and World, 1969), 270–71.

2. Reeves to Carson, February 23, 1943. All correspondence between Reeves and Carson cited in this chapter is located at the Harry Ransom Humanities Research Center, University of Texas, Austin (hereafter cited as HRHRC). Unless otherwise noted, dates of letters are included in the text.

3. Reeves to Carson, April 2, 1943, HRHRC.

4. Carson McCullers, "Love's Not Time's Fool," *Mademoiselle,* April 1943, 166–68. This text has not been published in any collection.

5. Reeves to Carson, April 25, 1943, HRHRC.

6. Reeves to Carson, May 3, 1943, HRHRC.

7. McCullers, "Love's Not Time's Fool," 167–68.

8. Carson to Edwin Peacock, no date or source given, quoted in *The Ballad of Carson McCullers,* by Oliver Evans (New York: Coward McCann, 1966), 97.

9. "Bebe" was the nickname of Carson's mother, Marguerite Smith.

10. Alfred Kazin to Aimee Alexander, New York City, February 3, 1971; also Alfred Kazin, interview with Virginia Spencer Carr, New York City, May 23, 1971, quoted in Carr, *Lonely Hunter,* 234.

11. Carson McCullers, *The Ballad of the Sad Café,* in *The Collected Stories of Carson McCullers* (Boston: Houghton Mifflin, 1987), 202.

12. Reeves to Carson, n.d., HRHRC.

13. Ibid.

14. Ibid.

15. Carson to Edwin Peacock, no date or source given, quoted in Evans, *Ballad*, 98.

16. "2d Ranger Infantry Battalion," in *Small Unit Actions*. American Forces in Action: Historical Division, War Department (Washington, D.C.: Government Printing Office, 1946).

17. Reeves to Carson, February 19, 1944, HRHRC.

18. Carson McCullers, "Illumination and Night Glare," transcribed in "The Unfinished Autobiography of Carson McCullers," 2 vols., by Carlos Lee Barney Dews (Ph.D. diss., University of Minnesota, 1994), 1:108.

19. Reeves to Carson, March 4, 1944, HRHRC.

20. Reeves to Carson, March 27, 1944, HRHRC.

21. Reeves to Carson, dated "Early June," HRHRC.

22. Reeves to Carson, June 10, 1944, HRHRC.

23. Reeves to Carson, June 20, 1944, HRHRC.

24. Reeves to Carson, July 14, 1944, HRHRC.

25. "Broadcast Carson McCullers on Nyack," July 1955, excerpted from *This Is America*, a series of special features about the communities of America hosted by John Pauker, HRHRC. In this series of radio interviews, several writers were invited to speak about the city or town in which they had chosen to live.

26. Reeves to Carson, September 17, 1944, HRHRC.

27. Robert Meltzer, "Normandy Interlude," *Collier's*, September 23, 1944, 24.

28. Ibid., 24, 27.

29. Reeves to Carson, September 23, 1944, HRHRC.

30. Reeves to Carson, November 9, 1944, HRHRC.

31. Carson to Reeves, November 12, 1944, HRHRC.

32. Carson to Reeves, November 22, 1944, HRHRC.

33. Virginia Spencer Carr, *The Lonely Hunter: A Biography of Carson McCullers* (New York: Doubleday, 1975; reprint, New York: Carroll and Graf, 1985), 244 (page citation is to the reprint edition).

34. Carson to Reeves, December 13, 1944, HRHRC.

35. Carson to Reeves, December 18, 1944, HRHRC.

36. Reeves to Carson, November 13, 1943, HRHRC.

37. Carson to Reeves, December 19, 1944, HRHRC.

38. Carson to Reeves, December 21, 1944, HRHRC.

39. Carson to Reeves, December 27, 1944, HRHRC.

40. Carson to Reeves, January 4, 1945, HRHRC.

41. Carson to Reeves, January 9, 1945, HRHRC.

42. Carson to Reeves, January 5, 1945, HRHRC.

43. Carson to Reeves, January 6, 1945, HRHRC.

44. Carson to Reeves, January 5, 1945, HRHRC.

45. Carson to Reeves, January 6, 1945, HRHRC.

46. Carson to Reeves, January 7, 1945, HRHRC.

47. Carson to Reeves, January 10, 1945, HRHRC.

48. Carson to Reeves, January 14, 1945, HRHRC.

49. Ibid.

50. Carson to Reeves, January 17, 1945, HRHRC.

51. Carson to Reeves, January 24, 1945, HRHRC.

52. Carson to Reeves, January 27 and February 8, 1945, HRHRC.

53. Carson to Edwin Peacock, March 26, 1945, HRHRC.

54. Carson McCullers, *The Heart Is a Lonely Hunter* (Boston: Houghton Mifflin, 1940), 108.

55. Carson McCullers, *The Square Root of Wonderful* (Boston: Houghton Mifflin, 1958), 23.

56. Ibid., 18–19, 21.

57. Carr, *Lonely Hunter,* 254.

58. McCullers, "Illumination and Night Glare," transcribed in Dews, "Unfinished Autobiography," 1:85.

59. Author's interview with John Brown, May 1993.

60. Jacques Tournier, *À la recherche de Carson McCullers: Retour à Nyack* (In search of Carson McCullers: Return to Nyack) (Paris: Éditions Complexe, 1990), 96–97.

61. Ibid., 96.

62. See Elizabeth Ames's account of this episode in Carr, *Lonely Hunter,* 259.

63. Gerald Clarke, *Capote: A Biography* (New York: Simon and Schuster, 1988), 96.

64. Ibid., 97–98.

5. Frankie "the European"

1. In the play that Carson McCullers based on this novel, the length of the action was reduced to a weekend in 1945, with allusion being made to the atom bomb dropped on Japan.

2. Carson McCullers, *The Member of the Wedding,* in *The Collected Stories of Carson McCullers* (Boston: Houghton Mifflin, 1987), 257.

3. Ibid., 261.

4. Ibid., 265.

5. Ibid., 258.

6. Ibid., 261.

7. Ibid., 325.

8. Eudora Welty, *Delta Wedding* (New York: Harcourt, Brace and Company, 1946).

9. Oliver Evans, *The Ballad of Carson McCullers* (New York: Coward McCann, 1966), 114–15.

10. McCullers, *Member,* 257.

11. Ibid., 285.

12. Ibid., 296, 301.

13. Ibid., 358.

14. René Lalou, "Carson McCullers et la communion humaine" (Carson McCullers and human communion), preface to Marie-Madeleine Fayet's French translation of *The Member of the Wedding* (1949; reprint, Paris: Livre de Poche, 1990), 14–17.

15. Margarita G. Smith, introduction to *The Mortgaged Heart,* by Carson McCullers (Boston: Houghton Mifflin, 1971), xi.

16. Evans, *Ballad,* 10.

17. Ibid., 125.

18. Ibid., 119.

19. Siegfried Sassoon, English poet (1886–1967), denounced the "butchery" of World War I, notably in his collection entitled *Counter-attack and Other Poems* (New York: Dutton, 1918).

20. Edmund Wilson, "Two Books That Leave You Blank," *New Yorker,* March 30, 1946, 80.

21. McCullers, *Member,* 372.

22. Ibid., 386–87.

23. Wilson, "Two Books," 80.

24. Edmund Wilson, *Memoirs of Hecate County,* 1st ed. (New York: Octagon Books, 1946).

25. Quoted in *The Lonely Hunter: A Biography of Carson McCullers,* by Virginia Spencer Carr (New York: Doubleday, 1975; reprint, New York: Carroll and Graf, 1985), 260 (page citation is to the reprint edition).

26. Clarke, *Capote,* 100.

27. Ibid., 101.

28. Tennessee Williams, *Memoirs* (Garden City, N.Y.: Doubleday, 1972), 106–7.

29. Carr, *Lonely Hunter,* 274.

30. Tennessee Williams, "Praise to Assenting Angels," quoted in Smith, introduction to McCullers, *The Mortgaged Heart,* xvii–xviii.

31. Tennessee Williams, "The Author," *Saturday Review,* no. 44 (September 23, 1961): 14.

32. Georges-Michel Sarotte, "Carson McCullers et le groupe" (Carson McCullers and the group), *Masques,* no. 21 (spring 1984): 46–49. Georges-Michel Sarotte is the author of an essay on male homosexuality in the American novel and theater, *Comme un frère, comme un amant* (Like a brother, like a lover) (Paris: Flammarion, 1976).

33. Tennessee Williams, "The Author," 15.

34. Tennessee Williams, quoted in Carr, *Lonely Hunter,* 275.

35. Carson McCullers, preface to *The Square Root of Wonderful* (Boston: Houghton Mifflin, 1958), vii.

36. Williams, "The Author," 15.

37. Williams, *Memoirs,* 108.

38. Author's interview with Henri Cartier-Bresson, July 1995.

39. Janet Flanner, quoted in Carr, *Lonely Hunter,* 281.

40. Carr, *Lonely Hunter,* 382.

41. Claude Roy, *Nous* (We) (Paris: Gallimard, 1980), 298.

42. Author's interview with André Bay, July 1995.

43. Author's interview with John Brown, May 1993.

44. Ibid.

45. Carson McCullers, "The Vision Shared," in *The Mortgaged Heart,* 262–63.

46. Carson McCullers, "When We Are Lost," in *The Mortgaged Heart,* 287. This poem first appeared in *New Directions in Prose and Poetry* 10 (December 3, 1948). It then was published with certain revisions in *Voices* 149 (September 1952). It was also recorded for MGM records under the title "When We Are Lost What Image Tells?"

47. Lalou, "Carson McCullers et la communion humaine," 7–10.

48. Cyril Connolly to Carson, April 30, 1947, HRHRC.

49. Constance Webb, *Richard Wright: A Biography* (New York: Putnam, 1968).

50. Carson to Marguerite Smith, July 28, 1947, HRHRC.

51. Jordan Massee, introduction to "Notes on Carson McCullers by Jordan Massee," unpublished journal, p. 1.

52. Carson McCullers, "The Sojourner," in *The Mortgaged Heart,* 144, 146.

53. Carr, *Lonely Hunter,* 291.

54. Ibid., 192.

55. Ibid.

6. Five Hundred Days on Broadway

1. *Quick,* December 17, 1947. The other best writers named were Norman Mailer, John Hersey, Arthur Schlesinger Jr., Jean Stafford, and Peter Viereck. Tennessee Williams, Arthur Miller, and Truman Capote came in second.

2. Virginia Spencer Carr, *The Lonely Hunter: A Biography of Carson McCullers* (New York: Doubleday, 1975; reprint, New York: Carroll and Graf, 1985), 295 (page citation is to the reprint edition). According to the *Mademoiselle* article, Merit Awards went to young women for whom "1947 meant signal achievement." The other winners were Barbara Ann Scott, figure skater; Anahid Ajemian, concert violinist; Toni Owen, fashion designer; Santha Rama Rau, diplomat and writer; Elizabeth M. Ackermann, research chemist; Mildred L. Lillie, municipal judge; Shirley Adelson Siegel, executive director of the Citi-

zens' Housing Council of New York; Anne Waterman, university professor; and Elaine Whitelaw, director of women's activities for the National Foundation for Infantile Paralysis ("*Mademoiselle* Merit Awards," *Mademoiselle,* January 1948, 118–19).

3. Carr, *Lonely Hunter,* 295.

4. Carson McCullers, preface to *The Square Root of Wonderful* (Boston: Houghton Mifflin, 1958), viii.

5. Reeves to Carson, August 8, 1945, HRHRC.

6. Carr, *Lonely Hunter,* 296.

7. Carson to Tennessee Williams, Valentine's Day (?), 1948. Translated from the French edition.

8. "How I Began to Write" first appeared in *Mademoiselle,* September 1948. Like the previously cited "When We Are Lost," "The Mortgaged Heart" was first published in *New Directions in Prose and Poetry* 10 (December 3, 1948), then appeared with certain revisions in *Voices* 149 (September–December 1952), and was reprinted in *The Mortgaged Heart.*

9. Tennessee Williams, *Memoirs* (Garden City, N.Y.: Doubleday, 1972), 108–9.

10. Carr, *Lonely Hunter,* 313.

11. *New York Times,* October 27, 1948, quoted in Carr, *Lonely Hunter,* 313.

12. Carson to the editors of the *Columbus Ledger Enquirer,* February 26, 1948, HRHRC.

13. Carson to Tennessee Williams, May (?), 1949. Translated from the French edition.

14. Ibid. "10" is numerical shorthand for "Tenn," Tennessee Williams's nickname.

15. Jordan Massee, "Notes on Carson McCullers by Jordan Massee," unpublished journal, March 17, 1949.

16. Ibid.

17. Ibid.

18. "I never had any inclination to join the Communists. For one thing, I'm just not a natural born joiner. The only club I belong to is The American Academy of Arts and Letters. Most of the people are older than I, but they are all extremely distinguished. There is not too much formality and when I'm able I enjoy going to their meetings" ("Illumination and Night Glare," transcribed in Dews, "Unfinished Autobiography," 1:157).

19. Carson to Tennessee Williams, May (?), 1949. Translated from the French edition.

20. Carson to Tennessee Williams, June (?), 1949. Translated from the French edition.

21. Carson to Tennessee Williams, December (?), 1949. Translated from the French edition.

22. Carson McCullers, "Loneliness . . . an American Malady," *This Week,* December 19, 1949; reprinted in *The Mortgaged Heart.*

23. McCullers, "Loneliness . . . an American Malady," in *The Mortgaged Heart,* 260.

24. Ibid., 260–61.

25. McCullers, "Illumination and Night Glare," transcribed in Dews, "Unfinished Autobiography," 1:120–21.

26. Brook Atkinson, review of *The Member of the Wedding,* by Carson McCullers, *New York Times,* January 6, 1950; reprinted in *New York Theatre Critics' Reviews* 11 (1950): 398.

27. William Hawkins, "Waters, Harris Roles Spark 'Wedding,'" *New York World-Telegram,* January 6, 1950; reprinted in *New York Theatre Critics' Reviews* 11 (1950): 399.

28. Howard Barnes, review of *The Member of the Wedding,* by Carson McCullers, *New York Herald Tribune,* January 6, 1950.

29. Wolcott Gibbs, "Brook and River," *New Yorker,* January 14, 1950, 44.

30. John Mason Brown, "Plot Me No Plots," *Saturday Review of Literature,* January 28, 1950, 27.

31. Ibid., 29.

32. George Jean Nathan, *The Theatre Book of the Year* (New York: Knopf, 1950), 164–66.

33. Harold Clurman, "Theatre: From a Member," *New Republic,* January 30, 1950, 28–29.

34. Carson to John Van Druten, February 5, 1950, HRHRC.

35. Carson McCullers, "The Vision Shared," in *The Mortgaged Heart,* 263–64. This text was first published in *Theatre Arts,* April 1950.

36. Ibid., 265.

37. Gerald Weales, *American Drama Since World War II* (New York: Harcourt, Brace and World, 1962), 174–79.

38. Carr, *Lonely Hunter,* 351.

39. Elizabeth Bowen, quoted in Carr, *Lonely Hunter,* 360.

40. Félicie Dubois, *Tennessee Williams, l'oiseau sans pattes: Portrait* (Tennessee Williams, footless bird: A portrait) (Paris: Balland, 1992), 141.

41. "Notes on Carson McCullers by Jordan Massee," October 21–22, 1950, 32–37.

42. Ibid., 35.

43. Ibid., 37.

44. Ibid., 38.

45. Edith Sitwell to Carson, November 21, 1950, quoted in Carr, *Lonely Hunter,* 365–66.

46. Carson McCullers, *The Ballad of the Sad Café: The Novels and Stories of Carson McCullers* (Boston: Houghton Mifflin, 1951).

47. Carson McCullers, "A Domestic Dilemma," in *The Collected Stories of Carson McCullers* (Boston: Houghton Mifflin, 1987), 151.

48. Ibid., 156.

49. Ibid., 157.

50. Charles Poor, *New York Times,* May 24, 1951.

51. Coleman Rosenberger, review of *The Ballad of the Sad Café,* by Carson McCullers, *New York Herald Tribune,* June 10, 1951, 13.

52. *Time,* June 4, 1951, 106.

53. "Chambers of Horrors," *Times Literary Supplement,* July 25, 1952, 340.

54. V. S. Pritchett, review of *The Ballad of the Sad Café,* by Carson McCullers, *New Statesman and Nation,* August 2, 1952, 137–38.

55. She mentions that episode in an autobiographical passage from "Illumination and Night Glare" in distinctly less enthusiastic terms, seeing it not at all as something "romantic" but rather as a kind of blackmail used by Reeves, who "threatened to jump overboard if I didn't take him back" (McCullers, "Illumination and Night Glare," transcribed in Dews, "Unfinished Autobiography," 1:177).

56. See Carr, *Lonely Hunter,* 375.

57. Carson to Reeves, n.d., HRHRC.

58. Carson to Reeves, August 7 [1951], HRHRC.

59. Carson to Reeves, n.d. [summer 1951], HRHRC.

60. Carson to Reeves, n.d., HRHRC.

7. *"Tomorrow I'm Going West"*

1. Carson to Fred Zinnemann, January 30, 1952, HRHRC.

2. Author's interview with André Bay, Paris, July 1995.

3. Author's interview with John Brown, Paris, May 1993.

4. Carson McCullers, "Illumination and Night Glare," transcribed in "The Unfinished Autobiography of Carson McCullers," 2 vols., by Carlos Lee Barney Dews (Ph.D. diss., University of Minnesota, 1994), 1:111–12.

5. Carson to Tennessee Williams, December (?), 1949. Translated from the French edition.

6. In French *et six* (and six) sounds like the last two syllables of "Tennessee."

7. Author's interview with André Bay, Paris, 1995.

8. Gerald Clarke, *Capote: A Biography* (New York: Simon and Schuster, 1988), 233–34.

9. Ibid.

10. McCullers, "Illumination and Night Glare," transcribed in Dews, "Unfinished Autobiography," 1:112–13.

11. Otto Frank to Carson, June 8, 1952, HRHRC.

12. Carson to Audrey Wood, August 1, 1952, HRHRC.

13. Fred Zinnemann to Carson, January 3, 1953, HRHRC.

14. Carson to Fred Zinnemann, January 27, 1953, HRHRC.

15. Carson McCullers, interview by Hans de Vaal, *Litterair Passport,* April 1953, HRHRC.

16. Carson to Rita Smith, March 23, 1953, HRHRC.

17. Dennis Cohen to Carson, August 17, 1953, HRHRC.

18. Letter from Andrée Chédid to Carson, March 4, 1953, HRHRC. Except for the complimentary close, the letter was written in English.

19. Janet Flanner, quoted in *The Lonely Hunter: A Biography of Carson McCullers,* by Virginia Spencer Carr (New York: Doubleday, 1975; reprint, New York: Carroll and Graf, 1985), 394–95 (page citations are to the reprint edition).

20. Tennessee Williams, *Memoirs* (Garden City, N.Y.: Doubleday, 1972), 245.

21. Jacques Tournier, *À la recherche de Carson McCullers: Retour à Nyack* (In search of Carson McCullers: Return to Nyack) (Paris: Éditions Complexe, 1990), 237.

22. Williams, *Memoirs,* 245.

23. Simone Brown to Carson, October 22, 1953, HRHRC.

24. Madame Joffre to Carson, September 21, 1953, HRHRC.

25. Reeves to Carson, November 21, 1945, HRHRC.

26. Jack Fullilove to Jacques Tournier, June 1977, quoted in Tournier, *À la recherche,* 21.

27. Oliver Evans, *The Ballad of Carson McCullers* (New York: Coward McCann, 1966), 161.

28. See Carr, *Lonely Hunter,* 402–3.

29. Clarke, *Capote,* 251.

30. Janet Flanner to Carson, December 5, 1953, HRHRC.

31. Dr. Robert Myers to Carson, n.d., HRHRC.

32. Carr, *Lonely Hunter,* 404–7.

33. Ibid., 407.

34. Natalia Danesi Murray to Carson, n.d., HRHRC.

35. Robert Myers to Carson, n.d., HRHRC.

36. Interview with Tennessee Williams, New Orleans, January 31, 1972, quoted in Carr, *Lonely Hunter,* 403, 409.

37. Carr, *Lonely Hunter,* 408.

38. Jordan Massee, quoted in Carr, *Lonely Hunter,* 409.

39. Telephone interview with Whit Burnett, December 15, 1970, quoted in Carr, *Lonely Hunter,* 415.

40. Francis Price to Virginia Spencer Carr, October 26, 1972, quoted in *Lonely Hunter,* 415.

41. Carson McCullers, "The Haunted Boy," in *The Mortgaged Heart,* 169, 171. This story was first published in *Mademoiselle* 42 (November 1955).

42. Carson McCullers, *The Square Root of Wonderful* (Boston: Houghton Mifflin, 1958), 115.

43. Ibid., 153.

44. McCullers, preface to *Square Root,* viii.

8. Something from Tennessee

1. Carson McCullers, untitled article on Georgia, n.d., HRHRC.

2. Ibid.

3. Ibid.

4. Ibid.

5. Margarita G. Smith, editor's note, *The Mortgaged Heart,* by Carson McCullers (Boston: Houghton Mifflin, 1971), 285.

6. Gerald Clarke, *Capote: A Biography* (New York: Simon and Schuster, 1988), 141.

7. Ibid., 155–56.

8. Oliver Evans to Carson, August 1, 1963, HRHRC.

9. Ibid.

10. Virginia Spencer Carr, *The Lonely Hunter: A Biography of Carson McCullers* (New York: Doubleday, 1975; reprint, New York: Carroll and Graf, 1985), 433 (page citation is to the reprint edition).

11. Robert Walden, quoted in Carr, *Lonely Hunter,* 428–29.

12. Carson McCullers, *Reflections in a Golden Eye* (Boston: Houghton Mifflin, 1941), 12.

13. René Micha, "Carson McCullers ou la cabane de l'enfance" (Carson McCullers, or childhood's cabin), *Critique,* no. 183–84 (August–September 1962): 707.

14. Remarks of Leon Edel made to Aimee Alexander in Honolulu, Hawaii, May 28, 1971, quoted in Carr, *Lonely Hunter,* 438.

15. Françoise Sagan, *With Fondest Regards,* trans. Christine Donougher (New York: E. P. Dutton, 1985), 45–61.

16. Tennessee Williams, "On Meeting a Young Writer," *Harper's Bazaar* 55 (August 1954), as cited in Carr, *Lonely Hunter,* 443–44.

17. Carson McCullers, "Who Has Seen the Wind?" *Mademoiselle* 43 (September 1956); reprinted in *The Mortgaged Heart* (Boston: Houghton Mifflin, 1971).

18. McCullers, "Who Has Seen the Wind?" in *The Mortgaged Heart,* 182.

19. Ibid., 178.

20. Ibid., 179–80.

21. McCullers, "Illumination and Night Glare," transcribed in Dews, "Unfinished Autobiography," 1:128–30.

22. Arnold Saint Subber, quoted in Carr, *Lonely Hunter,* 451.

23. Albert Marre, quoted in Carr, *Lonely Hunter,* 453.

24. McCullers, "Illumination and Night Glare," transcribed in Dews, "Unfinished Autobiography," 1:126–27.

25. John Chapman, review of *The Square Root of Wonderful*, by Carson McCullers, *New York Daily News*, October 31, 1957; reprinted in *New York Theatre Critics' Reviews* 18 (1957), 202.

26. Wolcott Gibbs, review of *The Square Root of Wonderful*, by Carson McCullers, *New Yorker*, November 9, 1957, 102–3.

27. Brooks Atkinson, review of *The Square Root of Wonderful*, by Carson McCullers, *New York Times*, October 31, 1957; reprinted in *New York Theatre Critics' Reviews* 18 (1957), 200.

28. Harold Clurman, review of *The Square Root of Wonderful*, by Carson McCullers, *Nation*, November 23, 1957, 394.

29. Author's interview with Floria Lasky, May 1995.

30. Louis Kronenberger, *The Best Plays of 1957–1958* (New York: Dodd, Mead, 1958), 12–14.

31. George Freedley, *Library Journal*, June 1, 1958, 1800.

32. Anon., release announcement for *The Square Root of Wonderful*, by Carson McCullers, *Kirkus*, May 1, 1958.

33. McCullers, preface to *Square Root*, ix–x.

34. Tennessee Williams, *Memoirs* (Garden City, N.Y.: Doubleday, 1972), 108.

35. Tennessee Williams, quoted in Carr, *Lonely Hunter*, 459.

36. Carson McCullers, *The Member of the Wedding*, in *Collected Stories of Carson McCullers* (Boston: Houghton Mifflin, 1987), 287.

9. The Ultimate Rebellion

1. Flannery O'Connor, letter to an anonymous correspondent, in *The Habit of Being*, ed. Sally Fitzgerald (New York: Farrar, Straus and Giroux, 1979), 115–17.

2. Virginia Spencer Carr, *The Lonely Hunter: A Biography of Carson McCullers* (New York: Doubleday, 1975; reprint, New York: Carroll and Graf, 1985), 469 (page citation is to the reprint edition).

3. Dorothy Salisbury Davis, quoted in Carr, *Lonely Hunter*, 469.

4. Carson McCullers, "Illumination and Night Glare," transcribed in "The Unfinished Autobiography of Carson McCullers," 2 vols., by Carlos Lee Barney Dews (Ph.D. diss., University of Minnesota, 1994), 1:172–75.

5. Didier Anzieu, "Beckett et Bion" (Beckett and Bion), *Revue française de psychanalyse*, no. 5 (1989): 1405–14.

6. Author's interview with Mary Mercer, Nyack, May 1995.

7. Ibid.

8. Robert Lantz to Mary Mercer, February 24, 1970, HRHRC.

9. Author's interview with Mary Mercer, Nyack, May 1995.

10. Transcription of "Meditations During Analysis," by Carson McCullers, April 2, 1958, HRHRC.

11. Ibid., April 11, 1958.

12. Ibid., April 14, 1958.

13. Carson to Carol Reed, May 10, 1958, HRHRC.

14. Ibid.

15. Author's interview with Mary Mercer, Nyack, May 1995.

16. Ibid.

17. Mary Mercer to Rita Smith, July 6, 1970, HRHRC.

18. Carson McCullers, *The Member of the Wedding,* in *The Collected Stories of Carson McCullers* (Boston: Houghton Mifflin, 1987), 378.

19. Thomas Lask, "Readings from Swift to Faulkner," *New York Times,* May 4, 1958.

20. Carson McCullers, "The Flowering Dream: Notes on Writing," in *The Mortgaged Heart* (Boston: Houghton Mifflin, 1971), 276, 278–81.

21. Gabriel Marcel, review of the French adaptation of *The Member of the Wedding,* entitled *Frankie Addams, Les Nouvelles littéraires,* December 18, 1958.

22. André Bay to Carson, May 31, June 12, 13, July 16, 1958; Carson to André Bay, June 18, 26, July 19, 1958, HRHRC.

23. Audrey Wood to Carson, June 16, 1958, HRHRC.

24. McCullers, "Illumination and Night Glare," transcribed in Dews, "Unfinished Autobiography," 1:133–34.

25. Author's interviews with Marielle Bancou, Paris, 1994 and 1995.

26. Ibid.

27. Carr, *Lonely Hunter,* 477.

28. Carson McCullers, "Isak Dinesen: *Winter's Tales,*" *New Republic,* June 7, 1943, reprinted in *The Mortgaged Heart;* "Isak Dinesen: In Praise of Radiance," *Saturday Review,* March 16, 1963, reprinted in *The Mortgaged Heart.*

29. Judith Thurman, *Isak Dinesen: The Life of a Storyteller* (New York: St. Martin's Press, 1982), 423–25.

30. Ibid.

31. Carr, *Lonely Hunter,* 481.

32. Carson to Tennessee Williams, April 1949. Translated from the French edition.

33. Raphaëlle Rérolle's interview with Arthur Miller, June 1995.

34. McCullers, "In Praise of Radiance," 217–72.

35. Margarita G. Smith, introduction to McCullers, *The Mortgaged Heart,* xii.

36. McCullers, "The Flowering Dream," 276.

37. Carson to Thornton Wilder, August 23, 1959, HRHRC.

38. Carson to Mary Tucker, November 7, 1959, HRHRC.

39. Jordan Massee, "Notes on Carson McCullers by Jordan Massee," unpublished journal, 69.

40. McCullers, "The Flowering Dream," 279.

41. Carson to the directors of the Columbus Public Library, August 21, 1961, HRHRC.

42. Granville Hicks, "The Subtler Corruptions," *Saturday Review of Literature,* September 23, 1961, 15.

43. Whitney Balliett, review of *Clock Without Hands, New Yorker,* September 23, 1961, 179.

44. Jean Martin, "Ways of Telling It," *Nation,* November 18, 1961, 411–12.

45. Rumer Godden, "Death and Life in a Small Southern Town," *New York Herald Tribune,* September 17, 1961.

46. Gore Vidal, "The World Outside," *Times Literary Supplement,* October 20, 1961, 52.

47. See Carr, *Lonely Hunter,* 433.

48. Carson McCullers, *Clock Without Hands* (Boston: Houghton Mifflin, 1961), 1.

49. Evans, *Ballad,* 186–87.

50. Margaret B. McDowell, *Carson McCullers* (Boston: Twayne, 1980), 98.

51. Ibid., 97.

52. Ibid., 115.

53. Ibid., 115–16.

54. Rex Reed, "Frankie Addams at 50," *New York Times,* April 16, 1967, sec. 2:15; reprinted in *Do You Sleep in the Nude?* (New York: New American Library, 1968).

10. *"The Dour Desire to Endure"*

1. McCullers, *Clock Without Hands* (Boston: Houghton Mifflin, 1961), 241. (Chapter 10 takes its title from a French poem by Paul Éluard, "Le Dur Désir de durer.")

2. Ibid.

3. Jordan Massee, "Notes on Carson McCullers by Jordan Massee," unpublished journal, December 28, 1961, 78.

4. Frederick R. Karl, *William Faulkner: American Writer* (New York: Weidenfeld and Nicolson, 1989), 1029–30.

5. Oliver Evans, *The Ballad of Carson McCullers* (New York: Coward McCann, 1966), 190.

6. Author's interview with Henri Cartier-Bresson, July 1995.

7. Massee, "Notes on Carson McCullers by Jordan Massee," June 8, 13, 1962.

8. Frank Tuohy, "Writers and Patrons: Cheltenham Festival," *Spectator,* October 12, 1962, quoted in *The Lonely Hunter: A Biography of Carson McCullers,* by Virginia Spencer Carr (New York: Doubleday, 1975; reprint, New York: Carroll and Graf, 1985), 518 (page citation is to the reprint edition).

9. Transcription of Jane Howard's interview with Carson McCullers, BBC, *Bookstand,* November 28, 1962, HRHRC.

10. Ibid.

11. Carson McCullers, "The Dark Brilliance of Edward Albee," *Harper's Bazaar,* January 1963, 98. The passage quoted here comes from Carr, *Lonely Hunter,* 502.

12. Edward Albee, "Carson McCullers — the Case of the Curious Magician," *Harper's Bazaar,* January 1963, 98.

13. Marjory Rutherford, "New Broadway Hit for Carson McCullers?" *Atlanta Journal and Constitution Magazine,* September 29, 1963, 10; quoted in Carr, *Lonely Hunter,* 503.

14. Carson McCullers, written responses to Mrs. Robert E. Rutherford, *Atlanta Journal,* August 20, 1963, HRHRC.

15. Carson to Elizabeth Schnark, May 28, June 26, July 3, 1963, HRHRC.

16. Dawn Pepita Simmons, quoted in Carr, *Lonely Hunter,* 520.

17. Carson to Dawn Langley Simmons, "Gordan" (Gordon Langley Hall), HRHRC.

18. Carson to Dawn Langley Simmons, "Gordan," June 13, 1963, HRHRC.

19. Carson to Dawn Langley Simmons, June 23, 1963, HRHRC.

20. Carson to Dawn Langley Simmons, July 2, 1963, HRHRC.

21. Carson to Dawn Langley Simmons, July 8, 1963, HRHRC.

22. Carson to Dawn Langley Simmons, August 12, 1963, HRHRC.

23. Carson to Marielle Bancou, n.d., HRHRC.

24. In his dissertation ("The Unfinished Autobiography of Carson McCullers," Ph.D. diss., University of Minnesota, 1994), Carlos Lee Barney Dews provides a number of important details regarding the nature of Carson McCullers's autobiographical materials and their probable chronology:

> In 1958, enthusiastic about the therapeutic possibilities of memory and wanting to share the unique way she experienced creative inspiration, Carson McCullers began to write an autobiography. This autobiography would be more straightforward than the oft-noted one played out beneath the surface of her fiction. Between 1958 and her death at age 50 in 1967, McCullers would attempt this autobiographical project at least three times, giving it a different title each time. Her first attempt, "The Flowering Dream," developed into an essay on creativity and the writing process published in *Esquire* magazine in December 1959. Her second attempt, "Illuminations Until Now," a fifty-page handwritten draft, was permanently put aside sometime before 1962. Her final attempt came very near the end of her life, a period previously considered unproductive. . . . Working during the four months before her death, McCullers dictated, to a series of paid secretaries and volunteers from a nearby college, what was destined to be an unfinished first draft of a work she had come to call "Illumination and Night Glare." . . . McCullers never finished her story of alternating inspiration and despair. (1:1)

. . .

There was some confusion, following McCullers's death, between the "meditations" written when she was in treatment with Mary Mercer and the manuscripts of "The Flowering Dream." It appears that McCullers used the title "The Flowering Dream" to describe a number of projects over a span of at least ten years and that "The Flowering Dream" owes its genesis to the meditations McCullers recorded and had transcribed during her treatment with Mercer. It is perhaps most helpful to consider these meditations as an early draft of "The Flowering Dream." (1:10–11)

A revised version of Dews's dissertation, *Illumination and Night Glare: The Unfinished Autobiography of Carson McCullers,* was published by the University of Wisconsin Press in 1999.

25. Carson to Oliver Evans, August 12, 1963, HRHRC.

26. Mary Mercer to Rita Smith, July 6, 1970, HRHRC.

27. Carson McCullers, *Sweet as a Pickle, Clean as a Pig* (Boston: Houghton Mifflin, 1964).

28. Richard Burton to Carson, August 11, 1965, HRHRC.

29. McCullers, "Illumination and Night Glare," transcribed in Dews, "Unfinished Autobiography," 1:106–7.

30. Ibid., 1:164–65.

31. Author's interview with Mary Mercer, May 1995.

32. McCullers, "Illumination and Night Glare," transcribed in Dews, "Unfinished Autobiography," 1:160–61.

33. Marlon Brando, quoted in Carr, *Lonely Hunter,* 527.

34. Marlon Brando to Carson, n.d., HRHRC.

35. Telegram from John Huston to Carson, January 5, 1967, HRHRC, quoted in Carr, *Lonely Hunter,* 527.

36. Terence de Vere White, "With Carson McCullers: Terence de Vere White Interviews the American Novelist at the Home of Her Host, John Huston," *Irish Times* (Dublin), April 10, 1967, 12.

37. McCullers, "Illumination and Night Glare," transcribed in Dews, "Unfinished Autobiography," 1:171.

38. Rex Reed, "'Frankie Addams' at 50," *New York Times,* April 16, 1967; reprinted as "Carson McCullers" in *Do You Sleep in the Nude?* (New York: New American Library, 1968), 38–43.

39. The White House to Carson, June 23, 1967, HRHRC.

40. McCullers, "Illumination and Night Glare," transcribed in Dews, "Unfinished Autobiography," 1:167–68.

41. Ibid., 1:107, 123–24.

42. Carr, *Lonely Hunter,* 522.

43. Carson to John Huston, July 31, 1967, HRHRC, paraphrased here in Carr, *Lonely Hunter,* 534.

44. McCullers, "Illumination and Night Glare," transcribed in Dews, "Unfinished Autobiography," 1:168–70.

45. Ibid., 1:179.

Epilogue: "She Was Ageless, Carson Was"

1. Terry Murray, quoted in *The Lonely Hunter: A Biography of Carson McCullers,* by Virginia Spencer Carr (New York: Doubleday, 1975; reprint, New York: Carroll and Graf, 1985), 415 (page citation is to the reprint edition).

2. Author's interview with Mary Mercer, Nyack, May 1995.

WORKS ABOUT
CARSON McCULLERS

I. Bibliographies

Leary, Lewis, comp. *Articles on American Literature, 1950–1967.* Durham, N.C.: Duke University Press, 1970.

Phillips, Robert S. "Carson McCullers, 1956–1964: A Selected Checklist." *Bulletin of Bibliography* 24 (September–December 1964): 113–16.

Pownall, David E. *Articles on Twentieth Century Literature: An Annotated Bibliography, 1954 to 1970.* New York: Kraus-Thomson, 1973–1980.

Shapiro, Adrian, Jackson R. Bryer, and Kathleen Field. *Carson McCullers: A Descriptive Listing and Annotated Bibliography of Criticism.* New York: Garland, 1980.

Stewart, Stanley. "Carson McCullers, 1940–1956: A Selected Checklist." *Bulletin of Bibliography* 22 (January–April 1959): 182–85.

II. General Studies

Bain, Robert, Joseph M. Flora, and Louis D. Rubin Jr., eds. *Southern Writers: A Biographical Dictionary.* Baton Rouge: Louisiana State University Press, 1980, pp. 290–93.

Carr, Virginia Spencer. "Carson McCullers." In *Contemporary Authors: A Bio-bibliographical Guide to Current Writers, American Novelists.* Vol. 1, edited by James J. Martine. Detroit: Bruccoli Clark/Gale Research, 1986, pp. 239–45.

———. "Carson McCullers." In *Fifty Southern Writers After 1900: A Bio-bibliographical Sourcebook,* edited by Joseph M. Flora and Robert Bain. Westport, Conn.: Greenwood, 1987, pp. 301–12.

Carr, Virginia Spencer, and Joseph R. Millichap. "Carson McCullers." In *American Women Writers: Bibliographical Essays,* edited by Maurice Duke, Jackson

R. Bryer, and M. Thomas Inge. Westport, Conn.: Greenwood, 1983, pp. 297–319.

Eisinger, Chester E. *Fiction of the Forties.* Chicago: University of Chicago Press, 1963, pp. 243–58.

Elliott, Emory, ed. *The Columbia History of the American Novel.* New York: Columbia University Press, 1991, pp. 429–30.

Gosset, Louise Y. *Violence in Recent Southern Fiction.* Durham, N.C.: Duke University Press, 1965, pp. 159–77.

Hassan, Ihab H. *Contemporary American Literature, 1945–1972: An Introduction.* New York: Ungar, 1973, pp. 66–69, 152–55.

——. *Radical Innocence: Studies in the Contemporary American Novel.* Princeton, N.J.: Princeton University Press, 1961, pp. 205–29.

Hoffman, Daniel, ed. *Harvard Guide to Contemporary American Writing.* Cambridge, Mass.: Belknap/Harvard University Press, 1979, pp. 186–87, 354–55, 365, 374, 412.

Kazin, Alfred. *Bright Book of Life: American Novelists and Storytellers from Hemingway to Mailer.* Boston: Little, Brown, 1973.

Kirkpatrick, D. L., ed. *Reference Guide to American Literature.* Chicago: Saint James, 1987, pp. 379–80.

Malin, Irving. *New American Gothic.* Carbondale: Southern Illinois University Press, 1962.

McBride, Mary. "Loneliness and Longing in Selected Plays of Carson McCullers and Tennessee Williams." In *Modern American Drama: The Female Canon,* edited by June Schlueter. Rutherford, N.J.: Fairleigh Dickinson University Press, 1990, pp. 143–50.

Moers, Ellen. *Literary Women.* Garden City, N.Y.: Doubleday, 1976, pp. 45, 108–9, 247.

Weales, Gerald Clifford. *American Drama Since World War II.* New York: Harcourt, Brace and World, 1962, pp. 174–79, 198–99.

III. Biographical Works

Carr, Virginia Spencer. *The Lonely Hunter: A Biography of Carson McCullers.* New York: Doubleday, 1975. Reprint, Carroll and Graf, 1985 and 1989.

——. *Understanding Carson McCullers.* Columbia: University of South Carolina Press, 1990.

Cook, Richard M. *Carson McCullers.* New York: Ungar, 1975.

Edmonds, Dale. *Carson McCullers.* Austin, Tex.: Steck-Vaughn, 1969.

Evans, Oliver Wendell. *Carson McCullers, Her Life and Work.* London: P. Owen, 1965. Reprinted as *The Ballad of Carson McCullers,* Coward McCann, 1966.

Graver, Lawrence. *Carson McCullers.* Minneapolis: University of Minnesota Press, 1969.

Kiernan, Robert F. *Katherine Anne Porter and Carson McCullers: A Reference Guide.* Boston: G. K. Hall, 1976.

McDowell, Margaret B. *Carson McCullers.* Boston: Twayne, 1980.

Westling, Louise. *Sacred Groves and Ravaged Gardens: The Fiction of Eudora Welty, Carson McCullers, and Flannery O'Connor.* Athens: University of Georgia Press, 1985.

Williams, Tennessee. "This Book." Introduction to *Reflections in a Golden Eye,* by Carson McCullers. New York: New Directions, 1950, pp. vii–xvii.

IV. Interviews

"Behind the Wedding: Carson McCullers Discusses the Novel She Converted into a Stage Play." Interview with Harvey Breit. *New York Times,* January 1, 1950: sec. 2, p. 3.

"Carson McCullers Completes New Novel Despite Adversity." Interview with Nona Balakian. *New York Times,* September 3, 1961: 46.

"The *Marquis* Interviews Carson McCullers." *Marquis* (Lafayette College) 5–6 (1964): 20–23.

"'Frankie Addams' at 50." Interview with Rex Reed. *New York Times,* April 16, 1967: sec. 2, p. 15.

"With Carson McCullers: Terence de Vere White Interviews the American Novelist at the Home of Her Host, John Huston." Interview with Terence de Vere White. *Irish Times* (Dublin), April 10, 1967: 12.

INDEX